1600
PENNSYLVANIA
AVENUE

1600 PENNSYLVANIA AVENUE

PRESIDENTS AND THE PEOPLE, 1929-1959

BY

Walter Johnson

Little, Brown and Company

BOSTON   TORONTO

Published simultaneously in Canada
by Little, Brown & Company (Canada) Limited

PRINTED IN THE UNITED STATES OF AMERICA

For Bette

Foreword

O forest of a land,
With your broad continents of night and day,
Sea of a land, endless and asking land,
How may we begin to know you with any song,
How may we say one word and utter your name?

STEPHEN VINCENT BENÉT *

The years since the stock market crash have been years of extraordinary, and often bewildering, change. The creeping chaos of the depression, the drama of the New Deal, Adolf Hitler and the Japanese, the struggle for control of American foreign policy, the expansion of American power in the war, the founding of the United Nations, the death of Franklin D. Roosevelt, the dropping of the atom bomb, the menacing Soviet Union, the Truman Doctrine and the Marshall Plan, the limited war in Korea, the rapid decline of European empires and the emergence of new sensitive nations in Asia and Africa, the hydrogen bomb with its total destructive power, rockets and space satellites, made other eras seem uneventful. Never before in American history had developments outside the borders of the nation so dramatically influenced American decisions.

Although the continuity of ideas and institutions is an important theme in the history of a nation, the recurring domestic and international crises after 1929 shook cherished traditions and forced extraordinary alterations in the attitudes of the American people. Called upon to do many things they had previously resisted, they made their first fundamental effort to adjust their democracy to the realities of a new age. Under the impact of the depression, they adapted the institutions of business and finance to democratic ends, achieving an enormous economic and political transformation of

* *Western Star* (New York: Rinehart & Co., 1943); copyright by Rosemary Carr Benét.

American society. After the isolationism of the mid-depression years, they made portentous decisions in world politics and quickly accepted the implications of world leadership. Despite a restlessness over the new position of the nation and, at times, a reluctance to part with older ways, the American people made the transition not without dignity.

Pivotal point of the reshaping of the role of the government in the economy and the nation in world decisions was political, particularly presidential, leadership. From the austere Quaker, international engineer, businessman, and humanitarian to the patrician, country gentleman, politico-statesman, to the hard-bitten Midwestern self-made man and party politician, to the professional soldier, famed as a conciliator and unifier of a brilliant group of Allied generals, the type of leadership furnished the nation was strikingly varied.

Although there are many ways of describing these years of profound change, I analyze in this book what leadership did and did not, could and could not, achieve in aiding the adjustment of the nation to the twentieth century. While much was accomplished, much was left undone; the words of Herman Melville are apposite: ". . . the world's a ship on its passage out, and not a voyage complete. . . ."

W. J.

Contents

1600
PENNSYLVANIA
AVENUE

BOOK ONE

Politics of Drift: Hoover

1. Crisis in American Democracy

Thousands of war veterans streamed into Washington through the warm, lazy days of June, 1932. Some came in rattletrap trucks, others in dilapidated jalopies. Still others arrived in boxcars, for, as the depression had gone on and on, the railroad police had been unable to cope with the thousands of idle men who roamed across the country riding the rails.

Many of them set up camp on the Anacostia mud flats across the Potomac. They scavenged the city dump heap and built miserable shacks from egg crates, packing boxes, pieces of corrugated iron, and rusty fence-wire. Others occupied some vacant land and unused government buildings on Pennsylvania Avenue just below the Capitol. By mid-June, fifteen to twenty thousand, some with their wives and children, had straggled into Washington.

They were there to demand immediate payment of the Soldiers' Bonus — "adjusted service certificates" which were to mature in 1945. Seventeen months before, Congress, over President Hoover's veto, had passed a law allowing veterans to borrow up to half the value of their certificates. But the demand for cash payment at once, led by Democratic Congressman Wright Patman, of Texas, gathered momentum. On June 15, 1932, the Patman Bonus Bill, calling for payment of nearly two and a half billions, passed the House. On the evening of June 18, as the Senators voted, thousands of ragged veterans packed the plaza before the Capitol. When word reached them that the Senate had voted down the bonus, there was growling, tension, and a mood of uncertainty. Then their elected leader, W. W. Waters — a thirty-four-year-old unemployed canning factory superintendent from Portland, Oregon — spoke to them, a band struck up "America," and they dispersed quietly.

During the next few days some of them left Washington on their own. Five thousand others, using travel funds which the President had asked Congress to appropriate, left for home during July. Desperate and bewildered, the others remained. In their hopeless search for security they had no better place to go. Extra guards were placed around the White House, its gates were chained, and the surrounding streets cleared. To the harassed, tired President in the White House, the Bonus Army was a hateful, daily reminder of the ferment of dissatisfaction, bitterness, and distress that was abroad in the nation.

July 28, 1932, was destined to be a day seared on the memory of Americans for years to come. General Pelham D. Glassford, Washington Superintendent of Police, whose understanding of their problems had won the respect of the veterans, was ordered to clear them out of the unused government buildings below the Capitol. One hour after the police started to execute this order, a scuffle broke out. A shower of bricks hit the policemen and they in turn began to club some veterans with nightsticks. General Glassford rushed into the fray and stopped it. Two hours later, however, when two veterans rushed a policeman, the policeman pulled his gun and fired. Before Glassford could stop the shooting, two veterans were killed and a number of policemen were injured.

Then, late that hot July afternoon, down Pennsylvania Avenue marched four companies of cavalry, four companies of infantry, several tanks, and a machine-gun contingent. The veterans and a large crowd that had gathered at the disputed area cheered the troops as they approached. Suddenly the cavalry charged the crowd with drawn swords, and "men, women, and children fled shrieking across the broken ground, falling into excavations as they strove to avoid the rearing hoofs and saber points." Meanwhile, the infantry adjusted their gas masks and hurled tear-gas bombs into the crowd. A reporter saw "dozens of women grab their children and stagger out of the area with streaming, blinded eyes." [1]

The troops moved on to Anacostia, scattering veterans and homeward-bound government clerks. When they crossed the Anacostia bridge, they tossed tear gas into a booing crowd. Then they set fire to two improvised barracks. Soon the veterans began firing their own shelters, and the Washington sky was aglow.

The Bonus Expeditionary Force was dispersed. Although many had been injured, the United States Army successfully completed its operation without a death. President Hoover, who had ordered out the Army under General Douglas MacArthur, did so at the request of the District of Columbia Commissioners.[2] General MacArthur said on September 28, 1932, "That mob . . . was a bad looking mob. It was animated by the essence of revolution." And he added that, if the President had not acted, "I believe that the institutions of our Government would have been severely threatened." Hoover told the press that the Bonus Expeditionary Force by July 28 contained a minority of veterans while the rest were Communists, hoodlums, and ex-convicts.

Although writers at the time pointed out that there were some Communists, they insisted that the great majority were simply veterans, ordinary Americans down on their luck. What is dramatically clear is that the routing of the Bonus Expeditionary Force by the Army left a bitter taste. Many citizens were shocked that any Americans, dispossessed by the depression, should be treated in this way. There seemed to be no genuine leadership, no statesman able to cope with the tragedies of an industrialized nation deep in depression.

Novelist Sherwood Anderson, in an open letter to the President, put into words the thoughts of many. After describing people eating from garbage cans, sleeping on park benches or in the mud under bridges, and the majority who wanted work but could not find it, he said: "I am wondering, Mr. President, if men like you, men now high in our public life, captains of industry, financiers — the kind of men who seem always to be closest now to our public men — I am wondering if all of you are not nowadays too much separated from the actuality of life. Everything has been very highly organized and centralized in America. Perhaps you have been organized and centralized out of our common lives."[3]

2.   Collapse of the New Era

Yet how optimistic the nation had been just four years before. Prosperity had come to the land and blessed it. When Secretary of Commerce Herbert Hoover accepted the presidential nomination in 1928, he observed:

> We in America today are nearer to the final triumph over poverty than ever before in the history of any land. The poorhouse is vanishing from among us. We have not yet reached the goal, but, given a chance to go forward with the policies of the last eight years, we shall soon, with the help of God, be in sight of the day when poverty will be banished from this nation. There is no guaranty against poverty equal to a job for every man. That is the primary purpose of the policies we advocate.

The booming economy of the 1920s, the dazzling prospects of the new technology for industry, the booster mentality of millions, the national mania for speculation on the stock market, all produced a firm belief in a new era in which Americans would be free of poverty. The new science and the new wealth opened broad vistas of a certain and advancing prosperity. And the American businessman and financier were celebrated for their wisdom, energy, divine impatience, guts, and vision. The ten-year period from 1919 to 1929 had shown the greatest increase in the national income the country had ever known. Industrial production rose 45 per cent and the value of the gross national product 43 per cent.[1] Little wonder, then, that in a New Year's editorial on January 1, 1929, the *New York Times* wrote: "It has been a twelve month of unprecedented advance, of wonderful prosperity . . . If there is any way of judging the future by the past, this New Year may well be one of felicitation and hopefulness."

Yale economist Irving Fisher assured the nation that we were dwelling upon "a permanently high plateau" of prosperity, while John J. Raskob — General Motors executive and Chairman of the Democratic National Committee — explained in the summer of 1929 that if a man invested $15 a week in good common stocks and allowed the dividends to accumulate, at the end of twenty years he would have an income from his investment of about $400 a month. "He will be rich," added Raskob. "And because income can do that, I am firm in my belief that anyone not only can be rich, but ought to be rich."

Newspapers and periodicals everywhere reported the same almost monotonous stories of the nation's prosperity. The undoubting confidence in the soundness of the economy rested on production and more production with voracious consumption. Dollars in the right quantity, place and time were all that were needed. But, in 1929, there was a serious problem of underinvestment which hampered economic expansion. And purchasing power was too unevenly distributed among the twenty-seven million families to sustain even current levels of production. The median family income was $1700.[2] But the Brookings Institution estimated that the minimum cost of the basic necessities for a family, including rent, was $2000. And sixteen million families — some 60 per cent of the total — were below this minimum standard. Although the idea of proper diets, in this year of food surpluses and seeming prosperity, was moderate, 74 per cent of the non-farm families could not afford an adequate diet. "It is this handling of every penny till the skin is worn off your fingers that kills," said a white-collar worker. Others had desires which were better left unfulfilled in 1929: "It's the never being able to take a flyer on the stock market."

There were many nuances to America's new era. Agriculture was languishing. Farm prices dropped 30 per cent between 1919 and 1929. Only 10 per cent of the farm families had incomes over $2600 a year, while 50 per cent earned less than $910. Even in Detroit, center of one of the most exciting industries of the new era, prosperity was illusory. The auto worker was paid a phenomenally high wage, $7 a day — when he worked. A social worker described the resulting situation in a terse report: "Ralph B., ten years in the automobile industry. Forty-one years old. His earnings for 1927 were $621.77, for 1928, $708.50, and for 1929, $903." [3]

If prosperity was not universal in 1929, the psychology of it was. America had always lived on its expectations. In spite of the depressed areas of the economy in 1929 — seldom discussed in the literature of the day — the nation had the highest standard of living in the world. Expanding technology offered a vision of abundance never before attained by man. The future was dazzling. When Herbert Hoover, in 1928, expressed the nation's desire for "two chickens in every pot and two cars in every garage," these seemed easily within reach.

Stock market speculation, during 1928 and 1929, delayed a necessary readjustment in the economy. The inflation in stock prices created the illusion of a prosperous economy. Actually, a number of components were in trouble by 1928. Speculation delayed what might have been a mild recession and then, when the crash came, converted it into the awful cataclysm of the depression. Part of the weakness in agricultural prices was that the middle-class market was far smaller in 1929 than it became after 1941. Profits, rent, and interest increased 45 per cent between 1920 and 1929 but went largely to the upper income group; wages and salaries rose only 13 per cent. Technological advances reduced the cost of production during the decade, but consumer prices were not reduced accordingly. And the labor movement was so weak that it failed to benefit proportionately from rising industrial productivity. Investments abroad were declining, too, and this directly affected foreign ability to continue to purchase American goods. Added to this was a weak banking structure at home and abroad. And there were shady practices in some holding companies and investment trusts.

The stock market boom, by postponing a readjustment, enabled stock speculators to stimulate a consumer boom, particularly in luxury goods; and it helped business to maintain capital expansion at a level unjustified by general conditions. The overbuilding of commercial and office structures was one such indication. The stock market boom was fed from many sources. Increases in stock dividends began to catch up with profits by the middle of the 1920s. Thus the advantages of investing in stocks became apparent to more and more people. Since there was no legal requirement as to the amount of cash needed to buy stock on margin, more and more people entered the market. And the speculative fever was contagious in an atmosphere of getting rich quickly and of faith in the new era.

The Federal Reserve system in August, 1927, made speculative credit even more plentiful. To encourage business at home, but largely to enable Britain to stay on the gold standard and France to get on it, the New York Federal Reserve Bank lowered the rediscount rate on loans from 4 to 3.5 per cent and purchased government securities in the open market. Secretary of Commerce Herbert Hoover protested in vain. Many since have agreed with him that the Federal Reserve Board, by failing to disallow this action, bears considerable responsibility for the stock market speculation. "I do not attribute the whole of the stock boom to mismanagement of the Federal Reserve System," Hoover wrote later. "But the policies adopted by that system must assume the greater responsibility." [4]

In the '20s, the Federal Reserve system lacked the power to set margin requirements; and there was no Securities and Exchange Commission to police the issuance, buying, and selling of securities. When credit inflation was added to the optimism of the day, it set the stage for what President Hoover has termed "wicked manipulations and promotions of stocks." The fact that a great part of the stock buying was done on credit gave the boom its momentum. Nearly three fourths of the money came not from the banks but from individuals and corporations. This rise in speculative credit tightened credit for regular business operations. The Federal Reserve Board was divided over what action to take in 1928. One group wanted to tighten money to check speculation, but others felt that, since there was no inflation elsewhere in the economy, the speculation should be allowed to ride itself out.

On February 2, 1929, the first group had its way. The Board warned that a member bank "is not within its reasonable claims for rediscount facilities when it borrows either for the purpose of making speculative loans or for the purpose of maintaining speculative loans." This warning was weakened, however, when Calvin Coolidge in the closing days of his presidency issued a statement assuring the country that prosperity was "absolutely sound" and that stocks were "cheap at current prices." It was one of the few times that the taciturn President had spoken on such questions, and it happened at an unfortunate moment.

The tightening of credit by Federal Reserve banks drove money rates up to 20 per cent, and for a moment it seemed as though speculation might be curbed. But Charles Mitchell of the National City

Bank of New York made the audacious announcement that his bank would lend $25 million at rates beginning at 15 per cent. The action taken by Federal Reserve banks was not stringent enough to check stock speculation, but the raising of interest rates made money too tight for business. In its unsuccessful attempt to kill the stock boom, the banks handcuffed business by freezing it out of money for expansion.

By the summer of 1929, business was turning downward. Even before the crash in October, powerful deflationary forces — declining construction, declining farm prices, and declining consumer purchases of durable goods — were already at work. The crash further deflated all values and the banking structure was almost destroyed. Banks had nearly 25 per cent of their assets in loans against stocks and 10 per cent in loans on real estate. The precipitous decline in stock and real estate values crippled the banks. The quoted value of all stocks listed on the New York Stock Exchange on September 1, 1929, was eighty-nine and a half billion dollars. By July, 1932, the quoted value had fallen to fifteen and a half billion.

In spite of weaknesses in the economy, a prosperity-minded America rode blissfully through the summer and early autumn of 1929. The day after Labor Day the stock market dropped sharply. The next few weeks the market was ragged. And by Saturday, October 19, the market was behaving badly. Three and a half million shares changed hands — the second heaviest Saturday trading in history — with some stocks off forty points and even powerful General Electric down nine.

On Monday, six million shares were traded and, by now, many margin accounts had been sold out. The losses on Wednesday, October 23, were unprecedented. When the market opened the next morning — "Black Thursday" — orders to sell deluged the Stock Exchange. Nearly thirteen million shares of stock changed hands. By noon panic gripped the market. To the rescue came the heads of the National City Bank, Chase, Guaranty Trust, Bankers Trust, and J. P. Morgan. They agreed to pool resources to support the market. Richard Whitney, floor broker for Morgan's, placed substantial orders at several points above current bids. Confidence revived for the moment. Then on Tuesday, October 29, sixteen and a half million shares were traded. Westinghouse dropped nineteen points; American Telephone and General Electric twenty-eight; Allied Chemical thirty-five; and the *New York Times* industrial averages were down forty-three points. Prices fell with regularity day after day until they reached their bottom for 1929 on November 13. Some thirty billion dollars — a sum almost as large as the cost of World War I to the United States — had disappeared in the crash.

Even though the new era was disintegrating, reassuring statements were issued by economists, bankers, business executives, and public officials. The *Literary Digest,* in describing the prevailing note of confidence, termed the crash "the prosperity panic of 1929." President Hoover seemed to say the final word: "The fundamental business of the country, that is, production and distribution of commodities, is on a sound and prosperous basis."

Expectations had been so aroused that people refused to accept the crash as the end of the new era. If there had been great losses, Christmas buying would bring an improvement. If holiday sales were small, the New Year would usher in the revival. If the New Year failed to live up to the promise, spring expansion would round the corner to recovery. The *Literary Digest* summed up expert opinion on May 15, 1930: "President Hoover is right in saying, 'We have now passed the worst.'" It was the belief, as Denis W. Brogan has suggested, "of Paradise Mislaid, not Paradise Lost."

As unemployment reached over four millions, the *Saturday Evening Post* for September 13, 1930, sustained the faith. More jobs awaited the intelligent and the resourceful than people believed. "What happened yesterday is finished. Today is always the threshold of the future, with all its unlimited prospects." But most editors bade a relieved farewell to 1930. And Will Rogers observed on New Year's Day, 1931: "If we could have eaten and digested 'optimistic prediction' during 1930 we would have been the fattest nation on earth." Even though Washington had the deep-seated conviction that conditions were going to be better in 1931, 1930 had been such a bad year for both profits and prophets that "the country suffers . . . from 'overprediction,'" Mark Sullivan wrote.

By the spring of 1931, the *Brooklyn Times* had had enough. When the big men "predict better times, and nothing happens, they just predict some more." And former President Coolidge, the personification of the golden age, said flatly in his daily newspaper column: "This country is not in good condition."

At the turn of 1932, even those most hopeful in previous years had finally given up. "Where are the prophets of yesteryear?" asked the *Literary Digest*. "The last soothsayer has crawled away to his corner," replied the *New York Herald Tribune*. And the *New York Times* explained that the prevailing condition in the financial community was "one of complete bewilderment" and an "inability to predict at all."

Now America's mental attitude had swung a full cycle. The tradition of hope and faith in progress had been violently shattered. In the new era the nation had talked of abolishing the Rainy Day only to have the skies open and the torrent fall. Creeping chaos had replaced rosy hopes. "No business as usual" had become the national slogan. Although the average citizen could still crack jokes at his troubles, he knew he was up against it. Any optimistic predictions met the popular response, "Oh yeah?" [5]

---

3.   The Deepening Depression

Statistics reveal in stark and heartless detail what happened to the productive economy after 1929. The Federal Reserve Board index of economic activity averaging 100 for the years 1923-1925 showed industrial production at 119 in the boom year 1929. By 1930 the average fell to 96; to 81 in 1931; to 64 in 1932; and to 60 in March, 1933. Construction reached its peak in 1928 when the index stood at 135. The index dropped 18 points in 1929. The decline thereafter was monotonous; to 92 in 1930; to 63 in 1931; to 28 in 1932; and to 14 by March, 1933.

The production of automobiles and trucks fell from 5,358,000 in 1929 to 2,389,000 in 1931. This had far-reaching effects. In 1930 this single industry used 82 per cent of the nation's rubber, 55 per cent of its plate glass, 15 per cent of its iron and steel, 30 per cent of its aluminum, and 24 per cent of its lead.

U. S. Steel's profits fell from $197,531,349 in 1929 to $13,000,000 in 1931, and then to a deficit of $12,729,000 in 1932. General Motors' dropped from $247,317,000 in 1929 to $96,000,000 in 1931. Sears, Roebuck's from $30,057,000 in 1929 to $12,169,000 in 1931. Over two thousand business firms failed each month during 1931 and 1932. The worst month, January, 1932, saw 3458 failures representing liabilities of $96,860,000.

Only a few firms increased their profits. Notable were Cities Service, from $36,477,000 in 1929 to $48,975,000 in 1930; and P. Lorillard Company (Old Gold), from $3,614,000 in 1930 to $4,846,000 a year later. Times might be tougher and tougher for more and more people, but the public had not given up cigarettes and driving. This prompted Will Rogers to remark: "We got more wheat, more corn, more food, more cotton, more money in the banks, more everything in the world than any nation that ever lived ever had, yet we are starving to death. We are the first nation in the history of the world to go to the poorhouse in an automobile." [1]

The threatened collapse of the banking structure after 1929 magnified the uncertainty and the growing despair. Although the Federal Reserve system, established in 1913, had been a significant step toward a sounder banking system, many banks had failed even in the years between 1920 and 1928. Bank suspensions in 1928 totaled 491. The next year 642 failed. Then, in 1930, 1345 banks with deposits of $864,715,000 closed their doors; in 1931, 2298 banks with deposits of $1,691,510,000; in 1932, 1456 banks with deposits of $715,626,000. [2] Savings were frequently the only resource of many people in times of sickness, old age, or unemployment. Eighty per cent of the unemployed in 1929 relied mainly on their savings to carry them along. The wiping out of savings by bank failures after 1929 heightened the tragedy when work became scarce and jobs were lost.

It was the worker — blue- and white-collar alike — who bore the brunt of the depression. One year after the crash, five million were unemployed. By January, 1931, there were two million more. The total reached ten million a year later. By Labor Day, 1932, over twelve million were out of jobs. Another million was added to the rolls of the unemployed by March 4, 1933. [3] One third of the nation's workers were unemployed by this time. Two thirds still had jobs, but some were working part-time and others were employed in other than their normal occupations. The loss of a sense of security for these workers in strange and temporary jobs was frightening. Even the skilled and veteran workers who held their jobs had little peace of mind as businesses of every type and size failed. And there seemed to be no end in sight. The depression just lengthened and lengthened.

Even the wealth of a New York City was little protection in the crisis. Over a half million people applied to relief agencies for aid in 1931. By April, 1932, three quarters of a million people were receiving aid. But no funds were available for the one hundred and sixty thousand individuals whose incomes averaged only $8.20 a month. The local relief system simply broke down under the expanding load and applicants at the rate of seven hundred families a day were being turned away. By September, 1932, it was estimated that there were over a million and a half needy in the city.

Unemployed men selling apples at street corners became a common sight. Others waited patiently in long breadlines every day at eighty-two places for the eighty-two thousand free meals which were handed out. Over 26 per cent of the apartments and tenements on the lower East Side were vacant in February, 1932, as families shared and doubled up in crowded quarters. Malnutrition among children increased from 18 to 60 per cent between 1928 and 1931.

New York City was a "busted Babylon." Only twenty-eight plays were running in the city's eighty-six legitimate theaters in December, 1931. Hotels averaged 50 per cent of occupancy. (One grim joke described the room clerk's asking a customer if he wanted the room "for sleeping or jumping.") The new Waldorf Astoria was 60 per cent filled at a six-dollar minimum. Elevators in the Empire State stopped running from the forty-second to the sixty-seventh floor. And vaudeville theaters forbade their performers to joke about the depression or President Hoover. Before they did this, however, it was standard for a comedian to appear on the stage with a vacuum cleaner, pull out his empty pockets, and say "Hoover cleaned us all."

Across the country the story was much the same. There were the apple sellers, the long breadlines, and unemployed sleeping in parks or in clusters of crude shanties — "Hoovervilles," their occupants called them — made of cartons or scraps of wood thrown up on vacant lots. Weekly food orders doled out to families on relief in August, 1931, averaged $7 per family in sixteen cities; $4 in four cities;

$1.50 to $2 in one city; and $3 every other week in another city. As the number of applicants increased, the amounts for each family had to drop.

In Philadelphia a reporter found over two hundred families in a few city blocks who were six to eighteen months behind on their rent. By March, 1932, over fifteen hundred dwellings a month were being sold at public auctions. Thousands of small grocers went bankrupt. They sold food on credit to those who were hard up, and then were unable to pay the wholesaler. One storekeeper explained the crisis: "Eleven children in that house. They've got no shoes, no pants. In the house, no chairs. My God, you go in there, you cry, that's all. What can you do? Let them go hungry?"

By 1932 the steel towns were on the verge of panic. In Donora, Pennsylvania, where American Steel and Wire normally employed 4500, only 277 were at work in March, 1932, while 2500 drew relief of $3.50 a week from the company for "made work." Owing to extraordinary local optimism, no action was taken to combat the depression in Youngstown until early 1931. Finally an abandoned police station was turned into a flophouse for homeless men who had been sleeping in the city incinerator. The city's relief program, finally undertaken, granted a family $1.50 a week. The Mayor described one case: "Father of ten drowns self . . . out of work two years . . . was born in Youngstown and was employed by the Republic Iron and Steel Company for twenty-seven years as a hot mill worker."

The automobile city of Detroit led the nation in unemployment. The unemployed were not only auto workers but ministers, lawyers, bank tellers, dentists, and "two families after whom streets are named." "Middletown" — Muncie, Indiana — provided its unemployed with free seeds and vacant lots for "self-help" in 1930. The city's Social Service Bureau furnished coal to 4727 families in the winter of 1930-1931. Although Community Fund receipts rose, the relief rolls rose faster than Middletown's defenses. By 1932 almost one third of the city's families were on relief.

In Chicago, schoolteachers and other municipal employees went without pay for a large part of 1931 and 1932. At one time the city reached the ludicrous situation of attempting to sell for unpaid taxes the homes of its own employees who were unable to pay because the city had not paid their wages. Private relief funds intended to last a year were exhausted in four months. The sight of men, women, and children foraging in garbage cans was an everyday occurrence.

In Davenport, Rock Island, and Moline all relief funds were exhausted by May, 1932. Some of the larger manufacturing companies paid the grocery bills of men long on their payrolls. International Harvester kept its tractor plant running until April, 1932, though it had no market. Every available space — freight yards, warehouses, abandoned stores — was overflowing with tractors. While city residents went hungry, farmers in the nearby countryside burned their corn and returned to the use of horses. The economic system had, indeed, gone mad. "Malthus never contemplated a condition when there would be too much to eat and too few eating it," wrote the *Louisville Courier-Journal*.

Los Angeles had 98,000 unemployed by January, 1931. The figure reached 151,000 a year later. The city was the mecca for the thousands of young men wandering footloose across the country. It accommodated 11,000 boys a month in 1931 but limited its hospitality to eight nights. It was estimated that 200,000 youths were drifting about the country that year. Five thousand passed through New Orleans every month. As many as seven hundred a day came through Kansas City on freight trains. Atlanta announced thirty-day sentences in the city jail or on the chain gang for any caught in Fulton County but actually gave temporary shelter to a large number despite the harsh law.

Industrial areas of the South felt the depression as fully as any Northern city. Here the economic catastrophe struck hardest at the Negro or, in the Southwest, the Mexican-American. In Charleston, South Carolina, Negroes were 49 per cent of the population, but 70 per cent of the unemployed. In Memphis, Negroes were 38 per cent of the population and 75 per cent of the unemployed. And Houston did not accept relief applications from Negroes or Mexican-Americans: "They are being asked to shift for themselves." Discrimination, however, was not restricted to the South. "The first to be fired and the last to be hired" was the Negro's unfortunate fate in Northern urban areas as well. In Chicago, Negroes were 4 per cent of the population but accounted for 16 per cent of the unemployed; in Philadelphia 7 per cent of the population and 25 per cent of the jobless.

Ethnic and religious tensions were increased. The '20s — with the Red Scare, the Ku Klux Klan, the new immigration laws, and the emotions engendered by the 1928 presidential campaign — had been a difficult decade for the recent immigrant. Now to all this tension was added the struggle for jobs. During the decade after 1930, for the first time in American history more people left the country than entered it. Foreign-born workers suffered unemployment more severely than native-born whites. Thirty-eight per cent of Boston's unemployed, for instance, were foreign-born. Older residents now eagerly sought undesirable jobs gladly left to immigrants in prosperous times. During the depression decade, some recent immigrants found an outlet for their frustration and discontent in ethnic organizations. Some Negroes turned to Father Divine, while George Christian's White Shirts, William Dudley Pelley's Silver Shirts, Father Coughlin and the Christian Front, the German-American Bund, and Detroit's Black Legion furnished an outlet for the hates and bitterness of some native whites.

Social workers found their first white-collar charity cases unforgettable. Many applicants refused to give their names and asked the social worker not to let their wives or children know they were getting relief. Reactions to the depression varied within groups, within families, and with individuals. Some white-collar workers, reflecting the high aspirations aroused by the new era, became not only bitter and resentful, but, as the depression lengthened, lost hope. In one such group of previously self-sufficient families registered as new cases by a Baltimore social agency between 1930 and 1932, forty-nine of the seventy-nine families had strained relations between husband and wife. Seventy-two of these families had used up all their savings and were in debt beyond all expectation of being able to repay. Children in seven families had left school, 80 per cent had purchased no new clothes, and many adolescents embarrassed over worn shoes stopped going out to social activities.

But the depression had far different effects for the families — a majority — that did not need outside aid. A Pittsburgh study of over a hundred white-collar and professional families discovered that the majority increased their family activities — bridge, checkers, Ping Pong, talking and planning, eating together, listening to the radio, and going to church more. A sense of community spirit developed; people were more friendly and helpful to one another. They no longer were worried about "keeping up with the Joneses." They read more and they discussed national issues more.

Although attitudes toward the depression varied with employment status, even those who held jobs were not without worries. A study of employed engineers in New York City in 1932 (three out of every ten were unemployed) indicated that 25 per cent feared being laid off at almost any time while another third felt a general anxiety over their work. The same survey reported that one third of the unemployed engineers and 19 per cent of those employed felt that the country needed a dictator; 65 per cent of the unemployed and 43 per cent of the employed blamed the government for much of the depression; while 68 per cent of the unemployed and 45 per cent of the employed said that the employers thought only of profits.

"Nothing at present," "Come back in two or three months and we might have a job," "We are not adding to our force this year" — these were the disheartening words of urban America in depression. Meanwhile, conditions in the farm areas were desperate. Agricultural prosperity depended heavily on the buying power of urban America and overseas purchasers. Even before 1929, the use of more and more farm machinery had produced a surplus. The depression added a crushing weight to the farmer's troubles. Between 1930 and 1934 nearly a million farmers lost their farms. And gross income of agriculture fell from $11,941,000,000 in 1929 to $5,331,000,-000 by 1932.

The tragedy of drought augmented the farmer's plight. Damage was severe in a belt stretching from Texas to Maryland in 1930. In the Dust Bowl the soil began to blow away, fields drifted into dunes — burying fences and machinery; and the air was so thick with dry, choking dirt that the visibility on highways at times resembled that in a London fog. There had been droughts on the Great Plains before, but nothing like this. Farmers in their misery pulled up stakes and joined the thousands of unemployed urban workers restlessly moving across the continent.

The drought was so severe in states like Arkansas that even subsistence farming could not produce enough to eat. One Red Cross worker described taking pack mules to reach an isolated cabin to find a "gaunt family subsisting on cornmeal and blue milk. A skeleton cow stares at you, a dead mule lies over in the field. Clothing is in rags. 'No, Ma'am, we ain't hongry . . . There's folk worse off'n us.' " Relief aid was even less adequate than in urban areas. A family of five received $5 worth of food a month to keep "the wrinkles out of their bellies." The wrinkle-removing formula was:

36 pounds of flour	$ .90
24 pounds of split beans	.70
12 pounds of cracked rice	.35
2 pounds of coffee	.30
24 pounds of meal	.55
½ gallon of molasses	.35
Lard and bacon	1.75
Baking powder	.10
	$5.00[4]

The value of farm crops in 1930 was 28 per cent less than the year before. Each of the next two years was even worse. The staggering decline in prices made the value of the 1931 crop less than half that of 1929. By 1932, wheat was selling in Kansas for twenty cents a bushel. In Nebraska, county commissioners bought corn for fuel at $8 a ton since coal cost $12. "Iowans have figured out that corn from ten acres will, if used as a fuel, keep a farmhouse warm through the winter," observed the *Detroit News*. "In time, as we have been saying, things will automatically right themselves. The next forward step is for a Kentucky miner to learn how to eat coal."

Farm credit dried up, mortgage foreclosures became frequent, and one Department of Agriculture agent wrote that farmers were "particularly sore" at the "seeming indifference of urban people and public officials." The anger in the farm country boiled to the edge of violence in Iowa in 1932. The wheat belt, the Dust Bowl, and depressed Southern agriculture all were more accustomed to trouble, more acquainted with grief — and more placid under calamity. But not the Iowa farmer with better soil, more rainfall, bigger crops, and greater prosperity. He was loaded with mortgages from purchasing land and machinery. Though he could turn to more than adequate subsistence farming, he refused to accept it. The Iowa farmer demanded the same comforts, privileges, and social status as the doctor, the lawyer, the preacher, and the merchant in the town. Nurtured on the belief that the independent farmer was the noblest creation of God, essential to the democratic way of life, the solid Iowa middle-class farmer would not accept the status of a peasant.

They were conservative men, but now they were ready to strike back. They organized a Farm Holiday to prevent the delivery of farm products at less than production costs. At 5 A.M. on August 15, 1932, barricades of spiked logs and cables were stretched across country roads near towns throughout northern Iowa. At Sioux City, the point of major effort, two thousand farmers patrolled the roads with clubs and pitchforks. They turned back cattle shipments, they dumped milk or confiscated it for free distribution. Only a few truckers evaded the barriers, two trains were stopped, and Sioux City ate out of cans. The strikers occasionally jostled armed deputies who roamed the roads, but there was little violence. One reporter wrote that the tense way the farmers talked and their determined faces "give you the feeling of Paul Revere rousing the countryside. They themselves bring in references continually to their own American Revolution. 'We aren't so different from the Boston Tea Party, boys. Those fellows weren't keeping the law.' "

Farm strikes spread in neighboring states. Although they failed in their immediate objective, they were a warning of the need for action to prevent smoldering discontent from becoming a raging prairie fire. Meanwhile, the Farm Holiday attempts to thwart farm mortgage foreclosures met more immediate success. Large gatherings of farmers in many communities prevented sheriffs from posting notices of foreclosure sales. Or at foreclosure auctions, the neighbors threatened outsiders, then bid in themselves, bought the animals and equipment at bedrock prices, and gave them back to the dispossessed farmer. At one foreclosure sale in Nebraska, cows went for ten cents, horses for twenty-five and tractors for fifty. The dispossessed owner received his animals and equipment back for a total cost of fifteen dollars. At a foreclosure in Iowa, fifteen hundred farmers gathered to restrict the bidding. The holder of the $2500 mortgage collected just $42.05. By election day in 1932, Kansas editor William Allen White wrote in the *Saturday Evening Post*: ". . . belief in force rather than in reasonable political procedure . . . was boiling in Iowa . . . seething in Oklahoma, southern Minnesota, and Wisconsin. When the American farmer comes out to the road with a club or a pitchfork, the warning flag is out." [5]

In spite of growing uncertainty and misery, the orderliness of the country in 1930 and 1931 had been notable. But by 1932, many were losing patience. Four persons were killed and twenty-nine stoned or shot in a "Hunger March" probably instigated by Communists in Detroit in March, 1932. There was a riot before the Home Relief Office in New York City in January; a demonstration of twenty thousand in Chicago in February; and smaller demonstrations in Philadelphia, Charleston, West Virginia, Boston, and St. Louis in the next few months. Then, in the summer, the Bonus Expeditionary Army and the Farm Holiday demonstrated that the mood of many had changed from dismay to desperation. The Railroad Brotherhoods admonished in May, 1932, that unless unemployment and distress were checked, disorder would result. And William Green, head of the American Federation of Labor, warned: "Revolutions grow out of the depths of hunger."

The cataclysm of 1929 plunged the nation from the greatest decade of material prosperity any nation had ever known into a period of despondence, doubt, and frustration. The depression brought a more serious questioning of American institutions than any event since the Civil War. The experience burned itself deeply into the American conscience. Many hallowed beliefs were shaken. The illusion that American capitalism led a charmed life and the legend of the omnipotence of Wall Street were punctured. Bankers, brokers, and businessmen alike suffered a rude drop in prestige.

The crash and the depression also shook the belief that the nation was unique. We had been a people set apart; a new people in a new world. We had been able to build a government and a society from the ground up without the heavy hand of the past encumbering us. We had developed the dynamic of political freedom and political equality; we had a class structure that was mobile, with economic opportunity as a birthright; we had been a dynamic revolution from our birth. Other nations surely would recognize the superiority of our institutions and adopt or imitate them. We had always been a caravan on the march. The future, not the past, held our Garden of Eden.

This legend had hypnotized Americans for generations. With hard work, thrift, plain food, and log-cabin virtue, you could attain success. Horatio Alger had been a byword. "From farm boy to financier," "From log cabin to the White House" were treasured American myths. Poverty was a virtue because it stimulated diligence and frugality and culminated in success. To be born to adversity and to rise out of it was the familiar American success story. To have made your own way in life gave you a great advantage over the rich man's son who never learned to work or to value a dollar.

The depression tarnished the success legend. The trusty old formulas of honesty, toil, and integrity did not get you on the top any more. Energetic, industrious people wanted work, but there was none. Even the doctrine of thrift was jolted as bank after bank closed its doors. Frank A. Vanderlip, former president of the National City Bank of New York, pointed out in the *Saturday Evening Post* on November 5, 1932, that the depression had made changes in our language: "No longer is it an apt metaphor to say anything is 'as safe as a bank.'"

People began to date events from the catastrophe of the crash and the long-lasting depression: "No, we haven't had one since the depression," "I used to, but that was before the depression," "He's been like that ever since the depression." In an act of desperation in 1931 the public cheerfully sang "Life Is Just a Bowl of Cherries," but the next year the grimmer situation produced "Brother, Can You Spare a Dime?"

The shock of the depression shattered the American self-image. At the close of World War II, a publisher wrote on a book jacket that the author had achieved success "in spite of degrading hardships of poverty" as a child. *In spite of* — what a revolution in thinking for a people who had been nurtured on the value of having a childhood of adversity. For generations campaign managers had stressed the background of poverty from which their presidential candidate had come — or they invented one. But no attempt was made to invent one for Franklin D. Roosevelt. When the promoters of Wendell Willkie tried to sell that dynamic corporation lawyer as a poor little Hoosier boy, the public roared at Harold L. Ickes's barbed reference to "the barefoot boy from Wall Street." In that public response perished the politician's trust in poverty as the mother of virtue and the nurse of success. Ever since 1900, in fact, the conviction had been growing that poverty was a civic disease, a breeder of crime and corruption, rather than of character. The poor boy was underprivileged rather than advantaged. The depression further undermined the older image. People became cynical about Horatio Alger, and the emphasis moved in the 1930s to a craving for security.

The great achievement — the epic of America — had been the conquest of a rich, vast, stubborn, and at times brutal continent. We began as explorers, empire builders, pilgrims, refugees, and we had been on the march ever since. From farm to farm, from farm to city, from state to state, from job to job we had kept moving. We were a nation of itching feet. Mobility had been the lubricant of our society. " 'Scuse our dust," "You've got to be a go-getter if you expect to get ahead," "Your Uncle Dudley's going places," "I'm on my way," "Don't sell America short" — all symbolized an America that was always moving on and up.

But by the autumn of 1931, many were doubting the faith they had always proclaimed. "Is America growing old? Have we — the young adventurers, the Innocents Abroad, the pioneers, the buccaneers, the racketeers — slumped into that sad maturity which submits to events, accepts the universe?" asked Anne O'Hare McCormick in the *New York Times*.

The inertia in the country, wrote Mrs. McCormick, made skilled workmen hang around day after day hoping for odd jobs; the unemployed meekly accept the dwindling weekly handouts of relief agencies; led salesmen to question their own sales talk; large and small depositors alike to withdraw money from the banks and hoard it; made Big Business tycoons timid in their planning; and led political leaders to become timid, poor in ideas, and lacking in initiative.[6]

The nation had had depressions before. But never had so many questioned, as they did after 1929, whether it was the right road we were traveling.

The country was suffering from a mental deflation as well as an economic one. Gilbert Seldes, another contemporary observer, called 1929-1932 years of breaking idols and abandoning faiths.[7] Our sunlit confidence was now clouded. Buoyant optimism and simple faith turned sour, cynical, and disbelieving. Many felt we would have permanent unemployment. Some writers embraced Communism and there was much discussion of Russia's Five Year Plan. Some businessmen, too, came to disbelieve in the future, and others favored a dictatorship. By 1932, some people wondered if this would be the last election and others believed it was America's last chance to save democracy.

Many foresaw the end of the long, dynamic expansion of the economy, the very foundation of the epic of America. The average American must now modify his ambitions. He would not rise. Instead he would have to take his place in a world more rigid and stratified than Americans had ever known. Permanent stagnation became the fear. We had not only lost faith in the past, but now some were in the mood to deflate the future.

From the vantage point of 1955, *Fortune* recalled how the depression split America mentally; how it robbed rational men of their ability to be rational about economics; how it degraded and stultified American capitalism and turned some of the nation's creative minds to specious promises of fascism, technocracy, social credit, socialism, and Communism; and how it brought despair and hunger to millions and planted blind resentment in their hearts. But, most of all, "It did something that no foreign enemy, national disaster, or old-fashioned 'panic' had ever done: it paralyzed, for years, America's growth." [8]

---

4. Ineptness in the White House

It was a grim irony of history that Herbert Hoover, the prophet of prosperity in 1928, presided over the nation in its years of travail. Until he entered the White House, his career epitomized the American success story. Orphaned at ten, he worked his way through Stanford University and soon was a mining engineer in Asia and Africa. Before the Great War of 1914, he had successfully managed a score of mining and other business enterprises in four continents, imposing order through his integrity, singlemindedness, and administrative genius.

With admirable efficiency he directed relief for the Belgians after the war broke out. Called to be Food Administrator by Woodrow Wilson in 1917, he soon made his name a household word. At the close of the war, Hoover's distribution of food and his direction of the mines and railroads of central Europe had won him widespread recognition. As Secretary of Commerce in the cabinets of Harding and Coolidge he increased the prestige of his Department immeasurably. Its functions were expanded and its services aided business in eliminating economic waste.

Within a year of his victory over Alfred E. Smith, the stock market crash posed a situation radically different from that faced by his immediate predecessors. Hoover's difficulties in coping with the depression during his trying years in the White House were increased, however, by his failure to grasp the full powers of the presidency. He viewed the office largely as administrative and government itself as more of a science than an art. While such attitudes made him a successful cabinet member, they limited his effectiveness in the White House. He never was able to use the presidency as a pulpit to rally Congress and the public to vigorous action under his leadership. For all his ability to work with business and financial leaders, he was unable to reach the average citizen who yearned for leadership from Washington. He did extend the government into the economy with the Reconstruction Finance Corporation, but this was remote from the individual person grappling with unemployment and the problems of feeding his family.

Hoover failed to project the image of the presidency as an institution which could help create what the people wanted. With his distant, austere personality he was unable to put into memorable words what the people were striving to achieve. The public, as a result, watched Hoover struggle with the depression, as Gerald Johnson has remarked, "without ever identifying themselves with the protagonist; most of us never felt that we had a penny on Hoover." [1]

Although Hoover could administer the machinery of government with great skill and efficiency and knew the world of business, he was unable to lead his party and Congress or to mold and guide public opinion. "I was convinced that efficient, honest administration of the vast machine of the Federal government would appeal to all citizens," he has written. "I have since learned that efficient government does not interest the people as much as dramatics." [2] Strong, imaginative leadership together with the drama of a cause were lacking. There were no hours of triumph for him in the presidency, none in which he could feel the applause and encouragement of a whole nation.

Hoover had had less prior experience in politics than any president since General Grant. He lacked the skill to handle the variety of groups a president must work with to secure legislation. And his uncertainty with and apparent dislike of politicians clearly hampered his conduct as President. He lacked the instincts of a politician; as a result, he failed as a party leader. His political ineptness led crusty H. L. Mencken to comment in May, 1931, that to the country "Lord Hoover is a flop."

His lack of support from his own party in the Senate was highlighted early in 1931 when Republican Senators remained quiet while the Democrats launched a scathing attack on him for an entire week. "Mr. Hoover is most poisonously unpopular in Washington," wrote T. R. B. in the *New Republic*. "Never have I seen the time when there was meaner talk about the occupant of the White House than there is today." [3] Much of the mean talk about the President actually originated with Old Guard Republican Senators on Capitol Hill.

He was not a dynamic public figure who believed in rallying the public to help him push a program through Congress as Theodore Roosevelt and Woodrow Wilson had done. "I had little taste for forcing Congressional action or engaging in battles of criticism," he has written. He felt that Congress had been weakened by the increasing ascendancy of the executive. The independence of the legislature was an article of faith with him. He recommended the fields where legislation was needed but he left its formulation to Congress. A case in point was the Hawley-Smoot tariff. He asked for a limited revision of rates. A single Senate vote was needed to secure a resolution calling for this, but he failed to use his influence to swing this vote and the way was then opened for widespread upward revision. By 1931, the President was more active in guiding legislation through

Congress, but by now he did not have a reliable majority to work with. Faced with divisions in Republican ranks and hostile Democrats thirsting for victory in 1932, he was unable to regroup his lines with Congress. Hoover was not the man to wheedle or cajole. Increasingly he gave the impression that he viewed Congress as a nuisance and all criticism of himself as merely partisan politics.

Had the President been able to maintain good relations with the Washington newspaper correspondents, he might have established a friendly channel to public opinion to offset his difficulties with Congress. As Secretary of Commerce he had had the good will and warm respect of the reporters. By the middle of his presidency, however, his association with the correspondents was described as "rapidly degenerating into open warfare." A series of blunders turned the press corps against him. "He resorted to high-handed measures and a rank antagonizing of the correspondents which brought down a storm of protest," Leo Rosten has written. Hoover bitterly complained of newspaper stories to the home offices, and it was believed he brought about the removal of some correspondents.

With his political inexperience, he was unable to develop the protective armor he needed to ignore newspaper criticism. He was fretful and moody under attack, and White House press conferences and newspaper releases became barren of news. To the correspondents he appeared an aloof, chilly figure who was "easily annoyed, and plainly peevish under the constant surveillance of the working press."

The fury welling up from the grave plight of the nation, the difficult situation with Congress, and partisan attacks from the Democrats might have been lessened somewhat by rapport between Hoover and the correspondents. The faulty handling of both newspaper reporters and Congressmen furnished plentiful ammunition for the Democratic National Committee. Charles Michelson, the Committee's publicity director, laid down a continuous barrage of charges. The "smear Hoover" campaign was cruel, hard-hitting, and effective. Much of it was unfair and contributed to the image of Hoover as a do-nothing President.[4]

When he entered the White House, Hoover's ambition was to be known as the great social engineer who could organize and manipulate the forces of production and distribution to serve human welfare.

In his lifetime since 1874, he had seen a remarkable rise in both American production and the standard of living. After the close of the depression of 1893, he had watched the American economy develop with no major dislocation. And he inherited from the post-Civil War giants, who had built the booming American industry, their faith that the system worked. He had a dedicated belief in the America that had produced such an economic system, and he saw more clearly than most businessmen and bankers the power for good that lay in the industrial revolution of the twentieth century.

The collapse of the world that had shaped his philosophy did not alter his faith in the American system. He did not feel that a major adjustment was necessary in America between democracy and capitalism. He was driven, therefore, to look abroad for the source of the trouble. While stating to Congress in December, 1930, that the "origins of this depression lie to some extent within our own borders through a speculative period," he insisted that the depression already would have been conquered had this been the basic problem. "The major forces of depression now lie outside of the United States." Europe was the plague spot. Even before the depression, he had an acute case of xenophobia. In his memoirs he explains that the United States had developed something new in history but that "out of the boiling social and economic caldron of Europe, with its hates and fears, rose miasmic infections which might greatly harm or even destroy what seemed to me to be the hope of the world."

Hoover's belief that in the new age that had developed the United States could no longer go its own way oblivious to developments elsewhere was profoundly right. But he was profoundly wrong in his interpretation that economic troubles abroad were the *major forces* generating our own depression. While Europe became the scapegoat to President Hoover, such is the perverseness of a democracy that, at home, the people cast him and the Republican party in that very same role.

As the depression developed and lengthened, the President could not conceive that there was anything fundamentally wrong with America. It was not that he believed the American system required no changes. He has written that the nation needed reforms in the antitrust laws, in the regulation of electric power, in the railroads, in the stock market, and in banking when he took office; but he felt that the depression had to be cured before "we could take the shocks of so widespread a Federal action." Nor did he view the American way as a system of laissez faire. There had to be economic justice as well as political and social justice. "It is as if we set a race," he explained during the 1928 campaign. "We, through free and universal education, provide the training of the runners; we give to them an equal start; we provide in the government the umpire of fairness in the race. The winner is he who shows the most conscientious training, the greatest ability, and the greatest character."

Hoover viewed the federal government as an umpire assisting in the achievement of economic justice. After the stock market crash, he encouraged voluntary action by business to maintain production and wages. He did bring federal leadership to a depression for the first time in American history, but he shied away from federal compulsion over business when voluntary promises could not be kept.

Nor did he believe in government in business. When Congress passed the Muscle Shoals bill in 1931, establishing a public corporation to control floods in the Tennessee Valley and produce cheap electric power, his veto was a stern rebuke: "I am firmly opposed to the Government entering into any business the major purpose of which is competition with our citizens . . . That is not liberalism; it is degeneration."

He was convinced that the government should not aid people directly with relief grants. It could help people to help themselves, and no more. Hoover was a man of unwavering principle. Through the throes of depression, he maintained his basic ideas intact. He was not indifferent or insensitive to the suffering of the unemployed, but it seemed to him that there were steps which must not be taken.

After the stock market crash, Secretary of the Treasury Andrew W. Mellon advised the President to keep hands off and let the slump liquidate itself. "Liquidate labor, liquidate stocks, liquidate the farmers, liquidate real estate," said Mellon.[5] This philosophy, that the economy was best served if the government did nothing, had been the American reaction in previous depressions. The core of business thinking was the self-regulating economy. If the economy were left alone by government and other power groups including labor unions, it would reach an equilibrium.[6]

Hoover, and a number of his advisers, disagreed. The nation was far more industrialized in 1929 than it had been in 1893 or 1873. It was not possible any longer for large numbers of unemployed to return to the farm. The government, Hoover believed, must help cushion the blows. While government should keep its activity down to a reasonable minimum, it could guide and stimulate private business initiative. It could also encourage local government and private charity to increase their humanitarian efforts. And it could maintain confidence in the future. In time, the sweeping public assurances from the White House that prosperity was just around the corner were met with derisive laughter.

The President knew in November, 1929, the seriousness of the economic situation. He held conferences with railroad presidents, leaders of finance, industry, trade, and labor. He explained that the crisis went deeper than the stock market crash. The depression, he predicted, would last for some time and two or three millions would be unemployed. He warned these leaders that the major responsibility for averting a catastrophe was theirs. He urged business to maintain production and refrain from severe wage reductions. In return, labor leaders were asked not to press for wage increases. The burden of the depression, the President insisted, must not be thrown on the workers. The liquidation of labor had been the policy of business in past depressions, but he explained that he was opposed to this. Wages should be maintained for the present but could be reduced later when the cost of living fell: "In any event the first shock must fall on profits and not on wages." The President also asked governors and mayors to join the federal government in increasing spending for public works.

When Congress convened that December, Hoover set forth his plans for expanding public works and described the encouragement he had given to voluntary efforts on the part of business and labor to meet the crisis. He was convinced, he told Congress, that "we have reestablished confidence" and that "the measures taken must be vigorously pursued until normal conditions are restored."

In the spring of 1930 Congress approved the expenditure of 750 million dollars for rivers and harbors, public works, and highways. For a few months business honored its pledge to maintain production and not cut wages. But beginning in May and June, 1930, since it could not produce for nonexistent markets, business had to slash production. Although wage scales were generally sustained until the summer of 1931, the increasing numbers of workers fired brought a drastic shrinkage in the total wage bill.

In spite of curtailment of production, Hoover stubbornly continued to talk as though his program were successful. During the summer of 1931, when unemployment was well over seven million and business was on the verge of radical wage cuts, the President observed that he had "steadily urged the maintenance of wages and salaries."

The worst actually seemed to be over in the spring of 1931. Industrial production increased slightly, bank failures lessened, and employment turned slowly upward. At this point, developments overseas checked the slight upswing. In May the largest bank in Austria suddenly closed its doors. All over Europe the financial structure trembled and business declined sharply. Europe's economy had been buoyed up in the 1920s by large American loans and sizable American imports. The depression brought a virtual cessation of both. And the passage of the highly protectionist Hawley-Smoot tariff in 1930 added to Europe's difficulty in earning dollars to pay its American obligations.

In June, 1931, Germany announced it was unable to meet its war reparation payments or its short-term obligations. Hoover, after enlisting the support of key members of Congress, proposed a moratorium on all intergovernmental debt and reparation payments. It was a statesmanlike step, but it did not stem the tide. In September, Britain was forced off the gold standard. Foreign investors unloaded their American securities and withdrew large sums of gold they had deposited in American banks. Americans, too, began withdrawing gold and hoarding it.

At this point the Federal Reserve Board decided to protect the gold standard in the traditional way. On October 9, it raised the rediscount rate from 1.5 to 2.5 per cent and one week later to 3.5 per cent. The outflow of gold was checked, but the step ended the chance of domestic recovery. Production declined, stock prices dropped rapidly, interest rates rose, and banks tightened credit starting liquidations all over again. Bank failures rose from 158 in August to 522 in October — the highest ever in any month. Unemployment rose from 7,778,000 in October to 8,908,000 by December, and to 10 million by January, 1932. Fear — "nameless, terrifying fear," Franklin D. Roosevelt called it later — gripped the nation.

The Federal Reserve authorities had succumbed to something approaching panic. Their strong deflationary measure came after two years of contraction, not inflation. Early in 1932, the Federal Reserve authorities reversed their October policy and undertook moderate credit expansion. Such a policy might have helped the previous October, but by now it was too late. The President, business, and financial leaders feared inflation. The years from 1900 to 1929 had seen generally rising prices. Inflation, then, seemed the chief threat to prosperity. And being more afraid of inflation than deflation, by their October action they produced a serious deflation which increased the severity of the depression.

The crash in Europe in 1931 deeply affected the depression in the United States as President Hoover has stated. But the failure to go off the gold standard, and the policy of tightening credit instead of moving toward inflation, made the American depression much more severe and long-lasting than that of those countries which went off gold in 1931. Hoover's past experience made him stick resolutely to the gold standard and to the hope of a balanced budget. He felt that only collectivists, fools, or knaves would tamper with these bulwarks of the American system.

With his belief that the depression was mainly of foreign origin, the President refused either to search for basic domestic causes of it or to develop domestic solutions that would check it. And his firm belief in the balanced budget — it was a bit out of balance in 1931 and 1932 — led him to resist massive government spending. He was opposed, he said, to "squandering the nation into prosperity." He refused to accept the contention that a government deficit need not be inflationary when the resources and workers of the nation were only partially utilized.

The Administration was forced to do more than encourage voluntary action by business when the depression deepened late in 1931. The economic structure now seemed in danger of toppling. At this point, the President accepted small and reluctant beginnings of the welfare state. Capital had to be rescued from imminent collapse and, then, stimulated by government aid. At his request, Congress chartered the Reconstruction Finance Corporation in January, 1932, to loan money to save railroads, banks, building and loan associations, and other financial institutions. "Its purpose," Hoover explained, "is to stop deflation in agriculture and industry and thus to increase employment by the restoration of men to their normal jobs."

Congress in January, 1932, also appropriated additional capital for Federal Land Banks and in July established home loan banks to enable building and loan associations, savings banks, and insurance companies to obtain money from them rather than to foreclose on homeowners. The President stood fast, however, against direct federal aid for the unemployed. Such a step ran counter to his principle that relief was the responsibility of voluntary agencies and state and local governments. "The moment responsibilities of any community, particularly in economic and social questions, are shifted from any part of the nation to Washington, then that community has subjected itself to a remote bureaucracy," he stated in February, 1931. "It has lost a large part of its voice in the control of its own destiny."

While few disagreed with this as a statement of political theory, many disagreed with it in the light of current reality. Although people were willing to contribute to community charities, local resources, both private and governmental, were not sufficient. Jacob Billikopf, a leading social worker, told the National Conference of Social Work in July, 1931, that community chests would certainly cooperate with the President's Emergency Committee on raising relief funds for the unemployed:

> But . . . I want to warn you . . . that we will be guilty of duplicity; we will be betraying the interests of the millions of unemployed . . . if . . . we should give the impression . . . that all a community has to do is to raise its chest quota . . . As a result of the policy of drift . . . our government will be compelled, by the logic of inescapably cruel events ahead of us, to step into the situation and bring relief on a large scale . . . Private philanthropy . . . is virtually bankrupt in the face of great disaster.[7]

When the demand grew in 1932 for generous grants of Federal money for public works, Hoover refused, saying: "It is generally agreed that the balancing of the Federal budget and unimpaired national credit is indispensable to the restoration of confidence and to the very start of economic recovery." In July, 1932, Congress passed a relief bill for direct aid to individuals and for a huge expansion of public works — only to meet a presidential veto. Hoover denounced the measure as "impractical," "dangerous" and "damaging to our whole conception of governmental relations." At the President's suggestion Congress then passed a relief bill authorizing the RFC to lend $300 million to states whose resources were exhausted and an additional billion and a half to states and municipalities for self-liquidating public works.

Twelve million were unemployed in July, 1932. Yet the President insisted that direct federal relief would weaken the moral fiber of the recipient. A growing segment of the vocal public considered his attitude harsh and inhumane. Many people intolerantly said that Hoover was against a dole for the unemployed but favored a dole for business. Hoover did not view the RFC as a dole. Rather he felt it was a necessary step to shore up a faltering system. Then, as the system steadied itself and began to function smoothly again, prosperity would spread from the railroads, banks, and big industrial units to the workers.

In 1932, opponents of Hoover denounced this as the "trickle-down" theory of wealth. And when the Democrats started firing their campaign guns, Hoover was in an impossible position. No democratic government could win public confidence when it was aiding big financiers and seemed to be disregarding the plight of millions of its humbler citizens. No matter how the President explained it, the explanation was inacceptable. A case in point involved General Charles G. Dawes, successful Chicago banker, Republican leader, and former Vice-President. Dawes agreed with Hoover that federal relief for the unemployed was a "violation of a fundamental principle of good government." From January to June 6, 1932, Dawes served as president of the RFC. He then resigned to devote himself to saving his bank in Chicago. The collapse of this major financial institution would have had wide repercussions. Late in June the RFC lent ninety million dollars to save the Dawes bank. The loan was a proper one and Hoover and the RFC acted correctly. During the presidential campaign, Hoover gave a long explanation of the necessity of the action and tried to make it clear that Dawes had not used his influence with the RFC to bail out his bank. But like the action against the Bonus Army at Anacostia Flats, it left a sour taste. "The situation demanded broad vision and comprehensive understanding of the problem, instant decision, bold and courageous action. Only by this was a major disaster averted," the President explained. Why, it was asked, did the President not recognize that helping the needy also required broad vision and bold and courageous action?

Hoover's inflexibility on basic economic questions was revealed in his attitude toward the farm problem. Before the stock market crash, Congress had established the Federal Farm Board to lend money to cooperatives to facilitate marketing of agricultural commodities and to control surpluses. This was essentially a long-range program. It assumed that there would be a gradual recovery for agriculture, as the non-agricultural segments of the economy continued to boom. The Farm Board by buying and storing surpluses would sustain prices until the market became normal. It was assumed that there was no problem of continual agricultural overproduction. The sharp decline in non-farm income which the depression brought was a blow which the Federal Farm Board had not been created to meet. Even without the depression, the program of the Board was inadequate. When domestic and foreign demand fell after 1929, the Farm Board found itself swamped with surpluses. While it bought some of the surplus, it lacked funds for a major effort. Finally, the Board tried to persuade farmers *voluntarily* to restrict production. This request for voluntary action was no more effective than the request for voluntary action to maintain business production.

Federal compulsion — acreage reduction in the case of agriculture — would come with the New Deal. President Hoover, with his belief that democracy and capitalism were not in need of serious readjustment, was as opposed to taking this step as he was to unbalanced budgets and abandonment of the gold standard. Once the depression reached its March, 1933, proportions, it could be checked only after prolonged suffering and by fundamental changes. By the time they came, the catastrophe was so widespread that the depression, with some alleviation, continued for the remainder of the decade.

5.   Repudiating the Republicans

By the time of his campaign for re-election in 1932, all the signs were against Hoover. Industrial production stood at just 50 per cent of the mid-1929 level, the value of the gross national product had fallen 40 per cent to $67 billion. Approximately twelve million were out of work. Several million more were working only part time and wages and salaries had fallen 40 per cent. Liquidations and failures were threatening such sturdy institutions as insurance, banking, and investment.

Although many Republican leaders had no enthusiasm for Hoover, the incumbent President could not be denied renomination. To have attempted it would only have created a greater party calamity than they already faced. After an apathetic Convention, many Republican politicians exerted little effort to help the nominee, while others deserted him. Senators George W. Norris of Nebraska, Hiram Johnson of California, Smith W. Brookhart of Iowa, Albert Gallatin Simms and Bronson Cutting of New Mexico, and Robert La Follette, Jr., and Governor Phil La Follette of Wisconsin renounced their national leader and campaigned for Roosevelt. The exodus of such liberal leaders made it easier for the opposition to label the Republicans as the reactionary party.

Early in October, the President delivered his first campaign speech in the state of his birth. Iowa Republican leaders carefully screened the audience against hecklers. But Farm Holiday leader Milo Reno prepared a less friendly reception "to let the world know that there's folks in Ioway who's sour'n hell on Hoover." Reno paraded two thousand shabby men, women and children through the streets of Des Moines with banners proclaiming: "In Hoover We Trusted; Now We Are Busted," "We Want Living Prices, Not Credit," "Hoover, Hyde [Secretary of Agriculture], Hell and Hard Times — the Republican 4-H Club."

The President was booed in Philadelphia and Salt Lake City. His reception in Detroit was worse. Several thousand bonus-seeking veterans, Communists, and disgruntled citizens surrounded his train at the station and heckled and jeered. "Down with Hoover, slayer of veterans," bystanders cried. At the Arena, banners derided the Administration's depression legislation: "Hoover's Record: Millions for Bankers, Hunger for Workers." Residents of other cities were not so blunt, but their reception could hardly have cheered the President. "I've been traveling with Presidents since Roosevelt," said one Secret Service agent, "and never before have I seen one actually booed, with men running out into the streets to thumb their noses at him. It's not a pretty sight."

Deeply convinced of the rightness of his policies, Hoover must have been shocked. Later in October, he was spurred briefly to an aggressive defense of his policies. He termed Democratic plans to employ ten million people on self-liquidating public works "a promise no Government can fulfill. It is utterly wrong to delude suffering men and women with such assurances." At Cleveland, he said: "There should be no fear at any deserving American fireside that starvation or cold will creep within their doors this winter." [1]

In New York City, the President described the New Deal as a "proposal of revolutionary changes which would undermine and destroy the fundamentals of the American system of government." When he closed his campaign at St. Paul, his reception was familiar by now and foreboding. Along the streets were the usual placards: "Billions for Bankers, Bullets for Vets," "Heroes in 1917 — Bums in 1932." Disturbed by such greetings, the President extemporized in his speech: "Thank God you still have a government in Washington that knows how to quell a mob." He was severely critical of Democratic plans: "Indeed, this is the same philosophy of government which has poisoned all of Europe. They have been the fumes of the witch's caldron which boiled in Russia and in its attenuated flavor spread over the whole of Europe and would by many be introduced into the United States."

Die-hard Republicans tried to help the President stem the Democratic tide. Henry Ford, on a nationwide radio broadcast, appealed for the "best man," "the very embodiment of common sense and reliability." And the Ford Motor Company notified its employees: "To prevent times from getting worse and to help them to get better, President Hoover must be elected." The Pennsylvania Railroad and several large Ohio rubber companies also suggested that their employees vote for Hoover. Secretary of Agriculture Arthur Hyde called Roosevelt "a common, garden variety of liar" and Secretary of the Navy Charles Francis Adams warned: "If Roosevelt is elected, the homes and lives of 100,000,000 American people might be in jeopardy."

When it had become clear early in 1932 that Hoover would seek re-election, newspapers focused their attention on the Democratic party. Since they felt that Hoover's chance of victory was slight, they demanded over and over that the Democratic candidate be a statesman who would lead the nation to recovery. They wanted no pussyfooting and no compromises. Most commentators by now were impatient with political necessity. They forgot in their angry comments about the Democratic front-runner for the nomination, Governor Franklin D. Roosevelt, that he had to win the nomination before he could run for president. As he carefully built his political strength in the months before the convention, the newspapers pictured him as no more than an adroit politician with no new ideas and offering no hope for the people. The paralyzed economic system had so sapped the tolerance of the commentators that they responded critically to Roosevelt's pattern of political behavior imposed by the political system.

To win the nomination, Roosevelt knew he had to win support from all sections and interests. This meant he had to compromise and deliberately be vague. To have proposed such a clear-cut plan as the commentators demanded might have lost all. But to the newspapermen, the emergency ruled out temporizing. Many of them were angry when Roosevelt developed a masterful campaign designed to win national support. More clearly than any other, Walter Lippmann set forth the commentator's image of Roosevelt when he described him as "an amiable man" who "is no crusader. He is no tribune of the people. He is no enemy of entrenched privilege. He is a pleasant man who, without any important qualifications for the office, would very much like to be President." And Frank Kent, respected elder statesman of political commentary, asserted in June, 1932, that there was no leader in sight for a nation that needed inspiring leadership: "What the people obviously want is a hero. We are in both parties and all factions, completely bereft of heroes." [2]

Roosevelt was unwilling to risk the progress of his political bandwagon to satisfy impatient intellectuals. He chose to win many moderately enthusiastic supporters rather than a few fanatic followers. There were many issues, including Prohibition and religion, hanging over from the '20s. Roosevelt skillfully maneuvered such issues into the background and thus avoided a divided party and a divided nation. Instead, in his pre-convention campaign, he kept the issue of the depression in the forefront. He spoke in eloquent words of the need for a planned recovery to restore economic balance. But he avoided a detailed program which would have reduced his area of flexibility and maneuver. Commentators, ignoring the political necessity in this, denounced him for proposing amorphous, glittering generalizations. A few, like the *San Francisco Chronicle* and H. L. Mencken, went so far as to write that the Democrats had nominated their weakest candidate.

The majority of Democratic politicians did not subscribe to the editorial writer's image of Roosevelt. He had the magic of a famous name; he had been re-elected Governor in 1930 by the staggering plurality of 725,000 — nearly twice as much as that "peerless" New York campaigner, Al Smith, had ever been able to roll up. And he had carried Republican upstate New York by 167,000 votes. His campaign manager, James A. Farley, diligently scoured the nation, shaking hands, writing letters, enlisting support for the front-runner, while back in Albany, Louis M. Howe, Roosevelt's faithful, untiring aide, coordinated the campaign.

Roosevelt by the spring of 1932 had strength in all parts of the nation. The West liked his support of public power. The East liked his opposition to Prohibition and his concern as Governor for the unemployed and the needy. To the South he was a dignified, Protestant country gentleman with a refined voice, who "could be trusted not to build a tunnel to the Vatican." Nevertheless, he faced practical political difficulties. Al Smith, the darling of the ethnic group voters in the big cities, had thrown his hat in the ring. Sensing a deadlocked convention, favorite-son candidates began to emerge. Immediately, the front-runner was exposed to attacks on all flanks.

William Randolph Hearst attacked one flank when he denounced Roosevelt as an internationalist and threw the support of his newspaper chain to John Nance Garner, Speaker of the House of Representatives. Roosevelt, who, as the vice-presidential candidate in 1920, had fought for the League of Nations, now ate his words. In a speech on February 2, 1932, after soothing the internationalists by attacking the Hawley-Smoot tariff and proposing a reciprocal trade program, he declared that the League today was not the League conceived by Woodrow Wilson. He would not now favor American participation in the League. This brought down upon him the scorn of the intellectuals, but the mass of the people, always suspicious of Europe and now fighting the depression, did not care. Roosevelt was already for them the symbol of the way out. Roosevelt's words brought a cessation of Hearst's attacks and ended the danger that his readers would desert the New York Governor. It seemed an essential political step toward victory.

The issues of Prohibition and corruption in Tammany Hall threatened to divide his supporters. He moved haltingly against Tammany during these months. And he supported repeal of the Eighteenth Amendment and the return of liquor-control to the states. He was wet but not wringing wet like Al Smith.

It was the depression, however, that Roosevelt intended to make the heart of his campaign. In a nationwide radio broadcast on April 7, 1932, he described the depression as a graver emergency than the World War. The Hoover Administration, while helping the top of our economy, had failed, he charged, to mobilize "the infantry of our economic army. . . . These unhappy times call for the building of plans that rest upon the forgotten, the unorganized but the indispensable units of economic power, for plans . . . that build from the bottom up and not from the top down, that put their faith once more in the forgotten man at the bottom of the economic pyramid."

Six weeks later at Oglethorpe University, in Georgia, the state Roosevelt considered his second home, he called for planning in the production and distribution of goods. The buying power of workers must be increased and the rewards for speculative capital reduced. "The country needs," concluded Roosevelt, "and, unless I mistake its temper, the country demands bold, persistent experimentation.

It is common sense to take a method and try it; if it fails, admit it frankly and try another. But above all, try something. The millions who are in want will not stand by silently forever while the things to satisfy their needs are within easy reach."

Roosevelt sensed that the dominant public mood demanded action from the White House. While Hoover seemed static, Roosevelt was a man in motion. Although his program was vague, it was in the liberal tradition of Theodore Roosevelt and Woodrow Wilson. His interest as Governor in agricultural relief, conservation, public power, social welfare, and unemployment relief pointed to this. Every survey indicated his appeal to the voter. As the Convention approached, however, there were dangerous roadblocks. He had the support of the South, except for Texas and Virginia, and of the West, except for California, leading H. L. Mencken to sneer that Roosevelt was supported by the yokels of the South and of the corn states. The East was more difficult. Tammany Hall was for Smith. Edward J. Flynn, leader of the Bronx, however, was for Roosevelt, as were most of the remaining state delegates. Massachusetts, Rhode Island, and Boss Hague's New Jersey were behind Al. Ohio, Indiana, and Illinois were all pledged to favorite sons.

When the delegates arrived at Chicago, Roosevelt was eighty votes short of nomination on the first ballot. Farley, Howe, and other Roosevelt lieutenants worked to persuade favorite-son candidates to withdraw. They raised the specter of a deadlocked convention as in 1924 when, after it had taken over a hundred ballots to nominate a candidate, the party had been left a shambles. In spite of their untiring efforts through hot, weary days, they were unable to shift any votes to the New York Governor. The nervous strain was close to the limit of endurance. The nominating speeches began on the afternoon of June 30, the fourth day of the Convention. They dragged on and on with "a merciless and unholy flood of oratory," Farley said. The delegates were hot — there was no air conditioning — and they were nearing exhaustion from the oratory, from the raucous demonstrations as each name was placed in nomination, and from the stale cigar smoke that hung like a fog over their heads.

Back in Albany, the Governor, his wife, his mother, and his legal aide and campaign consultant, Judge Samuel I. Rosenman, were glued to the radio. Out in the garage the reporters had set up their typewriters and special telephone lines had been run in. At Roosevelt's side was a direct phone to Howe's room in Chicago. He used it frequently. While the interminable seconding speeches were pouring over the radio, he advised Farley to push ahead with the balloting even though it was now early in the morning. The situation was too fraught with dangers to allow adjournment and a possible regrouping of strength by the Smith forces and the favorite sons.

The roll call started at 4:28 on the fifth morning. It took one hour and a half, since delegation after delegation demanded a poll of each member to reveal minority votes for candidates other than the one who had the unit vote of the entire delegation. Roosevelt's lines held and his total reached 666¼ votes — 104 less than the two thirds necessary, but 464½ ahead of Al Smith. Farley hoped for a switch in certain delegations before the results of the balloting were announced, but the bandwagon psychology did not work. On the second ballot, Farley threw in his meager reserve strength and Roosevelt's total reached 677¾. The third ballot was almost disastrous. Mississippi began to waver. It was held in line under the unit rule by the margin of one vote. Farley threw in his last reserves to reach 682 votes.

It was now 9:15 in the morning. The delegates had been in continuous session since the afternoon before. It was decided to adjourn the Convention until evening; and the delegates, exhausted from the bad air, the brass bands, the stale oratory, and the sleepless night, staggered back to their hotel rooms. Farley hurried to the Congress Hotel to confer with Howe. They agreed to stake everything on an attempt to win the support of John Nance Garner whose vote had jumped from 90¼ on the first ballot to 101¼ on the third. Farley met with Garner's manager, Congressman Sam Rayburn, who agreed to see what could be done.

Garner, in Washington, refused to answer a phone call from Al Smith, knowing that Smith wanted to pledge him to continue to block Roosevelt. William Randolph Hearst reached him through one of his reporters. Hearst disliked Roosevelt, but he hated Smith. He had been warned also by Farley and others that the deadlock might result in the nomination of Newton D. Baker, President Wilson's Secretary of War, whom he viewed as a dangerous internationalist. Hearst advised Garner to release his delegates to Roosevelt. Garner phoned Rayburn that the nomination should come on the next ballot. Later Rayburn phoned back that California would swing to Roosevelt but Texas would not unless Garner accepted the vice-presidential nomination. Garner, reluctant to leave the powerful post of Speaker of the House, nevertheless feared chaos at the Convention. He assented, saying, "Hell, I'll do anything to see the Democrats win one more national election."

The struggle was not over yet. Mississippi had cracked and gone over to the stop-Roosevelt forces. The most ardent Garner men, cheered by the increased vote on the third ballot, were canvassing delegates to switch to Garner. Sam Rayburn caucused Texas. The last-ditch Garner supporters fought a switch to Roosevelt. A number of them, rallying votes for Garner elsewhere, were absent from the caucus. After much wrangling, Rayburn persuaded the delegation to switch by a vote of 54 to 51.

When the Convention met that Friday night, the delegates anticipated another weary evening of balloting. Only a few knew about the maneuvering during the recess. When the roll call reached California, William G. McAdoo, Wilson's Secretary of the Treasury, spoke to the Convention. Eight years before, he had had a majority of the votes on ballot after ballot. But Al Smith's forces had held firm and McAdoo's chance had perished under the two-thirds rule. Now, in 1932, he ended Al Smith's last chance. "California came here to nominate a President," McAdoo told the Convention. "She did not come here to deadlock this convention or to engage in another disastrous contest like that of 1924." Then McAdoo cast California's 44 votes for Roosevelt. Mayor Cermak switched Illinois. All others fell in line except some diehard Smith followers who refused to make the nomination unanimous.

To indicate to the country that the Democratic candidate believed in spirited action and decisive leadership, in contrast to the months of apparent inaction and indecision from the White House, Roosevelt, ignoring the customary weeks of waiting to be informed of his nomination, flew immediately to Chicago to address the delegates.

Greeted by thunderous applause, Roosevelt pointed out that his flying to the Convention broke tradition. "Let it be from now on the task of our party to break foolish traditions." Warning against radicalism and reaction, he observed: "Ours must be a party of liberal thought, of planned actions, of enlightened international outlook, and of the greatest good to the greatest number of our citizens." He charged the Republican leadership with ignoring the domestic causes of the depression. In general terms he spoke of the need of government aid to agriculture, business, the unemployed, the regulation of the security markets, and the necessity for rigid governmental economy. It was not so much what he said as the way he said it. The calm, confident voice reassured a paralyzed nation that he would lead in the struggle to restore good times and to achieve a fairer share of the national wealth for all.

"I pledge you, I pledge myself, to a new deal for the American people," he concluded in his peroration. Like the phrase the "Forgotten Man," the "New Deal" caught on. It became the symbol for the Roosevelt program. It was to take its place in American politics with such earlier phrases as the "Square Deal," the "New Freedom" and the "New Nationalism," and after Roosevelt's death it would continue to evoke hope, enthusiasm, and bitterness. To the victims of the depression and to the youth of the decade of the '30s, the symbol was to have far-reaching effect in molding future political behavior.

Roosevelt demonstrated that autumn that he loved campaigning. He dismissed advice that a campaign might jeopardize his lead. He carried the attack to Hoover. And by his vigor he showed that whispering about his health was false. He had stumped the Midwest and the Pacific Coast by the time Hoover made his first campaign speech. James A. Farley, installed as chairman of the Democratic National Committee, working through his brother Elks, shaking hands, writing thousands of personal letters to party workers signed in green ink, far surpassed Republican organizers in energy and skill in conducting the nation-wide operation.

Roosevelt was received enthusiastically by large crowds wherever he went. Seventy thousand greeted him in Seattle, where he heard the Republican mayor call Hoover "a menace." At Los Angeles, thirty raggedly dressed supporters welcomed him at the station carrying placards: "Welcome to Roosevelt from the Forgotten Man." Two hundred thousand people crowded the streets as he toured the city. Through the Farm Holiday country of the Midwest he was met by thousands of deadly intent farmers. Chicago gave him a wild, roaring welcome with kerosene torches, horns, band music, and an old-fashioned parade. "It was truly a celebration," the *Chicago Tribune* sadly remarked. Detroit, soon to boo President Hoover, cheered Roosevelt lustily. "They liked his smile and the lift of his chin when he laughed," the *Detroit News* reported. By November 1, Roosevelt had traveled seventeen thousand miles and visited thirty-seven states. On election eve, the Governor turned to his only hopeless campaign — to win the votes of his conservative neighbors at Hyde Park.

At the close of the campaign, the *Nation* charged that neither party had proposed a "fundamental measure" that might "put us on the road to recovery." Roosevelt's campaign was exasperating to some writers. They wanted a clear blueprint for the future with a definite philosophy of government proposed. Roosevelt, on the other hand, was campaigning to win an election, not to erect a coherent system of political theory. He drew around him advisers reflecting left, right, and center. Before the nomination a Brain Trust of Raymond Moley, Rexford G. Tugwell, A. A. Berle — all professors at Columbia University — with Judge Rosenman, and Roosevelt's law partner Basil O'Connor, were his chief advisers on issues. After the nomination General Hugh "Old Ironpants" Johnson, Bernard Baruch, and many political leaders were added. The speech drafters were torn with dissension. Balanced budget advocates disagreed with those who insisted on spending for public works. High tariff men argued with proponents of a low tariff. Farm advisers were split over the merits of voluntary crop reduction as opposed to federal compulsion.

Roosevelt enjoyed listening to advice from all types of people. He liked to juggle ideas; to take one idea from one man and another from an opposing source and try to blend them. Raymond Moley has recalled his astonishment when Roosevelt told him to weave together two utterly different drafts of a speech on tariff policy.

Roosevelt had, in the words of Tugwell, "a flypaper mind." Roosevelt dug ideas and information out of people. The Brain Trust was a clearinghouse of ideas rather than a molder of Roosevelt's basic philosophy. ". . . the tapestry of policy he was weaving was guided by an artist's conception which was not made known to us," Tugwell has written. ". . . We were the journeymen, he the master craftsman." And Moley has explained: "I seemed to help crystallize his own ideas and inclinations, reflect them accurately, extend them where necessary, and present them congruously — in brief, to relieve him of a good deal of personal drudgery." [3]

During the campaign Roosevelt made appeals to a wide variety of groups. Before the Commonwealth Club of San Francisco he made the most complete statement of the philosophy behind the New Deal. He explained that every man had the right to a comfortable living, that wealth and products had to be distributed more equitably, that the average man had to have more purchasing power, and that there was the task "of adapting existing economic organization to the service of the people."

The speech was not quite a blueprint, but it showed the campaign was veering toward the left. A little later Roosevelt decided to take a tack to the right. Hugh Johnson drafted a strong economy speech. Roosevelt delivered it at Pittsburgh. He charged that Hoover was a spendthrift leading the nation to bankruptcy. He would bring Hoover's unbalanced budget into balance by reducing federal expense by 25 per cent. But he allowed himself a loophole: "If starvation and dire need on the part of any of our citizens make necessary the appropriation of additional funds which would keep the budget out of balance, I shall not hesitate to tell the American people the full truth and ask them to authorize the expenditure of that additional amount." [4]

Throughout the campaign Roosevelt changed pace and direction. This dismayed some of his supporters. It infuriated his opponents. Hoover growled that Roosevelt was a "chameleon on plaid" as he tried to grapple with this opponent who suddenly attacked, retreated deftly, then struck from the right, and a little later delivered a blow from the left. By the final weeks, Roosevelt's spirited campaign made him sound like a President in complete control of the situation while Hoover's harsh, belligerent tone made him sound like an uneasy, unsure contender.

For all of his criticism of the Hoover Administration, Roosevelt was careful in his speeches not to stir the emotions of the discontented and resentful. He did not arouse their passions or inflame their animosity. There was combustible material at hand. Roosevelt carefully avoided starting the blaze. He knew the delicate balance that had to be drawn. An attack on the Republican leadership for its failures must stop short of inflaming public bitterness. The mood of despair had to be manipulated into one of growing hope.

Roosevelt offered the people dramatic leadership, reform, and relief, but within the framework of orderly change. He stated his liberal philosophy succinctly in September, 1932: ". . . say that civilization is a tree which, as it grows, continually produces rot and deadwood. The radical says: 'Cut it down.' The conservative says: 'Don't touch it.' The liberal compromises: 'Let's prune, so that we lose neither the old trunk nor the new branches.' This campaign is waged to teach the country to move upon its appointed course, the way of change, in an orderly march, avoiding alike the revolution of radicalism and the revolution of conservatism." And, in the present crisis, he added, a President was needed whose interests were general, not special: ". . . . it needs to be reaffirmed," he said, "that the United States is one organic entity, that no interest, no class, no section, is either separate or supreme above the interests of all or divorced from the interests of all."

The 1932 election was America's reaction to adversity. The anger and frustration of an energetic people forced into idleness turned the Republican party out of power. Roosevelt carried forty-two states. He won 472 electoral votes to 59 for Hoover. He received 22,809,000 popular votes to Hoover's 15,758,000. In the crisis, the public retained its faith in the two-party system. The minor parties polled only 1,160,000 or 2.9 per cent of the total cast. The Communist party polled 103,000 of these and the Socialist party 885,000.

The *Chicago Tribune* remarked that Roosevelt's "personality and his ideas pleased the people. They were impressed by his good will and good faith." And the *Richmond Times-Dispatch* observed: "Tuesday's election has been termed a 'peaceful political revolution.' It is far more than that. It is a peaceful social revolution. Privilege rode too proudly. Then came Roosevelt with a magic phrase, 'The Forgotten Man.' "

The task of liberalism, Woodrow Wilson once said, was "to release the generous energies of our people." By 1932, the principle restrictive force binding the energies of the nation was an archaic economic organization that had throttled itself and reduced production to a trickle. Rigidity of thought in business had become a barrier to the achievement of a new era. The depression shattered public belief in the self-regulating economy. By 1932, the idea that government must assume responsibility for the welfare and security of its citizens was developing rapidly. The use of federal money for relief and for subsidies to stimulate purchasing power and employment was increasing — replacing the old concept of a self-regulating economy.

New ideas were needed to meet the depression in 1930, 1931, and 1932. But faith in American opportunity delayed the extension of governmental power over the economy. Then, after Hoover took the first halting step toward the welfare state, the public demanded more action, particularly governmental responsibility for the victims of the catastrophe.

Writers had asked in 1932 whether the two political parties could be revitalized to give them fighting programs, new names, and new aims. After March 4, 1933, as so many times before in American history, the political leadership that emerged was able to contain the inner stresses of a democratic society occupying a vast, rich continent. It was able to brake the disruptive forces short of the cleavage line and then start moving forward.

BOOK TWO

Politics of Resourcefulness: Roosevelt

---

6. "The Tremendous Entrance"

"It is good to be home," President Roosevelt told Congress in March, 1945, after his return from the Yalta Conference. "It has been a long journey," he added. "I hope you will also agree that it has been so far, a fruitful one."

It was a long and fruitful journey indeed from March 4, 1933, to April 12, 1945. During these years, Roosevelt was the principal actor in a mighty drama in which the American people experienced remarkable changes. After the interlude of the 1920s, capitalism was in the painful process of being adjusted to a democratic society and the dream of opportunity was being broadened to include nearly everyone. In world politics, the nation tortuously, sluggishly awakened to the Axis threat and then, during the war, became reconciled to the fact that it lived in an interdependent world.

Taking office at a time when the very foundations of the republic were threatened and when many were despairing of the ability of a democracy to meet the crisis, Roosevelt restored confidence and demonstrated that democratic government could be effective. He put the government clearly at the service of the people and the people responded. He awakened in millions of citizens a new sense of citizenship. The artistry with which he spoke to the nation convinced the public that they could trust him. He strengthened the natural and human resources of the nation. And he brought relief, reform, and, in a slower fashion, recovery.

Roosevelt's long and fruitful journey began, to use the words of Walt Whitman, with a "tremendous entrance." Confusion and despair were the keynotes of the closing days of the Hoover Administration. Unemployment soared to a new high, farm prices continued to decline, and, most terrifying of all, the nation's banking system was collapsing. By March 4, thirty-eight states had ordered their banks closed and in the remainder the banks operated under restrictions. All seemed to depend on the new President. ". . . no President . . . ever came to greater opportunities amid so great an outpouring of popular trust and hope," the *New York Times* wrote on March 3.

Between election and inauguration day — the last time the date would be the fourth of March — Hoover and Roosevelt carried on an undercover duel. Roosevelt met with his opponent, exchanged correspondence, and his aides worked with Hoover's associates, but Roosevelt was careful not to allow Hoover to commit him to the policies of the outgoing Administration. Above all, Hoover wanted Roosevelt to promise that he would not tamper with the gold standard. Roosevelt refused. Ever since those trying days, Hoover has insisted that Roosevelt's failure to agree with Hoover's "sound" policies unsettled business confidence and increased the severity of the depression.

Roosevelt's refusal to be committed was partly based on the fact that he had no legal powers until March 4. More important, he did not want any of the distrust and the hatred of Hoover to be transferred to him. Above all, he wanted to arrange the stage and his "tremendous entrance" on it according to his own plans. Robert E. Sherwood has written: "No cosmic dramatist could possibly devise a better entrance for a new President — or a new Dictator, or a new Messiah — than that accorded to Franklin Delano Roosevelt . . . Herbert Hoover was, in the parlance of vaudeville, 'a good act to follow.' " [1]

Clouds of gloom and despair hung heavy over the nation on the morning of inauguration day. At 4 A.M. Governors Herbert Lehman of New York and Henry Horner of Illinois, upon urgent entreaties from Washington, closed the banks in their states. Washington, itself, seemed a beleaguered capital in wartime. At midnight, March 3, the retiring, weary President said to a group of friends: "We are at the end of our string. There is nothing more we can do."

Roosevelt arrived in Washington on March 2. From the moment he arrived, the city took on almost a visible aura of hope. His calm, cheery confidence had already impressed the public. While the nation had shaken with fear on hearing the news that an assassin had tried to shoot him in Miami on February 15, the President-elect's poise had been undisturbed. His courage impressed the nation and increased the public's growing faith in him.

"This is a day of national consecration," the new President said in the opening words of his inaugural address. A hundred thousand somber spectators saw the President's uplifted chin, his confident smile, while countless millions heard the beautifully modulated words on their radios.

"This is preeminently the time to speak the truth, the whole truth, frankly and boldly," the President continued. "Nor need we shrink from honestly facing conditions in our country today. This great Nation will endure as it has endured, will revive and will prosper. So, first of all, let me assert my firm belief that the only thing we have to fear is fear itself — nameless, unreasoning, unjustified terror which paralyzes needed efforts to convert retreat into advance."

The difficulty, he explained, was not that we were stricken by a plague of locusts. There was plenty at our doorsteps but the "rulers of the exchange of mankind's goods" had failed through their stubbornness and incompetence. "The money changers have fled from their high seats in the temple of our civilization. We may now restore that temple to the ancient truths." Social values more noble than monetary profit must be restored. And restoration required more than a change in ethics. "This Nation asks for action, and action now. Our greatest primary task," he told the audience that now seemed to be stirring with hope, "is to put people to work." Along with this, farm prices had to be raised, foreclosures stopped, government costs reduced, relief activities unified, banking and credit regulated to end "speculation with other people's money." "We must act and act quickly," he stressed.

He called for the nation to be a good neighbor and supported restoration of world trade, but the establishment of a "sound national economy" came first. To go forward, "we must move as a trained and loyal army willing to sacrifice for the good of a common discipline." He was prepared, he told the audience, "to recommend the measures that a stricken Nation in the midst of a stricken world may require." In the event Congress failed to act, "I shall not evade the clear course of duty that will then confront me. I shall ask the Congress for the one remaining instrument to meet the crisis — broad Executive power to wage a war against the emergency, as great as the power that would be given to me if we were in fact invaded by a foreign foe."

After this note of grim warning, he shifted to a tone of hope and confidence. "We face the arduous days that lie before us in the warm courage of national unity; with the clear consciousness of seeking old and precious moral values; with the clean satisfaction that comes from the stern performance of duty by old and young alike. . . . We do not distrust the future of essential democracy," he continued. "The people of the United States have not failed." They ask for "direct, vigorous leadership," for "discipline and direction under leadership. They have made me the present instrument of their wishes. In the spirit of the gift I take it."

As he finished, he waved to the spectators and smiled his electrifying smile. Mrs. Roosevelt said to reporters afterwards: "It was very, very solemn, and a little terrifying. The crowds were so tremendous, and you felt that they would do anything — if only someone would tell them what to do." Back at the White House, Roosevelt plunged into a series of conferences. Congress was called into special session. The President proclaimed a bank holiday.

On March 9, as Congress hastily assembled, the President sent an emergency banking bill to the Hill. After forty minutes of debate, it was passed without a dissenting vote. The Republican floor leader told the Representatives: "The House is burning down, and the President of the United States says this is the way to put out the fire. I do not know that I am in favor of all the details carried out in this bill, but whether I am or not, I am going to give the President of the United States today his way. He is the man responsible and we must at this time follow his lead." After three hours' discussion in the Senate, the bill passed at 7:46 P.M. by a vote of 73 to 7. At 8:37 P.M. Roosevelt signed the measure.

On March 10 the President asked Congress to reduce government expenses and cut veterans' benefits. The message, in a crisis tone, warned that the nation was on the road to bankruptcy. Lobbyists for veterans deluged the Congress with telegrams. Revolt started in Democratic ranks. One leader pointed out that the new President studied the *Congressional Record*: "I warn you new Democrats to be careful where your names are found." Ninety Democrats deserted, but sixty-nine Republicans backed the President and the bill passed. While opposition was growing in the Senate, the President, in his first fireside chat on March 12, talked to the nation about banking. It was an immense success.

The next day, as the Senate considered the economy bill, the President sent a seventy-two-word message asking for modification of the Volstead Act to legalize the sale of beer and light wines. One newspaper remarked: "As the hart panteth for the running brook, the Democratic majority pants for beer." The President's timing was masterful. Protracted argument over the economy bill would delay the return of beer. The Senate passed the economy bill on the 15th and the beer bill on the 16th.

The President was acting. "The whole country is with him," Will Rogers said on March 5, "just so he does something. If he burned down the capitol we would cheer and say 'Well, we at least got a fire started anyhow.'" Ten thousand telegrams reached the White House the first week. Hope swept the nation. The stock market, after a nine-day suspension, reopened on the 15th. Excitement was high, stock prices climbed, and the ticker closed that day with "Happy days are here again." By now, too, sound banks with 90 per cent of the national banking resources were reopening and a surge of deposits indicated that faith in the banking system was being restored.

Fifteen days after Roosevelt had assumed the presidency, Anne O'Hare McCormick noted in the *New York Times*: "The yearning of America is for action, almost any kind of action. Roosevelt makes a flying start by satisfying that long-balked appetite . . . Two weeks of Roosevelt have changed the atmosphere of the capital, have raised the morale of the country . . . no President in so short a time has inspired so much hope."

Sensing the public elation, Roosevelt decided to hold Congress in session and push ahead with additional legislation. Government workers, struggling to keep up with the pace of these hectic days, grew gray-faced from lack of sleep, and newspapermen became groggy under the strain. There was a frenzied quality about these early New Deal days which obscured the fact that the original Brain Trust, and more recent advisers to Roosevelt, had drafted plans to meet various aspects of the crisis both prior to the campaign and between November and March.

Up to March 16, the legislation had been essentially defensive and conservative. Slashes in the budget pleased conservative Lewis W. Douglas, Director of the Budget. Bankers were delighted that Roosevelt had not nationalized the banks, a step which would have met only slight public resistance. But it was not all conservativism. On March 16, Roosevelt made a decision that veered toward the left. He sent to Congress the Agricultural Adjustment Act to increase farm prices and pay benefits to farmers in exchange for reduction of acreage. Farm pressure groups had at last achieved the fruits of more than thirty years of agitation. Working through the two-party system, after having failed with third-party movements in the late nineteenth century, they had succeeded in establishing the concept that farming was a special interest deserving special treatment. While some conservatives were reeling from the impact of the AAA proposal, the President asked Congress for the creation of a Civilian Conservation Corps which would put a quarter of a million young men to work planting trees, fighting forest fires, and cutting trails through the National Parks. The same day he requested five hundred million dollars for federal grants to the states for direct relief to the unemployed. An eleemosynary revolution was under way. Hoover had gone no further than loans to states and cities for self-liquidating public works. Now the biggest relief program in American history, to be financed by the federal government, was launched.

On March 29, the President sent Congress a bill to establish federal supervision of the security exchanges. Full publicity for new stock issues would be required and commercial banks would have to separate themselves from the sale of stocks. The measure also required that all member banks of the Federal Reserve system insure their deposits under the Federal Deposit Insurance Corporation. This was a major step in restoring confidence in the banking structure. Hysterical runs on banks became a thing of the past. Deposits were insured up to $2500 (later to $5000, then to $10,000), and money hoarded at home returned to the banks.

On April 10 Roosevelt asked Congress to create a Tennessee Valley Authority. It would not only produce power more cheaply than private utilities, but it would work on flood control, soil erosion, reforestation, navigation, and industrial development. Senator George Norris's long struggle for public operation of Muscle Shoals had been won.

On April 13, the President requested legislation to save small homeowners from mortgage foreclosures by readjusting payments to lower interest rates. On April 20, Roosevelt officially took the nation off the gold standard. On May 4, he asked for emergency railroad legislation to encourage financial reorganization, the prevention of waste, and the duplication of service.

Thirteen days later, the President asked for the passage of the National Industrial Recovery Act. He had planned to delay this legislation until his advisers could agree, but Congress was clamoring for action. A bill drafted by Senator Hugo Black of Alabama to spread work and purchasing power by reducing the work week to thirty hours had already passed the Senate. Unless he acted, Roosevelt knew that he would lose control of the legislative process to those who were more radical than he. Hastily, his advisers drafted the legislation.

It was designed, the President told Congress, for "a great cooperative movement throughout all industry in order to obtain wide reemployment, to shorten the working week and to prevent unfair competition and disastrous overproduction." The second section of the bill provided for a public works program of over three billion dollars. Although the NIRA was severely attacked in the Senate, particularly by liberals who charged that it was too favorable to business, it became law on June 16.

The first Hundred Days of the New Deal were now over. Roosevelt, thriving on the crisis, had emerged as the chief legislator, head of his party, and the unifier of the nation. Rallying public support to a degree unique in American history, he had launched an experimental program designed to achieve a more democratic economic and social system.

It was a program of trial and error. And of inconsistencies. The economy bill had been deflationary. The farm bill had been inflationary. While some were puzzled by such contradictions, the public mood was reflected in the popular tune "Who's Afraid of the Big Bad Wolf?"

The public, perhaps, did not comprehend all that the President was trying to do. They did understand, however, that he was different from Hoover. His laughter and great smile expressed the difference. The previous Administration had been grave, prudent, serious-minded, and hesitant. Roosevelt was neither hesitant nor fearful. Nor was he omniscient. He could try and try and try. The public welcomed the difference in a wave of joy. Hope and triumph replaced cynicism and despair.

The criticism of Roosevelt in 1932 as a pleasant man without much ability proved to be a boon. Their expectations had not been aroused as he approached the presidency. The public tended to underestimate, rather than overestimate, him. Then, the action that quickly followed his inaugural address came as sheer surprise. The eulogies in the press, the surprised and pleased comments of reporters, the flow of mail to the White House and to Congress were an incalculable asset. It was good fortune for him that he entered office a grossly underrated man — "a pill to cure an earthquake," sneered British Socialist Harold Laski. Had he been hailed as a messiah in 1932, his rapid actions might not have thrilled the country. The country had not responded, in fact, it laughed bitterly, when Hoover had called for a restoration of confidence. When Roosevelt said the "only thing we have to fear is fear itself," it electrified the nation, jarred the solidifying pessimism, and evoked a rebirth of hope.

7. Remaking the Face of the Nation

"For three years everything wore out and by the end of 1932 you could have said that the nation was down at the heel," *Fortune* remarked. Then, between 1933 and 1936, the New Deal speedily altered the face of the nation. On the farms, in the towns, in the great cities, in the forests and on the rivers, in business, in labor, in money and banking, and in government itself a vast transformation was under way.

In his haste to broaden opportunity and provide new hope, Roosevelt pursued reform and recovery with vigor although, at times, erratically. But the appalling conditions of the unemployed, the dead weight of over thirteen millions out of work, took precedence over every other problem. The resulting federal spending for public works and work relief brought the nation public construction on a scale undreamed of in the past.

The Public Works Administration, under the careful supervision and scrutiny of Harold L. Ickes, sponsored over thirty thousand projects. These were impressive and almost endless in their variety: a $42,000,000 sewer tunnel — the world's largest — for Chicago; a water supply system in Cleveland; a modern hospital for Florence, South Carolina; the Juniata Housing Project in Philadelphia; Boulder Dam; school and college buildings; a sewerage treatment plant at Springfield, Ohio; a Memorial Hall of Records at Annapolis; the Hillside Housing Project in the Bronx; new post offices; the completion of New York City's Triborough Bridge; strategic highways; parks; slum clearance; and the restoration of historic landmarks.

The various relief agencies, too, had a wide range of projects and activities: serving school lunches; flood and hurricane disaster relief work; raking leaves; instruction of illiterates; adult education classes in arts and crafts; a $40,000,000 airport for New York City; and the construction of schools, hospitals, libraries, and other public buildings. Work was found for people of every skill and occupation including white-collar workers, teachers, artists, musicians, actors, and writers.

A Federal Theater Project, begun in 1935, continued until 1939, when it was abolished in a blaze of controversy. It sponsored vaudeville troups, marionette companies presenting fairy-tale classics to enraptured audiences of children, minstrel shows, and dance groups. Among its highly successful productions for the legitimate stage were *Run Little Children* in Los Angeles, the swing *Mikado* in Chicago, *Murder in the Cathedral* in New York City, and an all-Negro *Macbeth*, with voodoo witch scenes.

By 1936, 4300 muralists, portrait painters, print makers, and sculptors were at work in schools, post offices, hospitals, and government buildings. Much of it was angry art depicting a great nation sunk in the throes of economic calamity.

Musicians and singers gave hundreds of performances and stimulated community musical activities. Scholars engaged in research projects and the preservation of historical records. Writers produced the valuable American Guide Series describing each of the states in detail. Meanwhile, the National Youth Administration kept many students in college and high school by paying them for part-time work in libraries and museums. As late as 1940, some four hundred thousand students were receiving NYA aid.

Unemployed youth flocked to the Civilian Conservation Corps which, in 1933-1934, employed about one million. When the program closed in 1941, some two and a half million men had been enrolled. Working from some 1500 camps the CCC planted over a billion and a half trees, strung over seventy-five thousand miles of telephone wires, spent nearly five million man-days fighting forest fires, broke thousands of trails through the national parks, and undertook innumerable pest and insect control projects.

When Roosevelt took office, one newspaper warned that "what this relief business needs is less RFC and more PDQ." Speedy improvisation was necessary to aid the real victims of the depression. Harry Hopkins, boss of the relief program, stated his concept of his duties succinctly: "I'm here to see that people don't starve." The Federal Emergency Relief Administration gave relief funds to the states, advised them on how to spend the money, and insisted that no wage rate be lower than thirty cents an hour. Decentralized control under the FERA led to different practices in different states.

Hopkins recommended cash payments to people on relief and deplored relief in the form of food or clothing as demoralizing for the recipients. But most communities had already established relief in kind, and continued the practice. Beginning in December, 1933, the government distributed surplus commodities through the FERA.

In the year 1933, 60 per cent of all public relief money came from the federal government. States like South Carolina, Arkansas, and Mississippi became virtually relief dependencies of FERA, drawing over 99 per cent of their relief funds from Washington. Although the Southern states drew the highest percentage of their relief funds from FERA, five Northern industrial states spent 42 per cent of the ERA's money. Sharecroppers in west Tennessee, where *previous* yearly incomes had ranged from nothing to $35, received wages up to $4.80 a week under FERA. They were furnished, in addition, surplus canned goods, rice, beans, and molasses. They received a little dental and medical care, and some overalls, underwear, and cotton dresses. One social worker reported: "Occasionally we had money to buy a few shoes. Once we had about a hundred dollars to spend for washboards, tubs and the like for six hundred families. (One old woman cried over the gift of a coffee pot.)" And a North Carolina social worker pointed out that FERA produced "a slight rise in living standard. While standards are still wretchedly low, they are better than many of these Negroes knew during the prosperity era. No longer does Sam Johnson, colored, 'Chaw wheat bread only on Saddy nights.' " [1]

The FERA not only established a minimum hourly wage for relief work, which in depressed areas like the South meant a higher standard of living than in the past for many citizens, but it also instigated a social policy of enormous significance for the future. Relief had to be given to all needy persons without discrimination because of race, color, religion, political affiliation or participation in industrial disputes. Striking workers, recent immigrant groups, and minorities in general were to be treated as full citizens. Equality of opportunity, even in relief, was the firm policy of the New Deal. This policy was in sharp contrast to previous relief policies in the South as far as Negroes were concerned. The results were immediately apparent. One North Carolina landlord complained: "I don't like this welfare business. I can't do a thing with my niggers.

They aren't beholden to me any more. They know you all won't let them perish."

By late 1933, it was clear that the FERA and the Public Works Administration were not sufficient to tide America's needy over the coming winter. Roosevelt decided to launch the Civil Works Administration to put four million more men to work. Even with these new jobs, three out of every four of the unemployed still not on relief could not be absorbed. Mayors from many large cities urged Congress, to no avail, to increase the CWA to eight million jobs.

At first, the CWA paid unskilled labor forty cents an hour in the South and fifty cents an hour in the North for a maximum of thirty hours a week. White-collar workers were paid the prevailing wage of the community for a thirty-nine-hour week. Hopkins's desire to pay real wages for real work brought the CWA into direct competition with private employment. Men left part-time or poor-paying jobs to work for the CWA. Employers were not impressed with the contention that private pay was too low. "High wages is ruining 'em," one Southern employer complained. Under pressure the CWA reduced the maximum hours of work permitted and accepted the local prevailing wage rate with a minimum hourly rate of thirty cents.

Within two weeks of its inception in November, 1933, CWA was employing a million and a half workers. They were set to street and road work, raking leaves, repairing buildings, and a variety of other projects where labor was the chief ingredient. The speed and scope of the CWA meant inevitable waste and some graft. In California, for instance, several thousand men were assigned roadwork without picks or shovels. Critics immediately leveled the charge of "boondoggling." "Most of the work we do might as well remain undone," wrote one CWA worker. "We dig ditches and fill them up again. We cut down a hill and build another somewhere else." Yet, he felt a grudging appreciation. He was not happy, but he had a job. The important thing was not what he was doing but that he was doing something.[2]

In many communities, CWA funds were the first substantial infusion of money into the economic bloodstream in several years. By January, 1934, Middletown was receiving thirty-three thousand dollars a week for 1800 workers. And a Georgia social worker remarked that the CWA wage scale "has worked a social revolution in the South comparable only to the emancipation of the slaves." In response to the bitter criticism of waste, Roosevelt ordered the CWA to end by the spring of 1934. Despite the flaws in the program, editorials urged that the CWA continue. "There is no doubt," the *Literary Digest* reported, on February 3, 1934, "that public opinion, as represented by the newspapers, thoroughly indorses the CWA in practise."

The CWA did achieve its main goal of carrying the unemployed through the first winter of the New Deal. Hurriedly set up under emergency conditions to employ surplus labor, it left concrete accomplishments in its wake. For all the idleness and inefficiency of the road workers, *Better Roads*, the national road builder's magazine, stated that the bulk of the CWA roadwork was of high order. Beneficial work on schools, particularly Negro schools, was accomplished. "CWA ends after Brightening Up Nation," the *Literary Digest* concluded on April 21, 1934.

At the time the CWA was ending, 4,600,000 families were on relief. Estimates of the unemployed not yet on relief ranged from three to ten million. "Our relief measures do little for a family until it becomes destitute," one economist wrote. The demise of the CWA did not mean that the federal government was abandoning responsibility for the unemployed. A half billion dollars was appropriated to continue the activities of FERA, and in the winter of 1934-1935 the agency employed nearly two and a half million workers a month.

While the federal government under the New Deal willingly accepted responsibility for aid to the unemployed, there was uneasiness over direct relief. It seemed un-American. With scorn people referred to it as the "dole." During the first year, only approximately one fourth of the federal relief funds went to work relief. Many resented their inability to perform work for the aid they received. They wanted something to do. At a rate of more than one a day, delegations from all over the nation came to Washington to demand relief jobs, not handouts in cash or in kind.

On January 4, 1935, Roosevelt asked Congress to reorganize the relief program and withdraw the federal government from direct relief. This, hereafter, would be the business of the states and localities, while the federal government would provide work for needy "employables" estimated by the President to number three and a half million of the five million families then on relief.

The creation of the Works Progress Administration, with an initial budget of nearly five billion dollars, marked the final step by the federal government from direct relief to work relief. Approximately two and a half million workers were on WPA payrolls in 1936. At no time did the WPA employ as many as the CWA had done. Nor did it provide work for all the three and a half million "employable" families, a minimum estimate at best, for whom the President accepted responsibility.

The WPA drew fire from all sides. The return of direct relief to the states and localities was opposed by social workers since the states were "totally unprepared to take over the relief load in wholesale fashion." In general, recipients of direct relief were less well off after 1934 than they had been under the FERA. At the same time, organized WPA workers agitated for increased wages. Private employers complained that the WPA competed with them for workers. And the National Economy League questioned both the cost and the usefulness of the agency.

In spite of the criticisms and the mistakes, by 1935 employment relief had evolved from the inadequate, chaotic private charity and local governmental programs of the Hoover era into organized public responsibility with financing by the federal government. But even so, there were gaps in relief work as programs were changed. None of the programs provided jobs for all who wanted them. It was difficult to plan large programs well in view of the need for haste.

Although persons on relief suffered from the uncertainties and inadequacies in the program, the income they received was of immeasurable benefit in carrying families through the crisis. Work relief, also, contributed to preserving worker's skills. By keeping workers active at their skills, a reservoir of productive activity was maintained until the time when the economy started to boom.

Equally if not more important was the fact that the federal government was willing to act and to assume responsibility in a new field.

There had never been a venture in the past quite like federal relief. By 1935, most Americans agreed that the federal government had the responsibility of aiding the victims of economic disaster. This marked the reversal of a long pioneer heritage. The traditional emphasis on individualism and self-reliance had assumed that the industrious and frugal would be able to save money to carry them through depressions, unemployment, and old age. But the sweeping away of jobs after 1929, the collapse of many businesses, and the bank failures created a universal fear of insecurity.

Stronger and stronger grew the demand for a government guarantee of security in old age. The population was aging. The ability of families to provide for elderly relatives largely had disappeared in the depression. One morning, a retired, almost destitute, former city health official, looked out of his window in California and saw three old women searching a garbage pail for scraps of food. Immediately, Dr. Francis E. Townsend launched a crusade that won the support of thousands of old people. He proposed that the government should pay a pension of $200 a month for every person over sixty who agreed to stop work and spend the money within thirty days. He sent his plan to a local newspaper in September, 1933. A thousand Townsend Clubs were organized within a year, and at least another thousand were formed by 1935.

The President appointed a committee in 1934 to study the question of social security legislation. When his plan was presented to Congress, it seemed so moderate and safe in comparison with the Townsend Plan that many critics reluctantly accepted it. The Social Security Act of August, 1935, created a system of old-age and survivors' insurance, in effect a plan of compulsory savings to which employers and employees made equal contributions. And grants were provided for those too old for active work. And a federal-state system of unemployment insurance, financed by a tax on payrolls, was included to furnish laid-off workers with payments for a few weeks.

It was a modest beginning. In time, benefits were increased and the majority of the working population came under the old-age insurance plan. This marked a distinct break with the past. Old age and unemployment were now accepted as national problems to be provided for on a permanent basis.

Between his election and his inauguration, Roosevelt and his advisers had been developing plans not only for relief but for rehabilitation and reform. Late in January, 1933, the President-elect and Senator George W. Norris visited the site of Wilson Dam in the Tennessee Valley where they watched water pouring unused through the spillways. Roosevelt called Norris to his side for photographs, and said: "This should be a happy day for you, George." Tears came to the eyes of the rugged Nebraskan as he replied: "It is, Mr. President. I see my dreams come true." Roosevelt explained to reporters:

> We have an opportunity of setting an example of planning, not just for ourselves but for the generations to come, tying in industry and agriculture and forestry and flood prevention, tying them all into a unified whole over a distance of a thousand miles so that we can afford better opportunities and better places for living for millions of yet unborn in the days to come.

During the Hundred Days, the Tennessee Valley Authority was authorized to buy real estate, build dams, reservoirs, power houses and transmission lines, develop navigation, produce fertilizers and explosives, and produce, sell, and distribute power. By 1934, the valley was throbbing with activity. Dams were going up, thousands of CCC workers were planting trees and building terraces for flood control, whole cities were being built to house workers, and agricultural experiments to develop new crops were under way.

The country watched the TVA with fascination. The *Literary Digest* labeled it "a prevision of utopia." Conservatives muttered about socialism and private power companies prepared for complicated sieges in the courts that lasted for years before the scope of TVA was determined. Meanwhile in the Valley a new era was dawning. The lives of the people and the economies of seven Southern states were changing more rapidly and more profoundly than at any time since the Civil War and Reconstruction. Free at last from the ravages of floods, with a reviving agriculture, and cheap electric power reaching into homes that never before had electricity, the people of the Valley now attained a life never conceived in the past. And the great reservoir of harnessed power after 1939 sparked the development of an expanding industrial complex which was to be valuable in the war.

Per capita income in the Valley by 1940 had increased 73 per cent over that of 1933, while the increase in the country as a whole was only 56 per cent. Bank deposits between 1933 and 1939 increased 76 per cent as compared to 49 per cent for the entire country. But the significance of the experiment lay not alone in economic statistics nor in the building of dams, roads, hospitals, schools, and farm land reclaimed from erosion. Contrasting the doleful past with the fruitful present, the *Decatur* (Alabama) *Daily* on May 18, 1943, stated: ". . . *the significant advance has been made in the thinking of a people.* They are no longer afraid. *They have caught the vision of their own powers.*"

While the New Deal in general centered more and more power in Washington, the TVA marked a significant reversal of this trend. Although it was established as a government corporation, the members of the three-man board lived in the Valley and had the authority to act without continual recourse to Washington. Wisely, the TVA's experts worked closely with the local chambers of commerce, trade unions, farm organizations, and governmental officials. Grass roots participation became as notable a feature of the TVA as the new dams and transmission lines. Decentralized administration, with active citizen participation, made the TVA a notable experiment in an age of increasing centralization.[3]

The TVA attracted world-wide interest and study. At home, some urged similar planning for the Missouri River Valley, the Columbia River basin, and the Central Valley of California. Important public power projects were undertaken in many areas including Bonneville in Oregon, Grand Coulee in Washington, and Fort Peck in Montana, but none of them with TVA's comprehensive plan for regional development. These public power projects of the New Deal greatly expanded the use of electric power in industry, on the farms, and in the homes. The Public Works Administration lent funds to municipalities for publicly owned power stations, and the Rural Electrification Administration, created in 1935, made loans to rural cooperatives to build transmission lines. The policy of making electricity available to rural areas by public action became an integral part of national farm policy. In 1929, only 580,000 farms had electricity. By 1941, nearly half of the over four million farms had it. Since then, rural electric lines have continued to spread rapidly, bringing revolutionary changes to farm operations and to the modes of rural living.

The New Deal's varied activities in agriculture brought a striking change in point of view to rural America. The individualistic farmer turned to the federal government to rescue him from an appalling crisis. The most striking phenomenon was agriculture's new dependence on the federal government.

Early in 1933, farmers were desperate. Cotton sold for a nickel a pound, a hog ready for market brought only three dollars, and prices for cattle did not cover the cost of shipping them to market. Ed O'Neal, powerful leader of the Farm Bureau Federation, warned a Congressional Committee in January, 1933: "Unless something is done for the American farmer, we'll have revolution in the countryside in less than twelve months."

The Farm Credit Administration, created on March 27, 1933, met a pressing emergency by refinancing farm mortgages. It was an important and practical emergency step, but it also significantly improved the nation's farm credit for more normal times. The Agricultural Adjustment Act of May, 1933, attracted far more attention than the expansion of farm credit, and it involved a drastic departure from past practices. The Hoover Farm Board, through exhortation, had unsuccessfully tried to reduce production. The AAA reduced production by paying the farmers to plant fewer acres of specified crops.

President Roosevelt, Henry A. Wallace, Secretary of Agriculture, and advisers like Rexford G. Tugwell sought to bring about a balance between industry and agriculture. Limiting farm production, it was believed, would result in farmers' achieving a parity of purchasing power equal to 1909-1914 levels, a period particularly favorable to farmers in relation to industrial prices. Higher farm prices meant higher prices to consumers, but the New Dealers justified this in the light of the increased purchasing power of the farmer which would enable him to buy more city-made goods.[4]

The AAA faced a host of difficulties. The most difficult immediate emergency was that the law had been passed after crops were already in the ground. Drought cut the prospective wheat crop, but cotton was about to have a banner year. It was decided to pay cotton farmers to plow under ten million acres. A million cotton farmers joined the scheme, and one reporter wrote that only the mule objected: "For all his years the mule has been trained to walk between the rows and not to tread on the cotton plants. Recently the Brain Trust asked this conservative to trample on the rows as he dragged the destroying plow. Many a mule's hide, through which he receives his education, has suffered in learning the strange lessons of the New Deal." [5]

The mule's hide was a small matter, and somehow plowing up cotton, although preposterous enough, hardly seemed harmful. It was not the same as destroying food. Hogs were threatening to flood the market. The AAA bought six million pigs. One hundred million pounds of pork were processed and distributed by relief agencies. Twenty-one million pounds of lard were manufactured. But what the public remembered was how much pork was dumped, burned, or buried, and that about 85 per cent of the pigs slaughtered were converted into inedible products. People were hungry. Was this the best the New Deal could devise? It was the most unpopular action ever taken by the AAA and it furnished political ammunition for campaigners for years to come.

With the conclusion of the hog-buying program, the AAA's emergency activity ended. Nothing like the plow-up or the killing of hogs would happen again, officials vowed. Plans for payment for acreage reduction now moved apace. But Mother Nature intervened. The massive droughts of 1934 and 1936 confused the policy, results, and analyses of the New Deal's farm program. Rescue and relief had to replace reduction of crops.

The "Dust Bowl" of the past had been confined to one hundred counties in Colorado, New Mexico, Kansas, Oklahoma, and Texas. As the dry death spread in 1934 and 1936, it came to include the entire region from the Canadian border to Mexico. It embraced 756 counties in nineteen states. "Okies," "Arkies" and thousands of other refugees fled the stricken land. "There is a story current in southwest Kansas," a social worker recorded, "about a man who, hit on the head by a raindrop, was so overcome that two buckets of sand had to be thrown in his face to revive him." [6] Americans could still laugh — a little.

Corn belt, wheat belt, and range country alike suffered. Over one-half million heads of farm families needed relief aid in 1936. The Farm Resettlement Administration, headed by Tugwell, became a disaster relief agency of major proportions. The Department of Agriculture, however, noted one grimly cheerful sign: "Those who have any grain are heartened by higher wheat prices."

Government payments to farmers under the AAA from 1933 to 1936 amounted to nearly one and a half billion dollars. The net income of farmers rose approximately three and a half billion dollars for the same period. But increased prices for farm products were mainly the result of short crops during the drought years and the reduction of farm inventories. Meanwhile, rural relief and better credit facilities enabled many to weather the storm. It was clear by 1936 that the farm program was more successful as a humanitarian venture than as a stimulus to recovery in the economy as a whole. Most important of all, the legislation firmly established the concept of federal responsibility for agriculture on a scale undreamed of even by the agrarian agitators of the past half-century.

---

8.   Washington — Center of the Country

In the first year of the New Deal, while the Federal Emergency Relief Administration, the Civilian Conservation Corps, and the Agricultural Adjustment Administration provided the bread for the victims of the depression, the National Recovery Administration furnished the circus. In July, 1933, a campaign was launched to bring all industry under a mass contract to shorten hours, increase wages, and stop price-cutting. Old army veteran General Hugh Johnson, the NRA administrator, could not resist the temptation of another nationwide mobilization effort like that of 1917. Government printing presses poured out millions of copies of a placard showing a flaring blue eagle and the words "Member" and "U.S." in blue and "N.R.A." and "We Do Our Part" in red over a white background. With employers displaying this emblem to prove their patriotism, the ballyhoo began.

Johnson launched the drive on August 27, with an unprecedented simultaneous radio appeal over the combined networks of the National Broadcasting Corporation and the Columbia Broadcasting System by celebrities from radio, Hollywood, and the theater. The next day, women across the country canvassed their sister housewives to urge them to patronize only those employers who displayed the blue eagle. Then individual cities seized the torch. New York City's performance was the largest and most spectacular. Over a million and a half spectators watched a parade of 250,000 marchers. There were drummer girls in red, white, and blue and a cadet corps that played "Over There," "Keep the Home Fires Burning," and "There's a Long, Long Trail." It was "a demonstration of confidence and enthusiasm such as had not been seen for half a generation," remarked the *New York Times*.

Across the nation that autumn there were parades and great demonstrations of enthusiasm for the NRA. General Johnson allowed the country no rest. H. L. Mencken commented:

> The problem before the General was to hustle, bump, and kick the great masses of the plain people up from the Slough of Despond to the topmost roof-garden of the New Jerusalem, and to that patriotic business he brought a technic so stupendous that the historian can only contemplate it in a boozy sort of silence, like that of Cortez upon his peak in Darien.[1]

While the hopes of the nation did not deserve such ridicule, there had been too much ballyhoo. When NRA did not live up to the confident prediction that it would launch the nation on the road to recovery, public opposition grew and almost everyone breathed a sigh of relief when the Supreme Court in 1935 found it unconstitutional.

Roosevelt viewed the NRA as a joint effort by business, labor, and the consumer to revive industrial activity. The role of the government was to be a broker among these competing groups. He was not committed to broad national economic planning nor to deficit spending to the degree some of his aides were. For all of his willingness to take advantage of a situation, there were certain things he would not do. He would not revolutionize the economy nor would he pursue wide-scale government expenditures to the degree suggested by the British economist John Maynard Keynes. The NRA, as the President understood it, was a modest measure intended to spread work and maintain wages without heavy investment by the federal government. His chief concern was the depression. The NRA, he believed, would increase urban consumer purchasing power just as the AAA was to accomplish the same end for agriculture.

At the outset, trade association leaders, reformers, and a forceful chief executive, whatever their divergent aims, combined to support the NRA. Many big business men were happy at the suspension of the antitrust laws and the guarantee of fair competition, some of Roosevelt's aides were pleased at the opportunity to reorganize the economy, labor leaders were delighted with the minimum wage and maximum hour provisions and the right of collective bargaining.

Most of the codes were prepared by trade associations, which by 1935 covered seven hundred different types of industries and businesses, with twenty-two million employees. Business and labor leaders reached bargains in the drafting of the codes, but the consumer representatives had little influence. As the codes became operative, business found itself in a web of frequently conflicting regulations. A California auto-supply operator's reaction was typical of the situation faced by small business: "I'm working under eight different codes, no two alike. That means if a man changes a tire he's on a forty-four hour week, but if he fills a battery he's on a forty-hour week. You can't coordinate these variables in the small business."

A minority of powerful business firms dominated the authorities responsible for the administration of the codes under General Johnson's general supervision. Small business was underrepresented, while labor and the consumer were virtually excluded from membership on the code authorities. The NRA, unsure of its legal grounds, hesitated to coerce violators of the codes. And the sheer volume of administrative detail gradually made the agency unworkable. Public enthusiasm for NRA wore off, and disillusionment set in at failures in enforcement and bureaucratic delays. Idaho's William E. Borah clamored for a return to the anti-trust laws. Secretary of Agriculture Wallace pointed to the farmer's dissatisfaction over the way the NRA had led to price increases. And Harry Hopkins said to Johnson: "Hugh, your codes stink."

In September, 1934, General Johnson — sick, suffering from emotional strain, and his patience exhausted — resigned as administrator. In May, 1935, the Supreme Court held the NRA invalid. It is difficult to determine whether the NRA actually contributed to recovery since other governmental activities also were fighting the depression. Employment did increase after March, 1933, as did industrial payrolls. A study by the Brookings Institution credited the NRA with the re-employment of 1,750,000 persons, but this analysis in general was critical. It charged that the agency had the effect of restricting production below what the economy otherwise would have attained.

Even its most severe critics had little to say against the boost in morale the NRA gave in 1933. And significant progress against child labor was achieved. The labor provisions for minimum wages, maximum hours, and collective bargaining had psychological effects long beyond the duration of the NRA. Until 1933, employer groups were dominant in their struggles with labor. But Section 7a of each NRA code, with the statement that "employees shall have the right to organize and bargain collectively through representatives of their own choosing," started a reversal in labor's fortunes. The adoption of the Wagner Labor Relations Act in 1935 completed the transition from the past. It gave the federal government power to interfere authoritatively in industrial relations.

The trade union movement had been in the doldrums in the 1920s. By March, 1933, the American Federation of Labor had dropped to 2,127,000 members, no more than it had had twenty years before. Some of labor's new strength came without direct, conscious encouragement from Roosevelt. He had little to do with Section 7a which had been framed by Congressmen and labor leaders to induce labor to join the NRA. And General Johnson stated frankly in July, 1933, that the NRA "would not be used as an instrument for the unionization of any industry. . . . The purpose of the Act is not to unionize labor nor does labor have to join a company union."

Nevertheless, Roosevelt's militancy during the Hundred Days stirred the trade union movement into action. Shaggy-browed John L. Lewis plastered thousands of posters through the mining regions stating: "President Roosevelt Wants You to Join the Unions." Surprised A. F. of L. leaders reported there was a grass-roots demand by workers for union membership. Workers flocked into the United

Mine Workers, the International Ladies Garment Workers Union, the Amalgamated Clothing Workers, and into embryonic unions in rubber, steel, auto, and other mass-production industries.

The A. F. of L., dominated by craft union leaders, could not meet the challenge. The Federation wanted to parcel out the militant new membership craft-by-craft dividing an industry among the Electricians, the Pipe Fitters, the Carpenters and a host of other craft unions. The young grass-roots union leaders and a few leaders of the A. F. of L. objected, recognizing that this would lead to weakness and disunity in dealing with great industrial combines.

At the 1935 Federation Convention, Lewis led an unsuccessful fight to persuade the Federation to launch an all-out drive to organize the mass-production workers into industrial unions. The struggle between craft and industrial unionism was dramatized for the public by a fist fight on the Convention floor between William Hutcheson of the Carpenters and Lewis of the Miners. Blows were exchanged, and as the two grappled, they went down amidst collapsing chairs. And the strained peace between the craft and industrial spokesmen collapsed with the chairs.

Hutcheson headed the largest craft union and Lewis the largest industrial union in the Federation. Both had risen to power by ruthlessly suppressing opposition. Both were Republicans. Hutcheson was the principal labor leader in the Liberty League. He knew that successful industrial unionism would cripple the old craft leaders' domination of the labor movement. Lewis, on the other hand, had seen his membership dwindle away under the impact of the depression. With the NRA, vigorous organizing campaigns brought the union from a little over one hundred thousand to over four hundred thousand in two years. If his gains in coal were to be held, Lewis knew that the hostile steel industry had to be organized. He pled with the Convention to "adopt a policy designed to meet . . . modern conditions in this industrial nation." And with his thunderous voice he said: "Now, prepare yourselves by making a contribution to your less fortunate brethren, heed this cry from Macedonia that comes from the hearts of men. Organize the unorganized."

In the fall of 1935, Lewis, Philip Murray, Sidney Hillman, David Dubinsky, and many others formed the Committee for Industrial

Organization within the Federation. A new labor organization — to be expelled from the Federation in 1937 — was under way.

The growth of organized labor as a great new power in American life was accelerated by the passage of the National Labor Relations Act in July, 1935. In February, Senator Robert Wagner of New York introduced this bill designed to establish a permanent law outside the NRA to guarantee collective bargaining to workers through unions of their own choice. Employers were prohibited from interfering with this right and forbidden from lending support to company unions. Under the NRA, employers resisted the efforts of the National Labor Board to establish definite rules for collective bargaining. And whether collective bargaining must operate through independent unions or company unions was never clarified. This prompted some labor leaders to denounce the whole process as the "National Run Around."

The President at first was cool to Wagner's proposal. He viewed labor from the position of a patron and a benefactor. He wanted to help people, not necessarily trade unions. Wages, hours, and working conditions should be improved, but he was not consciously interested in forging organized labor into a powerful economic and political force.

The Wagner Bill passed the Senate on May 16 by a large vote. Eight days later Roosevelt came out for the bill. House passage seemed certain, and the President probably wanted to gain credit for it. By this time, too, conservative opposition to the New Deal was irritating Roosevelt. Early in May, Chamber of Commerce leaders, who had been friendly, now broke with him. When the Supreme Court invalidated the NRA on May 27, this merely reinforced the President's decision to make the Wagner legislation a must bill. After it passed the House in July, it became possible for organized labor to develop massive economic power and growing political strength. By 1937, the CIO had thirty-two unions with 3,718,000 members and total union membership reached 7,218,000.

While federal relief, TVA, AAA, and the NRA attracted the attention of the public, important changes were occurring also in monetary policy, banking, and finance. Determined to raise domestic prices, Roosevelt took the nation off the gold standard in April, 1933. While the dollar immediately depreciated on foreign exchanges, the domestic price level moved upward. Director of the Budget Lewis W. Douglas fought domestic inflation, lamenting "the end of Western civilization"; but the President, urged on by other advisers, including Henry J. Morgenthau, Jr., George F. Warren, and Frank A. Pearson, embarked upon a course of national currency management. When the World Monetary and Economic Conference met in London in June and July to stabilize currency exchange, restore international trade, and return to the international gold standard, the President was turning to domestic action as the first priority to end the depression. Roosevelt torpedoed the Conference when, to the shock of some of the members of the American delegation, he denounced the Conference for ignoring fundamental economic ills in favor of artificial stabilization of a few currencies. "The sound internal economic system of a nation," he insisted, "is a greater factor in its well-being than the price of its currency in changing terms of the currencies of other nations." While internationalists denounced this nationalistic path, British economist John Maynard Keynes hailed it as "magnificently right."

Following the theory that the best way to achieve recovery was through controlled inflation, the dollar was devalued to its 1926 purchasing power. By January, 1934, Roosevelt achieved the "commodity dollar" now theoretically equal in purchasing power to the dollar of 1926. And the gold content of the dollar had been reduced by 41 per cent. This monetary management failed to speed recovery appreciably. Large increases in the money supply and in bank credit did not occur and prices failed to rise significantly. Shifting somewhat from the 1933 emphasis that recovery could be gained by domestic monetary manipulation, Roosevelt in 1934 supported attempts to revive international trade through lower tariffs.

If the public was perplexed over the technical aspects of controlled inflation and the commodity dollar, it was ardent in its support for government action against bankers and stock speculators. During the early months of the New Deal, a Senate banking committee and its dapper counsel, Ferdinand Pecora, ruthlessly pursued Wall Street's biggest names. While a publicity agent posed a midget on the once dignified knee of J. P. Morgan, the committee revealed that Morgan and Company partners had paid no income taxes in 1931 and 1932. The committee exposed practices which, while legal, seemed morally wrong, particularly to a people in a depression. The juggling of capital gains and losses to avoid income taxes, the revelation of huge profits from selling securities, which later lost most of their value, only increased the public belief that bankers and financiers were rogues. The public demand for government policing of financial markets did not have to be created by Roosevelt; it was already a powerful reality even among many conservatives. The revelation that banks had underwritten a number of shoddy stock issues in the bull market and then sold the stock to their depositors resulted in the Glass-Steagall Act of June, 1933, separating commercial banking from investment banking. And a Board of Governors replaced the old Federal Reserve Board. The new Board was granted greater control over credit and over the whole Federal Reserve system. In 1934, to prevent a repetition of the sale of fraudulent stocks and bonds, Roosevelt moved against the "unscrupulous money changers" mentioned in his inaugural address. The Securities and Exchange Act, passed against a din of hostile propaganda from Wall Street, established a commission empowered to draw up rules to govern operations on the Stock Exchanges. All corporations issuing new securities had to register with the Securities and Exchange Commission and divulge corporate information which Wall Street insiders always before had considered "their own business." And, under the Public Utility Holding Act of 1935, the SEC was granted the power to limit utility holding companies to an integrated power system, and to supervise the payment of dividends and the acquisition of securities and assets by their operating companies.

Powerful Wall Street and business interests fought the SEC, claiming that its powers were destructive of the private enterprise system. The President of the New York Stock Exchange, Richard Whitney, was outspoken in his attacks. In 1938, Whitney was sent to the federal penitentiary for misappropriating securities belonging to a customer. This revelation about such a pillar of the financial community only increased the public belief in the need for close supervision and control of stock transactions. Now Wall Street itself became more cooperative with the SEC.

The regulation of Wall Street and the new banking laws were the result of misdeeds and inadequacies in the financial world exposed by the collapsing economic structure. The transfer of power from Wall Street to Washington after March, 1933, signified for many citizens that the nation now had a government that governed.

The radical shift in authority to Washington was accomplished rapidly and easily. The *New York Times* observed on November 10, 1938:

> . . . an increasing number of Americans, irrespective of party line, have come to regard, as both necessary and desirable, a larger share of responsibility on the Government's part in the policing of financial markets, in the achievement of essential social reforms and in the attainment of a generally higher standard of living for underprivileged people. For that quickening of the American conscience which has brought about this change in point of view, credit must be given to Franklin D. Roosevelt.

---

9. The Roosevelt Coalition

Chicago's astute political boss, Mayor Edward J. Kelly, said to me in 1940: "Roosevelt is the greatest precinct captain I've ever known. He has made the job of our workers easy. They have only to mention the name Roosevelt, and the results are sure." With the fireside chats he turned the nation into a precinct. Many of the leaders of the big city machines had no particular personal affection for Roosevelt, nor did they care much about the New Deal. But these leaders discovered that supporting Roosevelt was a matter of self-preservation and a means of perpetuating their own power. The President brought into the Democratic party many who previously had voted Republican or who simply had never voted before. The use of the magic name Roosevelt enabled city leaders to elect their local candidates and stay in power themselves

As President, Roosevelt worked closely with the leaders of the same city machines that had fought his nomination in 1932. He ignored the old progressive attack on political machines and bosses, an attack which in the years before the First World War had cost progressives the support of the immigrants in the big cities. Roosevelt was the new version of the big city boss. Just as the bosses had aided the recently arrived immigrants to find work and housing, he helped people adjust to new conditions. The WPA, the PWA, the CCC, the AAA, and the social security system on a broader and more organized scale extended the humanity of the city bosses. This aid, however, Roosevelt institutionalized in the federal government. And by so doing, he contributed to the weakening of city machines.

With the transfer of many of the social welfare functions of the machines to the federal government, the voters were less indebted to the local political leader for favors. If out of work, they could draw unemployment insurance. If in retirement, they had old-age insurance. The prosperity that came later with World War II further weakened the city machines. Not only did many able precinct captains leave political jobs for more remunerative employment in industry, but prosperity built a new urban middle class that no longer needed the services of the party machine. In fact, many of this class resented the dependence of their immigrant parents on the machine, and demonstrated their growing resentment in postwar voting behavior.

The New Deal attracted many different types of adherents. Roosevelt's strong action to meet the crisis won the support of people who had not followed politics closely and who had not heretofore felt themselves politically effective. He gave them a sense of belonging. Roosevelt spoke for those who lived on the ragged edge or who feared they might be ground down to that level. He called upon them to help him make the government an agency for the general welfare. Although his conservative critics, at the time, charged that he was setting class against class, Roosevelt's relief and reform measures brought to the disinherited and the lower income groups a chance to rise on the social and economic ladder. Many who supported Roosevelt were victims of the depression rescued by New Deal measures. Some, particularly the youth, were molded by the depression. Many of them did not need federal relief. They supported Roosevelt because they favored reforms to prevent the evils of future depressions.

The memory of the depression, the way most people held the Republican party responsible for it, and Roosevelt's peaceful social and economic revolution bound voters to the Democratic party until 1952. Roosevelt championed the demands of virtually every group except big business. There was nothing new in a President's sponsoring legislation that favored various elements of society. But what was new about the New Deal was the size of the groups it served. Agriculture and labor, alone, were far more broadly based groups than the manufacturing, commercial, and financial interests which had been favored in the decade of "normalcy." These pressure groups had money, but the ones favored by the New Deal had votes.[1] The captains of industry now had to share power with the new militant unions, the farm pressure groups, and the rapidly expanding power of the government itself.

Unhappy critics denounced the New Deal's aid programs as "handouts." One of the most biting attacks on Roosevelt's "handouts" appeared in the old *Life* for May, 1936. There was a full-page cartoon with the caption "A Mad Tea Party." Roosevelt was the Mad Hatter, Farley the March Hare, Congress the Dormouse, and Alice the public. Roosevelt was pouring tea (dollars) into cups marked CCC, WPA, TVA, ABC, etc., frequently missing the cups, with the dollars flowing all over the table and onto the ground. The concluding stanza of the verses accompanying the cartoon read:

> The March Hare kept on blaring and The Hatter kept on pouring.
> The maiden kept on staring and The Dormouse kept on snoring.
> The tea continued spilling, and so Alice asked The Hatter:
> "Who's going to pay for all of this?" Her question pleased the latter.
> He pointed to his hat and said, his sunny smile upon 'er,
> "The checks — this style — in Wonderland are paid by guests of honor."
> "Well, *I* give up," she answered, more in self-reproach than malice,
> "One of us is crazy." And the Dormouse murmured "Alice."

Such criticism ignored the attempt being made to achieve a more just social order. Farmers, factory workers, white-collar workers, immigrants, Negroes, the unemployed, and the aged were receiving a greater share of the American bonanza than ever before.

The people who elected Roosevelt in 1940 would vote for him "for a fourth and a fifth term as readily as for a third," Samuel Lubell concluded in his perceptive book, *The Future of American Politics*. The urban population were the chief supporters of the Roosevelt revolution. Between 1881 and 1900 nearly nine million immigrants entered the country; between 1900 and 1914, another thirteen million. The significance of these numbers did not escape Roosevelt. He understood the remark of Tammany boss Tim Sullivan, that the America of the future "would be made out of the people who had come over in steerage and who knew in their own hearts and lives the difference between being despised and being accepted and liked."

Despite hardships in early years, the elevator of mobility carried many immigrants, and particularly their children, upward. The depression struck the children of prewar immigrants just as they were becoming adults and dealt a violent blow to their aspirations. Roosevelt's relief measures succored them, his reform measures revived their hopes, and his leadership awakened "the climbing urban masses to a consciousness of the power of their numbers." In election after election, by their dedication to Roosevelt, they made the Democrats the majority party of the nation.

By 1920, for the first time, a majority of the population was living in cities. Not only the newer immigrants but Southern whites and Negroes flowed into Northern cities. The birth rate of the less privileged far outnumbered that of the well-born. Between 1936 and 1944 over twenty-one million potential new voters reached the age of twenty-one. Most of them came from poorer Democratic families. In 1928, Al Smith represented the revolt of the underdog urban immigrant against the older American stock from the United Kingdom, Scandinavia, and Germany. The older stock in the Northern cities held aloof from the newer stock in 1928. Four years later they began to shift and by 1936 many of them combined with newer immigrants to form the essential core of the new Democratic party.

Roosevelt's relief and reform measures, and the organization of both native Americans and immigrant workers by the CIO, were powerful forces that fused lower income groups into a voting bloc regardless of their national origin. Grim economic necessity suppressed the racial and religious antagonisms that had divided these groups in the past. Roosevelt, in 1932, failed to carry a dozen cities with a hundred thousand population or more, but in 1936 each one of them gave its vote to him, whether the population was predominantly foreign-born or native American, Catholic or Protestant.

Many of the minorities which occupied so prominent a place in the New Deal's legions were "have-nots" in the mid-'30s. But returning prosperity lifted many of them into the middle income group. They formed, in the postwar era, a powerful new middle class, largely Democratic until 1952. This social revolution under the New Deal, by stimulating and speeding up the development of a middle class among the minorities, steered the nation away from divisive class conflict.

Republican leaders frequently attributed their defeats to the fact that Roosevelt was just too clever a politician. But these leaders failed to realize that the Democratic party under Roosevelt was reaching groups the Republicans had long ignored. Negroes and Southern whites in the Northern cities, and the Irish, Polish, Italian, and Jewish urban dwellers found the Democratic party more in sympathy with their aspirations. The Republican party had absorbed the emerging leaders of the German and Scandinavian communities but had scorned the immigrants from Eastern and Southern Europe. During the 1920s, Republican leaders largely ignored the drive for recognition and position welling up from the recent immigrants in the urban centers. But the Irish leadership of the Democratic city machines was more sensitive to this, as was Roosevelt in the next decade.

Rhode Island was a case in point. Here Americans of Italian ancestry, with faith that prosperity and Republican rule were synonymous, had in election after election given their votes to that party. During the 1920s, middle class leaders began to arise in the Italian group, but the Yankee leadership of the Republican party provided no adequate recognition for them. Beginning in 1930, the Democrats began to shake Republican supremacy and, as this happened, patronage was carefully shared with Italo-Americans, Franco-Americans, and other minorities. In 1934, Republican control was shattered with the fusion of Irish and Italian forces.

The growing importance of the Northern Negro vote was one of the most significant elements in the emergence of the urban population in the depression decade. The Negro, remaining true to tradition, did not desert the Republican party in 1932. While Tammany and the Pendergast machine in Kansas City delivered the Negro vote, elsewhere traditional loyalty to the Republican party held. In Chicago, which had the second largest Negro population in the North, Roosevelt received only 23 per cent of the Negro vote. By 1936, a political revolution was under way. Roosevelt received 49 per cent of the Negro vote in Chicago. In city after city that year, the Negroes shifted to the Roosevelt banner. In 1940, Chicago's Negroes gave Roosevelt 56 per cent of their votes, a percentage somewhat lower than his strength among Negroes in New York, Detroit, and Philadelphia. Four years later Roosevelt received 65 per cent of the Negro ballots in Chicago. Although the Negro vote in Chicago in 1940 for Roosevelt had reached 56 per cent, this was still lower than the Democratic vote in the city as a whole. By 1944, however, Roosevelt's 65 per cent margin in Black Metropolis made the Negro vote more Democratic than that of the rest of the city.

It was significant that during the difficult days of the 1930s the Communist party had no more appeal for Negroes than for other underprivileged groups. Although the Communists ran a Negro for vice-president in election after election, the Negroes shifted to Roosevelt, not to the Communists. For the Negroes, who were replacing the immigrants as the less privileged element in the North, the New Deal opened the way for advancement, more equal opportunity, and fuller participation in the benefits and responsibilities of American life.

Again, the Republicans in the 1920s had been largely indifferent to the emerging leadership in the Negro community. The Democratic party after 1932 slated a growing number for elective offices, and in 1934 Chicago sent its first Negro Democrat, Arthur W. Mitchell, to Congress. Four years before, he had been registered as a Republican. And Roosevelt appointed far more Negroes to important posts than had previous presidents. The Negro community regarded this as a significant step toward their recognition as full citizens.

In many ways, the New Deal had a more direct and immediate impact on Negroes than on any other group. In the North, since they were "the first to be fired and the last to be hired," Negroes generally had been out of work longer than the white worker. The vast majority were at the lowest wage level and few had been able to accumulate savings. The CCC, FERA, WPA, and NYA meant much to Negroes. In 1939 alone, more than a million made their living from the WPA. Nearly a third of the federal public housing projects were occupied by Negro families. In the South, AAA payments and rural relief activities affected large numbers of Negroes. Although discrimination occurred in the local administration of most New Deal measures in the South, older patterns were breached in a substantial way.

The Fair Labor Standards Act of 1938, establishing a minimum wage for industrial workers — agricultural and domestic workers were excluded from its provisions — provided opportunity for Negroes. During the early days of the depression most unions had tightened their racial exclusion policies. When the CIO launched its campaign to organize the mass-production industries it opposed racial discrimination, and Negroes became active members of many local unions. Increasing industrial employment now opened the benefits of the Social Security system to Negroes.

The mass movement of Negroes to the Democrats between 1932 and 1936 was in response to Roosevelt's humanitarian program. Negroes appreciated economic aid and recognition by the New Deal. They also appreciated Eleanor Roosevelt's championship of equal rights. When race-conscious Southerners attacked her as a busybody, such attacks, like those on her husband by conservative businessmen, only solidified support for the New Deal from the many new groups which had joined the Democratic party.

In 1940, for the first time, the Democratic platform mentioned the Negro by name and opposed "discrimination in government service and benefits, and in the national defense forces." It also pledged "to uphold due process and the equal protection of the laws for every citizen, regardless of race, creed, or color." The following year, under pressure from A. Philip Randolph, head of the Pullman porters' union, who planned a march on Washington by thousands of Negroes to demand that the government prevent discrimination in defense industries, the President issued Executive Order 8802 forbidding "discrimination in the employment of workers in defense industries or Government because of race, creed, color, or national origin." And a Committee on Fair Employment Practices was created to investigate complaints of discrimination. Although much discrimination continued, the FEPC had a salutary effect. Some employers and unions revised their policies to avoid unfavorable publicity.

The growing influence of Negroes in the Northern Democratic party and the significance of the Negro vote to continued Democratic victories began to make some Southern whites restive. In 1936, Southerners had lost their hundred-year-old veto power over Democratic presidential nominations when the two-thirds requirement was replaced by a simple majority. And by 1940, their party was baldly appealing for Negro votes. A growing fear that Northern Negroes might become more important to the national wing of the party than Southern whites began to shake traditional party loyalties.

The civil rights plank in the Democratic platform in 1944 reflected the delicate balancing of forces within the party: "We believe that racial and religious minorities have the right to live, develop, and vote equally with all citizens and share the rights that are guaranteed by our Constitution. Congress shall exert its full constitutional powers to protect those rights." The absence of any statement about a permanent Fair Employment Practices Commission, anti-poll tax and anti-lynching legislation, or discrimination in the armed services antagonized some Negro leaders. But the Negroes gave their votes to Roosevelt by an even larger majority than in 1940.

---

10. Champion Campaigner

Roosevelt created a powerful sense of national unity during 1933. He believed that the President should guide men with diverse views and interests into a national harmony. The phrase "a concert of interests" with the government in the leading position was one he used many times. He told a convention of bankers in October 24, 1934: "You will recognize, I think, that a true function of the head of the Government of the United States is to find among many discordant elements that unity of purpose that is best for the Nation as a whole. Government by the necessity of things must be the leader, must be the judge of the conflicting interests of all groups in the community, including bankers. The Government is the outward expression of the common life of all citizens."

Many bankers and industrialists, who had been so influential in the past decade, did not relish this doctrine. By 1934, the era of good feeling came to an end. Many business leaders and newspaper publishers now expressed their alarm over the growing power of the government, relief expenditures, the mounting national debt, the epidemic of strikes, and the growth of unions. Odgen Mills, Roosevelt's Hyde Park neighbor and Hoover's Under Secretary of the Treasury, accused the New Deal of "fostering revolution under the guise of recovery and reform." And the Brain Trusters were scathingly attacked as dangerous radicals trying to destroy private enterprise.

The President struck back during the 1934 congressional campaign. In a fireside chat on September 30, he said:

> In our efforts for recovery we have avoided, on the one hand, the theory that business should and must be taken over into an all-embracing Government. We have avoided, on the other hand, the equally untenable theory that it is an interference with liberty to offer reasonable help when private enterprise is in need of help . . . I am not for a return to that definition of liberty under which for many years a free people were being gradually regimented into the service of the privileged few.

The results that November reversed the old generalization that the President's party loses strength in a mid-term election year. Instead, the Democrats increased their control of the House from 313 to 322 and, even more startlingly, in the Senate from 59 to 69.

Although by 1935 production had increased, unemployment had been reduced, and people were better off than two years before, there was still misery in the land. Spokesmen now tried to rally the underprivileged with simple, emotional appeals. The most important was Senator Huey Long, "the Louisiana Kingfish," with his Share Our Wealth Society. Long blamed the woes of the nation on the big moneyed interests and on the New Deal. The Senator attacked Roosevelt as "Prince Franklin," lambasted his Administration, referred to "Lord Corn Wallace," "Chicago Cinch Bug" Ickes, and accused Farley of profiteering. His Senate office became the national headquarters of his movement and he promised free homesteads, cheap food, veterans' bonuses, limitation on fortunes, and a minimum annual income of $2000 for all. Every man would be a king with Huey the "Kingfish." Long's power spread to neighboring states, and he sought allies to help him toward the presidency.

One such ally he found in the priest, Father Charles Coughlin, who broadcast from the Shrine of the Little Flower in Royal Oak, a suburb of Detroit. Through radio Father Coughlin built a nationwide following. One speech in 1932 attacking Hoover brought him over a million letters. In 1934, he organized his own network embracing twenty-six stations across the nation. By 1935, his admiring listeners were giving him enough money to pay for his radio time, to build a $750,000 shrine, to maintain a clerical force of over two hundred, and to support his Radio League of the Little Flower and its offshoot, the National Union for Social Justice.

Although Coughlin had at first hailed the New Deal as "Christ's Deal," his program was far more extreme than Roosevelt's. He wanted to nationalize banking and natural resources; he was a violent isolationist; and his demands for currency inflation went far beyond Roosevelt's actions. By 1934 he turned against the President and classed him with the "godless capitalists, the Jews, Communists, international bankers, and plutocrats."

In 1935, Coughlin joined Huey Long and the Hearst press to block the ratification of the World Court by the Senate. Paul Leach reported in the *Chicago Daily News* (January 30): "Mr. Long with his Share-the-Wealth clubbers and the doughty, outspoken Father Coughlin with his National Union for Social Justice are bigger men today politically as a result of the World Court vote than they were yesterday morning."

The assassination of Long in his state capitol in September, 1935, however, removed the most dangerous of the demagogues. And the following year Roosevelt's personal appeal and his promise of more

New Deal measures to come reduced the numbers Coughlin could swing to his new political party.

Opposition from the wealthy and from anti-labor businessmen irritated Roosevelt more than the attacks of the agitators. The most conservative elements formed the Liberty League in August, 1934, to "combat radicalism, preserve property rights and uphold and preserve the Constitution." Powerful business figures including some of the du Ponts, J. Howard Pew, and Sewell L. Avery joined the League along with such conservative Democrats as Al Smith, Jouett Shouse, and John W. Davis. In April, 1935, leaders of the Chamber of Commerce, who had been generally sympathetic to the New Deal, broke with Roosevelt. And a month later the Supreme Court invalidated the Railroad Retirement Act, the NRA, and the Frazier-Lemke Farm Mortgage Act.

Roosevelt slashed at the Court's decision on the NRA, terming it a "horse-and-buggy definition of interstate commerce." Next month he insisted that Congress pass certain bills. While these conformed to Roosevelt's general concept of assisting the underdog, and reforming the system in order to remove abuses, they also reflected his reaction to the attacks on him that were welling up on the right and on the left.

The Wagner Labor Relations Act, the Social Security Act, and the Public Utility Holding Act were passed speedily. On June 19, he asked Congress for an inheritance tax, gift taxes to prevent evasion of the inheritance tax, an estate tax, increased income taxes on "very great individual incomes," and a corporation income tax graduated to the profits of corporations.[1] In his message to Congress, Roosevelt recommended this legislation to check the growing concentration of economic power, to reduce "social unrest and a deepening sense of unfairness," and to encourage the wider distribution of wealth by increasing the tax burden on the upper class and the large corporations.

The Revenue Act was denounced by leaders of the business community as a "soak the rich" bill, a more sophisticated version of the Share-the-Wealth plan. Publisher Roy W. Howard wrote the President in September that many businessmen who had once supported him were now hostile and frightened. The tax bill they viewed as "revenge on business." Roosevelt replied: "The tax program of which you speak is based on a broad and just social and economic purpose. Such a purpose, it goes without saying, is not to destroy wealth, but to create broader range of opportunity, to restrain the growth of unwholesome and sterile accumulations and to lay the burdens of government where they can best be carried." His basic program, he added, had now reached substantial completion. The "breathing spell" which Howard had suggested, Roosevelt said, was now here.

Events in 1936, however, seemed like no breathing spell to business leaders. By now, the President's "concert of interests" included few from the leaders of finance and business. He was at first surprised and later indignant that so many people of wealth had turned against him. Attacking Roosevelt as a "deserter" of their class, some became obsessed with their hatred of "That Man."

It could be argued, however, that Roosevelt's class was betraying him. Taking power when the nation was in a dangerous stage of demoralization, he had channeled the tides of discontent and preserved, with some alterations, the system of private capitalism. He had adopted the classic conservative doctrine of reform in order to preserve. But his business opponents, seeing their power and privileges weakened by the increase of the power of the government, the rise of trade unions, and the new strength of the urban masses, failed to see any wisdom in Roosevelt's course.

Part of Roosevelt's political success was the result of the bad judgment and the incredible ineptness of his conservative opposition. They deluded themselves into thinking they knew what the country wanted, prompting sharp-tongued Harold L. Ickes to taunt them as representing the grass-roots of the country clubs. Assuming they could frighten the voters away from the New Deal by denouncing it as socialism or communism or as a threat to property and liberty, they defended the old system without realizing the public was no longer devoted to it. Still mistaking the class interest of business for the national interest, they thought they could win votes by denouncing government spending as wasteful "boondoggling." Roosevelt knew better. When he visited a town, he would ask the crowd: "How do you like your new school?" When a shout of approval met the question, he drove home his point. "It's always the school in another town that's a boondoggle. In the next county the doubters say your school was a waste of government money." [2]

Roosevelt's detractors on the right were held responsible by the vast majority of the public for the disaster that had overwhelmed the nation. It was, as a result, a political advantage to the President that his class regarded him as a traitor. By their attacks on him, they helped convince the majority that Roosevelt, despite his background, belonged to them and not to their enemies. Stanley High, a White House assistant, described in the *Literary Digest*, on April 14, 1934, how he explained the New Deal to a "luncheon of prominent Detroit women." The women were extremely hostile. When the talk was over, the waiters sent one of their number to him. "We wanted you to know," the waiter said, "that we heard your speech and that we noticed, also, how these people look at it. We just thought that we would tell you that the folks in the kitchen are all for you."

During 1936 Roosevelt maneuvered skillfully to counteract the Liberty League's influence among less affluent citizens who traditionally had voted Republican. He contrasted what the Liberty Leaguers wished to return to with the security that the average citizen now had. Before the Jackson Day Dinner on January 8, 1936, he remarked that he would use the same language if he were speaking to a Republican audience or a Progressive, Independent, or Farmer-Labor gathering. Charging that a minority of people in business and finance were ganging up against the people's liberties just as they had in Jackson's day, Roosevelt said: "Our enemies of today are the forces of privilege and greed within our own borders."

At Roosevelt's suggestion, the Democratic National Committee took the offensive against the Liberty League, branding it a "millionaires' union" and "the American Cellophane League because it's a du Pont product and you can see right through it." On June 27, when Roosevelt delivered his speech accepting renomination, he set forth the strategy to be followed in the campaign. He stated that he viewed himself not only as a candidate of the Democratic party but as a national leader with a "grave responsibility." He thanked the Democrats and "those of other parties . . . who on so many occasions have put partisanship aside." Saving America from the crisis was "not a mere party task," he continued. "It was the concern of all of us. In our strength we rose together."

Political tyranny had been wiped out at Philadelphia on July 4, 1776, Roosevelt told the crowd, but the development of modern civilization created problems of economic tyranny: ". . . out of this modern civilization economic royalists carved new dynasties . . . There was no place among this royalty for our many thousands of small business men and merchants . . . They were no more free than the worker or the farmer." As the crowd roared its approval, Roosevelt continued: "The collapse of 1929 showed up the despotism for what it was. The election of 1932 was the people's mandate to end it. Under that mandate it is being ended." With rising fervor in his voice as the crowd responded to his words, Roosevelt increased the tempo of the attack: "These economic royalists complain that we seek to overthrow the institutions of America. What they really complain of is that we seek to take away their power." Near the close of the speech, the President observed:

> In the place of the palace of privilege we seek to build a temple out of faith and hope and charity. It is a sobering thing, my friends, to be a servant of this great cause . . . There is a mysterious cycle in human events. To some generations much is given. Of other generations much is expected. This generation of Americans has a rendezvous with destiny . . . here in America we are waging a great and successful war. It is not alone a war against want and destitution and economic demoralization. It is more than that; it is a war for the survival of democracy. We are fighting to save a great and precious form of government for ourselves and for the world . . . I join with you. I am enlisted for the duration of the war.

Shortly after the speech, Roosevelt went on a cruise and left the Republicans to talk themselves out before the climax of the campaign had arrived. He knew that the cumulative effect of the past three years was enough of a campaign for the moment. Then, in late August and early September, he made a "nonpartisan" tour of the drought area. It was a huge political success. Thousands of people heard him speak, and he conferred with hundreds of party leaders.

Roosevelt's sense of timing was never better. He left the main burden of the campaign to others until the last five weeks. By this time, the Republican campaign had passed its peak and was sagging badly. The nominee, Governor Alf M. Landon of the liberal wing of the Kansas Republican party, tried to avoid being identified with the Liberty League. But leading Democratic members of the League, including John W. Davis, James Reed, Joseph B. Ely, and Al Smith, campaigned for Landon. The violence of their attacks, Walter Lippmann wrote, was "literally manna from Heaven" for Roosevelt.

At the same time, Landon tried to escape the embraces of Herbert Hoover. But, in the closing weeks of the campaign, Landon was overshadowed by Hoover's increasingly bitter denunciation of the New Deal. Hoover's attack made it all the easier for the President to make it a campaign against Hoover once again and to reawaken the memories of 1932.

Late in October, sensing the militancy of the crowds who came to hear him, Roosevelt began to promise the extension of the New Deal. Closing his campaign at Madison Square Garden before an impassioned crowd, he charged: "For twelve years this Nation was afflicted with hear-nothing, see-nothing, do-nothing Government . . . Powerful influences strive today to restore that kind of government with its doctrine that that Government is best which is most indifferent. . . . Never before in all our history have these forces been so united against one candidate as they stand today. They are unanimous in their hate for me — and I welcome their hatred."

A roar burst from the crowd and the President then pledged, among other things, to continue to improve working conditions; to curb monopoly; to aid the farmers; to provide useful work for the needy unemployed; to work for cheaper electricity, low interest rates, sounder home-financing, for reciprocal trade among nations, and for the wiping out of slums. "For these things," he concluded, ". . . and for a multitude of others like them, we have only just begun to fight."

While the *Literary Digest* predicted a Landon victory, James A. Farley confidently announced that Roosevelt would carry every state except Maine and Vermont. As the returns rolled in confirming Farley's judgment, the President said, with a wicked twinkle in his eye: "I knew I should have gone to Maine and Vermont, but Jim wouldn't let me." Roosevelt received 27,478,945 votes to Landon's

16,674,665, the largest popular plurality in history. In the Electoral College the vote was 528 to 8. The minor parties were swamped. Norman Thomas's Socialists received 194,000 votes, Earl Browder's Communists 80,000. The new Union party — backed by Father Coughlin, Dr. Francis Townsend, and Gerald L. K. Smith, a rabble-rousing Louisiana minister, who claimed the mantle of Huey Long — polled only 894,000 votes for their candidate, Republican Representative William Lemke of North Dakota.

It was a gigantic personal victory for Roosevelt. Running well ahead of Democratic candidates for Congress and Governor, he swept many of them into office with him. The House of Representatives increased its Democratic membership from 321 to 334 and the Senate added five more Democrats, bringing the total to 75. While the President did not win a majority of the upper income vote, he came close to it. His majority with middle and lower income groups was overwhelming. He easily won a majority of the votes of Catholics, Jews, and non-church members, and just carried the Protestant vote, being weakest among rural Protestants outside the South. In the past, the Northern urban Democratic party had been heavily identified as the party of Catholics, but by his leadership Roosevelt made it more desirable for non-Catholics to vote Democratic.

Roosevelt's greatest strength was in the cities. He could have been elected in 1932 and 1936 without his top-heavy urban majorities, but these majorities were indicative of the main forces behind the Roosevelt coalition. The Democratic party's continued strength in urban centers was essential to victory in 1940, 1944, and 1948. New York, Massachusetts, Pennsylvania, Maryland, Missouri, Illinois, Michigan, Ohio, Wisconsin, and California contained the twelve cities of a half million population or over. If these metropolitan areas gave sufficient votes to one candidate, he captured the electoral vote of the state. Urban Democratic pluralities from 1932 to 1948 were the dominant influence in the electoral vote of these ten states.[3]

They gave Roosevelt 212 electoral votes in 1940 and 193 four years later. With only 266 votes necessary for victory, these ten urban states held the key to presidential elections. In his four elections, Roosevelt's strength in the big cities combined with less urban

Northern states was such that he did not need the electoral vote of the South to win. With the exception of California, the ten urban states were located along the North Atlantic coast and in the Midwest. These two regions had been basically Republican from 1864 to 1928. The size of the Democratic majorities in the big cities ended this old political allegiance and made the Democratic party the majority party for the first time since 1860.

BOOK THREE

Limits to Leadership: Roosevelt

11. Political Miscalculations

A successful final term seemed in the offing for Franklin D. Roosevelt. But, by the end of 1937, his party was bitterly divided by his attack on the Supreme Court, and the economy had gone into a tailspin. Many of Roosevelt's difficulties in 1937-1938 were not unlike those faced by other presidents in their second terms. There was a jockeying within his party to influence the selection of the next presidential nominee. And, following the dominant presidential leadership of the first term, Congress began to reassert its power. But regardless of these factors, Roosevelt's difficulties stemmed directly from the surprising ineptness with which he himself, as well as his aides, dealt with Congress during his fight against the Supreme Court.

Although the Seventy-first Congress was torn by the Supreme Court issue and also rebuffed the President's proposal to reorganize the executive department, it did enact a number of significant laws. Congress passed the Farm Security Administration bill which lent money to tenant farmers to enable them to become farm owners. The FSA also promoted the withdrawal of submarginal land from production, established some thirty camps to house migratory farm workers, and helped farmers organize rural medical and dental care groups. Congress also established the United States Housing Authority to lend money to local governmental housing agencies and to establish standards of cost, construction, and eligibility of tenants. By 1941, when USHA turned to the task of housing defense workers, over five hundred projects had been constructed.

Early in 1938, Congress enacted the second Agricultural Adjustment Act authorizing soil conservation payments to farmers who agreed to restrict production of specific crops. And the President, by appealing to the public and exerting great pressure on Congress, also secured the last of the New Deal's labor legislation. The Fair Labor Standards Act, passed in May, 1938, established a minimum wage of twenty-five cents an hour which was to rise gradually to forty cents. The work-week was set at forty-four hours and to be reduced in three years to forty. Overtime was to be paid at the rate of time and a half. And, by forbidding the shipment in interstate commerce of goods manufactured by children under sixteen, the act ended the exploitation of children by industry and abolished the worst of the sweatshops. By 1939, some thirteen million workers were affected by the provisions of the law.

Growing opposition to Roosevelt's program in 1937-1938 may have in the long run proved to be salutary. It tempered and modified legislative proposals, allowing the country to absorb with less friction the continuing social changes. The opposition rendered the President a favor he did not appreciate by forcing him to defend and clarify his program. The ensuing debate broadened public understanding of the New Deal revolution. As a result, for all of the controversy in the postwar decade, no basic alteration of the social and economic measures of the Roosevelt era could be a practical political program.

The legislative achievements of 1937-1938 were overshadowed by Roosevelt's inability to win congressional endorsement for his Supreme Court plan. Throughout his career, Roosevelt had known the value of a "devil" in politics. The "money changers," the "economic royalists," and the public utility magnates had all been fully exploited. But in 1937, his turning on the Supreme Court was a serious blunder. His earlier "devils" had all discredited themselves in the popular mind during the crash of the new era. The Court, he was to discover, was different. It enjoyed the protection of the potent political myth that it was a non-political body, "a sacred institution on which politics must not lay its profane hands." [1]

When Chief Justice Charles Evans Hughes administered the oath of office to Roosevelt for the second time, the average age of those on the Court was nearly seventy-two. Willis Van Devanter (77) had been appointed by Taft. Wilson had appointed James C. McReynolds (74) and Louis D. Brandeis (80). Harding had appointed George Sutherland (74) and Pierce Butler (70). Coolidge had appointed Harlan F. Stone (64). Hoover had appointed the Chief Justice (74), as well as Benjamin N. Cardozo (66), and Owen J. Roberts (61).

Roosevelt had had no vacancies to fill during his first term. Before the advent of the New Deal, four of the Justices — Van Devanter, McReynolds, Sutherland, and Butler — had in their decisions established their abiding distrust of governmental control over economic life. Three members of the Court — Brandeis, Stone, and Cardozo — generally had favored federal and state attempts to regulate aspects of the economy. The other two members — the Chief Justice and Roberts — fell in between these two groups. In a number of the major decisions invalidating New Deal laws, the Court had split five to four or six to three.

By early 1937, a number of key New Deal measures were on the Court's docket. On February 5, the President called the Cabinet and congressional leaders to an extraordinary meeting. Only a few of his closest aides knew what he had in mind as he explained his plan. There was no mention of the recent decisions of the Supreme Court nor of the constitutional crisis created by them. Instead, Roosevelt talked of the problems of delay in federal court litigation, of the heavy burden on the Supreme Court, and of the need for a "constant infusion of new blood" into the courts. To achieve this, the President proposed he be empowered to appoint a new justice in any federal court when an incumbent failed to retire at the age of seventy. In the case of the Supreme Court, since six justices were over seventy, Roosevelt explained, its size could be increased to fifteen.

The dissimulation in this approach was obvious. Roosevelt's most consistent supporter on the Court was eighty-year-old Louis Brandeis. If justices over seventy were incapable of sound decisions, then Brandeis had been thinking unsoundly.

As the President read the message he was sending to Capitol Hill, the assembled congressional leaders sat as if stunned. When Roosevelt finished with his proposed legislation, Vice-President Garner and Sam Rayburn said nothing. Senators Joseph Robinson and Henry Ashurst indicated their approval. But there was little discussion. It was obvious to those present that Roosevelt was not seeking the opinions of his party's congressional leaders. On the way back to the Congress, Hatton Sumners, Chairman of the House Judiciary Committee, told his colleagues: "Boys, here's where I cash in." After the message was read to the Senate, Garner stood in the lobby vigorously shaking a turned-down thumb.

The President expected newspaper attacks on the plan, but he counted on the support of the public to push the measure through Congress. Usually aware of the need of preparing public opinion and the necessity of organizing congressional support in advance, he had been made too cocky by his personal election triumph over the Old Guard in 1936. Elated by his margin of victory over Landon, he now lost his customary political skill. His secrecy about the plan until February 5, his lack of consultation with congressional leaders until the last minute, his failure to make the Court an issue in the campaign, and the indirect and maladroit scheme he proposed split the country. The plan brought the first serious division in the New Deal coalition. Some liberals were shocked by Roosevelt's technique; and progressive Senators Hiram Johnson, Burton K. Wheeler, Joseph O'Mahoney, Tom Connally, Bennett Champ Clark, and Edward Burke all came out against it. George W. Norris announced at the outset that he was not in sympathy with the proposal, but in the end voted for it. As public and congressional opposition grew, congressional Republicans shrewdly stayed in the background and let the Democrats lead the attack.

Bar associations denounced the plan, New England town meetings protested, and mail flooded congressional offices. There was a deep reverence for the Court and an element of fear for the unknown in these letters, a fear increased by the rash of sit-down strikes that had just broken out. Part of the protest was stimulated by the Constitutional Government Committee headed by newspaper publisher Frank Gannett. Full-page advertisements appeared in newspapers, speakers attacked the plan over the radio, and copies of speeches were sent out by the thousands. But, as Emporia editor William Allen White wrote to Senator Norris, for the first time opposition to Roosevelt was coming "not from the plug hat section but from the grass roots."

Realizing that opposition was developing rapidly among many who had voted for him, Roosevelt shifted his approach and at last put the issue frankly. At a Democratic rally on March 4, he explained to the party faithful how his remedial measures had been struck down by the Court. And he warned: "If we would keep faith with those who had faith in us, if we would make democracy succeed, I say we must act — Now!" In a fireside chat five days later, he reminded his listeners of conditions four years before and charged the Supreme Court with failure to work with the executive and Congress to solve them. The Constitution, he stated, had to be saved from the Court.

By this date, however, it was too late. His plan already had suffered irreparable damage. And two weeks later the Chief Justice explained, in a public letter to Senator Wheeler, that the Supreme Court was abreast of its work and contended that a larger court would hurt its efficiency.

The Court itself delivered the final blow to Roosevelt's proposal. On March 29, it upheld by a five to four vote a minimum wage law of the state of Washington quite similar to the New York law it had invalidated ten months before. Justice Roberts switched sides, leading one reporter to observe, "A switch in time saves nine." All through the bitter struggle, the solemn, bewhiskered Hughes outmaneuvered the overconfident President. The Chief Justice worked closely with the opposition. His letter to Senator Wheeler was carefully timed to have maximum effect. And he knew weeks before March 29 that Roberts would switch, but he held up the case until its impact would be most devastating to the President's plan.

On April 12, the judicial revolution continued when the same five upheld the Wagner Labor Relations Act. And on May 21 the Social Security Law was upheld. Eleven days later Justice Van Devanter retired from the Court.

After the announcement of Van Devanter's retirement, Roosevelt told the Senate Majority Leader, Joseph Robinson, that he would accept a compromise bill. But Robinson had a difficult time winning votes necessary even for a compromise. On July 14, he dropped dead.

Those who had supported the measure out of personal loyalty to Robinson now withdrew their support. On July 20, Vice-President Garner, who had shown his disapproval of the measure by going to Texas during the key period of the fight in the Senate, told the President: "You are beat. You haven't got the votes."

Several years later Roosevelt remarked that while he had lost the battle, he had won the war. To a degree he was right. After 1937, the Court, by upholding social and economic legislation, completed the constitutional revolution started by itself during the struggle over the President's plan. And vacancies came so fast on the Court, after 1937, that Roosevelt appointed the Chief Justice and the eight associate justices. The fortuitous resignation of justices, rather than his own skill, enabled him to claim he had won the war and rationalize his excess of cleverness and miscalculations into victory.

The bitterness of the Supreme Court fight temporarily, at least, strained his relations with Congress and weakened his prestige with many of his supporters. Angered by his defeat, Roosevelt decided to make an attempt in 1938 to drive some of his conservative Democratic foes out of Congress. They not only had led the opposition to the court bill, but had also defeated his administrative reorganization bill, and were delaying the passage of the wages and hours bill. These Democrats, Roosevelt felt, were only too happy to envelop themselves in the Roosevelt mantle when they campaigned but after their election deserted his program.

He had been careful not to interfere in the 1934 and 1936 primaries, leaving to local leadership and local voters the determination of the type of Democrat to represent them. Although the 1938 purge attempt was represented as liberalism, it was provoked by irritation rather than by any well-thought-out plan on Roosevelt's part to make the Democrats a wholly liberal party.

Roosevelt's principal efforts to influence Democratic nominations were made in four states. In Kentucky, he urged voters to re-elect Senate Majority Leader Alben Barkley over Governor Happy Chandler on the basis of Barkley's greater experience. But in Georgia he drew the issue between conservatism and liberalism in urging the voters to defeat their influential Senator, Walter F. George. In Maryland, Roosevelt took the stump against Senator Millard Tydings. He accused Tydings of wanting to run "with the Roosevelt prestige and the money of his conservative Republican friends both on his side." In New York City, he urged voters to defeat Congressman John O'Connor, who, as Chairman of the powerful Rules Committee, had thwarted New Deal legislation.

Barkley won and O'Connor was defeated. But George and Tydings were renominated. Even with his abounding prestige, the President had assumed a difficult, if not impossible, task. With local and state patronage far more plentiful than federal, the basic power in primary elections lay in these units. Moreover, Senators such as George and Tydings, by doing favors for their constituents, had built a loyal following. Although supporters of Roosevelt for President, they would not support his primary fight which challenged the Senators' well-established personal relationships.

Roosevelt did not again attempt to purge conservative Democrats. While writers are in general agreement that Roosevelt's purge was a failure, the mere fact that he attempted it, and might attempt it again, may have had a cautionary effect on many congressional Democrats. A number may have voted with reluctance for the President's "must" legislation in order not to provoke him into supporting an opponent in a bitter, costly primary struggle.

In the 1938 congressional campaign, Roosevelt called for the election of a liberal Congress. Although the Democrats emerged with a heavy majority, Republicans showed important gains, increasing their representation in the Senate from 17 to 23 and in the House from 89 to 169. Heaviest Republican gains came in the Midwest and the Northwest. The collapse of both Governor Philip La Follette's Progressive Party in Wisconsin and the Farmer-Labor Party in Minnesota gave a boost to the Republicans as did the fact that the country was again deep in depression. Robert A. Taft was elected to the Senate seat from Ohio. Republicans won more than a dozen governorships, and the young, vigorous New York district attorney, Thomas E. Dewey, came close to upsetting Governor Herbert Lehman.

Republicans, in combination with conservative Democrats, now had enough votes to control the Congress. By 1939, however, the Congress could not have abolished the New Deal even had it desired to do so. It could, however, check further extension. And with world developments approaching a dangerous climax, Roosevelt now knew that if he further antagonized conservative Democrats, he would jeopardize their support of his foreign policy. Although he defended his domestic program in his annual message on January 4, 1939, he asked for no additional reform legislation, stating: "We have now passed the period of internal conflict in the launching of our program of social reform." The principal theme of the speech was the enormity of the totalitarian threat to peace and democracy.

12. The Economy in a Tailspin

The year 1937 was a turbulent one for the nation and for the world. Overseas, General Franco's forces besieged the Loyalist government in Madrid, the Japanese attacked North China, and Hitler turned Germany into an armed camp. At home, the country not only went through the bitter struggle over the Supreme Court bill, but also witnessed the climax of the most militant phase of the trade union movement, and, late in the year, the economy suffered a setback.

Industrial conflict marked the drive for unionization. During 1937 there were 4720 strikes and lockouts affecting 1,950,000 workers, two thirds of these over union recognition. The most startling were the sit-down strikes, first used by employees in a Western packinghouse in 1933 and developed on a large scale by Akron rubber workers in 1935. The workers simply remained in the plants but did no work. Not until November, 1936, at the Bendix plant in South Bend, Indiana, did employees, however, stay in the plant overnight. Late in December, a series of short sit-down strikes occurred in Michigan automobile accessory plants, and then came a forty-four-day strike against General Motors and Fisher Body plants in Anderson, Indiana, and Detroit, affecting over 150,000 workers. This was followed by an unexpected strike in Detroit's Chrysler plants idling 65,000 workers. Like an epidemic, sit-down strikes spread to Detroit hotels, restaurants, department stores, and other factories.

National union leaders, including John L. Lewis, were almost as unprepared as the public for these strikes welling up from militant local leaders and new union-minded workers. The chief concern of Lewis and the CIO early in 1937 was an impending strike in the steel industry. The demand of the auto workers for union recognition, however, forced the national leadership into support of the sit-down strikes against General Motors. The corporation denounced the strikers as revolutionaries and trespassers on private property, and requested Democratic Governor Frank Murphy to use the National Guard to dislodge them. Murphy refused. Instead, he encouraged mediation of the dispute. On January 29, General Motors secured an injunction ordering the strikers from the property. The strikers would not leave, warning that the use of force would "mean a blood bath of unarmed workers." Governor Murphy refused again to use the National Guard and increased his efforts to bring about mediation. President Roosevelt, too, brought pressure on General Motors. On February 11, the corporation agreed to recognize the United Automobile Workers as the sole bargaining agent for the workers.

With this momentous victory, the UAW now called a sit-down strike against Chrysler. Governor Murphy brought Lewis and Walter P. Chrysler together for talks and announced this time that he would enforce a court injunction against the strikers. Although the strikers were called out of the plants by Lewis, on April 6, Chrysler agreed to bargain with the UAW.[1]

Labor reporter Louis Stark, after interviewing sit-down strikers, wrote that they felt they had a property right in their job equal to any employer's property right. "Our hides are wrapped around those machines," one Fisher Body striker said. Businessmen were angered and frustrated by the sit-down technique. The President was annoyed both at the intransigence of employers and at the actions of the unions. In the midst of the controversy, he infuriated Lewis by issuing the statement: "A plague on both your houses." Public opinion gradually turned against the sit-down strikes. Union leaders, aware of their need for support from the public and the government, forsook the technique for well-organized membership drives and the traditional strike.

Faced with what threatened to be a long and costly strike, the United States Steel Corporation agreed on March 2 to recognize the Steel Workers' union, raise wages 10 per cent, and accept the forty-

hour week with time and a half for overtime. This was a milestone
in the history of labor. Big Steel, which in the past had been the
leader in fighting unions in the basic industries, had made an about-
face. With this victory, the union now went after the smaller companies. Inland Steel recognized the union but others refused. Strikes,
violence, and deaths followed. In Chicago the police killed ten
strikers in the "Memorial Day Massacre." A Senate subcommittee
charged Little Steel with violating both the Wagner Act and the
civil liberties of the strikers with the help of local police and the National Guard. The National Labor Relations Board, at the request
of the union, moved into the case and in 1941 required the companies to recognize the unions and to bargain in good faith.

CIO unions also organized the rubber industry, the textile mills
in the North, the longshoremen on the West Coast, and a dozen
other industries. By 1941, the CIO numbered over five million, the
A. F. of L. had over four and a half million members, and independent unions counted for another million. Counterbalancing the
power of big business now was the power of big labor. This achievement was the result not only of labor militancy. A favorable public
attitude, and the moral and legal support of the government, had
been essential.

The tensions and excitement created by the sit-down strikes and
the Supreme Court bill were hardly over when business took a turn
for the worse. By the autumn of 1937, the value of the gross national product was 5 per cent above its 1929 peak. Industrial production also had passed the 1929 peak. The working force, however,
had increased 10 per cent, and full employment required the gross
national product to be 25 per cent higher than in 1929.[2] And, in
spite of aid to the lower income groups, over 40 per cent of all
families had less than $1000 in cash income from July, 1935, to June,
1936, and 65 per cent less than $1500. Economists Roland S. Vaile
and Helen Conoyer observed: ". . . the total of all the incomes
distributed to 78 per cent of families with lowest incomes was insufficient to permit an average consumption equal to the scale suggested as adequate for 'bare subsistence.'"[3] But the improvement
since 1933 led many to feel the depression had ended. "Last week
with Depression vanishing into memory, the portents of Boom

drummed excitingly throughout the land," *Time* editorialized on December 14, 1936.

While optimism seemed the order of the day, there were weak spots. Over seven million were still out of work. Residential construction was still 40 per cent and industrial and commercial construction 50 per cent below the 1929 level. Capital spending on industrial and commercial construction and on producers' equipment had not recovered. One explanation of this, given at the time, was that the economy had "matured." It had reached a point of stagnation and great expansion was no longer to be expected. It is probably more accurate to say that business had not adjusted to all the changes since 1933. Unions had had to be accepted and wage rates had gone up 41 per cent since then. Stock market regulations and reforms in the credit system, necessary as they were, seemingly discouraged the floating of new stock issues. Higher taxes, too, altered the basis on which investments had been made. Profits, which had been unusually high in 1929, did not recover as fast as wages and production after 1933, another factor limiting expenditures for capital goods. And the bitter conflict between businessmen and Roosevelt, increasing after 1934, slowed adjustment to all these changes.

During 1936, when Roosevelt should have been worried about the continuing deflation, he decided instead that inflation was more to be feared. Although government spending was too small to counteract the decline in private spending, at the insistent advice of his Secretary of the Treasury, Henry J. Morgenthau, Jr., Roosevelt now decided to reduce deficits and move toward a balanced budget. As a result, between January and August, 1937, the government's contribution to the country's buying power was reduced by over three billion dollars and WPA rolls were slashed from three million to a million and a half workers. Meanwhile, the Federal Reserve system raised the reserve requirements of member banks by 50 per cent and Federal Reserve Banks bought government bonds on a wide scale to prevent monetary and credit inflation.

The slump started in September. Roosevelt was perplexed as to what course to follow. While Republicans talked of the Roosevelt depression, unemployment climbed to ten million by 1938. The President was torn between his desire to balance the budget and the advice he received from Marriner Eccles, Chairman of the

Board of Governors of the Federal Reserve system, and others, who urged a return to government spending. Morgenthau countered by insisting that advocates of spending had created a loss of business confidence. But Eccles felt that with the deflation, government spending was essential to check growing unemployment and to stimulate private enterprise.

In 1936, John Maynard Keynes had published his influential book, *The General Theory of Employment, Interest, and Money.* He denounced the doctrine that in a depression governments must let wages and prices fall, and balance budgets. Instead, he insisted that governments should at such a time unbalance the budget by heavy spending and concurrently reduce taxes. The economy could recover, he wrote, only by heavy consumer spending and investing by private sources or by the government. In February, 1938, he wrote Roosevelt from England that recovery was possible only through large-scale public works and the stimulation of investment in such durable goods as housing, public utilities, and transport.

In April, 1938, Roosevelt resumed government spending although not on the scale Keynes had recommended. While accepting emergency pump-priming, the President never adopted this theory in its entirety. Some of his advisers repudiated this altogether, others favored it only as a temporary measure. Some, believing that the economy had now "matured" and could not expand, saw no solution to the American problem in Keynesian ideas.

On April 14, 1938, the President sent a special message to Congress announcing that restrictions on credit were being eased and asked for increased appropriations totaling five billion dollars for the WPA, public works and other agencies.[4] Congress responded, but against considerable opposition.

After mid-1938 the economic situation showed a distinct improvement. Industrial production rose and unemployment began to decline. Government expenditures for national defense were now rising and orders from European governments for aircraft and other military equipment were a stimulus to increased production. There was still a lack of confidence in the future. Walter Lippmann observed: "We are undecided, nervous and torn because we are confronting the problems of the Twentieth Century with minds formed in the Nineteenth Century and attached to the smaller duties of a simpler past. . . . We are afraid of the fertility of the American earth, afraid of the productiveness of American capital and American labor, afraid of American influence in the family of nations, because we still cling to the mentality of a little nation on the frontiers of the civilized world, though we have the opportunity, the power, and the responsibilities of a very great nation at the center of the civilized world." [5]

When Hitler invaded Poland in the autumn of 1939, the "simpler past" disappeared and the productivity of American capital and labor were unleashed. Events, rather than any plan of F. D. R., brought recovery. Wartime expenditures by the government revealed to conservatives what massive government action would do to restore vigor to the economy. For those liberals who felt a permanent state of stagnation had been reached, wartime developments revealed the tremendous potential implicit in modern science and technology.

Americans quickly recognized the economic significance of the war. Stock prices soared. Employment in the steel industry rose 10 per cent that September. A million and a quarter men had returned to work by October. The tragedy in Europe, the American Federation of Labor said in October, was a more powerful "shot in the arm" to business than "any pump-priming" of the past six years.

The real boom came in May, 1940, as Hitler's divisions rolled across France. Roosevelt asked Congress for full-scale rearmament and called for fifty thousand planes a year, a figure laughed at by "practical people" as unrealistic. Congress soon authorized defense appropriations of over ten billions. From now on the government, instead of using an eyedropper as in the 1930s, ladled money into the economy. Keynes pointed out that the wealth-producing capacity going to waste in America was huge. He bemoaned the fact that it was impossible in peacetime for a democracy to spend enough to generate an enormous production and bring full employment. The war, he predicted, would teach Americans their productive strength. "Your war preparations," he wrote, "so far from requiring a sacrifice, will be the stimulus . . . to a greater individual consumption and a higher standard of living." [6]

13.   Public Opinion and Foreign Policy

In the turbulent '30s, the Good Neighbor Policy was the only aspect of the Administration's foreign policy which a majority of the public supported wholeheartedly. A public opinion favorable to such a policy had been developing during the '20s, when vocal elements protested American interference in the affairs of Latin American nations. During the next decade, as Europe and Asia moved toward war, improved relations with Latin America became essential to the national security. Both internationalists and isolationists supported the Good Neighbor Policy. Isolationists advocated closer hemispheric relations as an essential factor before regional isolation could be achieved. Internationalists believed that a united hemisphere could play a significant role in maintaining peace.

When President-elect Hoover toured South America before his inauguration, he saw how deep was the hatred of the "Colossus of the North." As President, he started to reverse past policies and launch the nation on the road to being the Good Neighbor. Roosevelt completed the transition. In his inaugural address he pledged the nation "to the policy of the good neighbor — the neighbor who resolutely respects himself and, because he does so, respects the rights of others — the neighbor who respects his obligations and respects the sanctity of his agreements in and with a world of neighbors." This policy was quickly translated into action. New treaties were drafted with Cuba and Panama which ended their status as protectorates. Marines were withdrawn from Haiti. At a Pan American Conference in December, 1933, Cordell Hull pledged that the United States would not intervene in the affairs of Latin America. And during 1933, the Monroe Doctrine was being transformed from the unilateral policy of the United States to the multilateral policy of the whole hemisphere. Roosevelt pointed out that the maintenance of constitutional government in nations of the Western Hemisphere was the concern of each nation. Only if, and when, the failure to maintain law and orderly processes affected the other nations of the continent did it become their concern. ". . . and the point to stress," Roosevelt said, "is that in such an event it becomes the joint concern of a whole continent in which we are all neighbors."

Three years later at a Pan American Conference at Buenos Aires, the President emphasized the Pan Americanization of the Monroe Doctrine when he said that any non-American state seeking "to commit acts of aggression against us will find a Hemisphere wholly prepared to consult together for our mutual safety and our mutual good." In 1938, at the Lima Conference, the nations repeated their pledge to consult one another to maintain peace, they condemned the racial and religious persecutions in Nazi Germany, and they denounced political activities by alien minorities in their midst.

The achievements of the Good Neighbor policy came none too quickly. Germany, Italy, and Japan tried to arouse Yankeephobia in Latin America to keep the hemisphere in turmoil. After the outbreak of war in Europe, the American nations established joint military, economic, and propaganda boards. Important military bases were made available to the United States for the protection of the hemisphere. After Pearl Harbor, many Latin American nations declared war, and all the countries except Argentina and Chile immediately severed relations with the Axis.[1] It was a far more united hemisphere than in 1917 when many nations had been uncooperative and even hostile to the United States. The completion of the Pan Americanization of the Monroe Doctrine came at the Chapultepec Conference early in 1945 when it was agreed that an attack on any American state would be an attack upon all. Two years later at Rio, the twenty-one American Republics established machinery to implement the Declaration of Chapultepec.

While the public rallied to Roosevelt's Good Neighbor Policy, the majority disagreed with his belief that American power should support the collective security efforts of Great Britain and France. But the steady march of aggression and Roosevelt's warnings of the menace of totalitarianism to American security brought a gradual change of attitude by 1939. By then, most Americans were sympathetic to extending aid to the Allies, short of war.

From his experience in the Wilson Administration, Roosevelt recognized the necessity of securing public understanding before his foreign policy could be accepted. During his first term, he realized that he would commit political suicide if his policy appeared to be too international. The temper of the time demanded isolation from the troubles of the world. Public opinion had to evolve from the belief that isolation was a protection from aggression to a realization that the Axis design was world domination.

Gradually and carefully, the President used the pulpit of the White House to alter public opinion. Although his inaugural address had contained only one paragraph on foreign affairs, by 1934 more and more about the world situation crept into his speeches. In some he ignored world events, but in the entire context of his speeches and press conferences over the next five years, there was increasing and hardening comment about the Axis nations. He understood, however, that public opinion could not be changed overnight. He knew what a leader could and could not accomplish. In his judgment, distortions in the public mind could be counteracted slowly as the aggressions of the Axis began to disturb the people. Roosevelt moved warily. As in domestic matters, he would tack with prevailing winds. While he seemed cautious, hesitant, and almost timid at times in his efforts to lead the country away from isolationism, he knew from his political experience that there were many routes to an objective. As a result, he would zig and then zag in the course he was pursuing to arouse the public to the Axis threat to American security. Occasionally, he misjudged the public temper as he did in his speech in October, 1937, calling for a quarantine of aggressor nations. Then he would retreat until the time was more propitious to warn again of the dangers of aggression.

His freedom of action to conduct foreign policy in accordance with his conception of the national interest was hampered until 1939 by the wide adherence to isolationism. Roosevelt understood the pluralistic forces — including physical isolationists, pacifists, agrarian liberals, and German- and Irish-American ethnic elements — gathered under the tent of isolationism. The complexity of the isolationist forces and their wide appeal in the early '30s forced the President to be cautious.

Growing disillusionment over American participation in the first war was a significant ingredient of this isolationism. During the

1920s, many writers insisted that Allied propaganda, American munitions makers, and international bankers had duped the nation into the war. Another current of isolationism flowed from Western agrarian liberalism. For thirty years prior to 1917, many Western Congressmen had attacked the power of Wall Street. When the nation entered the war, their spokesmen — Senators George W. Norris and Robert M. La Follette — transferred the domestic stereotype of "evil" Wall Street to world politics, placing the blame for American entry on their old domestic foe. After 1919, many of these liberals charged that our entering the war had killed reform at home. They demanded, therefore, that the nation stay out of future wars in order to proceed with domestic reform.

The intimate connection between isolationism and domestic liberalism was demonstrated in much of the vote La Follette received in his 1924 campaign for the presidency. When Roosevelt was seeking delegates to the 1932 convention and needed the support of Western liberals, he shied away from international issues. During his first term, his need of their support for domestic legislation was a factor that limited his foreign policy. Until 1939, in fact, domestic liberals were the leading spokesmen of the isolationist cause. After 1939, although Senators Burton K. Wheeler, Hiram Johnson, Gerald P. Nye, and Governor Philip La Follette were still featured speakers at isolationist rallies, the leaders of the America First Committee — the most influential isolationist organization — were economic conservatives who feared continuing social reforms.[2] This had not been the case, however, from 1933 to 1939, when progressives were in the front ranks of isolationism.

Some Americans of Irish and German ancestry, as well, were vocal members of the isolationist crew. Many had voted against the Democrats in 1920 and 1924 in protest against our part in the first war. In 1936, the Union Party headed by Congressman William Lemke drew its main support from German and Irish Catholics, "the most belligerently isolationist voters in the country," Samuel Lubell has observed in The Future of American Politics.

The depression spurred isolationist tendencies. Many tried to retreat more and more from Europe which they blamed for the depression. Unpaid war debts only confirmed the belief that foreigners were tricky and that Americans always were cheated. An intolerance of foreign peoples and a profound distrust of anything savoring of internationalism spurred the demand for withdrawal from the world.

The climax came with the work of the Nye Committee. On February, 8, 1934, Senator Gerald P. Nye of North Dakota proposed that the Senate establish a committee to investigate the munitions industry. Many magazine indictments of munitions makers appeared and pressures mounted on the Senate to approve Nye's resolution. In April, Nye was named chairman of the investigation. Roosevelt and Hull had approved the investigation since they knew it was impossible to fight the isolationist wave at this moment. But they were startled, in view of the Democratic majorities in Congress, that an isolationist Republican was placed in charge.

The press and radio gave the hearings wide coverage. And Nye toured the country proclaiming that the main cause of war was "the greediness of the dominant industrialists and financiers." This devil theory was stressed over and over again. It had a major impact on the public mind. The Federal Council of Churches of Christ announced that "a wave of moral indignation is sweeping through the churches" against those who would "jeopardize the peace of the world for the sake of private gain." And a rash of articles and books appeared. H. C. Engelbrecht published *One Hell of a Business* (1934); Walter Millis brought out *Road to War* (1935), a best-seller which lent support to Nye's position.

Americans now "knew" what "really" had forced them into the war. The "facts" of history had been revealed. The hearings, coinciding with Roosevelt's attack on "economic royalists," proved to be an immense liability to Roosevelt as the Axis powers extended their aggressions. The Committee exploited current prejudices against wealth in an irresponsible fashion and reinforced isolationist attitudes at a time when they had become archaic. It spread the belief that the nation's location rendered it safe from war in Europe or Asia. This encouraged the aggressors to think that American public opinion was unconcerned with their plans and they could proceed without interference from the Roosevelt Administration.

The President and the Secretary of State were in a difficult position. As early as 1934, American embassies in Berlin and Tokyo warned the State Department of the ambitious expansionistic plans of Germany and Japan. These reports implied action which Congress and public opinion would not accept. Hoover had faced the same problem when he asked Congress in January, 1933, to confer on the President the authority to limit or forbid shipment of arms "in cases where special undertakings of cooperation can be secured with the principal arms manufacturing nations." He contended that such a discretionary embargo would enable the United States to work together with other nations to prevent military conflict. Congress failed to adopt the measure. In March, 1933, Roosevelt asked Congress to pass a similar measure but Congress again refused to act.

In May, while Congress was considering this proposal, he moved to place the United States on the side of nations opposing aggression. He allowed Norman Davis, our representative at the Geneva Disarmament Conference, to give assurance that the United States would consult with other nations over any threat to the peace. And, if America agreed with the decision then taken, it would "refrain from any action tending to defeat such collective effort which these states may thus make to restore peace." This pledge was immediately attacked at home; and Roosevelt, who had considered appointing an ambassador to the League of Nations to implement this policy, decided not to risk arousing greater isolationist sentiment in this way.

With domestic recovery uppermost in the mind of the President and the country in 1933, these initial steps toward American participation in the maintenance of peace were weakened by the President himself when he adopted a policy of economic nationalism at the International Monetary Conference. The Reciprocal Trade Agreements passed by Congress in June, 1934, however, marked a shift away from this position. And that October the President suggested to Under Secretary of State William Phillips that a multilateral nonaggression pact be drafted with provisions for a trade boycott of an aggressor. This, however, died in the State Department.

The continuing veto power held by isolationists was demonstrated in the spring of 1935 when a proposal to allow American entrance into the World Court failed to pass the Senate. Roosevelt was stung by the rebuff. It was another indication that he had to move cautiously. He wrote Elihu Root that membership would come "but today, quite frankly, the wind everywhere blows against us." And he wrote Hoover's Secretary of State, Henry L. Stimson: "I fear common sense dictates no new method for the time being — but I have an unfortunately long memory and I am not forgetting either our enemies or our objectives."

The wind was blowing against Roosevelt's foreign policy when it became evident in August, 1935, that Italy was preparing to invade Ethiopia. The President asked Congress to pass legislation which would empower him to embargo shipment of arms to both sides if war broke out or to the aggressor nations only. But Congress instead listened to the Nye Committee where it had been emphasized that President Wilson had had too few restrictions before 1917 and, as a result, had been duped by "evil" forces. No President again should be allowed such freedom. Congress, therefore, proposed a mandatory arms embargo on both sides. When isolationists like Nye threatened a filibuster unless this were accepted, the President agreed, providing the bill would continue in force only until February 29, 1936.

It was a postponement of the showdown with the isolationists. But this mandatory embargo may well have made British diplomacy cautious. If she went to war with Italy, she would be unable to secure American arms. The danger was that the mandatory arms embargo would be applied to all circumstances and the aggressors could move without fear of even indirect American interference. After some hesitation, Roosevelt signed the Neutrality Act, but he warned that "the inflexible provisions might drag us into war instead of keeping us out."

The bill had passed Congress with nearly a unanimous vote. A veto might have been overridden and been a repudiation of Roosevelt's leadership then and for the future. Even if the veto had not been overridden, the threat of a filibuster would have delayed essential domestic legislation. Since the measure was to expire in six months' time, Roosevelt rationalized that collective security might not be seriously endangered. Roosevelt told reporters that the bill met the "needs of the existing situation." He could not yet stem the tide of isolationism, he implied.

The mandatory arms embargo, with no flexibility for the executive to discriminate between the aggressor and the victim, originated in Congress. It was guided through Congress by men of narrow provincial views who in most cases came from the least populous areas of the nation and had little understanding of the interdependence of the world.

In spite of his belief that the President was in a better position to interpret the true interests of the nation, Roosevelt knew he could not move without support. He had to give ground in order to salvage anything in the situation. Roosevelt's dilemma was increased by the political fact that many of the leaders of the isolationist bloc were key supporters of his domestic program. The reformer in the White House and the reformers in Congress disagreed sharply over foreign policy. The disagreement was not restricted to Congress. The Federal Council of Churches of Christ supported the Neutrality Act as did the National Council for the Prevention of War. And on August 16, 1935, a group of Democratic Congressmen told the Administration that "thousands and thousands of women's votes have been lost" over its refusal to come out for a mandatory arms embargo.

The arms embargo was enforced when Italy attacked Ethiopia. Since such items as scrap iron, oil, and trucks did not come under the designation of arms, Roosevelt and Hull issued a "moral" embargo warning citizens against transactions "of any character with either of the belligerent nations except at their own risk." They took this step to prevent the United States from becoming the "arsenal of the aggressor." Through this maneuver, not sanctioned by the law, the Administration attempted to achieve as much as it could for its policy of opposing aggression. And the State Department assured the League of Nations that "further action" would be taken if the League imposed an effective embargo on oil. Premier Pierre Laval of France, however, blocked such a move by the League. Instead, he and Sir Samuel Hoare, the British Foreign Secretary, agreed that Ethiopia should cede part of its territory to Italy. The publication of this plan created such a furor in Britain and France that Hoare and Laval resigned. And Roosevelt's and Hull's enthusiasm for cooperation with the League was chilled. In their minds, the Hoare-Laval plan placed a premium on aggression.

As the date for the expiration of the mandatory arms embargo approached, isolationist sentiment was stronger than it had been in 1935. The collapse of collective security in the Italo-Ethiopian war and the feverish militarizing of Germany threatened another conflagration. Unconvinced that a discretionary arms embargo would discourage aggressors, the public supported the mandatory embargo as the only means of avoiding involvement. And now, fearing war, pacifist groups, which had supported collective security efforts with the League of Nations, joined the isolationist forces.

The Administration, dropping any hope of securing flexibility in applying an embargo, agreed in 1936 to the extension of the Neutrality Act for another year. As the nation took refuge in its storm cellars, a group of Japanese militarists assassinated a number of moderate statesmen who had been exercising a restraining influence on the expansionists. On March 7, Nazi troops marched into the Rhineland. In July, General Franco launched his revolt against the Spanish government. Meanwhile, in America a new isolationist coalition was in the making. Father Coughlin praised Mussolini and Hitler over the radio and charged that Roosevelt was trying to lead the nation into war by favoring Great Britain, Loyalist Spain, and the Soviet Union. Some who had favored Roosevelt's domestic program but felt that he was too internationalist now started to drift to Congressman Lemke's Union Party.

At Chautauqua, New York, on August 14, 1936, Roosevelt bent before the isolationist gale. "I hate war," he told the crowd. "We shun political commitments which might entangle us in foreign wars; we avoid connection with the political activities of the League of Nations." But he did add the warning: "Yet we must remember that so long as war exists on earth there will be some danger that even the Nation which most ardently desires peace may be drawn into war."

Two events that autumn forecast the explosions that lay ahead. On October 25, Hitler and Mussolini formed the Berlin-Rome Axis. A month later, the Germans and the Japanese joined forces in the Anti-Comintern Pact aimed at the Soviet Union and its Communist apparatus in other nations. A new alliance of powerful military nations, determined to destroy the existing balance of power and establish fascist hegemony of the world, was now under way.

By this time, the Soviet Union, in the face of the growing threat from Germany and Japan, had reversed its policy toward the Western democracies. Instead of denouncing them as "capitalistic warmongers and imperialists," it was now trying to work with them to stop fascist aggression. For two years Soviet leaders had been moving gradually to a policy of collaboration with the Western powers.

Before this shift occurred, the United States and the USSR had established diplomatic and trade relations on November 16, 1933. There were many reasons for the American action. Business firms had been trading actively with Russia in the 1920s, and by 1930 the Soviet Union was the largest purchaser of American agricultural and industrial equipment. *Business Week* reported in June, 1932, that business was more in favor of recognition than the government, and the Scripps-Howard newspaper chain undertook a campaign for recognition that year. Liberal Republicans — including Senators Borah, Johnson, Brookhart, Norris, and La Follette — championed recognition. As the depression deepened, the prospect of increased trade with the Soviet Union speeded favorable action. In March, 1933, Al Smith advocated it and a majority of newspaper editors supported him. Recognition met with praise and the protests against it were swept under by a wave of approval.

The following year, the Russians, who had long charged that the League of Nations was an "organ of some imperialistic powers," joined it. In 1935, the Soviet Union signed mutual assistance pacts with France and Czechoslovakia pledging that in the event either party should be the subject of an unprovoked attack, the other would render active assistance.

The Communist party in the United States underwent a gradual shift as it adjusted to changing Soviet policy. In 1933, American Communists branded public works, the Civilian Conservation Corps, and the TVA as fascist preparations for war. But in 1934, they began to drop mention of the United States, France, and Great Britain as the chief enemies of the "peaceful" Soviet Union and attacked Japan and Germany instead. Then, in October, 1935, the Communist International laid down the policy of the popular front.

Georgi Dimitroff instructed the Communist parties to appeal not only to workers, but to the toiling farmers, to the middle class, and to all "anti-fascist and progressive elements." The issue was no longer socialism versus capitalism but "democracy" against fascism and the collective security of these nations against the fascist warmakers.

Under the new Soviet policy, American Communists now tried to "Americanize" themselves and broaden their appeal. They courted all types of movements. Ethnic groups, particularly those from countries having fascist governments or which were threatened by fascism, were wooed. Communists organized the National Negro Congress in 1936, dropped their earlier demand for a Negro republic in the South, and advocated the integration of American Negroes.

In 1935, the Communists dissolved their own union organization and helped John L. Lewis and the emerging CIO build the fast-growing industrial unions. They early infiltrated the American Youth Congress which had been organized by non-Communist liberals, and they were active in the formation of the American Student Union in 1935.

During the 1936 presidential campaign, Communist party candidate Earl Browder played on the theme of collective security against fascist aggression. Although Roosevelt was criticized because he had signed the Neutrality Law and would not aid the Loyalist government of Spain, Landon was denounced as more dangerous than Roosevelt. Browder announced that they would do everything possible to shift votes away from Landon "even though we cannot win their votes for the Communist Party, even though the result is that they vote for Roosevelt."

In New York the Communists achieved some success in infiltrating the American Labor party which had been organized in 1936 by labor leaders, liberals, and Socialists to support Roosevelt. Two years later party-liner Vito Marcantonio, nominated by the ALP, was elected to Congress, and the Communists withdrew their candidate for governor to support the ALP endorsement of Democratic candidate Herbert Lehman.[3]

With their growing "respectability" in the popular front days, the Communists succeeded in winning the support of a number of intellectuals. While some, embittered by the depression, had lent their support to the Communist party before 1935, many others did so after the popular front was launched. While some were attracted by the economic experiment in the Soviet Union and were disillusioned with American life, others were impressed by the Soviet opposition to the fascist aggressors. The American League Against War and Fascism, rebaptized in 1935 as the American League for Peace and Democracy, and the League of American Writers were two of the principal Communist front organizations appealing to intellectuals.

The mask of respectability soon began to slip, however, and the nakedness of the Communist parties as agents of the Soviet Union was more and more exposed. Many of the Americans who fought on the Republican side in the Spanish Civil War saw at first hand how the Communists conspired to destroy non-Communist liberals and tried to make the Spanish government a mere tool of Soviet policy. Stalin's ruthless purge from 1936 to 1938, in which he eliminated rivals and built his monolithic dictatorship, also shattered the illusions of some American intellectuals. The great disillusionment came, however, when Stalin signed a non-aggression pact with Hitler in August, 1939, and joined Germany in swallowing Poland. The disguise of anti-fascism and democracy was now torn off the Soviet Union and its Communist parties in other lands. The popular front had passed into the dustbins of history. Hosts of non-Communist intellectuals resigned from Communist front organizations and thousands of party members, including their best-known journalists and writers, left the party.

Although the 1930s would later be described by Eugene Lyons as *The Red Decade*, and politicians seeking power after the war would make much of the Communist menace in America under the New Deal, the number of writers and government workers who joined the Communist party or followed the party line was small. Their influence on the New Deal, too, was exaggerated.

14.   The High Tide of Isolation

When the Spanish Civil War broke out in July, 1936, the sympathies of many non-Communist liberals for the Republican government of Spain coincided with the demands of Communists and Communist front organizations for American support of the Spanish government. At the same time, many of the Catholic clergy in the United States denounced the Spanish government as "Communists" and supported Italian and German intervention in aid of Franco. While the Civil War stirred certain groups in the United States, the public as a whole was uninterested. A Gallup poll in January, 1937, revealed that 22 per cent favored the Loyalists, 12 per cent favored Franco, and 65 per cent favored neither or had no opinion.[1]

By the close of 1936, large numbers of international volunteers had arrived in Spain to aid the Loyalists. At the same time, organized units of Italian and German troops, flouting the non-intervention agreement signed with Britain and France in August, joined Franco's forces. The war was increasingly transformed into an international contest in which German and Italian fascists fought with Franco against an incompatible coalition of republicans, liberals, Communists, Socialists, and anarchists now openly aided by the Soviet Union.

Since the Neutrality Act did not apply to civil wars, the Administration asked Congress, when it convened on January 5, 1937, to enact legislation extending the arms embargo to both sides in Spain. The next day, with only one dissenting vote, Congress passed such a bill. Soon after its adoption Claude Bowers, the American ambassador to Spain, sent warnings that the arms embargo played into the hands of Franco, Hitler, and Mussolini. Under Secretary of State Sumner Welles expressed concern that a Franco victory would greatly enhance Mussolini's power in the Mediterranean. Socialist leader Norman Thomas and isolationist Senator William E. Borah opposed Roosevelt's policy as unjust and unneutral. Roosevelt, himself, became increasingly concerned with the sham of non-intervention. He considered extending the arms embargo to Germany and Italy but was dissuaded following unfavorable reactions from his ambassadors in London and Rome and from the British Foreign Secretary. Finally, in the spring of 1938 Roosevelt considered asking Congress to end the arms embargo on the Loyalist government.

In May, Senator Nye introduced just such a proposal. When the Senate Foreign Relations Committee asked the Administration for its position, Roosevelt rejected Nye's resolution. Harold L. Ickes recorded in his diary that the President explained to him that Democratic Congressional leaders were fearful that raising the embargo would mean the loss of "every Catholic vote" that fall. Ickes wrote in indignation: "This proves up to the hilt what so many people have been saying, namely, that the Catholic minorities in Great Britain and America have been dictating the international policy with respect to Spain." [2]

Ickes was only partly right. In addition to Roosevelt's concern that aiding the Loyalists would antagonize the Catholic Democratic vote, Cordell Hull and a number of influential foreign service officers were stubbornly opposed to lifting the embargo and running counter to the British policy of non-intervention. Hull had political support on Capitol Hill independent of Roosevelt, and by 1938 the President needed Hull's support to secure vital domestic legislation. And, although the Gallup poll found in December, 1938, that now 76 per cent sympathized with the Loyalists and only 24 per cent with Franco, the same poll revealed that only 24 per cent of those interviewed favored lifting the arms embargo.

In the spring of 1937, Congress passed a new neutrality bill retaining the mandatory arms embargo to both sides in a conflict. The Administration, however, did manage some aid for the Western democracies. Oil, scrap iron, rubber, cotton, and other such items were placed under a "cash and carry" embargo which allowed belligerent nations to secure such goods by paying cash and transporting them in their own ships. Winston Churchill observed that while the Allies could not count on American military assistance, the cash and carry provision had "the merit of rendering to superior sea power its full deserts."

The weakness behind the concept of the Neutrality Law was exposed when Japan launched its attack against North China in July, 1937. To apply it would prevent agricultural China from securing the arms necessary to combat industrialized Japan. Furthermore, the cash and carry plan would have enabled Japan to buy essential raw materials while virtually all trade with China would have been cut off. The Administration was in an anomalous position. If the law were enforced, it would aid Japan. The way out was not to enforce the law at all. Since no formal declaration of war had been made by either side, Roosevelt refused to invoke it. While this position did not go unchallenged, public opinion favored the President's decision. A Gallup poll early in October, 1937, revealed that the sympathies of 59 per cent were with China, 1 per cent with Japan, and 40 per cent with neither.

Knowing that the aggression in Asia was linked to aggression in Europe, Roosevelt spoke out boldly. In Chicago on October 5, 1937, he charged that international lawlessness threatened world peace. "It can engulf states and peoples remote from the original scene of hostilities . . ." he warned. "When an epidemic of physical disease starts to spread, the community approves and joins in a quarantine of the patients in order to protect the health of the community against the spread of disease. . . . There must be positive endeavors to preserve peace," he added. "We are adopting such measures as will minimize our risk of involvement, but we cannot have complete protection in a world of disorder in which confidence and security have broken down."

Although writers have described this speech as a "turnabout" in American policy and a "new departure," it was neither.[3] It was another attempt by Roosevelt to speed the transition of public opinion toward support of collective security. The speech, however, provoked a violent reaction. Pacifists charged that Roosevelt was trying to lead the nation into war. A poll showed a large majority in Congress opposed to joining the League of Nations in action against Japan. Hull, who had not seen the speech before it was delivered, was shocked at its language and remained silent as did other prominent Democrats.

Roosevelt and Under Secretary of State Sumner Welles decided to use the occasion of Armistice Day for a speech calling upon the nations of the world to reach agreement on principles of international conduct, the reduction of armaments, and on steps to improve economic relations among the peoples of the world. If this were accepted, the President planned to call a meeting of ten nations to draw up proposals to implement his ideas. The major objective, according to Welles, was to make it clear to Germany, Italy, and Japan that America would not remain indifferent if they persisted in preparing for world conquest.

But Hull registered a violent protest and insisted on sounding out the British first. The plan was abandoned when the Chamberlain government made it clear that it favored direct negotiations on its part with the Axis. "We must regard its rejection," observed Winston Churchill, "— for such it was — as the loss of the last frail chance to save the world from tyranny otherwise than by war."

The year 1938 was a year of crises. The fighting in Spain and China and new aggressions by Hitler kept the world in turmoil. Roosevelt, in a special message to Congress in January, declared that, since other nations were arming at an "alarming rate," national defenses must be increased in a vigorous fashion. Congress adopted the President's program without important changes. At the same time, the government began accumulating a stockpile of essential raw materials and assisted the British and French in obtaining weapons, particularly advanced types of aircraft.

In January, too, the Administration beat back an isolationist move which would have seriously handicapped presidential leadership of foreign policy and crippled growing support of the Western democracies. Representative Louis Ludlow of Indiana had been agitating since 1934 for a constitutional amendment that would require a declaration of war to be submitted to a popular referendum. This resolution was about to be debated in the House when Roosevelt and Hull intervened and succeeded in having the measure bottled up in committee.

During the next few months, American policy toward Japan stiffened. Japanese bombing of the civilian population of Chinese cities led the Department of State on July 1, 1938, to announce a moral embargo on the shipment of airplanes to Japan. This discriminatory embargo was a significant shift from the isolationist conception that embargoes should be applied impartially to each side. As Japanese armies pressed on, America extended a twenty-five-million-dollar loan to China to buy war supplies other than arms and munitions. And when Japan proclaimed its "New Order" in Asia in December, we refused to recognize it, adding that we would not admit the right of any power to constitute itself "the agent of destiny." While Japan moved ahead in China, Hitler plunged Europe into a war of nerves in March, 1938, when his troops seized Austria. Hull warned that the vital issue was whether brute force would prevail or whether the peace-loving nations could maintain law, order, and justice. If America turned its back on these nations, it would be left without a friend in a world of enemies. Isolation, Hull argued, was "a fruitful source of insecurity."

Germany next applied pressure on Czechoslovakia for cession of the Sudetenland provinces to Germany. To avoid war, for which Britain and France were ill prepared, Prime Minister Chamberlain flew to meet Hitler. And Roosevelt sent messages to the European governments urging a peaceful solution of the crisis. To forestall criticism of this at home, the President said: "The Government of the United States has no political involvement in Europe, and will assume no obligations in the conduct of the present negotiations." Then he added: "Yet in our own right we recognize our responsibilities as a part of a world of neighbors."

The French and the British leaders agreed to the dismemberment of Czechoslovakia in return for Hitler's promise that he would make no further territorial demands in Europe. A feeling of relief that war had been avoided swept over the American people, but at the same time they viewed the Munich agreement with disgust. Roosevelt now moved to increase the tempo of rearmament and Congress responded early in 1939 by increasing the budget of the army and the navy by two-thirds. In Britain and France, the governments shifted from their policy of appeasement and redoubled their defense efforts.

American feeling against Germany hardened after November, 1938, when Hitler intensified his ruthless persecution of German Jews. The President echoed public revulsion when he expressed amazement that "such things could occur in a twentieth-century civilization." Internationalist organizations increased their activities against isolationist pressure groups and warned that America could not stand aside in a conflict between the democracies and the Axis powers. If the war went into a stalemate, or if the Axis threatened to achieve domination of Europe, Asia, and Africa, the United States would be in a precarious position. The demand then for American intervention to protect the nation's security would be inevitable. It was wiser, therefore, these internationalists maintained, for the United States to take collective steps to prevent such a war from occurring.

From Roosevelt's viewpoint, public opinion must be prepared to support repeal of the arms embargo. If this could be achieved, the aggressors would realize that, while the nation still would not involve itself in military action, it would be available as an arsenal for the democracies. Such a step, he felt, would also encourage the democracies to resist the aggressors. He made a major attempt to crystallize public sentiment for repeal of the arms embargo in his annual message to Congress in January, 1939. It was carefully worded. He made it clear that he agreed with the public's desire to stay out of war, but he warned that no nation was safe "as long as any powerful nation refused to settle its grievances by arbitration." Then he said:

> At the very least, we can and should avoid any action, or any lack of action, which will encourage, assist, or build up an aggressor. We have learned that when we deliberately try to legislate neutrality, our neutrality laws may operate unevenly and unfairly — may actually give aid to an aggressor and deny it to the victim. The instinct for self-preservation should warn us that we ought not to let that happen any more.

Late that same month, however, there was a violent outburst, a warning that he still had to move cautiously in shaping public opinion to support his position. An American bomber crashed in California with an official of the French Air Ministry aboard. The news now came out that Roosevelt had allowed Allied officials to familiarize themselves with our latest military developments. Isolationists howled that a secret alliance had been signed. After the Senate Military Affairs Committee met with the President to discuss the situation, one Senator told the press that Roosevelt had said America's frontier now lay in France or on the Rhine. Isolationists immediately seized upon this statement as proof that the Neutrality Law should not be revised.

Some of Roosevelt's supporters now urged him to go to the country and explain that the one method of stopping Hitler was to warn him that the resources of the United States would be at the disposal of the democracies in the event of war. Roosevelt evidently feared that such an approach was still too daring. At his press conference on February 3, he branded the statement by the Senator a "deliberate lie" and said that the country was opposed to any entangling alliances.

In April, 1939, the President let the Chairman of the Senate Foreign Relations Committee know that actually he favored repeal of the Neutrality Act *in toto*. Senator Pittman rejected this but did support the replacement of the arms embargo with a cash and carry formula for war goods. But Pittman could not get this bill out of committee. The proposal to repeal the arms embargo ran into trouble in the House as well. The best that could be achieved was that "implements of war" — planes and tanks were so designated — could be had on a cash and carry basis. But arms and ammunition were still embargoed. The minority report objected even to this bill on the grounds that it gave the President "additional powers to be unneutral . . . No President has ever had such powers before . . . We are opposed to the President's policy of using the threat of our power to preserve a balance of power in Europe."

Roosevelt and Hull took what they could get. Reports from Europe were growing darker every day. Germany had absorbed Czechoslovakia in March, and Italy had conquered Albania the following month. Ambassador Bullitt warned from Paris that Hitler might launch a general war in the belief that the Neutrality Law would not be changed. "A change . . . at the present moment, therefore, would enormously strengthen the chance of peace," Bullitt concluded. With the outlook for a peaceful world growing dimmer every day, Roosevelt urged the Senate to take action on the House bill. But on July 11, the Foreign Relations Committee by a vote of twelve to eleven decided to give no further consideration to any neutrality measures during that session of Congress. Five Democrats joined seven Republicans in the majority vote. Among the opposition Democrats were Walter George and Guy Gillette. These Senators, observers felt, were still embittered at the President's attempt the year before to purge them.

The Committee's vote rocked the British and French governments. And it was a crushing defeat for Roosevelt. The Administration was now in a hopeless position. The cash and carry provision of the 1937 law had expired in May, but the mandatory arms embargo remained. The country was back to where it had been in 1935, but the world was rushing toward a cataclysm.

With public opinion polls revealing a majority favorable to the sale of arms and ammunition to the democracies, Roosevelt felt the difficulty lay in executive-legislative relations. Almost all Republicans and about a quarter of the Democrats were in a coalition to block him. Since Hull was popular on the Hill, particularly with conservatives, the President decided to emphasize the Secretary's leadership in the struggle. On July 14, in the hope of persuading the Senate to override the Committee's action, Roosevelt sent the Senate a statement by Hull setting forth the necessity of lifting the arms embargo.

When the message failed to secure action, Roosevelt and Hull called a conference of leading Senators from each party. Among those present at the White House that fateful night of July 18 were Vice-President Garner, Majority Leader Barkley, Key Pittman, Minority Leader Charles McNary, Deputy Minority Leader Warren Austin, and William E. Borah.

The President began by pointing out: "Our decision may well affect not only the people of our own country, but also the peoples of the world." He reviewed the alarming information from envoys in Europe and said revision of the Neutrality Law was essential. Borah, a stalwart isolationist cut from the familiar progressive pattern, dominated much of the discussion. He made it clear that he was unalterably opposed to lifting the embargo during that session of Congress and that he did not believe that war was likely in the near future. Hull replied: "I wish the Senator would come down to my office and read the cables. I'm sure he would come to the conclusion that there's far more danger of war than he thinks." To this Borah dogmatically replied: "So far as the reports in your Department are concerned, I wouldn't be bound by them. I have my own sources of information . . . and on several occasions I've found them more reliable than the State Department."

Hull was indignant at this arrogant reflection on the Department of State but, fearing he would explode, remained silent. Roosevelt continued to plead with the Senators but to no avail. As the meeting broke up, he wrote out a statement for the press placing responsibility squarely on the Senate: "The President and the Secretary of State maintained the definite position that failure by the Senate to take action now would weaken the leadership of the United States in exercising its potent influence in the cause of preserving peace among other nations in the event of a new crisis in Europe between now and next January."

The Administration had tasted one more defeat. It was, however, to be the last time isolationists were able to defeat Administration proposals although their opposition would have a cautionary effect on Roosevelt during the next two years.

Six weeks after the White House meeting, Germany invaded Poland. The United States had been unable to adapt itself to positive world leadership as the march of aggression brought the world to a second war in twenty-five years. But in the difficult months ahead, a combination of events overseas and strong presidential leadership were to bring the nation to a decisive position in world affairs.

15. Presidential Leadership and Foreign Policy

The struggle to influence public opinion was never more intense than from September, 1939, until that fateful Sunday morning when Japanese planes rained bombs on Pearl Harbor. The impact of the fall of France and the Battle of Britain; Churchill's stirring leadership of the British at their darkest hour; and Roosevelt's careful management of public opinion all augmented the majority that favored aid to the Allies even at the risk of war.

The Administration acted on the belief that it would be a threat to American security if Hitler won control of Europe, and possibly of Great Britain, and if Japan won hegemony over much of Asia. Aid to the Allies, therefore, was essential even at the risk of war; this the public supported. When the Gallup poll asked: "Do you think the United States *should keep out of war* or do everything possible to help England, *even at the risk of getting into war ourselves?*" the response was:

	Stay Out	Help England
May, 1940	64	36
June	64	36
July	61	39
August	53	47
September	48	52
November	50	50
December	40	60

But Roosevelt was acutely aware of the danger that isolationists could frighten the nation into repudiating the aid essential to the national security. In a letter to William Allen White in December, 1939, he set forth the dilemma that he was to face until December 7, 1941: "Things move with such terrific speed, these days, that it really is essential to us to think in broader terms and, in effect, to warn the American people that they, too, should think of possible ultimate results in Europe and the Far East." But, he added, "my problem is to get the American people to think of conceivable consequences without scaring the American people into thinking that they are going to be dragged into this war." [1]

He well knew the danger of being too far in advance of public opinion. But, at the same time, he realized that public opinion was not static. Over the radio, at his press conferences, and in public speeches he conducted a careful, steady campaign to shape public attitudes. He made sure that he had the votes before he asked Congress for legislation. And, when such support was not apparent, he implemented his policy by executive action.

Two weeks after Germany invaded Poland, the President issued a call for a special session of Congress to revise the neutrality legislation. An Administration analysis indicated support for this from some sixty Senators. Although Roosevelt preferred the repeal of the Neutrality Act, congressional leaders made it clear that this was impossible. They explained that while lifting of the arms embargo could be secured, cash and carry had to be substituted for it, loans to belligerents prohibited, and American merchant ships excluded from combat zones. Roosevelt accepted these proposals in order to achieve the removal of the embargo on arms shipments.

In his speech to Congress on September 21, 1939, the President carefully avoided mentioning the popular desire to aid the democracies and declared instead that repeal of the arms embargo would protect "the neutrality, the safety, and the integrity of our country, and at the same time keep us out of war." There is no reason to doubt the statement in Hull's *Memoirs* that he and the President believed that cash and carry offered "a better chance of keeping out of war than the old legislation because, if Britain and France won the war, we could remain at peace, whereas if Germany won, there was every likelihood that we would soon have to fight." [2]

Roosevelt, however, did not say this explicitly, for fear of providing the isolationists with additional ammunition. Overemphasis on the interdependency of the American and Allied causes might have precipitated a Senate filibuster and delayed repeal of the embargo. While Congress debated the President's proposal, pressure groups on both sides doubled their efforts to stir the public and sway votes.

On September 26, the Non-Partisan Committee for Peace Through the Revision of the Neutrality Law was formed to mobilize support for the Administration. This Committee was formed by the Union for Concerted Peace Efforts which had been organized in 1938. The Union was a committee of representatives from a number of collective security organizations which formed a central board of strategy. Among the organizations represented were the League of Nations Association, World Alliance for International Friendship Through the Churches, National Committee on the Cause and Cure of War, the League of Women Voters, and the American Association of University Women.

Hull suggested to leaders of this Committee that William Allen White, editor of the *Emporia Gazette*, would be ideal as national chairman. It was a logical choice in many ways. White came from strongly isolationist Kansas. He was widely respected by his fellow newspaper editors, well known to the reading public through his popular magazine articles and books, and had been important as a liberal Republican in the boom for Landon in 1936. Making White chairman proved to be a wise decision. His name attracted a nationwide following; and criticism of the Non-Partisan Committee as just another New York City organization was weakened by having a Kansan at its head.

Adopting traditional publicity techniques, the new Committee placed names of distinguished citizens on its letterhead, held rallies, sent letters and telegrams to Congressmen, and sponsored radio talks by such personalities as Al Smith, Monsignor John A. Ryan, and Mayor Fiorello La Guardia. White concentrated his efforts on trying to persuade Republican Congressmen to vote for the repeal of the arms embargo. "I would hate to have my party put itself in a posture where it can be charged that we played Mr. Hitler's game in the matter of the embargo," he told House Minority Leader Joe Martin. "If we fail to repeal the embargo and Hitler should win, we, as a party, will be vulnerable."

White supported the Administration's contention that involvement in the war was less likely under cash and carry. He did add, however, that next to America's desire to stay out of war was the desire for an Allied victory. He said in a radio speech:

> These European democracies are carrying our banner, fighting the American battle . . . We need not shed our blood for them now or ever. But we should not deny them now access to our shores when they come with cash to pay for weapons of defense and with their own ships to carry arms and materials which are to protect their citizens and their soldiers fighting our common cause.

Administration spokesmen in Congress, however, continued to gloss over the idea of aid to the democracies. Instead, they emphasized that cash and carry would help us stay out of war since such legislation would enable Britain and France to secure the arms and ammunition they needed to defeat Hitler. In November, the President's measure passed the Senate by 55 to 24 and the House by 243 to 172. Although the margin of victory was gratifying, the minority was still sizable and vocal. It was also partisan. Only six Republicans in the Senate and nineteen in the House voted for cash and carry.[3]

While the war remained quiet in the West during the next few months, the Soviet Union absorbed the Baltic nations and fought a winter war against Finland. In January, 1940, Roosevelt sent Sumner Welles to Europe to explore the chances for a negotiated peace. Welles concluded that only the conviction that America would come to the support of the Western democracies would give Hitler pause. But, Welles has added, it was clear at that time there was not "the remotest chance that our government could tell the Nazi government that this would prove to be the case. The great majority of the American people were altogether confident that they could keep out of the war." [4]

In April, 1940, Germany smashed into Denmark and Norway. Then on May 10, German divisions invaded the Low Countries and mounted a massive assault on the French. Five days later, German mechanized divisions sliced through the French line at Sedan. Within a week, they cut off French and British forces in Flanders. On May 28 King Leopold of Belgium surrendered.

During the next week, the British, pressing all types of boats into action, evacuated some three hundred thousand British and French forces from the beaches at Dunkirk. The *New York Times* said in an editorial on June 1, 1940: "So long as the English tongue survives, the word Dunkerque will be spoken with reverence. For, in that harbor, in such a hell as never blazed on earth before, at the end of a lost battle, the rags and blemishes that have hidden the soul of democracy fell away. There, beaten but unconquered, she faced the enemy."

On June 5, Germany launched an attack to crush France. Five days later Mussolini brought Italy into the war. And on June 22, with her defenses devastated, France signed an armistice with Germany.

The German penetration of the French lines, the near tragedy of Dunkirk, and the fall of France jolted the American people. During these hectic days, William Allen White and other leaders organized the Committee to Defend America by Aiding the Allies. White told the nation that it was necessary to arm Britain, since behind the British fleet "we could have two years in which to prepare for the inevitable attack of the totalitarian powers upon our democracy, which must come unless Great Britain wins this war."

Roosevelt worked closely with the Committee and it became one of the vehicles he used to apply public pressure on Congress. White wrote of his relationship with Roosevelt:

> I never did anything the President didn't ask for, and I always conferred with him on our program . . . He never failed us. We could go to him — any members of our executive committee, any member of our policy committee. He was frank, cordial, and wise in his counsel. We supported him in his foreign policy, many of us who voted against him in the election . . . He was broad-gauged, absolutely unpartisan, and a patriot in this matter if ever there was one.

Late in May, the White Committee urged the Administration to return military aircraft to the manufacturers who, in turn, would sell them to the Allies. Early in June, Roosevelt approved the release of planes to help the Allies counteract German air superiority.

On June 10, the President conferred with J. Pierrepont Moffat, who was to head the American legation in Canada. He urged Moffat to ask Canadian officials to seek assurances that the British fleet would not be surrendered. Moffat was also instructed to explain to the Canadians that, as a neutral, the United States could give almost as much help as it could as a belligerent. Whether we should become a belligerent, no one could tell, Roosevelt said. It was clear, he added, we would not unless Germany or Italy committed an overt act against us.

That evening, in a speech at the University of Virginia, the President declared: "Overwhelmingly we, as a nation — and this applies to all other American nations — are convinced that military and naval victory for the Gods of force and hate would endanger the institutions of democracy in the Western World, and that equally, therefore, the whole of our sympathies lies with those nations that are giving their life blood in combat against these forces." In the crisis, he explained, we would speed up rearmament and, at the same time, extend "the material resources of this nation" to the opponents of force.

With the collapse of France in the third week of June, Great Britain faced the Axis alone. William Allen White wrote: "The wave of sympathy for Great Britain that washed across this country found our Committee ready to energize its tide." On June 29 he conferred with the President. Roosevelt discussed the possibility of releasing destroyers to the hard-pressed British. For the next six weeks, the White Committee held rallies, ran advertisements in major newspapers, and put distinguished retired military figures on the radio to mobilize public support. And by the middle of August, 1940, a Gallup poll reported that 62 per cent of those interviewed favored the release of destroyers.

The President also asked White, who was close to Wendell Willkie, to confer with the Republican nominee about the exchange of the destroyers and try to persuade Willkie to influence Republican congressional leaders to favor it. While White was unable to bring the two men together to issue a public statement or even reach a private agreement, he was able to advise the President that his opponent favored the plan. But Willkie refused to try to influence Republican congressional leaders to support such legislation.

On July 11, a small group aroused by the dangers to the nation met at the Century Club Association in New York. To strengthen the defense of the hemisphere, it was proposed that destroyers be turned over to England in return for bases in British possessions in the Americas.[5] Three of the group — Clark Eichelberger, Herbert Agar, and Ward Cheney — afterwards discussed the proposal with the President. The following day at a Cabinet meeting there was general agreement with the idea.

Up to this point, the President and his advisers felt that legislation was needed to carry out the exchange. But without support from Republican leaders in Congress, Roosevelt feared such legislation might be defeated or delayed to the point where the transaction would have no value. Again the Century group proved to be fertile with ideas. On August 11, 1940, the *New York Times* published a letter signed by four leading lawyers — Charles C. Burlingham, Thomas D. Thacher, George Rublee, and Dean Acheson — analyzing the existing legislation and stating that the President by executive action could release the destroyers. Then a message reached the President from White about his further conversations with Willkie. White said he was confident that Willkie would not criticize the destroyer exchange in his speech accepting the Republican nomination and actually might say something favorable about it.

On August 13, Roosevelt decided to go ahead. The German air blitz against Britain was now on and the British position was desperate. The announcement that the arrangement had been completed was released on September 3. Willkie criticized the President for bypassing Congress with an executive agreement but stated publicly that he favored the aid. Although some isolationist newspapers accused Roosevelt of being a dictator, it was ironic that the isolationists had long advocated the acquisition of bases in the territory of European powers in the Western Hemisphere and one committee had been formed with the name Islands for War Debts Committee. By tying the British bases to the exchange of the destroyers, Roosevelt reduced much of the pressure of the isolationist attack. One isolationist Senator summed it up by saying: "Listen, you can't attack a deal like that . . . Roosevelt outsmarted all of us when he tied up the two deals."

After the destroyer transaction there was little left of American neutrality. The nation was now a non-belligerent ally. Public opinion rallied to the support of the destroyer exchange. It was clearly a national commitment, not only a presidential action. While the President may have delayed a few weeks in carrying out what Churchill had urged as a vital necessity as early as May, by delaying he avoided losing step with public sentiment.

At the same time that Roosevelt and the William Allen White Committee were mobilizing public opinion, a host of isolationist committees were attempting to turn the public against aid to the Allies. As in the case of the White Committee, the isolationists were highly diverse in their motivations and origins. The Socialists had the Keep America Out of War Congress. The Communist party — from the Soviet-German pact to the German invasion of the Soviet Union on June 22, 1941 — was a virulent exponent of isolationism, spreading the slogan "The Yanks Are Not Coming" across the nation and organizing the American Peace Mobilization. Fascist-oriented groups, including the German-American Bund, Father Coughlin's Christian Front, William Dudley Pelley's Silver Shirts, the American

Destiny party and others, although small and limited in appeal, added to the chorus. Three committees — the War Debts Defense Committee, the Make Europe Pay War Debts Committee, and the Islands for War Debts Committee — carried the names of Senators Lundeen of Minnesota, Robert A. Reynolds of North Carolina, and Representative Martin L. Sweeney of Ohio as officers. After the nation entered the war, it was revealed that the guiding hand behind these committees was George Sylvester Viereck, a Nazi agent.

The leadership in the struggle against intervention came, however, from none of these committees. The most influential isolationist organization ("non-interventionist," as its members preferred to be described) was the America First Committee. Chicagoan R. Douglas Stuart, Jr., son of the first Vice-President of Quaker Oats Company, founded this committee. With the aid of General Robert E. Wood, Chairman of the board of Sears, Roebuck and Company, Stuart obtained the support of a number of leading Midwest industrialists.

Although America First also received support from such former New Dealers as General Hugh Johnson and such progressives as Philip La Follette and Burton K. Wheeler, the leadership of the isolationist cause was now in the hands of economic conservatives, who feared that if the country went to war, Roosevelt would extend New Deal reforms. There were, of course, a great many economic conservatives in the Committee to Defend America by Aiding the Allies. While politically they were conservative, on world problems they had long been internationalist in outlook. Most of them were Easterners while the America First Committee was run mainly by Midwesterners.

The America First Committee challenged Roosevelt's contention that a British victory was essential to American security or that Britain was America's first line of defense. It urged, instead, an impregnable defense for America and fought aid short of war as weakening defense at home while it threatened "to involve America in war abroad." After the Lend-Lease Act was passed over its vocal opposition in March, 1941, the Committee tried to focus debate on the question of peace or war. Spokesmen charged that the Administration and the Aid the Allies Committee were trying to prepare the public for a declaration of war.

Wayne S. Cole has observed in his careful study, *America First: The Battle Against Intervention 1940-41*, that the Committee by defining the issue as war or peace was attempting to conduct the debate "on a much simpler basis than the views of most Americans actually justified." [6] Roosevelt saw to it that the foreign policy debate did not concentrate on the issue of war or peace but rather on the question of aid to Britain as essential to American security. He allowed America First no issue on which it could defeat him. His sensitivity to isolationist strength was such that he sought congressional authorization only for those measures for which he could achieve majority support. When he ordered naval patrols in the Atlantic in the spring of 1941, he did it by executive action. He told Secretary of War Stimson, who was urging more candor, that it was too dangerous to ask Congress for such authorization. That he was not overestimating the continuing strength of his opponents was revealed when the Selective Service Act was extended by the House in the summer of 1941 by a margin of just one vote, and the Neutrality Act was repealed less than a month before the attack on Pearl Harbor by a vote of only 50 to 37 in the Senate and 212 to 194 in the House.

During the 1940 presidential campaign, it was the nation's good fortune that both candidates agreed on the issue of foreign policy. Wendell Willkie was no solace to the isolationist forces. He believed in aid to the Allies and bluntly said so. Although as head of the Commonwealth and Southern Utilities Corporation he had fought the Tennessee Valley Authority, he was no economic Tory. He was a Wilson Democrat who had voted for Roosevelt in 1932. He endorsed major New Deal reforms but stated that the Republicans could administer them more efficiently. He was a dramatic, colorful figure as he toured the nation in his disheveled suits, necktie askew, hair falling down over his forehead, with his voice getting hoarser and hoarser as he attacked the "third term candidate." Although his campaign was not well organized, he gave the Republicans the type of dramatic leadership the party had lacked since the days of Theodore Roosevelt.

The President's sense of timing was never better than in 1940. While Willkie roared across the country, Roosevelt ignored him.

Roosevelt's strategy was sound. The public was much more concerned with the Battle of Britain than with the campaign. Day after day in late August, German armies of almost a thousand planes a day roared over the green fields of England and day after day the outnumbered Royal Air Force pilots fought, landed to refuel and reload, and fought again until exhausted.

September 7, the blitz of London started. That night two hundred and fifty Nazi bombers hit the city. For the next week London reeled under the assault, fires raged unchecked, streets were filled with debris, and uncounted bodies lay in the ruins. But the British people were unbowed and the RAF fought on.

The blitz shocked the world and mobilized more and more sentiment in the United States for support of Britain. On October 12, Roosevelt turned a routine Columbus Day speech into a vigorous aid to the Allies speech. He never alluded to the political campaign at home but expressed the public's sentiment for support of those fighting Hitler: "We have learned the lessons of recent years. We know now that if we seek to appease aggressors by withholding aid from those who stand in their way, we only hasten the day of their attack upon us."

Late in the campaign, Republican politicians persuaded Willkie to attack Roosevelt as a warmonger. Under their prodding, Willkie charged that the nation would be involved in a foreign war within five months if Roosevelt were re-elected and there would be a totalitarian government with a third term.[7] In the last ten days of the campaign, Roosevelt took the offensive. He praised New Deal reforms and sarcastically said of Republican appeals to the workingman: "The tears, the crocodile tears, for the laboring man and laboring woman now being shed in this campaign come from those same Republican leaders who had their chance to prove their love for labor in 1932 — and missed it."

At Madison Square Garden on October 28, he rallied his battalions with a shrewd attack on Republican isolationists. To charges that he had not adequately prepared the defenses of America, he quoted statements by leading Republican Congressmen before 1940 that the government was spending too much for defense. In citing the voting records of Congressmen Joseph Martin, Bruce Barton and Hamilton Fish, the three names fell into a euphonious pattern. The crowd roared as Roosevelt spoke the rhythmic sequence of Martin, Barton, and Fish.

In the last week of the campaign, insistent advice came from the Democratic National Committee and leaders around the country that the election would be lost unless Roosevelt gave solemn promises to mothers that the country would not go to war. Bowing to the pressure, Roosevelt said in Boston on October 30:

> And while I am talking to you mothers and fathers, I give you one more assurance. I have said this before, but I shall say it again and again and again: Your boys are not going to be sent into any foreign war.

Roosevelt's adviser, Judge Rosenman, has stated that always before and every time after this speech Roosevelt added the words that he had inserted in the party platform: "except in case of attack." When Rosenman suggested the addition of these words in the Boston speech, Roosevelt, sick and tired of the whole business, said: "It's not necessary. It's implied clearly. If we're attacked it's no longer a foreign war." [8]

The urgency of the war crisis and the return of prosperity were important factors in Roosevelt's re-election.[9] In spite of the emotion engendered by the third term issue, the strident attacks of the isolationists against his "warmongering," and lack of support from such former aides as James A. Farley, he held together most of the divergent elements in his coalition. And while he lost votes among Americans of German ancestry, he won the votes of some Republican interventionists who doubted that Willkie as President could lead his party away from isolationism. There is little doubt that the voting record of his party in Congress limited Willkie's appeal to the nationwide electorate.

16. Avoiding the Irrevocable Act

A month after Roosevelt's third-term victory, Winston Churchill warned him that German submarines were sinking an appalling number of Allied ships. Britain could mount an offensive only if

American naval forces kept the North Atlantic sea lanes open, he advised, and only if Britain had enough bombers and other equipment. And the time was approaching, Churchill added, when Britain could no longer pay for supplies.

Roosevelt at once began to prepare public opinion for the next step in his policy of aiding Britain. He opened his press conference on December 17 with a powerful statement of the vital role that Britain was playing in the defense of the United States. To solve the problem of Britain's lack of funds, Roosevelt suggested that America could either "lease or sell" supplies to Britain. Then, with his ability to explain issues in simple, dramatic terms, he told his parable of the garden hose. If a neighbor's house was on fire, you did not say to him: "Neighbor, my garden hose cost me $15; you have to pay me $15 for it." Instead you lent him the hose to help put out the fire and got the hose back afterwards. What he was proposing, Roosevelt added, was to substitute for the dollar sign a "gentleman's obligation to repay in kind."

Twelve days later, in a fireside chat, the President declared that the British fleet stood between America and Axis aggression:

> I make the direct statement to the American people that there is far less chance of the United States getting into war, if we do all we can now to support the nations defending themselves against attack by the Axis than if we acquiesce in their defeat, submit tamely to an Axis victory, and wait our turn to be the object of attack in another war later on.

Then, the President frankly faced up to the truth of what he and Willkie had avoided during the campaign:

> If we are to be completely honest with ourselves, we must admit that there is risk in any course we may take. But I deeply believe that the great majority of our people agree that the course I advocate involves the least risk now and the greatest hopes for world peace in the future.

Business-as-usual must go, he added. "We must be the great arsenal of democracy. For this is an emergency as serious as war itself." The newspaper reaction to the speech was overwhelmingly favorable and the mail reaching the White House was the greatest response to any speech Roosevelt had delivered.

The next week Roosevelt asked Congress to enact the Lend-Lease

Bill. He thus submitted to legislative debate the great question: Would the public support him even at the risk of war? The *Chicago Tribune* angrily attacked the bill as a measure that would take America into war and "destroy the Republic." The America First Committee mounted its greatest assault on his foreign policy and Senator Burton K. Wheeler charged that the bill was a "triple-A foreign policy: it will plough under every fourth American boy." This provoked Roosevelt into his only reply to his critics. He assailed the statement as "the rottenest thing that has been said in public life in my generation."

For weeks the merit of lend-lease was debated before Congress, in the press, on the radio, and from public platforms. Wendell Willkie, who had just returned from a visit to England, testified most effectively for it. On February 8, the House passed the bill by 260 to 165. Although some advised the President to press the Senate for an early vote, he wisely refrained. As a result, the lengthy Senate debate greatly enhanced public understanding. After the Senate passed it on March 8, by a margin of 60 to 31, House Minority Leader Martin and Senator Vandenberg pledged their cooperation, as did other Republicans. Wheeler and Nye led only a few die-hards in promising to continue their opposition.

Now that lend-lease committed the economic resources of the nation to aid in the defeat of the Axis, action was necessary in the Battle of the Atlantic. On March 25, Germany extended the North Atlantic war zone to the coast of Greenland. Nazi "wolf pack" submarines and airplanes were thrown into the struggle to prevent American supplies from reaching Britain. The outcome of the Battle of the Atlantic, Churchill warned, might determine the entire course of the war.

While Secretary of War Stimson, the Aid to the Allies Committee, and many leading citizens urged American naval convoys of ships to British ports, the President decided against this step. Instead, American shipyards were ordered to repair British ships, ten Coast Guard cutters were transferred to the British, and on April 10 the President decided to extend the area patrolled by the American Navy to the longitude along the east coast of Greenland. Naval ships would search out, but not attack, Nazi submarines up to this line and warn the British of their presence. And the President announced that Greenland was being placed under the temporary protection of the United States and that the Danish Minister in Washington had agreed to the establishment of American bases there. That same day, the President removed the ban against American shipping to the Red Sea to supply British forces in that area.

On May 27, in a fireside chat, Roosevelt proclaimed an unlimited state of national emergency. He pointed out that the Germans were sinking merchant shipping more rapidly than it could be replaced. As a result, he added, our naval patrols had been extended in the Atlantic: "Our patrols are helping now to insure delivery of the needed supplies to Britain. All additional measures necessary to deliver the goods will be taken . . . I will say that the delivery of needed supplies to Britain is imperative. I say this can be done; it must be done; it will be done."

On June 5, Roosevelt, to bolster British morale and assist further in the Battle of the Atlantic, ordered American forces to replace the British in Iceland. Although this action was not completed until July, it freed British troops for other theaters and extended American naval escort of convoys further to the east. Then, on June 22, 1941, the war took a new turn when Hitler invaded the Soviet Union. Although isolationist spokesmen opposed aid to the Soviet Union and wanted Hitler and Stalin to fight it out, the Administration on August 2 announced it would extend assistance "in the interest of the national defense of the United States."

On August 9, Roosevelt met with Churchill aboard a ship off Argentia, Newfoundland. Although the British attempted to secure a commitment promising American participation if the Japanese attacked British Far Eastern possessions, Roosevelt refused. He agreed, however, that British and Allied merchant ships could join American convoys to Iceland. He hoped still that by insuring that American supplies reached their destination we could avoid war. Before he had made a public announcement of this new policy, the destroyer U.S.S. *Greer*, en route to Iceland, was fired upon by a German submarine.

The President made this incident the subject of a fireside chat on September 11. He denounced the attack as piracy and as a deliberate attempt to sink the *Greer*. Henceforth, American naval and air patrols would protect all merchant shipping "engaged in commerce in our defensive waters," he announced. Our ships will not wait, he added, until the enemy has fired first: "From now on, if German or Italian vessels of war enter the waters, the protection of which is necessary for American defense, they do so at their own peril."

Roosevelt was misleading in his speech when he charged there was a deliberate attempt to sink the *Greer* without mentioning that the destroyer had been following the submarine for several hours and radioing its position to the British. But by the time of the incident, he was not acting without support from Congress and the public. Although the public still wanted to avoid sending troops overseas, they were in support of such steps as extending naval patrols, which meant that the line between short of war and actual war had lost its significance.

By now, the Neutrality Act was outmoded. On October 9, the President asked Congress to repeal the provisions prohibiting the arming of American merchant ships and forbidding American ships from sailing through combat zones and entering belligerent ports. The Senate accepted the President's recommendation on November 7. There was difficulty in the House, however.[1] At the request of Speaker Sam Rayburn and Majority Leader John McCormack, the President sent a letter on November 13 stating that failure to allow American ships to sail to belligerent ports would be disastrous. With the aid of this letter, they secured repeal that day by a vote of 212 to 194.

Although it was a close call, the nation had now come full cycle since the Neutrality Act of six years before. It stood ready to aid one side; it no longer placed restrictions on its shipping; and it backed up that claim by fire. Nevertheless, it is doubtful that the President could have led the nation any further. The impasse reached by December, 1941, might have continued indefinitely had the Axis so willed it.

In spite of the belief held by Secretary of War Stimson and others that it was in the nation's interest to declare war on the Axis, the strength of the isolationists could not be ignored by the President. He had to accept the fact that a powerful minority believed that an Axis-dominated Europe and Asia would not be a threat to American security. Roosevelt clearly felt that his policy had to stay within certain bounds set by this opinion. ". . . whatever the peril," Robert

E. Sherwood has written, "he was not going to lead the country into war — he was going to wait to be pushed in." [2]

Japanese leaders seized upon the war in Europe as a golden opportunity to carry out their dreams of expansion. When France fell, they forced the French to grant military bases in Northern Indo-China as a step in their conquest of British and Dutch possessions in the Far East. The Roosevelt Administration responded to this action on July 26, 1940, by placing an embargo on aviation gasoline, lubricants, and scrap iron to Japan and two months later by extending a new loan to China. On September 27, Hitler and Mussolini signed the Tripartite Agreement recognizing Japan's "New Order" in Greater East Asia and the three nations agreed to cooperate militarily, politically, and economically "if one of the three Contracting Powers is attacked by a power at present not involved in the European War or in the Chinese-Japanese conflict."

Throughout 1940-1941, we strove to avoid a clash in the Far East. Roosevelt explained in August, 1941, that he was trying to "baby the Japanese along." It was necessary, however, to take deterrent action which involved risks. Ambassador Joseph C. Grew insisted from the American Embassy in Tokyo that merely registering disapproval of Japanese actions was insufficient; words would not deter them. It was his hope, rather, he explained to Washington, that firm steps by America might lead the Japanese "to believe their hand is being overplayed."

The German invasion of the Soviet Union in June, 1941, freed Japan of concern over the Russians, and she moved into Southern Indo-China in July. The President impounded all Japanese assets in the United States, closed the Panama Canal to Japanese shipping, called the Philippine militia into service, and forbade the export to Japan of oil that could be made into aviation gasoline.

By the late summer and autumn of 1941, Ambassador Grew believed that Japan was faced with the necessity for either an "all out, do-or-die attempt on the part of her armed forces" or a settlement through negotiations. On August 18, it was suggested to Grew that Prince Konoye, the Prime Minister, wanted to meet with the President. Roosevelt at first was receptive to the idea. The situation in Japan was fluid, Grew explained, and through a meeting with

Konoye we might avert war. A successful meeting would be so dramatic, Grew believed, that it might be possible for Konoye to curb the militarists. Grew added that "there is little doubt that Prince Konoye would first of all request the cooperation of the United States in terminating the China Affair" and would probably be ready to agree to the eventual removal of Japanese forces from Indo-China.

On September 6, Konoye dined with Grew in great secrecy and affirmed his desire that a meeting be arranged. "It was unquestionably the strong measures taken by the United States, culminating in the freezing order of July 26, 1941, that had led him to see the handwriting on the wall and to realize that the best interests of his country then lay in conciliation with America," Grew has written.

Grew warned Washington that Konoye felt he could not commit himself on issues in advance since he feared that the military leaders would learn of this and prevent the meeting. But back in Washington, Secretary Hull and Stanley Hornbeck, Chief of the Division of Far Eastern Affairs, insisted that Konoye reach agreement on Japanese withdrawal from China as well as on a number of other issues before any meeting could be held. This delayed the proposed conference.[3]

Then, on October 16, Konoye was replaced as Prime Minister by General Tojo. Although negotiations still continued in Washington, on November 5 military leaders won the Emperor's consent to an attack if negotiations were not successful by the 25th. Three days before this date, the United States intercepted a message from Tokyo to their representatives in Washington extending negotiations until November 29 but warning that after that "things are automatically going to happen." On November 26 Hull sent a lengthy memorandum to the Japanese government setting forth the position of the two nations on disputed points. It was not an ultimatum, but simply a restatement of the conflicting positions. Grew, in Tokyo, welcomed it as a basis for further discussion.[4]

The following day the President approved the transmission to American commanders in the Philippines, Hawaii, and elsewhere of a "final alert" informing them of the diplomatic situation and telling them to be on guard against attack: "This dispatch is to be con-

sidered a war warning." The day before this warning was trans-
mitted, a Japanese task force left its base in the Kuriles and headed
for Hawaii.

On December 3, through cracking the Japanese code, the Administration learned that the Japanese Embassy in Washington was receiving orders to destroy most of its codes. This information was
radioed to the American commanders in the Pacific. On December
6, a reply from the Japanese government to Hull's note of November 26 began to arrive in Washington. When Roosevelt read the
first part he told Harry Hopkins: "This means war." The next morning soon after breakfast, the final part of the note was deciphered.
The Japanese were saying that all talk was at an end. Their intent
now seemed clear, but would they make a declaration before they
attacked? And where would they strike?

Washington did not expect an attack at Hawaii since defenses
had been strengthened there and it had been alerted. It seemed
logical to expect a Japanese move against Singapore and the Dutch
East Indies, avoiding an attack on the Philippines, Guam, or Hawaii. The Administration knew in the first days of December that
Japanese convoys were steaming southward, but it had not decided
on a course of action if the attack came upon non-American territory. Would the American people approve a declaration of war if
this occurred?

On December 6, the President decided to send a message to the
Emperor urging him to dispel the threat of war. Anticipating no reply, Roosevelt planned to address Congress on December 8 warning
Japan against further belligerent action. On the assumption that the
attack would come against Siam or Malaya, the speech was intended to convince Congress and the public that such an attack
would be a threat to American security and would require military
action by the United States.

While Washington officials were conferring Sunday morning over
the last section of the Japanese note, Japanese planes had already
taken off from their carriers for the attack on Pearl Harbor. At
11:50 A.M. in Washington (6:20 A.M. in Honolulu), General
George C. Marshall handed a message to his communications officer
warning Navy and Army commanders in the Pacific that at 1:00
P.M. the Japanese were presenting what amounted to an ultimatum:

"Just what significance the hour set may have we do not know, but be on the alert accordingly." Radio contact with Hawaii was temporarily suspended and the message was given to Western Union. It reached Hawaii at 7:33 A.M. While the messenger was en route to the headquarters of the commanding general, the first wave of Japanese bombs struck Pearl Harbor.

The American commanders were taken completely by surprise. Even a warning from a radar operator that planes were approaching Oahu had been ignored. Both in Washington and in Hawaii an attack on American territory was regarded as senseless.[5]

For this miscalculation the nation paid dearly. But for the Japanese, in the long run, it was even more costly. Their attack unified American public opinion to a degree that presidential leadership alone could never have achieved. And, in the next four years, Japan's dominance in Asia was destroyed.

At the close of the war, a new "devil theory of history" gained currency contending that Roosevelt had maneuvered the nation into war. Since Hitler was too wary to provide the President with a sufficiently provocative act, Roosevelt, it was said, deliberately based the Pacific Fleet at Pearl Harbor in an exposed position in order to provoke a Japanese attack. Some added that the Administration had evidence that Pearl Harbor was to be attacked and allowed it to happen.

This theory overlooked many relevant facts. On September 6, 1941, the Japanese High Military Command Conference with the Emperor decided that if diplomatic negotiations did not succeed in gaining Japanese demands, "We will immediately make up our minds to get ready for war against America." The plan for attack on Pearl Harbor was adopted in October and the plan for its execution was issued on November 5. The American fleet at Pearl Harbor was an obstacle, not a lure, to Japanese expansion, as Herbert Feis has pointed out.[6]

The actions taken in 1940-1941 in the Pacific and in Europe stemmed from the desire to sustain resistance to the Axis, not from a desire to get into war. The central problem for the Administration was to support the Allies as far as Congress and public opinion would permit and by diplomacy try to keep Japan from moving southward.

Roosevelt moved carefully with a public opinion shocked out of isolationism by the impact of war. He secured public backing before he released planes and destroyers in 1940, advocated lend-lease, and extended naval patrols in 1941. If such a policy had not been adopted, resistance to the Axis might have collapsed in 1940 or in 1941 and the national security been placed in the greatest jeopardy.

The choice prior to Pearl Harbor was not really peace or war: it was to support resistance to the Axis at the risk of war or face a Europe and Asia under hostile domination. No evidence has ever been produced by Roosevelt's critics that indicates he decided aid short of war was not sufficient. But he did know he could not move without an overt act. When the Japanese supplied this, Roosevelt rallied the American people for the task ahead with the same supreme, confident tone he had used in the domestic crisis of 1933.

Roosevelt did not lose control of his leadership of the nation by too hasty steps. As a result, he was in a favorable position after Pearl Harbor to emerge as a supreme architect of victory. Unlike Woodrow Wilson from 1914 to 1917, who failed to explain the interrelationship between our own security and that of the Allies, Roosevelt was continually educating the public mind. In spite of the fact he did not always advance as fast or as far as some advocates of collective security wished, his course prepared the nation better to fight the war and, afterwards, to accept world leadership. From 1934 to 1941, the country went through a difficult adjustment to the responsibilities of a great power in world affairs. Its weakness in not adjusting more rapidly may, in the long run, have proved to be a strength. The issues were raised and the significance of each step vigorously debated in the newspapers, over the radio, and from the platform. And the public came to realize that the old policy of isolation no longer was a safeguard of the national interest.

BOOK FOUR

Commander-in-Chief: Roosevelt

17. Production and More Production

The outbreak of war in Europe accomplished what Roosevelt's New Deal had failed to do. It removed the brakes from the American economy. Production soared. Between July 1, 1940, and December 31, 1941, we produced 23,223 airplanes, 1330 naval ships displacing 269,000 tons, 136 cargo ships displacing 1,551,000 tons, 4203 tanks and 120.4 million tons of steel.

Defense industries alone added three million workers between the fall of 1940 and the fall of 1941. By that date, unemployment had dropped to 3,600,000. Despite loud criticisms of the defense effort, the achievements of the eighteen months before Pearl Harbor were impressive. By December 7, 1941, war production was well under way, although it was not near the pace it would achieve later on in the war. When the bombs fell, the nation was still far from ready, but it was more ready than at any other time in our history.

Between September, 1939, and December, 1941, there was considerable fear in official, business, and labor circles that the nation would overproduce and a great crash would occur at the close of the war. The collapse that came after the first war was much in people's minds. The depression-born distrust of businessmen and financiers, increased by New Deal attacks, too, was prevalent. It was intensified by the wide acceptance of the nonsense, stimulated by the Nye Committee, that America had entered the first war because of the nefarious activities of munitions makers and international bankers. These attacks made some manufacturers wary, at first, of accepting defense contracts. And the boom in civilian business led many firms to prefer to do business as usual, with the result that they were slow to convert to defense work. Generally, businessmen felt the defense economy could simply be superimposed on the civilian economy.

The President had to integrate all elements into the defense effort. He had no specific authority to compel business firms to accept defense orders. He had the powers of persuasion and government contracts. Realizing that business might be induced to join the defense effort if its principal leaders were given a prominent place in the program, he appointed numerous "dollar-a-year men." In addition, he prevented Thurman Arnold and his trust-busters in the Attorney General's Office from prosecuting antitrust cases.[1]

In May, 1940, Roosevelt pledged in a fireside chat that there would be no cancellation of New Deal social gains. But he explained that the cooperation of the leaders of industry was vital to the defense effort. That month he appointed as the key figures on the National Defense Advisory Commission: William Knudsen, Danish-born President of General Motors; Sidney Hillman, Lithuanian-born President of the Amalgamated Clothing Worker's Union; and Edward R. Stettinius, Jr., Chairman of the Board of United States Steel. Leon Henderson, Chester Davis, Ralph Budd, and Harriet Elliott were other important members; and Donald Nelson of Sears, Roebuck was made coordinator of National Defense Purchases.

Roosevelt appointed men of competing interests — businessmen, labor leaders, and New Deal administrators — to spur defense production. Although no single group was satisfied with its degree of power, the production effort gained momentum. Most labor leaders were far from joyful over the way the defense program was run. Big business, they charged, was in the driver's seat. Nevertheless, organized labor in general supported the President's policies. A conspicuous exception was John L. Lewis who had broken with Roosevelt and resigned as head of the CIO after Wendell Willkie's defeat. The Communists, who had infiltrated segments of the labor movement, fought the production effort, too, until the Soviet Union was invaded on June 22, 1941.

Business leaders continued to have doubts about the Roosevelt Administration. A *Fortune* survey of executive opinion revealed that 75 per cent of those interviewed felt that the President was using the emergency as a pretext for pushing "still farther the more radical social and economic aims of the New Deal." [2] And businessmen in the government faced open hostility from many New Deal administrators who feared that these men would try to kill the social programs they had been unable to destroy from the outside. When the President appointed James Forrestal, of Dillon Read and Company, as a presidential assistant, the New Dealish *New Republic* was unhappy. "Just who is to run the rearmament program," the magazine asked. ". . . on its face Mr. Forrestal's appointment is the most marked step so far taken toward freezing the New Dealers out. But just how chummy can the New Deal be with Wall Street and still continue to be the New Deal?" [3]

After seven years of running the government, a number of New Deal administrators were allergic to new ideas. They showed little disposition to meet the demands imposed by the international situation. As a result, new agencies had to be created to assume the new responsibilities. When Sidney Hillman and William Knudsen, for instance, agreed that the normal mediation machinery of the Department of Labor was not adequate to prevent strikes, Hillman tried to persuade the Secretary of Labor to make changes, but Miss Perkins adamantly resisted. Finally, Hillman went to the President and secured authorization for the National Mediation Board, the forerunner of the War Labor Board.

Reconciling the competing demands of business, labor, the Army, and the Navy proved too difficult for the National Defense Advisory Commission. In January, 1941, Roosevelt replaced it with the Office of Production Management. Knudsen was made Director General, Hillman Associate Director General. These two men and the Secretary of the Army and the Secretary of the Navy formed the OPM board. Knudsen was a great industrial production engineer, but weak on broad public policy and as a public administrator. Nevertheless, he helped overcome business resistance to working with the Administration. While Knudsen and Hillman disagreed over the expansion of production, they kept their disagreement to OPM meetings. A number of trade union leaders attacked Hillman within the ranks of labor for not opposing Knudsen before Congress. Hillman refused, knowing that a public dispute would only prejudice the defense effort.

Hillman succeeded in bringing the competing labor factions together behind the defense program and united labor in support of the special rules under which it had to operate in war time. Leaders of the A. F. of L., the CIO, and the Railroad Brotherhoods sat together in his regular meetings for the first time since the CIO had been organized. While the unions tried to increase their newly won gains, Hillman worked instead to consolidate them and, realizing the larger issues involved, helped place limits on further gains. Naturally, some labor leaders resented this. At the same time, management felt that labor was trying to exploit the defense effort. The overriding loyalty of both Hillman and Knudsen to the national program and to the President lost them the support of their own special groups, and eventually both became expendable.

"The Battle of Washington" during 1940-1941 revolved around the dispute over the magnitude of production. The "all outers," consisting mainly of New Dealers led by Leon Henderson, with allies like Donald Nelson, contended that the nation could not avoid all-out involvement in the war and must, therefore, go all out for production. Before joining the defense effort, Henderson had participated in the activities of the Temporary National Economic Committee, investigating monopoly in industry. "He was naturally suspicious when he saw the men whose financial manipulations he had been studying suddenly appear in positions of great government trust," Herbert Emmerich, Secretary of OPM, has written. "Hillman was also leery of these men, but not nearly as suspicious as Leon. He was actually less doctrinaire than the New Deal economists and had the inner confidence to appraise the business leaders individually on their merits." [4]

Meanwhile the "go slowers" on production argued that involvement in the war could be avoided and, hence, it was not necessary to go all out for defense. They were mainly industrialists who feared that an overexpansion of productive capacity would leave them in a precarious position at the end of the emergency. To encourage industrialists to expand and to allay their fears that they would be left later with unused productive facilities, Congress suspended an 8 per cent limitation on profits from military and naval aircraft contracts. Congress also allowed the cost of new plants to be amortized for tax purposes over a five-year period. In addition, the Defense Plant Corporation of the Reconstruction Finance Corporation paid for new plants and leased these to industry with an option to buy after five years. To soften the protests of liberals, an excess profits tax was coupled with the tax amortization.

The "all outers" on production gained the upper hand by autumn, 1941. Leon Henderson, head of the Office of Price Administration and Civilian Supply, charged: "There has been far too much concern within industry over the dangers of expansion, too much willingness to accept shortages of raw materials, of plant capacity, of power, of freight cars." Roosevelt created a new agency, the Supply Priorities Allocation Board, dominated by "all outers." It was placed over the OPM in August with Vice-President Henry A. Wallace as Chairman and Donald Nelson as Executive Director. They soon succeeded in curtailing by 50 per cent civilian production in the automobile industry to free facilities for defense production.

Although the scars of the depression decade were far from healed as America stood on the threshold of war, the President furnished the leadership to rally public support for rearming the nation and aiding the Allies. He cast himself, as in 1933-1934, in the role of a broker among the competing groups. And as chief of state, despite inevitable friction, Roosevelt formed a concert of interests to defend American security.

Between 1939 and December 7, 1941, the nation underwent a profound transformation. The torpor which had possessed it for so long was now gone. "Paul Bunyan Is Back!" Louis C. Jones wrote:

> No bully ever pushed this boy about
> And no mad loon's agoin' to do it now
> He's in the factory towns and in the mines,
> He stalks along the regimental streets at night
> He spits upon his hands and adds his weight to ours.[5]

Once the nation was convinced that its survival required the production of more planes, guns, and ships than anyone had ever dreamed of before, it flexed its muscles, rolled up its sleeves, and went to work. While in the back of everybody's mind lurked the fear of postwar collapse, Americans turned to the immediate challenge posed by Hitler and Hirohito.

Although much was made of blundering and confusion in war-time Washington, the production achieved was remarkable. Roosevelt told Congress on January 6, 1942:

> Our task is hard — our task is unprecedented — and the time is short. We must strain every existing armament-producing facility to the utmost. We must convert every available plant and tool to war production. That goes all the way from the greatest plants to the smallest — from the huge automobile industry to the village machine shop.

The automobile industry, which had been slow to convert to war production, produced its last civilian car five days before Singapore fell to the Japanese. Now its assembly lines turned to producing fighter and bomber planes. But since conversion of existing facilities was not sufficient, the Defense Plant Corporation constructed machine tool factories, steel mills, aluminum plants, aircraft factories, plants to make high-octane gasoline for aircraft, and synthetic rubber plants. "Their output has changed the face of the nation," Henry F. Pringle wrote in the *Saturday Evening Post* (December 18, 1943), "for steel is being manufactured on Western deserts, magnesium on the Texas Gulf coast, and artificial rubber in Louisiana. Their postwar potentialities can alter radically the economics of the entire world."

War production reached its peak in November, 1943, when some six billion dollars' worth of munitions were manufactured. Up to this time, the critical shortage had been raw materials. But for the last eighteen months of the war, it became manpower, after the slack of unemployment had been absorbed and the armed forces continued to expand. Despite shortages, the nation produced 276,000 airplanes including more than 90,000 bombers, 71,000 naval ships including 65,000 landing vessels, 4800 merchant ships with a dead-weight tonnage of 50 million, and 80,000 tanks. "Without American production the United Nations could never have won the war," Stalin remarked. And General Dwight D. Eisenhower said: "America's record in production, as well as on the battle line, is one that will fill our histories forever."

Roosevelt time and again reorganized wartime Washington and was widely criticized for it. But it was not disastrous. The important question to him was not administrative planning but the participation of the entire nation in the war effort. Eliot Janeway has suggested that the President did not believe that his appointees had to organize the war effort particularly well since "the participation of the people would push it forward faster than any leader could lead it, and the spontaneous dramatics of democracy would organize it." [6]

In his press conferences, fireside chats, visits to factories and inspections of military installations, Roosevelt exhibited the same dramatic appeal, the same buoyant confidence that had rallied the public during the Hundred Days. He traveled overseas to Casablanca, Cairo, Tehran, and Yalta and paid surprise visits to the fighting forces. The common peril that faced the private and the President gave, as Gerald Johnson has observed, "a wonderful sense of solidity to the American." One of the popular stories of the war told of a flyer who shouted to his companions in a billet in Casablanca: "Don't drink any more of that whisky! Don't touch it! I took only one drink and looked out the window and saw Roosevelt in a jeep!"

Roosevelt's critics asserted that all he had to do as Commander-in-Chief was to let a production czar and the military leaders run the war effort. Roosevelt knew, however, that it was his responsibility to operate above the level of both military and civilian agencies and to balance the powers of each. In the depression years, he had tried to achieve a balance among business, agriculture, and labor; now it was his role to balance the civilian against the enormously expanding power of the military.

The creaking and groaning of the huge war effort, and the inevitable frictions produced by it, made the "Battle of Washington" seem to some newspaper readers almost as significant as the production battle itself. Mark Sullivan remarked in his column on March 25, 1942: "The atmosphere of Washington this week is not that of a foreign war. It is of domestic battle, the battle of the New Deal to keep and increase its power, of New Dealers to hold on to their offices."

While New Dealers had their battles with business-minded officials and with conservative Congressmen, industry struggled against industry for war orders, priorities, and allocations. And farm groups struggled against price controls; labor unions fought to block new regulations; individuals fought for power and prestige; and civilian spokesmen battled the Army and Navy for butter as well as for guns.

When the nation entered the war, Congress, dissatisfied with the defense organization, was on the verge of creating a new agency. On January 15, 1942, the Senate Special Committee Investigating the National Defense Program — the Truman Committee — described in its first annual report the "disappointing record" of the Office of Production Management and criticized the "ineptness" of its officials. Two days before the report was issued, the President replaced the OPM and the Supply Priorities and Allocation Board with the War Production Board. The WPB was given sweeping powers over the entire war economy. Roosevelt told Donald Nelson, appointed as the single head of the Board, that he was to "have complete and absolute control over the production of all implements of war and over all related activities." The WPB represented the establishment of complete civilian control over the home front, but Nelson failed to use all the power given him. As a result, the military moved into the vacuum he left. In addition, he failed to eliminate the administrative confusion responsible for shortages or to allocate priorities wisely.

Disturbed over production tangles, Roosevelt in October, 1942, called James F. Byrnes from the Supreme Court and installed him in the White House as Director of Economic Stabilization. In May, 1943, the President created the Office of War Mobilization with Byrnes as Director and "Assistant President" with command over all aspects of the economy. With this step, the domestic front was at last well directed and this skilled politician established a clear civilian dominance over the military on the home front.[7]

The struggle to control inflation was another controversial aspect of the "Battle of Washington." In July, 1941, the President asked Congress for authorization to control prices and rents, since there had been a 6 per cent rise in the cost of living in urban centers during the first six months of 1941 and farm prices had risen 35 per cent over 1939 levels. Congress failed to act, however, until January, 1942. Then the farm bloc, with its well-organized following in Congress, succeeded in prohibiting price ceilings on agricultural goods at less than 110 per cent of the parity price.

This loophole in the first price control act soon threatened the entire stabilization program. After food prices had risen 8 per cent between April and September, 1942, the President persuaded a reluctant Congress to pass a new act authorizing him to stabilize prices, wages, and salaries at the levels prevailing on September 15. Ceilings on farm goods could be set at parity or at the highest price they had reached between January 1 and September 15.

The Office of Price Administration in 1942 and after was the natural target for everyone. It reached into every transaction from the buying of a necktie to the buying of a house. Each pressure group vented its rage on OPA, and to the anti-New Dealers, the agency seemed to be the embodiment of "regimentation, boondoggling, and socialism." Its director, Leon Henderson, invited attack. A tough-minded economist, he loved to take on fights often even when they were unnecessary. When any group was rebuffed by the OPA, it turned to Congress for relief. Henderson did not tolerate Congressmen easily. When one asked a favor, he would slam down the telephone. He warned his staff against political involvement and publicly stated: "No one in OPA is going to be permitted to play politics with the war effort. I have always said that OPA is going to be run on non-partisan principles."

Congressmen protested, grumbling about lack of understanding among bureaucrats. In October and November, 1942, Congress investigated the OPA and was highly critical. Unless Henderson went, some Congressmen threatened to withhold all funds for the agency. Henderson resigned in December. While his foes were jubilant, many newspapers felt he had been "crucified to appease a group of Congressional critics"; a large corporation ran a full-page advertisement in many papers saying, "Henderson did an able, two-fisted job for every man, woman, and child in America"; and a Republican Senator from New England said, "Within six months they will be praying to have Henderson back."

Former Senator Prentiss Brown was appointed OPA director to improve relations with Congress. He was more lenient than Henderson, and by April, 1943, the cost of living was up almost 25 per cent over August, 1939. After nine months, Brown resigned with the laconic statement that he was "expendable" in the war on the home front. He was replaced by advertising executive Chester Bowles who remained in the post until 1946. Despite continuing attacks, the OPA held the line. From May, 1943, to August, 1945, the cost of living rose less than 3 per cent. All told, from August, 1939, to August, 1945, the cost of living rose 28 per cent. This was in sharp contrast to World War I, when from July, 1914, to November, 1918, the cost of living rose 60 per cent. When price controls were lifted in 1946, the cost of living spiraled. By 1948, it was almost 75 per cent higher than in 1940.

18.　Transforming the Social Fabric

In World War II — despite the title of General Eisenhower's book, *Crusade in Europe* — there was little of the crusading spirit. The enthusiasm of 1917, which had led Americans to march in the streets with flags, hold wild recruiting rallies, and sing such patriotic songs as "Over There," was missing. The havoc in Europe and Asia had a sobering impact. Disillusionment over World War I helped also to condition the response. People did not want to be victims of hysteria again, seduced by slogans and parades. And the depression had left its mark, as those unsure of their fate in hard times now had war added to their doubts about the future.

An adolescent thirst for glory was replaced by a grim determination to defeat the enemy. The justness of the cause was not doubted, but the nation fought with a deadpan face. Gerald Johnson has emphasized in *Incredible Tale* that cartoonist Bill Mauldin's two GIs, Willie and Joe, were average Americans who could laugh at the absurdities of Army life, but at bottom were melancholy types who found nothing funny about the war itself.

Also missing in World War II was the intolerance toward nonconformists and Americans of German background which had led to a curbing of civil liberties in 1917 and after. The American Civil Liberties Union reported in 1944 that "the third year of the war has maintained the extraordinary and unexpected record of the first two years in freedom of debate and dissent on all public issues."

But the uprooting of the West Coast Japanese-Americans was the exception to an otherwise favorable record on civil liberties. In the hysteria that followed Pearl Harbor, newspapers and Congressmen from the area clamored for the removal of the Japanese-Americans as disloyal. In February, the Commanding General of the Army ordered them into detention camps. It was tragic and unnecessary. In Hawaii, where the proportion of Japanese-Americans was far higher, the situation was handled with greater intelligence by the military. Leaders of the Americans of Japanese ancestry cooperated closely with the military and the Federal Bureau of Investigation; the few suspects were rounded up immediately after December 7, and then the Americans of Japanese ancestry went on to make a brilliant military record in the fighting in Europe.

Although there was a minimum of the crusading spirit, the nation surged with change. The miracle of production altered the outlook of the country. Destroyed was the depression-born mood of disbelief in the future expansion of the economy. After a long journey across the country in 1943, John Dos Passos observed:

> Our people are still frontiersmen . . . The people of this country can still change their occupations, their way of living, their settlements as easily as they can eat their breakfasts. We are still jacks of all trades, eager to learn new skills and adapt ourselves to new social arrangements.[1]

The value of the gross national product grew enormously during the war.[2] And per capita disposable personal income in real terms rose 44 per cent between 1939 and 1944.[3] Despite the fact that 42 per cent of the gross national product in 1944 was expended for war as against less than 2 per cent in 1939, civilian consumption of goods and services was actually 20 per cent higher in 1944 than it had been in 1939. Although expenditures for such durable goods as automobiles and new housing decreased, expenditures for non-durable goods and services increased.

". . . *the typical beneficiary of our present wartime prosperity,*" Frederick Lewis Allen remarked in 1944, "*is a middle-class or skilled-worker family, probably in war work, that was making something like two thousand dollars a year before Pearl Harbor and now is making something like three or four thousand.*"[4] Although the cost of living rose some 28 per cent between 1939 and 1945, the average weekly earnings of workers in manufacturing industries went up 86 per cent. The number of families earning less than $2000 a year declined; the number earning more than $5000 increased, but only slightly. The important increase came in the $2000 to $5000 bracket. Farmers, engineers, technicians, specialists of various types, and skilled workers in war industries were the principal beneficiaries of the war boom.

The relative share of the national income received by upper income groups fell gradually between 1929 and 1939 and sharply from 1939 to 1944. The average share of the national income before taxes going to the top 5 per cent of income recipients from 1919 to 1938 was 30 per cent. Between 1939 and 1944, there occurred the most precipitate fall in this percentage in American history. From 27.8 per cent in 1939, it fell to 18.7 per cent in 1944.

Before 1940, the average yearly proportion of Americans who filed income tax returns was less than 10 per cent. The war years brought a decided change. And in 1943, the year when the effective tax rate was highest for all groups, even people in the income bracket from $2000 to $3000 paid 10.5 per cent of their income in taxes. That year the $300,000 to $500,000 class (only 456 returns) paid 80.8 per cent of their income in taxes.

The American bonanza, increasing in size, was being shared with a larger and larger number of people. Income from wages and salaries increased in percentage terms far more than income from rents, interest, and dividends. The largest corporations, with huge war orders, on the average showed earnings no larger than in the prewar period. Dividend payments were generally modest. Excess profits taxes, renegotiation of war contracts, and the managerial desire to avoid public disapproval of war profiteering were all factors in this. These large corporations, however, consolidated their already powerful positions in the economy and retained resources to finance expansion in the postwar decade. The wartime earnings of some smaller companies, including the aircraft industry, were phenomenal compared to previous earnings. Many oil producers, who had a depletion allowance on income taxes, became millionaires.

Extravagant spending occurred in many places. Some was overt tax dodging, but much was the consequence of lavish company expense accounts. Money which otherwise would have gone to the government in taxes went into entertainment of clients and future customers on a sumptuous scale. Hotels, theaters, and night clubs

benefited hugely. The theme song became "The sky is the limit —
It's all on the government."

The insatiable demand for labor transformed the social fabric of
the nation. By late 1942, manpower was in short supply. The armed
forces, which had numbered about two million on December 7,
1941, reached a peak of over twelve million in June, 1945. Despite
this tremendous drain, employment actually increased from fifty million at the beginning of the war to fifty-five million by 1943. Young
people from fourteen to eighteen years, women, retired workers, and
marginal workers, who had little chance of finding jobs in the prewar
economy, swelled the ranks of the laboring force.

Nearly one million Southern Negroes migrated to Northern cities.
While the influx produced tensions in every city and a race riot in
Detroit in 1943, the war was a period of unprecedented advancement
for Negroes. By 1944, nearly two million Negroes were employed in
war plants. Although the Fair Employment Practices Committee,
created in 1941, was only a temporary agency, it established government responsibility for equality of employment opportunity without
respect to race, creed, or ancestry. It also stimulated some Northern
states to establish permanent committees for fair employment.

While unions swelled their membership from ten and a half to
nearly fifteen millions, and the rank and file increased their standard
of living impressively, the trade union movement lost considerable
standing with the general public. Farm owners, seeing their hired
help leave for industrial employment, became openly hostile to union labor. Meanwhile, John L. Lewis became almost a one-man
wrecking crew of labor's public relations. He called a series of work
stoppages in the coal pits in 1943, roared and bellowed in his own
inimitable fashion, and aroused public wrath against the union
movement in a way no campaign of the National Association of
Manufacturers ever had achieved. Congress, its temper aroused by
the recurring coal strikes, passed the Smith-Connally Act over the
President's veto in June, 1943. This legislation required a union planning a strike in a war plant to issue a strike notice to be followed
by a thirty-day cooling-off period. On the thirtieth day, the National Labor Relations Board was required to conduct a strike vote.
The President was empowered to seize any struck facility, and, once

a plant was in the government's possession, unions could be fined and their leaders imprisoned for continuing the strike. The law also prohibited political contributions by unions in federal elections.

Business, too, sometimes provoked the public, although never to the same degree as the coal strikes of 1943. The John L. Lewis of the business world was Sewell L. Avery of Montgomery Ward. When Avery refused to obey a War Labor Board directive in 1944 to extend a union contract, the President ordered the seizure of Ward's Chicago plant. Avery refused to vacate his office and had to be lifted bodily and carried from the scene by two soldiers. As he was being carried out, he turned to Attorney General Francis Biddle, who was supervising the seizure, and uttered the worst epithet he could conceive: "You New Dealer, you."

Despite the public anger created by the coal strikes, labor's record of performance was excellent. In a special issue to the GIs, *Life* (September 24, 1944) remarked: "As for strikes, there really haven't been many of importance. The man-days lost through strikes between Dec. 7, 1941 and the present amount to one-tenth of 1 per cent of the 22½ billion man-days worked."

The two major issues in wartime labor disputes were union membership and wage rates. The membership issue was compromised by resorting to the expedient of the maintenance of membership rule whereby all employees who were members of the union at the time the contract was signed had to maintain their union membership. While this was not as desirable to union leaders as the closed or the union shop, it was preferable to the open shop.

The wage policy followed by the War Labor Board was laid down in the Little Steel formula of July, 1942. Since living costs had risen 15 per cent from January 1, 1941, to May 1, 1942, wage rates were permitted to rise 15 per cent above the January, 1941, level. Although under this formula hourly wage rates were limited to a 15 per cent rise, with the abundance of overtime work the weekly pay check rose considerably more than 15 per cent. Labor members of the War Labor Board fought the Little Steel formula throughout the war, but it managed to survive although breaches were made in it through concessions on fringe benefits and portal-to-portal pay.

With fifteen million members by 1945, organized labor had

achieved a degree of economic strength that gave it, in John Kenneth Galbraith's words, "countervailing power." By the close of the war, unions were generally accepted and membership in them considered respectable. These gains, however, had not been achieved without a growing hostility, particularly among farmers, white collar, and professional people. A wave of strikes immediately following the war increased the demand for legislation to curb the power of labor leaders. The CIO itself was torn by an internal struggle between anti-Communists and Communists which sapped much of its energy. And many of the workers unionized in the war years were not particularly union-conscious. With the greater numbers and the prosperity of the workers, the militant quality that had characterized the CIO in depression days faded rapidly.

Farmers, still fearing surpluses after Pearl Harbor, were the slowest to increase production. Surpluses from the depression decade were plentiful, however, during this period. By the fall of 1942, farm spokesmen shifted from the depression psychology of limiting production to the war psychology of all out production; but, remembering the 1920 collapse of farm prices which had plunged agriculture into a depression, they feared the postwar period. To mollify the farm bloc, the Price Stabilization Act provided that the government would support basic commodity prices at 90 per cent of parity for two years after the close of hostilities, thus setting the pattern for postwar price supports.

With the possible exception of the lowest income labor group, farmers were the greatest beneficiaries of the war boom. The per capita income of persons in agriculture rose from $173 in 1939 to $554 in 1945. While the total national income increased 129 per cent in these years, the income from farming increased nearly 165 per cent. And this income was shared with fewer and fewer people since the farm population declined from 30,480,000 in 1939 to 25,190,000 by 1945.

Although farm employment dropped some 7 per cent, agricultural production increased nearly 25 per cent with a war-spurred revolution in American agricultural methods. During the farm depression of the 1920s and the great depression of the next decade, scientists and inventors had developed new machinery, fertilizers, insecticides, and high-yielding seeds. The war brought these and a widespread application of electrical power into general use in farming.

Farmers used their greatly increased income to pay off their debts, buy more land and equipment, and increase their bank deposits. While the number of farms decreased 6 per cent during the war, the number of farms with over a thousand acres increased 12 per cent. Agricultural prosperity was the result of full employment at home and the abnormally high export of foodstuffs. Per capita food consumption was considerably larger than in the depression years. Formerly low income groups ate better than ever before, particularly increasing their consumption of meat and milk. In spite of the boom in agriculture, the poorest 25 per cent of farmers gained little. The chief benefit to them was the draining off from small and poor farms of a considerable amount of surplus labor.

Congress, which had been dominated by the power of the executive during Roosevelt's first term and had started to reassert itself in the second, found itself submerged again in the third. Congress followed the President on the over-all planning of the war and on the building of a world organization. An excellent example of close congressional-executive collaboration involved appropriations to the Manhattan Project for developing the atomic bomb. When members of the Appropriations Committee raised questions about certain large unexplained funds, a small group of Congressmen were given confidential information by Roosevelt. In all, over two billions were authorized but the items were hidden in the appropriation bills. It was a well-kept secret throughout the war.

There were sharp differences, however, on the home front over labor, farm, and tax legislation. Congress was dissatisfied, too, over the use made of delegated powers, notably in the area of price controls. And committees, most importantly the Truman Committee, performed valuable services in exposing inefficiencies and inadequacies, profiteering, and needless shortages.

There was much conflict between Congress — which was in the control of conservatives — and New Dealers in the government. The New Deal emphasis on planning came under attack and Congress, by refusing to appropriate funds, killed the National Resources Planning Board in 1943. This proved unfortunate, indeed, in the light of the reconversion pitfalls which lay ahead. On the other hand, Congress worked well with the President on planning for the veterans. A committee of the NRPB, headed by Professor Floyd Reeves of the University of Chicago, made the basic study that materialized in the GI Bill of Rights.[5]

While some liberals viewed the war as a further opportunity to change the nature of the economy by legislation, some conservatives saw it as a golden opportunity to bring the New Deal to an ignominious burial. Both proved to be wrong. Full employment and the redistribution of income achieved the ends of Roosevelt's humanitarianism without the need of further legislation. And, regardless of the vindictiveness of some congressional attacks on specific New Dealers, Congress was in no mood to commit political suicide by repealing basic New Deal laws.[6]

During the war, Vice-President Wallace emerged as the darling of the liberals and the bête noire of the conservatives. In speeches and pamphlets, he described the need for full employment — sixty million jobs — at home and the perfection of democracy here and abroad. He lashed out at the concept being developed by Henry Luce of *Life*, *Time*, and *Fortune* that the coming century was the "American Century." On May 8, 1942, Wallace said: "Some have spoken of the 'American Century.' I say that the century we are now entering — the century which will come out of this war — can and must be the century of the common man . . . Those who write the peace must think of the whole world. There can be no privileged peoples . . . The people's revolution is on the march, and the devil and all his angels cannot prevail against it." In the middle of the speech, he explained that he had said half in fun and half seriously to the wife of the Soviet Ambassador: "The object of this war is to make sure that everybody in the world has the privilege of drinking a quart of milk a day."

Immediately, Wallace came under bitter attack as a hopeless dreamer, visionary, and troublemaker. But his Century of the Common Man had deep roots in the American past, and Wallace himself was an Old Testament prophet in the circuit-riding tradition. In July, 1943, after a bitter public vendetta between Wallace, as head of the Board of Economic Warfare, and Jesse Jones, as Federal Loan

Administrator, the President fired Wallace from the BEW. The *New Republic* (July 26, 1943) complained: "The President's action . . . is the most severe shock to his liberal followers since he has been in office. . . . The progressive movement will never be secure so long as it depends so largely on the whims and erratic impulses of a single individual." And *Time* (July 26) gloatingly quoted "One Wash. wag: 'They have just buried the last New Dealer.' "

The final blow seemed to fall that December when Roosevelt told a reporter, who remained after a press conference, that he wished journalists would stop using the term New Deal. But at his press conference on December 28, Roosevelt clarified his statement. The New Deal came into existence because the nation "was suffering from a grave internal disorder — awfully sick," and Dr. New Deal remedied the illness. When war came, Roosevelt added, Dr. New Deal, an expert on internal medicine, needed a partner, "Dr. Win-The-War," who was a surgeon. At the present time, Roosevelt observed, "principal emphasis, the overwhelming first emphasis should be on winning the war." But, he continued, "when victory comes, the program of the past, of course, has got to be carried on . . . it seems pretty clear that we must plan for, and help to bring about, an expanded economy which will result in more security, in more employment, in more recreation, in more education, in more health, in better housing for all of our citizens, so that the conditions of 1932 and the beginning of 1933 won't come back again."

Two weeks later in his message on the State of the Union, Roosevelt called Dr. New Deal back into action when he submitted an "Economic Bill of Rights." In 1945, in his final message on the State of the Union, Roosevelt recommended that Congress consider the postwar development of natural resources, an overhaul of the national highway system, construction of airports, an expanded social security system, and adequate health and education programs. The federal government, with the help of states, municipalities, business, labor, and agriculture, had to make the economic bill of rights a reality, he said. "Our policy is, of course, to rely as much as possible on private enterprise to provide jobs," he added. "But the American people will not accept mass unemployment or mere makeshift work. There will be need for the work of everyone willing and able to work — and that means close to 60,000,000 jobs."

19. The Inexorable Calendar of Elections

Although for a few months after Pearl Harbor the enormity of the danger facing the nation blanketed partisanship, the 1942 congressional elections gave a powerful rebirth to political controversy. That fall the Republicans capitalized on shortages in the economy, administrative bungling in Washington, and assorted irritations: farmers over price controls, workers over wage ceilings, small businessmen who felt that the lion's share of war orders was going to big business, and consumers who were facing increased rationing. The Republicans gained 47 seats in the House of Representatives, reducing the Democratic margin to 13; and they captured 8 seats in the Senate. New York elected Thomas E. Dewey Governor, placing him in a strategic position for 1944. Indifference and apathy had characterized the Democratic campaign, with the vote in New York the lowest in eight years.

After the Republicans had swept most local and state elections in the autumn of 1943, *Life* declared: "The U.S. is now a Republican country." While agreeing that Roosevelt still had immense prestige, *Life* announced that the Republicans were in a technically sound position to win the 1944 election, adding: "The Republican nomination is a rich prize and the candidates are scrambling hard for it." [1] Writing in *Look*, Wendell Willkie insisted that the Republicans could win only if they first won a victory within their own party. The party, he charged, was "corrupted by vested interests in its own ranks and by reactionary forces. It forgot its own great liberal tradition." To win the presidency, he added, the liberal wing had to win control of the party and make it the "great American liberal party." [2]

Willkie staked his own fortunes on the Wisconsin primary, an amazing political judgment on his part since the state organization was controlled by men hostile to his domestic liberalism and to his advocacy of American leadership in world affairs. After he was routed in the primary, he withdrew from the race. His failure to regain the nomination should not obscure the fact, however, that the bold espousal of his views contributed to the Republican Party's adjustment to the Roosevelt Revolution and to world politics and helped make it impossible for an Old Guard candidate to win the nomination.[3]

Even before Wisconsin eliminated Willkie, Governor Dewey had been emerging as the new Republican leader. He had proved to be an excellent vote-getter in New York; he was vigorous and youthful, moderately liberal and internationalist in his thinking, and he was an efficient administrator. ". . . he has an alert, highly disciplined mind . . ." Richard H. Rovere wrote in *Harper's Magazine*, May, 1944. "He is as humorless as a man can be . . . He has no apparent interest in general ideas, but within the limits of practicality his mind works shrewdly and quickly. He is, in fine, an excellent politician."

If the Old Guard had a candidate to stop Dewey, it was Governor John W. Bricker of Ohio. When reactionaries and isolationists rallied to Bricker, William Allen White wrote the last of the blistering editorials that had won him fame: "Surely the Republican Party cannot be so craven as to conspire to sneak into victory with no issue but Bricker and a bellyache. Bricker is an honest Harding-thumbs down."

Dewey's well-organized campaign could not be blocked. He was nominated on the first ballot with only one dissenting vote and Bricker received the vice-presidential nomination. While the platform denounced the Administration for inefficiency, waste, and bureaucracy, and for destroying private enterprise, it endorsed the basic Roosevelt policies in the fields of social security, labor, and agriculture and supported joining a world organization.

A week before the Democratic Convention, Roosevelt announced in a public letter to Robert Hannegan, Chairman of the National Committee, that while "All that is within me cries out to go back to my home on the Hudson River," "if the people command me to continue in this office and in this war, I have as little right to withdraw as the soldier has to leave his post in the line." Many party leaders, concerned over the President's health, anticipated that the vice-presidential nominee might become president. The ensuing bitter battle, waged publicly and privately for the vice-presidency left scars that had not faded by the postwar years. Vice-President Wallace had the vociferous support of extreme New Dealers and top CIO leaders, but his lack of tact had alienated many powerful figures. As presiding officer of the Senate he had failed to win the friendship of the Senators, and he had feuded with Jesse Jones and other Administration figures to the acute embarrassment of Roosevelt. Moreover, to many moderates, he seemed temperamentally unfit for the presidency.

Roosevelt was unwilling to go through a difficult convention fight to win renomination for Wallace. Although on July 14, Roosevelt wrote a letter stating that he would vote for Wallace if he were a delegate, he added: "I do not wish to appear in any way as dictating to the convention. Obviously the convention must do the deciding." Before this date James F. Byrnes had been emerging as a powerful candidate. He had discussed it with Roosevelt and decided to become a candidate when the President explained that he would express no preference other than his statement about Wallace. But Sidney Hillman, head of the Political Action Committee of the CIO, protested to Roosevelt and warned that the South Carolinian was unacceptable to labor and to Negroes.

The CIO had launched its Political Action Committee in 1943 to counteract the apathy of workers and to defeat unfriendly Congressmen in 1944. It trained union members in the techniques of registering voters, ringing doorbells, and discussing issues. This work increased the influence of the CIO in the 1944 selection of Democratic candidates. After Hillman's talk with Roosevelt, the President instructed Robert Hannegan to seek Hillman's approval of the vice-presidential nominee. "Clear it with Sidney" became a slogan much used by the Republicans to create the impression that the Democrats were controlled by the unions.

At a White House conference on July 11, Roosevelt discussed possible candidates with party leaders including Edward J. Kelly, Frank Walker, and George Allen. According to the President's aide, Judge Rosenman, after all candidates had been evaluated, the President settled on two men. At Hannegan's suggestion, Roosevelt wrote a letter — dated July 19 — saying he would be happy to run with either Senator Harry S. Truman or Supreme Court Justice William O. Douglas.

July 19 was the opening day of the Convention and only three or four people knew of the existence of this letter. Truman, who was supporting Byrnes, was not one of them. After Hannegan showed him Roosevelt's letter, he continued to work for Byrnes until the latter withdrew from the race. Truman, surprised he was Roosevelt's official choice, finally told Roosevelt's lieutenants he would run, but said characteristically: "Why the hell didn't he tell me in the first place?"

Although Wallace led on the first ballot, Truman won on the second. Elected to the Senate in 1934, with the support of the notorious Kansas City boss, Tom Pendergast, Truman had voted consistently for New Deal measures. Not until his wartime activity as Chairman of the Senate Committee Investigating the National Defense Program had he attracted public attention.

In 1944, the problem was to find a man who would hurt the President the least. "Truman was the only one who fitted. . . . He just dropped into the slot," Edward J. Flynn has recalled.[4] He was acceptable to Roosevelt, to party and labor leaders, to his fellow Senators, and to Negroes. *The St. Louis Post-Dispatch*, which had long been a foe of the Pendergast machine, said of Truman on October 24, 1944: "Hating his political origin as it does, this newspaper is among those which freely pay tribute to the Senator for his accomplishments. We hold that as candidate for the vice-presidency he has outlived his unwholesome past and now stands up as a public servant who has served the public with exceptional courage, integrity, and ability."

During the campaign, Dewey charged that the Roosevelt Administration was composed of tired, quarrelsome old men. Dewey seemed to be gaining momentum as he toured the nation reiterating in his well-trained voice the tired old men theme and promising the New Deal with a better administration. It was a well-organized campaign, but no warmth flowed from the candidate.

The Republicans stung Roosevelt with the charge that government was in the hands of "tired old men." When the President returned from a visit to the Pacific theater of the war, he spoke to the nation from aboard ship in the Bremerton Navy Yard. The wind was blowing and it was difficult for Roosevelt to turn the pages of his manuscript. He delivered the speech in a halting, tired manner. It seemed to confirm the charge that he was failing in health and had lost his old vigor.

To counteract this impression, he opened his campaign with one of the most masterly political speeches of his career before the Teamsters' Union on September 23. "Well, here we are together again — after four years — and what years they have been!" he began. "You know, I am actually four years older, which is a fact that seems to annoy some people. In fact, in the mathematical field there are millions of Americans who are more than eleven years older than when we started in to clear up the mess that was dumped in our laps in 1933." As he heaped ridicule on the Republican leaders, he delivered a paragraph that derailed the hitherto well-planned Dewey campaign:

> These Republican leaders have not been content with attacks on me, or my wife, or on my sons. No, not content with that, they now include my little dog, Fala. Well, of course, I don't resent attacks, and my family doesn't resent attacks, but Fala *does* resent them. You know, Fala is Scotch, and being a Scottie, as soon as he learned that the Republican fiction writers in Congress and out had concocted a story that I had left him behind on the Aleutian Islands and had sent a destroyer back to find him — at a cost to the taxpayers of two or three, or eight or twenty million dollars — his Scotch soul was furious. He has not been the same dog since. I am accustomed to hearing malicious falsehoods about myself — such as that old, worm-eaten chestnut that I have represented myself as indispensable. But I think I have a right to resent, to object to libelous statements about my dog.

Roosevelt's sarcasm enraged Dewey. Two days later he started swinging wildly, shouting: "He asked for it, now we'll let him have it." Over the next weeks the bitterness of Dewey's attacks grew. It was just what Roosevelt wanted. As one Democrat said, the campaign after the Fala speech was between "Roosevelt's dog and Dewey's goat."

Out of some forty-eight million votes cast, Roosevelt was re-elected by a margin of three and a half million. In the closest of his four elections, he polled just under 54 per cent of the major party vote. Roosevelt lost some support among farmers and workers, but he gained strength with white collar and business people and among Negroes. While Republican spokesmen and labor leaders alike emphasized the power of the Political Action Committee, both overrated it, at least, in the presidential election. Roosevelt's vote in 1944 among workers dropped from 1940. And the National Opinion Research Center found that for every person more likely to vote for Roosevelt because of PAC backing, eleven were less likely to vote for him.

Surveys indicated that a majority of voters believed that the war would be won faster with Roosevelt and that he could build a solid foundation for peace better than Dewey. Only on the question of management of domestic affairs after the war did Dewey approach the President in the public favor.[5]

---

20. The Victorious Coalition

Two weeks after the Japanese attack on Pearl Harbor, Winston Churchill arrived in Washington to forge the bonds of Anglo-American unity and lay plans for the eventual defeat of the Axis. The extraordinary degree of Anglo-American cooperation was symbolized by the close relationship between Churchill and Roosevelt. The mutual respect and esteem that each had for the other appear even in the formal messages they exchanged. "It is fun to be in the same decade with you," Roosevelt ended a long serious cable to the Prime Minister during one of the darkest hours of the war. And Churchill wrote in 1950: "I formed a very strong affection, which grew with our years in comradeship, for this formidable politician who had imposed his will for nearly ten years upon the American scene, and whose heart seemed to respond to many of the impulses that stirred my own." [1]

Both of them were men of immense personal magnetism. They exultantly surmounted the supreme crisis and their respective publics responded to their leadership. As politico-military craftsmen on a global scale, they established, in the words of Robert E. Sherwood, "an easy intimacy, a joking informality and a moratorium on pomposity and cant — and also a degree of frankness in intercourse which, if not quite complete, was remarkably close to it. But neither of them ever forgot for one instant what he was and represented or what the other was or represented." [2]

Roosevelt learned how tenacious and stubborn Churchill could be, while the Prime Minister discovered how difficult it was, at times, to pin down the "artful dodger" on specific points. During 1942, while America was still in the initial stage of mobilizing its strength, Churchill's power to influence decisions was at its height. By late 1943, when American military power surpassed that of the British, Churchill had to accept the American viewpoint on many disputed issues. Roosevelt, sensitive to the relative decline in British power, conceded on some issues to Churchill in return for more fundamental concessions.

Nothing resembling the Anglo-American economic and military planning and the joint administration of activities was ever achieved with the Soviet Union. At best, the Russians were only half an ally. Not until near the close of the war was something of a coordinated military strategy developed. Even then, always beneath the surface, lay the shadow of distrust. The Soviets never supplied the United States with such detailed information about their military forces or economic conditions as did other nations receiving lend-lease supplies. Soviet officials made many blunt demands, they refused to exchange information, and they were suspicious and secretive. They revealed their distrust of the British and Americans many times, particularly over the delay in establishing the second front in Normandy, which they interpreted as indicating that the Western Allies wanted Germany and Russia to bleed each other white. As a result, it was believed in Washington that any request from Western leaders for detailed information would only confirm the Russian suspicions.

The Stalin purges, the Nazi-Soviet Pact, and the war against Finland created widespread distrust of Soviet intentions in America. But during 1942-1943, as the Russians suffered immense losses and carried, in Churchill's words, "the main burden" of the war, most Americans came to view them as an heroic ally, a view encouraged by official propaganda. And the Administration adopted the most favorable interpretation of the difficult relations with the Russians. It believed that they were doing more than their share of the fighting, and, since America was unable to commit its full strength until the invasion of France in 1944, the President felt that he was not in a strong position to bargain with Soviet leaders over more military information or details of the postwar settlement. At the heart of the Administration's unwillingness to demand information from the Rus-

sians was the fear that if pressed too much they might make a separate peace with Germany. Significant pressure was exerted on Roosevelt by the Joint Chiefs of Staff to avoid this danger. And early in
1945, when this hazard had passed, the Joint Chiefs insisted that the
President persuade the Russians to enter the war against Japan.[3]

Military leaders exerted a powerful and, many times, decisive influence on foreign policy decisions. The Joint Chiefs of Staff had direct
access to the President, and he seldom overruled these advisers. Admiral William D. Leahy, personal Chief of Staff to the President, and
General George C. Marshall, Army Chief of Staff, were the dominant
influence on more major foreign policy decisions than Cordell Hull.
In fact, Roosevelt tended to ignore Hull except in the planning of
the world organization. Hull was not present, for instance, at the
Casablanca, Cairo, and Tehran Conferences, nor did he attend military discussions between Roosevelt and Churchill even when these
had significant diplomatic repercussions.

Roosevelt not only ignored the Secretary of State, but he also had
a deep-seated prejudice against career diplomats. His close friend Sumner Welles has written that "it was very rare indeed that President
Roosevelt could be persuaded to bring into White House conferences on foreign policy any of those State Department specialists
who had devoted a lifetime to the study of some particular country
or region, and who could have given him the detailed information
and authoritative viewpoint that he very frequently lacked." [4] Roosevelt's devotion to personal diplomacy, his heavy reliance on the
Chiefs of Staff, and on such personal advisers as Harry Hopkins,
weakened the influence of the Department of State and contributed
to its already low prestige with the Congress and the public.

When Hull resigned late in 1944 and was replaced by Edward R.
Stettinius, Jr., liaison between the White House and the Department improved. The Department was kept better informed of White
House decisions, and Department officials played a somewhat more
important role than previously. But even so, military leaders continued to exercise pre-eminent influence. There never was throughout the war a systematic coordination of foreign policy with military
planning.[5]

Many of the policies recommended by the Joint Chiefs were political as well as military in their ramifications, but seldom were the

political aspects considered by the military. Embedded in the American military tradition, and for that matter in the thinking of most citizens, was the concept of the non-political military officer who fought for victory as an end in itself. The political and social conditions resulting from military victory were considered outside the province of the military man.

The British and the Russians operated differently. Both were alert to the fact that war is an extension of politics in another form and constantly had in mind the impact of strategic military decisions on the postwar power structure.

The difference between the American and British attitude came to the fore over the invasion of Europe. Roosevelt favored a massive attack across the English Channel as the quickest way to win the war. The British favored in 1943 an attack through the Balkans — the soft "underbelly" of Europe. This British policy was politico-military and was intended not only to defeat Hitler, but by the presence of British and American soldiers to close the Balkans off from the Red Army. The British, after tenacious opposition, finally had to agree at the Quebec Conference in August, 1943, that the invasion of Normandy had priority over operations in Italy and the Mediterranean. Churchill, however, doggedly continued to urge a companion invasion of the Balkans with a landing in the Trieste-Fiume area and a push into Austria. By 1944, it was too late to save the Balkans from Russian control, but Churchill hoped that such an attack would mean that Central Europe could be liberated by the Western Allies.

In March and April, 1945, when the war against Germany was nearly over, the British political-military strategy again ran into determined American opposition. General Eisenhower decided against an advance on Berlin since it was no longer an important military objective. Churchill's protests were ignored and the Joint Chiefs agreed with Eisenhower that "the single objective should be quick and complete victory." [6] In his final report, Eisenhower wrote: "Berlin no longer represented a military objective of major importance . . . military factors, when the enemy was on the brink of final defeat, were more important . . . than the political considerations involved in an Allied capture of the capital."

General Omar N. Bradley later wrote: "As soldiers we looked naively on this British inclination to complicate the war with political foresight and non-military objectives." [7] Unlike the Russians and the British, the Americans subordinated the political complexion of the peace to the destruction of the enemy's armed forces and a quick victory and failed to assess correctly the strategic and political importance of Berlin.

The American view of the postwar era was optimistic. It was assumed that the American experience could be translated into world application; that peace, prosperity, individual freedom, and justice could be given universal meaning and receive ready acceptance. The President crystallized the support of the nation for membership in a world organization, and his idealism was a potent force in other free nations as well as among people under Axis tyranny. While the American insistence on a world organization was a significant contribution to world politics, it was also true that the Administration and leaders of public opinion in general were voicing millennial hopes. They stimulated the expectation that an international organization was the solution to the maintenance of peace. As a result, part of the poswar disillusionment with the lack of effectiveness of the United Nations stemmed from the wartime overemphasis on what it could accomplish.

During the war, as far as most Americans were concerned, international relations became nearly synonymous with international organization. In the spring of 1943, Republican Senators Ball and Burton and Democratic Senators Hatch and Hill introduced the B_2H_2 resolution calling for the organization of the United Nations with a military force to suppress aggression. That summer ten teams of Senators and Representatives toured the country on behalf of the resolution. On September 21, a resolution sponsored by Representative J. W. Fulbright of Arkansas, expressing congressional approval of the creation of "appropriate international machinery," passed the House with only 29 votes opposed. On November 5, the Senate passed a comparable resolution — the Connally Resolution — by a vote of 85 to 5. In the summer of 1944, both party platforms, with somewhat different phraseology, approved American participation in a world organization.

With these assurances from both parties, the Department of State initiated the Dumbarton Oaks Conference in Washington in late August to discuss the world organization with the British and the Russians. Although no Congressmen were included in the American delegation, leaders of both Houses were given day-by-day résumés of the proceedings. When the Republican presidential nominee issued a statement expressing concern that the interests of small nations might be ignored by the Big Three, Hull invited him to consultations. Instead, Dewey appointed John Foster Dulles, international lawyer and chairman of the Commission on a Just and Durable Peace of the Federal Council of Churches, to represent him.

After the election, bipartisanship in building the world organization was enhanced by the "conversion" of Senator Arthur H. Vandenberg from isolationism. On January 10, 1945, Vandenberg told the Senate that he favored maximum American cooperation "to make the basic idea of Dumbarton Oaks succeed. I want a new dignity and a new authority for international law." In the course of the speech, he criticized unilateral actions by the Soviet Union and Great Britain which were at variance with American peace aims, and urged the Administration to speak out against them. He also recommended that unilateral decisions resulting from military necessity be temporary and subject to postwar revision. For all his critical tone, he extended a hand to the President by saying at the close of his speech: "I do not wish to meddle. I want only to help, I want to do my duty."

A few weeks later Roosevelt appointed Vandenberg a member of the American delegation to draft the United Nations Charter at San Francisco. The culmination of the efforts of Roosevelt and Hull to build congressional and public support for a world organization came in the Senate on July 28, 1945, when only two Republican isolationists — Langer and Shipstead — voted against membership in the United Nations.[8]

Shortly after Pearl Harbor, Russia's postwar demands were explained bluntly, and in detail, to Anthony Eden. Stalin demanded, among other things, a Soviet-Polish boundary based on the Curzon line, parts of Finland and Rumania, all of the Baltic States, the transfer of East Prussia to Poland, the detachment of the Rhineland from

Germany, and heavy German reparations. Eden made it clear that he could not enter into secret agreements without consultation with the British War Cabinet and the United States.

The Roosevelt Administration refused, at this point, to negotiate on these questions and expressed its opposition to any territorial settlements until the war was won. The President felt that discussions over "local" questions might split the coalition and delay victory. Moreover, in view of the degree of isolationist sentiment in the past decade, he doubted whether the American people would be willing to remain involved in European problems at the close of the war, and he believed that the public would demand the withdrawal of troops from Europe. He wrote Churchill on November 18, 1944: "You know, of course, that after Germany's collapse I must bring American troops home as rapidly as transportation problems will permit."

Assuming from past experience that the public would not accept long-term commitments in Europe and hoping that discord among the Big Three might be lessened, Roosevelt pushed the plans for establishing the United Nations organization before the end of hostilities.

The American attempt to postpone territorial settlements until the war ended ran afoul of the immediate demands of the war. Zones of military operation hardened into postwar spheres of influence. In March, 1942, the President proposed that the British assume responsibility for the Middle East, the United States for the Pacific, and both operate jointly in the Atlantic theater. And, by 1943, Italy, Greece, Turkey, the Mediterranean area, and East Central Europe were added to the sphere of British responsibilities.

The American Joint Chiefs of Staff decided in the autumn of 1943 that the nation should take no responsibility "in the Balkans including Austria." It was not until December, 1944, at the insistence of Ambassador John G. Winant, American representative on the European Advisory Commission, that they reluctantly agreed to a zone of occupation in Austria. Philip E. Mosely, from his experience as Winant's alternate on the European Advisory Commission, has written that the opposition of the military to accepting American responsibilities in spheres outside their own theaters of command left the Department of State "adrift, to 'make do' the best it could by means of notes and exhortations." [9]

In the spring of 1944, as the Red Army began to roll into Eastern Europe, the British accepted Soviet domination of the areas captured by the Russians in return for Soviet acceptance of British paramount interests in the countries bordering the Mediterranean. Churchill proposed in April that Russia have controlling interest in Rumania and Britain in Greece. Nurtured in the idealism of Woodrow Wilson, Cordell Hull reacted violently against such manifestations of "power politics" and "spheres of influence." Staking all on a world organization, like so many of his fellow countrymen, he underestimated the importance of power and spheres of influence in the postwar world. At Hull's insistence, Roosevelt objected to the plan. Two days later, however, Churchill persuaded Roosevelt to accept it for a three-month period. That October, Churchill and the Russians agreed that the Soviets were to have preponderance in Bulgaria, Rumania, and Hungary, while they were to share power equally in Yugoslavia.

By late 1944, the American policy of postponing the settlement of specific issues was no longer feasible. The impending victory of the Allied forces required agreement by Churchill, Roosevelt, and Stalin on the treatment of nations liberated from Hitler's tyranny and on the plan to be imposed on defeated Germany. In addition, it was necessary for the Big Three to settle their differences over the structure of the world organization. And the Joint Chiefs of Staff pressed for a high-level conference to plan the final blows against Germany and to bring the Russians into the Japanese war.

---

21. Yalta: Myth and Reality

When Churchill, Roosevelt, and Stalin met in the Soviet Crimea in February 4-11, 1945, the military situation placed drastic strictures on Western diplomacy. In December, 1944, German forces had counterattacked against the Western Allies and created a "Bulge" in northern France, driving American forces back to the Meuse. The German attack upset planning for the Allied spring offensive and created a spirit of gloom. In mid-January, 1945, Eisenhower informed

General Marshall, who was soon to leave for the Yalta Conference, that the forces under his command might defeat Germany provided the Soviet offensive went well. At Malta, where the British and Americans met en route to Yalta, General Bedell Smith, Eisenhower's Chief of Staff, told Secretary of State Edward R. Stettinius, Jr., that there was an outside chance that the Russian advance might be at an end. Even if the Germans lost Berlin, there was the possibility, he said, that they might retire to southwest Germany and conduct guerrilla fighting for months or even years. He emphasized that to Eisenhower the necessity of coordinating his drive with that of the Russians was of the utmost importance.

The Soviet Union had launched its winter attack on January 12. By the first of February, Soviet forces had moved northward from Warsaw to the Baltic, cutting East Prussia off from the rest of Germany. Other Russian troops pushed westward to the Oder River. When the Big Three met at Yalta, Poland was in the hands of the Russians and their advance units were less than one hundred miles from Berlin. Meanwhile, Allied forces had not yet crossed the Rhine.

The military achievements of the Red Army restricted what Roosevelt and Churchill could achieve by diplomacy. On January 8, Churchill telegraphed Roosevelt: "This may well be a fateful Conference, coming at a moment when the Great Allies are so divided and the shadow of war lengthens out before us. At the present time I think the end of this war may well prove to be more disappointing than was the last." And at Malta, Stettinius has written that Churchill "expressed utter dismay at the outlook of the world . . . it was his opinion that future peace, stability, and progress depended on Great Britain and the United States remaining in close harmony at all times." [1]

The Yalta Conference was the second meeting of Roosevelt, Churchill, and Stalin, but it was the first time they reached basic agreements on postwar problems. Yalta, too, was the first time that the military leaders of the three nations discussed in detail future operational plans.

At the Conference, Churchill demonstrated his deep understanding of the need of checking the further expansion of Soviet power. Tensions were frequently at a danger point over such questions as

Poland and Germany. Churchill's brilliant oratory was countered by blunt objections from Stalin. Roosevelt served as conciliator between the two. Although as moderator he reduced tensions, most of his maneuvering was designed to lend support to Churchill's position.

In addition to his role as conciliator, Roosevelt clearly and forcefully set forth the American position on the issues under discussion Stettinius has written:

> I wish to emphasize that at all times from Malta through the Crimean Conference . . . I always found him to be mentally alert and fully capable of dealing with each situation as it developed. The stories that his health took a turn for the worse either on the way to Yalta or at the Conference are, to the best of my knowledge, without foundation. The President's ability to participate on fully equal terms day after day in the gruelling give-and-take at the conference table with such powerful associates as Churchill and Stalin is the best answer to these stories.

The Polish issue was the most explosive of all the questions discussed at Yalta. With Soviet troops in command of Poland, it was not a question of what Roosevelt and Churchill would allow Russia to do in Poland, but rather what they could persuade Stalin to accept. The sheer facts of the situation required Churchill and Roosevelt to agree to the Curzon Line as the Russo-Polish boundary. They refused, however, to approve Stalin's demand that the German-Polish boundary be the Western Neisse River. The question of the Polish government produced the most bitter disagreement. Stalin insisted on the recognition of the Soviet puppet Lublin government. When he failed, he tried to win approval for an enlarged Lublin government. Roosevelt and Churchill insisted that the Lublin government had to be reorganized to include democratic Poles from both inside and outside Poland. Stalin finally agreed. He also acquiesced to the British and American demand that free elections be held at an early date to select a government representative of the people.

In addition, Roosevelt and Churchill also persuaded him to accept the Declaration on Liberated Europe pledging the Big Three "to form interim governmental authorities broadly representative of all democratic elements in the population and pledged to the earliest possible establishment through free elections of governments responsive to the will of the people." Roosevelt, however, refused to present to the Conference a State Department recommendation for a European High Commission to supervise liberated areas. He objected to "another organization" and his political adviser James F. Byrnes remarked that it would be unpopular if American troops had to remain and accept responsibility for European internal matters because of such a Commission.

Ambassador W. Averell Harriman had warned the Department of State from Moscow prior to Yalta that when the Russians used such terms as "friendly" and "independent" government they meant something quite different from the American interpretation. But under the prevailing military circumstances, Roosevelt and Churchill secured what was attainable. American diplomacy was operating on the assumption clearly stated in the official briefing papers:

> We must have the support of the Soviet Union to defeat Germany. We sorely need the Soviet Union in the war against Japan when the war in Europe is over. The importance of these two things can be reckoned in terms of American lives. We must have the cooperation of the Soviet Union to organize the peace.

And Churchill has written: "What would have happened if we had quarrelled with Russia while the Germans still had three or four hundred divisions on the fighting front? Our hopeful assumptions were soon to be falsified. Still, they were the only ones possible at the time." [2]

Although Roosevelt and Churchill were unwilling to allow the problem of liberated Europe to rupture relations with the Soviet Union, they blocked Russia's demands for dismemberment of Germany. They postponed any implementation of such a plan at Yalta, although they agreed that the Big Three "will take such steps, including the complete disarmament, demilitarization and the dismemberment of Germany as they deem requisite for future peace and security." Stalin demanded that Germany be stripped of its industry and the Soviet Union be rebuilt with German equipment. One of the myths about Yalta is that the United States supported a plan prepared by Secretary of the Treasury Henry Morgenthau, Jr., to dismember and to deindustrialize Germany. At a meeting in Quebec on September 15, 1944, Roosevelt and Churchill agreed in part with it. But shortly after the Quebec Conference both abandoned even limited concurrence with it.

At Yalta, Roosevelt and Churchill refused to accept deindustrialization and postponed the question of reparations. Roosevelt, but not Churchill, agreed that a Reparations Commission should consider the Russian demand of twenty billion dollars in its initial studies, although only as a basis for discussion.

Stalin also wanted the western Polish boundary at the Western Neisse River, and the Ruhr and Saar separated from Germany. Churchill and Roosevelt refused. The demands which were met fully were those proposed by the British and the Americans. Stalin agreed to a French zone of occupation carved from the British and American zones. Reluctantly, he agreed to the inclusion of France on the German Control Commission intended to integrate the administration of Germany.

The boundaries of the zones of occupation were not drawn at Yalta. The European Advisory Commission, established after the Tehran Conference (1943), drafted the zones. The Department of State recommended three zones of occupation — France was not yet included — drawn in such a way that each would touch Berlin. The War Department rejected this. Then the War Department also rejected a British suggestion of a corridor between the Western zones and Berlin. The American military insisted that it was not possible in 1944 to predict what roads, canals, and railroads would be usable. Access to Berlin, they stated, was a military matter to be left to military representatives to be determined at the proper times.[3]

The agreement on the zones of occupation and on the administration of Berlin was signed by British, Russian, and American representatives in the fall of 1944. The Big Three at Yalta confirmed the agreement with the addition of France as an occupying power. On June 29, 1945, General Lucius D. Clay, as General Eisenhower's representative, and General Sir Ronald Weeks, as the British representative, negotiated an oral agreement with Marshal Georgi Zhukov on access to Berlin. "We did not wish to accept specific routes which might be interpreted as a denial of our right of access over all routes," General Clay has written. Instead, Clay and Weeks "accepted as a temporary arrangement" the allocation of a main highway and rail line and two air corridors, but they reserved the right to reopen the question in the Allied Control Council. "I must admit," Clay has added, "that we did not then fully realize that the requirement of unanimous consent would enable a Soviet veto in the Allied Control Council to block all our future efforts."

Although no record was kept at the meeting, Clay has written: "I dictated my notes that evening and they include the following: 'It was agreed that all traffic — air, road and rail . . . would be free from border search or control by customs or military authorities.'" At the time of this meeting, British and American troops occupied a sizable part of what became the Soviet zone. "I think now," Clay added, "that I was mistaken in not at this time making free access to Berlin a condition of our withdrawal into our occupation zone . . . However, I doubt very much if anything in writing would have done any more to prevent the events which took place than the verbal agreement which we made. The Soviet Government seems to be able to find technical reasons at will to justify the violation of understandings whether verbal or written." [4]

Roosevelt, according to his Secretary of State, had no illusions about the Russians at Yalta. He knew the difficulties of working with them. "He worked in the hope and faith that a stable world order could be achieved," Stettinius has written. "He did not have the illusion, as his enemies have charged, that world peace could be achieved easily or by appeasing the Soviet Union." Roosevelt hoped that if a world organization could be formed in which the Soviets could participate in good faith there would be a possibility of peace and Big Three unity after the war.

The Russians and the British never had Roosevelt's consuming faith in a world organization. At the Dumbarton Oaks Conference in 1944, the plans submitted by them were fragmentary compared to the detailed structure proposed by the United States. At Yalta, as a result of the President's steady insistence, the Big Three agreed to call a conference at San Francisco that April to draft the UN charter. The Russians, who had demanded sixteen votes in the UN Assembly in the Dumbarton Oaks discussions, found Roosevelt resolutely opposed. They modified their position and received three instead. Finally, after much objection, they accepted the American position on voting in the Security Council. Each of the Big Three agreed on the need of a veto by the permanent members of the proposed UN Security Council on questions involving economic and military sanctions. The United States believed, however, that the veto should not apply to cases involving the peaceful settlement of a dispute to which a big power might be a party. When the Russians at last acceded, the American delegation felt that a significant concession had been made. And Roosevelt hoped that through the United Nations injustices which had developed out of wartime military exigencies might be corrected.

At the time of the Yalta Conference, not only had Western forces not yet crossed the Rhine, but, in the Pacific, Japan was far from defeated. The struggle for the Philippines was under way and the savage battles for Iwo Jima and Okinawa lay ahead. The Chiefs of Staff insisted that the Soviet Union must help in the Far Eastern War. Even with this aid, they estimated that the war would not end until about eighteen months after the close of the European war. At the Moscow Conference in October, 1943, Stalin had told Hull that Russia would join in the Pacific war after the defeat of Germany. This statement was repeated at Tehran in December, but by this time Stalin was attaching some political "strings" to it. In October, 1944, Ambassador Harriman and General John R. Deane, American Military Attaché in Moscow, pressed for a specific commitment. Stalin made it clear that it would be three months after the defeat of Germany before his forces could take action. And Soviet participation would be contingent on the clarification of political questions. Although these demands were not spelled out in detail, the outline of what Russia desired was clear weeks before Yalta.

The Far Eastern situation was not discussed at the large formal sessions of the Big Three. While the Joint Chiefs discussed military plans with Russian officers, Roosevelt and Stalin negotiated the political questions.[5] Stalin told Roosevelt that Southern Sakhalin and the Kurile Islands must go to the Soviet Union. He also demanded Dairen at the terminus of the South Manchurian Railroad. Roosevelt replied he preferred that it be internationalized. Stalin added that the Russians wanted a long-term lease of the Manchurian railroads. Roosevelt tried to delay by saying he had not discussed this with Chiang Kai-shek. He told Stalin, however, that he favored they be leased under a joint and equal Chinese-Russian commission. Stalin replied that if his conditions were not met "it would be difficult for him and Molotov to explain to the Soviet people why Russia was entering the war against Japan."

In the conversations, Stalin agreed to American bases in Siberia and he also recognized Chiang Kai-shek as the head of China. Roosevelt, in view of the insistence by his Joint Chiefs that Russia join the war, tried to limit Russia's demands. He was aware of the danger that the Soviet Union might wait out the war, while the United States crushed Japan at a great cost in lives, only to march Soviet troops into Manchuria and North China and establish "People's Republics."

In the Far Eastern Agreement signed by Roosevelt, Stalin, and Churchill on February 11, the Soviet Union received South Sakhalin, the Kurile Islands, and the naval base of Port Arthur. Stalin agreed to Roosevelt's recommendation that the Manchurian railroads be jointly operated by a Chinese-Soviet company, the port of Dairen be internationalized, and that China retain full sovereignty over Manchuria. Although it was acknowledged that these decisions required the concurrence of Chiang Kai-shek, the Agreement stated: "The Heads of the three Great Powers have agreed that these claims of the Soviet Union shall be unquestionably fulfilled after Japan has been defeated." The Soviet Union also expressed its readiness to sign a pact of friendship and alliance with the Nationalist Government. To insure that Russia's decision to enter the war would not be released prematurely by the Nationalists, it was decided that Roosevelt would discuss the Agreement with Chiang only when the Soviet Union was ready to strike.

Soon after Yalta, the Russians refused to grant the promised bases in Siberia to American forces. In June and again in August, in discussions with Chinese officials they demanded Soviet control of the Manchurian railroads and Dairen, in violation of the agreement. They soon stripped Manchuria of its industrial resources and helped the Chinese Communists gain power. After the war, bitter controversy raged in the United States over the Far Eastern Agreement, and Roosevelt was charged with deliberately "selling out" Nationalist China to the Communists.

Stalin was in a position to drive a hard bargain in view of the insistence of the Joint Chiefs that Russian aid in the Far Eastern War was essential. Although there is some evidence that Navy and Air Force leaders believed that Russian entrance was not necessary, the Army definitely believed otherwise.

Admiral Ernest J. King has written that he and Admiral Chester W. Nimitz felt that the defeat of Japan could have been achieved by sea and air power alone, but they reluctantly acquiesced in a decision to attack the home islands. At Yalta, however, King was agreeable to the entry of the Soviet Union in the war since Russian engagement of Japanese forces in Manchuria would hasten Japan's capitulation.[6] In assessing the military advice given Roosevelt, it must be remembered that the atomic bomb was an unknown quantity in February, 1945. And Roosevelt's personal Chief of Staff, Admiral Leahy, has written that he did not have much confidence in its practicability.

When Soviet violations of the Declaration on Liberated Europe were discussed with President Truman on April 25, the military leaders then present pleaded for patience with the Soviet Union since they feared that firm action by America might be used by the Russians as an excuse to stay out of the Far Eastern War. And as late as the Potsdam Conference, after the first atomic bomb had been exploded at Los Alamos on July 16, the military continued to insist that the Soviet Union had to be brought into the war.[7]

Except for the Kurile Islands, the Soviet Union did not receive in the Far Eastern Agreement anything it could not have taken without an agreement. Russia did agree to China's retaining full sovereignty over Manchuria and to a pact of friendship with Chiang Kaishek. From mid-1943 on, Chiang had sought Soviet recognition of his government hoping thereby to deprive the Chinese Communists of Russian support. As a result, Stalin's agreement at Yalta to recognize the Nationalists as the authority in China seemed of great import to the American delegation.

There is no doubt that Roosevelt overestimated the possibilities of postwar cooperation with the Soviet Union. His hope that secure boundaries and membership in an effective world organization would end Russian aggrandizement proved unwarranted; as did his belief that the Soviet Union might need a generation to recover from the devastation of war.

At Yalta, Roosevelt and Churchill were confronted by a changed balance of power, with Russia rather than Germany dominating Central and Eastern Europe. The concessions to the Soviet Union reflected this. They could have refused to make any agreements, but this would have been a blow to Western morale at the time. Moreover, if there had not been an honest effort to work with the Russians at Yalta, it would have been difficult subsequently to rally public opinion in opposition to Russian defection from the agreements. Although they refused many Russian demands, Roosevelt and Churchill hoped by minimum concessions to win their cooperation both to speed the end of the European war by coordinating a Russian attack with the Allied spring offensive and to terminate the Japanese war early, thereby preventing huge American casualties.

Immediately following Yalta, most American and British newspapers praised its accomplishments highly. But within three years, the Conference had become a symbol of evil, a symbol to many of appeasement and of betrayal. Some critics wrote penetrating attacks on Roosevelt's injudicious optimism about future Soviet collaboration with the United States and Great Britain to underwrite a peaceful world. Other critics created myths about Yalta, either engendered by emotionalism or by shrewdly calculated political advantage. Many Americans had traditionally believed that power politics, spheres of influence and secret diplomacy were evil. As the cold war dashed hopes for a peaceful world, rather than face the realities of world politics, some of them searched for "devils." [8]

Many of the attacks stemmed from resentments and frustrations of ethnic groups in the United States. As early as February 14, 1945, Representative Alvin E. O'Konski of Wisconsin denounced the agreements on Poland as a betrayal and the Polish American Congress for years reiterated the charge. Politicians played upon the emotions of those Americans whose ancestry traced back to nations behind the Iron Curtain. In his pre-convention campaign in 1952, Senator Taft charged in Milwaukee on March 29: "No peoples have suffered more from this Administration than the Polish people. The agreements made at Yalta betrayed every interest of the Polish people as if they had never existed." And during the campaign, Republican orators dealt regularly with the theme of the liberation of people behind the Iron Curtain. Although talk of liberation frightened America's

Allies, much of it was designed to "liberate" the vote of Americans of Polish descent from the Democratic party.[9] In this it succeeded.

Attacks on the Yalta settlement became an integral part of Republican politics. Although this trend started before 1948, after the defeat of Governor Dewey it was a rising crescendo, until the 1952 Republican platform called for the repudiation of the Yalta agreements. The defeat of the Nationalist Chinese in 1949 was attributed by some Republicans to the Yalta Conference. And when Alger Hiss was convicted of perjury in 1950, the inference of a tie between Democrats and treason was drawn. Senator Dworshak of Idaho asked on the floor of the Senate (April 12, 1951): "Is it not true that the Yalta Conference is one of the few occasions when we had a display of bi-partisan policy, because, at that time, the late President represented the Democratic Party, while Alger Hiss represented the Communist Party?" To which Senator Dirksen of Illinois intoned: "That is correct."

Senator Malone and others stated emphatically that Hiss was the key figure behind the Far Eastern Agreement. The chief responsibility Hiss had at Yalta was to work on the legal aspects of the world organization. There is no evidence that he was involved in the negotiations leading to the Far Eastern Agreement, but in the emotion-charged atmosphere of 1949 and immediately after, the myth-makers remodeled history to their satisfaction and "proved" that Hiss was the master mind.[10]

After the Eisenhower Administration took office in 1953, some Republican leaders urged the publication of the Yalta discussions believing that they would embarrass the Democratic party with minority groups in the large cities. When the Department of State yielded to the pressure and published the papers in 1955, the staff of the Senate Republican Policy Committee prepared a fifty-one-page mimeographed "analysis" designed for campaign use.[11] But the publication of the official papers produced little new fuel for domestic partisanship. Nothing of importance was revealed that had not already been discussed in a number of books. By this time, the public was weary of the Yalta issue and its usefulness as a domestic political issue seemed at an end.

Intimately associated with the partisan aspect of the attacks on Yalta was the attempt to tarnish the reputation of Roosevelt. *Life*

(September 6, 1948) captioned a picture of Yalta: "High Tide of Appeasement Was Reached at Yalta Conference." Former Ambassador William C. Bullitt charged in the same issue that Roosevelt had difficulty "in formulating his thoughts, and greater difficulty in expressing them consecutively. But he still held to his determination to appease Stalin." *Time* (March 28, 1955) insisted: "From beginning to end of the Yalta record there is an almost total absence of recognition that justice is the only enduring restraint upon power, the only basis for order." [12]

The Roosevelt Administration, itself, contributed to the belief that Yalta was evil. The decision that the United States and Great Britain would support two extra votes for the Soviet Union in the United Nations Assembly was not published at the conclusion of the Conference. The President wanted to discuss it with congressional leaders, and there was some hope in the Department of State that Russia might be persuaded to withdraw the request. When this was "leaked" to the press late in March, 1945, it gave rise to the charge that there were other secret agreements. Then, when the Far Eastern Agreement was released to the newspapers, the suspicion of still further secret agreements increased. Although the publication of the Yalta records in 1955 revealed that all the agreements had been known for years, suspicion had flourished for a decade.

---

22. The Art of Presidential Leadership

The great change that had taken place in public communications was an immense asset to Roosevelt during his years in the White House. His personal talent for making the most of technological opportunities enabled him to rally support for his program in peace and war. Through the press conference and over the radio, Roosevelt established a new relationship between the President and the public. The press conferences and the fireside chats generally were relaxed, but at the same time they provided the means for a serious discussion of many issues. They enabled Roosevelt to carry on a "dialogue" with the people.

While Hoover had held only 66 press conferences, Roosevelt held 337 in his first term, 374 in his second, 279 in his third, and eight in the few weeks of his fourth. He created a New Deal for Washington correspondents, with the invaluable assistance of his press secretary, Stephen T. Early, and generally won their understanding and support although their owners were hostile. With only 40 per cent of the newspapers supporting him in 1932 and fewer and fewer in subsequent elections, Roosevelt counteracted editorial attacks by blanketing them with news stories and creating a position of affirmative leadership for himself.

At some press conferences, he was suave and amiable; at others, impatient and irritable. But over the years of his presidency, he achieved an effective relationship with the working press. Much of the success of the early New Deal and the growth of the image of Roosevelt as a leader who believed in action was the result of the steady flow of information to the Washington correspondents. They liked him. Raymond P. Brandt, Chief of the Washington bureau of the *St. Louis Post-Dispatch*, has written that Roosevelt transformed "the presidential press conference from the comatose institution he inherited from Herbert Hoover to a distinctly American device for informing the nation of what the President is contemplating and the President of what the nation is thinking." [1]

In addition to the press conference, he used radio as a direct means of reaching the whole country. "Mr. Roosevelt," Arthur Krock observed, "is the best showman the White House has lodged since modern science made possible such an effective dual performance." He capitalized upon the possibilities of radio in a way his immediate predecessor had not. By sitting before the microphones and simply saying "My Friends," he established a friendship with his listeners. There was magic in these words as Roosevelt spoke them. When he was campaigning, he would add to "My friends" the statement "You and I know . . ." and convince his listeners that they shared his insights and his prejudices. As had no previous president, he involved the common man in politics. Everybody, whether critical or adulatory, was caught up in the drama of the New Deal. Roosevelt's close associate Samuel I. Rosenman has observed that the greatest source of the President's strength was his ability to "explain to the people the most intricate problems of government. He could do it by the use of simple language and by the clear, confident, and persuasive tone of his voice."

Roosevelt's era of domestic change and war was rich in raw material for the press and radio. It became part of his job to furnish big stories frequently and small stories constantly. Roosevelt set a style. Daniel J. Boorstin has suggested that "perhaps never again would any man attain the Presidency or discharge its duties satisfactorily without entering into an intimate and conscious relation with the whole public." [2]

The personality — the voice, the expression, the gesture, the influence of the face — gained greater and greater importance during Roosevelt's day as against the formally constructed sentence, the sharpened definition, and the grandiose idea. Photographs in the press and the newsreel had begun to make the face of the President more familiar than his words even before 1930. During the next decade new inventions made indoor and candid photography much easier. No longer was the posed, stilted picture of the President the principal means of showing him to the public. In the 1930s not only tabloids but other papers, as well, gave more space to pictures. And in 1935 the Associated Press began its wirephoto service. *Life*, the spectacularly successful picture magazine, began publishing in 1936. Its circulation reached a million within a year, two million within two. *Look* appeared a year later and soon had a circulation of a million. Full-time professional news photographers now appeared and were soon at least as important as the newsreporter. The aggressive news photographer became a commonplace in the American political scene. If, by chance, one was not present at a public event, an amateur photographer was sure to be there and his work, too, found a ready market. The technological apparatus, by which literary style has become overshadowed by the personality in American politics, would be completed soon with the rapid growth of television which added the living image to the living word.

Not only did Roosevelt use the radio and the newspaper to reach the public, but his Administration watched the public response carefully. Letters to the President reached a new volume. In McKinley's time about a hundred letters a day came to the White House. Roosevelt received 450,000 in response to his First Inaugural Address. He received regular reports on this mail. Ira R. T. Smith, chief presidential mail clerk for many years, has written: "Whenever there was a decrease in the influx of letters we could expect to hear from him or one of his secretaries, who wanted to know what was the matter — was the President losing his grip on the public?"

Editorial opinion, also, was summarized for him and the President watched current trends closely. Public opinion polls developed in the New Deal decade, and, in addition, specialists in "opinion research" were hired by the government to inform the President what people favored or opposed. In addition, a wide range of people had access to the White House. The information that Roosevelt gained from them about the nation's aspirations he carefully balanced with what reached him through government sources. And there was Eleanor Roosevelt.

Mrs. Roosevelt played a far more active role than had the wife of any earlier President. She became a figure of both domestic and international significance. She undoubtedly broke more traditions than her husband. She held a weekly press conererence for newspaperwomen and many of these yielded news of the first importance. Not only did she preside over the White House with distinction and charm, but she did an amazing amount of speaking and writing. By 1940, her newspaper column "My Day" was appearing in 135 papers. She wrote a number of books, did radio programs, and conducted a question and answer page for *Woman's Home Companion*.

Gerald Johnson has remarked that she did things no President's wife "could do without disaster, yet disaster never followed." Reckless and brutal attacks on her by such writers as Westbrook Pegler made little impression. Her passionate concern for the underdog made her one of the most valuable assets of the New Deal. The dispossessed and the disinherited found their champion in Eleanor Roosevelt. Playwright and former Republican Congresswoman Clare Boothe Luce said of Mrs. Roosevelt in 1950: "Now the plain fact is, Mrs. Roosevelt has done more good deeds, on a bigger scale, for a longer time, than any woman who ever appeared on our public scene. No woman has ever so comforted the distressed — or distressed the comfortable."

When she returned from a trip, her husband questioned her closely. She seemed to be everywhere and into everything. In March,

1933, she visited the encampment of the second bonus army quite unexpectedly, had lunch with the men, who, when she left, called "Good-by and good luck to you." After that she seemed to turn up in the most unlikely places. One of the most pertinent cartoons the *New Yorker* ever carried showed a coal miner deep in the bowels of the earth, glancing over his shoulder and saying to his startled companion: "My God, here comes Mrs. Roosevelt!"

When Roosevelt entered the White House, his attitude toward the institution of the presidency, as well as his views toward public relations, differed radically from that of his immediate predecessors — Harding, Coolidge, and Hoover. Like his distant relative, Theodore, he loved the presidency. It challenged his imagination. He saw himself as not only Chief of State — the unifying symbol of the nation — and head of government, but chief legislator and head of party as well.

The presidency, he explained in 1932, was a pulpit. It was, he added, "pre-eminently a place of moral leadership. All our great Presidents were leaders of thought at times when certain historic ideas in the life of the nation had to be clarified. . . . Without leadership alert and sensitive to change," he stressed, "we are bogged up or lose our way, as we have lost it in the past decade." [3]

Roosevelt demonstrated that he was a political evangelist who could make issues vivid to the public. He proved that a powerful President, willing to use the full authority of his office, could guide, mold, and unify the nation for action. His keen sense of the public mood, his unprecedented gift of being able to appeal to millions of people enabled him to mobilize public support for most of his policies. And he knew how to focus that support on Congress. As chief legislator and head of party, he flattered, begged, and pressured reluctant Democrats to obtain support for his legislation. He was willing also to utilize such groups as the Committee to Defend America by Aiding the Allies to mobilize public support for his policies and encouraged such groups to exert pressure on Congress.

In his first term, he had a Democratic Congress that wanted a New Deal on a broader plane than he did. The majority wanted much more inflation, more benefits for veterans and farmers, larger appropriations for public works, and a more rigorous policy toward business and finance. This Congress was constantly trying to push him further to the left. But he generally outmaneuvered Congress or compromised when a clear victory was not possible.

During the first two years of his second term, his relations with Congress were strained and a number of his major proposals were defeated. But by 1939 foreign policy issues relegated domestic questions to the background. In the world crisis, Roosevelt again became chief legislator and party leader and guided the Congress and the public away from neutrality to the policy of aiding the Allies. He succeeded, with minor exceptions, from 1933 to 1945 in welding the amorphous Democratic party, with its conflicting forces, into an effective instrument for national policy. He contained the divergent forces of a vast continent and mobilized them in depression and war. By so doing, he contributed significantly to a readjustment of American attitudes toward the role of the government in the economy and toward the role of the nation in world politics.

Unlike his predecessor, Roosevelt had had a variety of political experiences which aided him in meeting the exacting requirements of the presidency. He had served in the New York State Legislature for two years before joining the Wilson Administration as Assistant Secretary of the Navy. In 1920 he was the Democratic candidate for the vice-presidency. From 1928 to 1932, as Governor of New York he was in charge of a state which contained most of the diverse forces found in the entire nation. New York was an ethnic league of nations. And, although the financial and industrial forces were most powerful there, the state had important agricultural activities as well. Since New York, like so many states, was districted in favor of the rural as against the urban population, he had to work with a Republican legislature. And his own party was torn internally between Tammany in New York City and the anti-Tammany forces of the remainder of the state. He had started in politics as a foe of Tammany. Part of his political education was to learn that, at times, he needed Tammany support. Part of Tammany's education was that they needed Roosevelt to win. Out of this came an uneasy sort of alliance typical of those a President must lead in the White House.

By the time he reached the presidency, Roosevelt knew the intricate machinery of politics and government. He knew the deftness required to make the system function, not smoothly always, but in spite of delays function for the greater good. An "artful dodger" — so he was described by playwright Robert E. Sherwood. And it was true that Roosevelt consistently maneuvered to escape commitment to doubtful political positions even when this involved questions of loyalty and consistency. He knew how to compromise, to proceed slowly, often even deviously, but he also knew when to be daring.

His was not an elaborate economic or political philosophy. His lack of commitment to any rigid doctrine made it possible for him to move fast in a crisis. As President, he borrowed ideas from the past, from planners like Tugwell and Berle, from advocates of trust-busting and of government spending to revive purchasing power, and, for a short time, at least, from those who advocated retrenchment in government. Always he let his mind range. He liked politicians as well as people outside the party machinery and could work with both. He brought into the federal government new men — lawyers, professors, social workers, politicians — with varying ideas, with exciting plans and dreams. From all of them he derived rich inspiration.

Roosevelt's death on April 12, 1945, stunned the nation and the Allied world. Men and women wept openly as they watched the funeral train roll north from Warm Springs to Washington for a simple service in the East Room of the White House and then continue its journey to Hyde Park. Senator George Aiken of Vermont remarked: "The world can ill afford to lose him at this time." And Winston Churchill said he was "the greatest American friend we have ever known, and the greatest champion of freedom who has ever brought help and comfort from the new world to the old. . . . It is a loss, indeed a bitter loss to humanity that these heartbeats are stilled forever."

President Truman proclaimed April 14, the day of the funeral, a day of mourning and said: "His fellow countrymen will sorely miss his fortitude and faith and courage in the time to come. The peoples of the earth who love the ways of freedom and hope will mourn him." A young Congressman observed: "He was the only person I ever knew — anywhere — who was never afraid. God, how he could take it for us all." And an army private spoke for his generation:

"America will seem a strange, empty place without his voice talking to the people whenever great events occur."

Less than a week after Roosevelt's death, Carl Carmer put into verse the intimacy that the President established with the people:

> . . . I never saw him —
> But I *knew* him. Can you have forgotten
> How, with his voice, he came into our house,
> The President of the United States,
> Calling us friends. . . .[4]

For the first time in American history, the President had been a voice from kitchen tables, the living room, and the counters of lunchrooms and bars. And his skill in projecting himself and his ideas of presidential leadership created the fixed idea in the minds of friend and foe alike that the New Deal was a far more rigid, comprehensive program than it actually was.

Foreign observers of American society frequently have remarked that the mass public is a deadening influence incapable of meeting a crisis, and a force opposed to enlightened progress. The pressing circumstances from 1933 to 1945 and Roosevelt's artistry in leadership generally turned this "weakness" into a positive strength. A happy coincidence of personal qualities and technological opportunities rallied the public to meet the challenges of depression and war.

BOOK FIVE

Price of Survival: Truman

23. Ushering in the New Age

Although the American delegation left the Yalta Conference feeling that the Big Three would work together to secure a lasting peace, disillusionment quickly set in. By the time Roosevelt spoke to Congress on March 1, 1945, the Yalta agreements were being contravened. The Russians postponed granting military bases to the United States; they forced a puppet government on Rumania; and they delayed the reorganization of the Lublin government. Roosevelt cabled Stalin on April 1 that merely enlarging the Lublin government could not be reconciled with the Yalta agreement. And the day he died he sent a message to Churchill on the Polish question and closed with the words: "We must be firm, however, and our course thus far is correct."

After Germany surrendered in May, the rift in the Grand Alliance continued to grow. At the San Francisco Conference, the American and Soviet delegations wrangled over many questions and the disruption of the Conference was averted only by an appeal from Truman to Stalin. Truman sent Harry Hopkins to Moscow in May to join Ambassador Harriman in frank talks with Stalin. In the conversations, Stalin at last agreed to admit non-Communist Poles to the Polish government and to meet with Truman and Churchill at Potsdam in mid-July to discuss outstanding problems.

This conference marked the last meeting of the leaders of the Grand Alliance. They agreed to establish a Council of Foreign Ministers to prepare peace treaties for Italy and the Balkan nations,[1] and issued a declaration calling for the immediate surrender of

Japan. Reluctantly, the Americans and British accepted Polish occupation and administration of conquered German territory east of
the Neisse River until a peace conference could settle the western
boundary of Poland. Agreement was reached on the disarming and
demilitarization of Germany, the elimination or control of German
industrial potential for war, denazification measures, the punishment of war criminals, and the reorganization of the judicial and
educational systems. These decisions reflected the necessity of doing
something with the defeated enemy rather than any accord over
long-range German policy.

The basic Soviet demand at Potsdam was for unconditional recognition of the Soviet-dominated governments in Hungary, Rumania, and Bulgaria. Truman refused and declared that no recognition was possible until free governments were established "without
pressure from beyond their borders." Stalin's response was blunt:
"any free elected government would be anti-Soviet and that we cannot permit."

The location of military forces at the close of the war was the decisive factor in the divergent fates of Eastern and Western Europe.
Philip E. Mosely has written: "The strategy of coalition called for
the assignment of military 'spheres of responsibility,' and these, as
the Cassandras of the State Department warned over and over, were
likely to harden into postwar 'spheres of influence' and into competition and conflict between them . . . By the end of 1946, against
unyielding Soviet insistence on transforming East Central Europe
into a closed preserve, the American government had a heap of
broken Soviet promises to point to as a reminder that hope, divorced
from power, is not a policy." [2]

When Truman returned, Potsdam had already faded into the
background. At breakfast time on August 6, a B-29 roared over
Hiroshima and dropped an atomic bomb. One plane with one bomb
destroyed more than a raid of two thousand B-29s. The new bomb,
with a destructive power equivalent to twenty thousand tons of
dynamite, killed between seventy and eighty thousand people and a
hundred thousand more were injured. Three days later a second
atomic bomb was dropped on Nagasaki. On August 14, the Japanese surrendered.

Before the dropping of the bomb on Hiroshima, the Japanese Cabinet had been planning to surrender but could not persuade the Army leaders to agree. They still balked on August 11, but the Emperor insisted and issued an Imperial Rescript ordering the armed forces to surrender. Months before this action, peace feelers had been emanating from Japan.

On May 28, 1945, after the great devastation of Tokyo by B-29 attacks, Acting Secretary of State Joseph C. Grew discussed the peace feelers with Truman. "The greatest obstacle to unconditional surrender by the Japanese," he told Truman, "is their belief that this would entail the destruction or permanent removal of the Emperor and the institution of the Throne. If some indication can now be given the Japanese that they themselves, when once thoroughly defeated . . . will be permitted to determine their own future political structure, they will be afforded a method of saving face without which surrender will be highly unlikely."

Truman expressed his interest in the suggestion but asked Grew to discuss it with the Secretaries of War and Navy and the Chiefs of Staff. These leaders considered it inadvisable at that moment to pursue the question. The bloody fighting in Okinawa was still going on, and the military leaders feared that such a declaration by the President would be interpreted in Japan as a confession of weakness. As a result, Grew's proposal was, for the time being, dropped. "If surrender could have been brought about in May, 1945," Grew has written, "or even in June or July, before the entrance of Soviet Russia into the war and the use of the atomic bomb, the world would have been the gainer."[3]

A few days after the dropping of the atomic bomb, a Japanese official standing in the rubble of Hiroshima said:

All this from one bomb; it is unendurable.

And a number of scientists at the University of Chicago, who had been instrumental in the development of the new bomb, pointed out that in a relatively short time many nations would be able to accumulate large stocks of atomic bombs. Then they warned:

Even though our population and our industry are dispersed to a large number of small towns, enough bombs probably can be made, sooner or later, to destroy a large fraction of even such small towns. Enough bombs may, in fact, be accumulated to lay waste a significant fraction of the land area of this country.

---

24.   Man of Great Decisions

The postwar decade was crammed with anxiety, recurring crises, rapid and complicated change. For its own survival, the nation abandoned its separateness and became the leader of the Atlantic Community. Any belief that the nation was not part of the Atlantic Community was shaken in 1947 when President Truman assumed the British role as defender of Turkey and Greece against Russian expansion and in 1948 when economic aid was extended under the Marshall Plan. The old aloofness perished when he took the lead in forming the North Atlantic Treaty Organization.

Never before had Americans been asked to do so many things at variance with their traditions. They accepted economic responsibilities far outside their previous scope. Americans who had resented any suggestion of European interference in the Western Hemisphere engaged actively in planning for European unity. They established military bases around the globe and fought a limited war in Korea to check Communist aggression. As a result, their taxes assumed new proportions; the machinery of government was greatly expanded; and military expenditures claimed an unprecedented proportion of the national income. Little wonder that many Americans adrift from their secure past turned angrily on their leaders.

Relationships in the postwar world were strangely altered. The Atlantic and Pacific Oceans that had once seemed insurmountable barriers against aggression suddenly became avenues of hostile approach, the once friendly sky a medium in which danger lurked. No longer could Americans view with detachment events in Iran, Vietnam, and India. The assumption that with postwar recovery in Western Europe the Atlantic Community would be the world's power center was invalidated by the emergence of a bipolar system with power concentrated in Moscow and Washington. Stalin created a new Russian empire, making satellites of the nations of Eastern Europe; while the United States took the initiative in attempting to contain further Soviet expansion.

In Asia, the Middle East, and Africa the revolution against colonialism brought the disintegration of old empires, sapping the strength of once-powerful European nations. Many of the new nations remained uncommitted in the bipolar struggle. With their anti-Western feeling, their demand for a better way of life, and their insistence on being recognized as equals by white Westerners, the uncommitted nations added a new dimension to world politics.

A revolution in technology was another factor that shaped the postwar world. Until 1949, the atomic monopoly of the United States was a deterrent to the Red Army's overrunning Western Europe. When the Soviet Union developed a bomb that year, an alarming race in nuclear weapons was launched. The explosion of a terrifying hydrogen bomb by the United States in 1952 and one by the Soviet Union the next year accelerated the race in nuclear weapons. The ramifications of this struggle for nuclear mastery shook the world power structure, straining the alliances on both sides of the Iron Curtain.

The new relationships in the postwar decade forced rapid adjustments in American attitudes. Those who resisted adapting argued that the Western Hemisphere could still be a fortress, that America could maintain its separateness, that the nation need not be concerned with the views of its allies. They were still imbued with the belief in America's omnipotence and moral superiority. Among their spokesmen were Herbert Hoover, Senators Robert A. Taft and William Knowland. But their irritability and belligerence indicated that they, too, had doubts that America was as singular as it once had been.

A smaller but equally vocal group of citizens insisted that the new age demanded world government. Twelve days after the dropping of the bomb on Japan, Norman Cousins's "Modern Man Is Obsolete" was published in the *Saturday Review of Literature*. A group headed by Chancellor Robert M. Hutchins of the University of Chicago drafted a constitution for world federalism and published a journal, *Common Cause*. They warned that the choices lay between world government and world catastrophe. Some apologized for American prosperity, contending that it separated the nation from the fraternity of man.

As the decade advanced, government policy and public opinion felt a new influence. It emanated from writers who reinterpreted America's history as the development of the western frontier of the Atlantic Community and called for careful diplomacy as the surest pursuit of the national interest. Walter Lippmann's *U. S. Foreign Policy: Shield of the Republic* (1943) was a vigorous attempt at such a reinterpretation. George F. Kennan, diplomat and historian, admonished:

> If you say that mistakes of the past were unavoidable because of our domestic predilections and habits of thought, you are saying that what stopped us from being more effective than we were was democracy as practiced in this country. And, if that is true, let us recognize it and measure the full seriousness of it — and find something to do about it. A nation which excuses its own failures by the sacred untouchableness of its own habits can excuse itself into complete disaster.[1]

And America's intoxication with moral abstractions came under attack from Professor Hans J. Morgenthau. "The illusion that a nation can escape, if only it wants to, from power politics into a realm where action is guided by moral principles rather than by considerations of power . . . is deeply rooted in the American mind," he charged. During the early years of the republic, he observed, there were leaders who understood the realities of power politics. It was a fruitful period for Americans to restudy before moral abstractions came to influence attitudes toward the world. "The choice," he declared, "is not between moral principles and the national interest, devoid of moral dignity, but between one set of moral principles, divorced from reality, and another set of moral principles, derived from political reality." [2] These writers and others sought to focus attention on our need to recognize that world politics and power politics were synonymous and that peace should be pursued through accommodation and flexibility. Increasingly during the postwar decade, beginning with the adoption of the Truman Doctrine, the dominant elements in both the Democratic and Republican parties advocated some of the realism of this position.

The months between the close of the war and the Truman Doctrine were months of uncertainty and lack of clear direction in
foreign policy. The President's sudden termination of lend-lease aid
at the end of the war had a nearly disastrous impact on the Western
Allies when their need of financial assistance was acute. And the
wartime alliance was further imperiled when military coordination between Britain and America was allowed to lapse. Meanwhile, the
Soviet Union consolidated its hold on Eastern Europe, encouraged
political sabotage by Communist parties in France, Czechoslovakia,
and Italy, supported civil war in Greece and China, exerted pressure
on Turkey and Iran.

Truman's policy toward Russia gradually stiffened and, as it did,
the alliance with Western Europe was rebuilt. He told Secretary of
State Byrnes on January 5, 1946: "I'm tired of babying the Soviets."
Russian demands were resisted by an increasingly firm policy in-
cluding the insistence that Soviet troops withdraw from Iran.[3] In
1946, however, Truman had not yet abandoned hope for the unity
of the three great powers. Meanwhile, two other positions crystal-
lized. At the urging of the President, Winston Churchill spoke at
Fulton, Missouri, on March 5, and challenged the concept that the
United Nations had to function on the basis of great power unity.
Instead, he advocated the organization of free nations to confront
Soviet power. Unless the non-Communist nations led by the United
States organized a bloc, revolutionary Communism would expand,
he insisted:

> From Stettin in the Baltic to Trieste in the Adriatic, an iron
> curtain has descended across the continent . . . In front of the
> iron curtain which lies across Europe are other causes for anx-
> iety . . . Communist fifth columns are established and work in
> complete unity and absolute obedience to the directions they re-
> ceive from the Communist center . . . the Communist parties or
> fifth columns constitute a growing challenge and peril to Christian
> civilizations . . . I do not believe that Soviet Russia desires war.
> What they desire is the fruits of war and the indefinite expansion
> of their power and doctrines . . . From what I have seen of our
> Russian friends and allies during the war, I am convinced that
> there is nothing they admire so much as strength, and there is
> nothing for which they have less respect than for military weak-
> ness.

Some Congressmen and newspapers expressed concern that Church-ill's idea would wreck the UN, destroy the unity of the Big Three, and precipitate a war.[4]

Some leaders not only denounced Churchill's recommendations, but they also assailed Truman's policy of firmness. A member of his own Cabinet, Henry A. Wallace, declared on September 12 that America was not trying to meet Russia halfway. "Enemies of yester-day and false friends of today continually try to provoke war be-tween the United States and Russia . . ." he charged. "Russia must be convinced that we are not planning for war against her and we must be certain that Russia is not carrying on territorial expansion or world domination through native communists." He added ex-temporaneously: "I realize that the danger of war is much less from Communism than it is from imperialism." [5]

The reaction in the country and abroad was violent. What policy was the United States following, that proposed by Wallace or by Byrnes? The Secretary of State, in Paris negotiating with the Rus-sians, sent a message saying that the American position toward the Russians was being undermined at the conference table by such divided counsels. If the President was not clear in his own mind that a cabinet member should refrain from criticizing foreign policy, Byrnes warned that he would have to resign. And Senator Vanden-berg, who had been working closely with Byrnes at Paris, said: "We can only cooperate with one Secretary of State at a time."

On September 20, 1946, Truman ousted Wallace from the Cabinet. At the presidential press conference, on the afternoon before Wal-lace's speech was delivered, a reporter with an advance copy quoted Wallace as saying: 'When President Truman read these words he said that they represented the policy of his administration." That is correct, Truman replied to the reporter. When another reporter asked if the speech did not represent a departure from Byrnes's policy, Truman said the two were right in line. At a special press conference following the speech, Truman allowed no questions. He remarked that he had meant only to approve Wallace's right to express his opinion, not the actual opinions themselves. In 1955, Truman stated he had not read Wallace's speech. Wallace has stated that he and the President went over it page by page. Whatever the truth of the mat-ter, the incident indicated that Truman, as yet, was not in full control of his Administration. But his subsequent firing of Wallace suggested that he was taking hold and demonstrating the courage needed in the office.

In February, 1946, months before Wallace left the cabinet, George Kennan, then second in command at the American Embassy in Moscow, expressed his thoughts on Soviet policies in a lengthy dispatch to Washington. He wrote: "The Kremlin's neurotic view of world affairs is the traditional and instinctive Russian sense of insecurity. . . . Russian rulers . . . have learned to seek security only in patient but deadly struggle for the total destruction of rival power, never in compacts or compromises with it." While the Soviet rulers were expressing centuries-old Russian nationalism, equipped with the apparatus of international Communism, that movement had become "more dangerous and insidious than ever before." He warned that they would try to disrupt and paralyze the West. The problem of coping with Soviet power, Kennan added, was the greatest task our diplomacy had ever faced. The first step was to recognize the Soviet for "what it is" and the second was to tell the American public the truth about it. "I am convinced that there would be far less hysterical anti-Sovietism in our country today if realities of this situation were better understood by our people."

By the close of 1946, continued Russian pressure on Turkey and Greece helped mold a new policy. At a cabinet meeting on September 25, 1946, a State Department paper advocating aid to friendly countries, including Greece and Turkey, was endorsed. Then in February, 1947, the hard-pressed British government notified Washington that it would be unable to continue further economic and military aid to Greece and Turkey. If Greece fell to the Communists, the Soviet could penetrate into the Eastern Mediterranean and the Middle East.

The Truman Administration moved quickly. Congressional leaders were called to the White House. Some Republican leaders in the Eightieth Congress were visibly unhappy as Secretary of State George C. Marshall explained the need of economic aid but he insisted that the choice was "between acting with energy or losing by default." As the meeting broke up, Vandenberg said: "Mr. President, if that's what you want, there's only one way to get it. That is to make a personal appearance before Congress and scare hell out of the country."

On March 12, Truman told Congress:

> . . . it must be the policy of the United States to support free peoples who are resisting attempted subjugation by armed minorities or by outside pressures . . . we cannot allow changes in the *status quo* in violation of the Charter of the United Nations by such methods as coercion, or by such subterfuges as political infiltration.

He proposed $400,000,000 in economic and military aid for Greece and Turkey and proclaimed American policy for the next decade: "The seeds of totalitarian regimes are nurtured by misery and want . . . They reach their full growth when the hope of a people for a better life has died. We must keep that hope alive. If we falter . . . we may endanger the peace of the world — and we shall surely endanger the welfare of our own Nation."

In the public discussion that followed, it became clear that there was wide support for the Truman Doctrine. Vandenberg told newspapermen after the speech: "The President's message faces facts and so must Congress . . . In such a critical moment the President's hand must be upheld . . . We must either take or surrender leadership." To allay fears that such action would destroy the UN, the Senator drafted a new preamble for the bill bringing the aid program "as far as possible within the United Nations," pointing out that the UN had recognized the seriousness of the Greek situation but was "not now in a position to furnish" the aid required. He and Tom Connally, minority leader of the Senate Foreign Relations Committee, also inserted in the bill a statement permitting the UN Assembly or Security Council to terminate the American program whenever "action taken or assistance furnished by the United Nations makes the continuance of such assistance unnecessary or undesirable." [6]

Attacks on the bill came from the two extremes in Congress. Senators Pepper and Taylor argued the aid should go through the UN, and they denounced direct American aid as bailing out a decadent monarch and British imperialism. Right-wing Republican Senators, including Kenneth S. Wherry, C. Wayland Brooks, and George W.

Malone, predicted that the program would lead to war or bankrupt the nation. But the moderates prevailed, and the Senate in April by a vote of 67 to 23 and the House in May by a margin of 287 to 107 approved the Truman Doctrine.

While Congress debated the Truman Doctrine, the economic situation in Western Europe, shaky since the war, began to deteriorate badly. Winston Churchill said of Europe on May 14: "It is a rubble-heap, a charnel house, a breeding-ground of pestilence and hate." Newspapermen, government officials, and Congressmen who visited Europe warned that France and Italy were seriously threatened by an internal Communist threat. Dean Acheson, in a forewarning of what was needed, said in Mississippi on May 7: "Since world demand exceeds our ability to supply, we are going to have to concentrate our emergency assistance in areas where it will be most effective in building world political and economic stability, in promoting human freedom and democratic institutions."

Secretary Marshall turned to his Policy Planning Staff for recommendations. George Kennan, who had been brought home from Russia to head this Staff, was disturbed over certain weaknesses in the Truman Doctrine: chiefly, its truculence, its defensive reaction to Communism, its indiscriminate offer of aid to any nation opposing the Soviets. The Policy Planning Staff, rejecting both war and the indefinite expansion of Communism as acceptable policies, recommended the containment of the Soviet Union. The approach, they felt, should not be primarily military nor merely anti-Communistic. The emphasis should be on economic aid to create healthy societies. But such aid, they advised, could only be effective to nations desiring to stay non-Communist and willing to help improve their own economies.

They recommended to Marshall a massive American aid program for all of Europe with no ideological distinctions. When fear was expressed that the Soviet Union might join the program, Kennan argued that it was the best way to demonstrate that the program was not mere anti-Communism. In addition, it would force the Soviet Union either to decline to help or agree to make a real contribution to the revival of Europe.

To win support for the new policy among leaders of public opinion, Kennan published an article, "The Sources of Soviet Conduct," in the July issue of *Foreign Affairs*. Although he used the pseudonym Mr. X, it quickly became known that the author was Kennan. The article reflected many of the views expressed in his dispatch of February, 1946, and the discussions in the Policy Planning Staff leading to the Marshall Plan. He cautioned that America would find the Russians hard to deal with for a long time and that the basis of policy toward the Soviet Union must be "a long-term, patient but firm and vigilant containment of Russian expansive tendencies." American blustering, he predicted, would only place Russia in a position where "it cannot afford to yield even though this might be dictated by its sense of realism." To deal with Russia, "demands on Russian policy should be put forward in such a manner as to leave the way open for a compliance not too detrimental to Russian prestige." Soviet pressure against free institutions could "be contained by the adroit and vigilant application of counter-force at a series of constantly shifting geographical and political points, corresponding to the shifts and maneuvers of Soviet policy," he added.

The United States, he wrote, was not limited to merely holding the line against Soviet expansion, but could influence developments within Russia and throughout the international Communist movement by creating "among the peoples of the world generally the impression of a country which knows what it wants, which is coping successfully with the problems of its internal life and with the responsibilities of a World Power, and which has a spiritual vitality capable of holding its own among the major ideological currents of the time." But, he insisted, "exhibitions of indecision, disunity and internal disintegration" in the United States "have an exhilarating effect on the whole Communist movement."

Secretary Marshall, speaking at the Harvard Commencement exercises in June, 1947, said that if European nations would plan their recovery in common, they would receive speedy help from the United States. To counteract charges at home and abroad that American aid would split the world into two camps, Marshall added: "Our policy is directed not against any country or doctrine but against hunger, poverty, desperation, and chaos. Its purpose should be the revival of a working economy in the world so as to permit the emergence of political and social conditions in which free institutions can exist."

At a conference of Great Britain, France, and the Soviet Union on June 27, the Russians made it clear that they would not join in the program. By so doing, they simplified the Administration's task in securing congressional approval. The Soviet satellites, too, rejected invitations to a general conference in July attended by sixteen Western European countries. After a series of studies these nations recommended that twenty-nine billion dollars was necessary over a four-year period. Meanwhile, the Administration had appointed a nonpartisan Advisory Council, headed by Averell Harriman, to study the question. In December, President Truman asked Congress to appropriate seventeen billion dollars over a four-year period.

A Committee for the Marshall Plan was formed, with Henry L. Stimson as its National Chairman, to mobilize public support for the President's proposal. Local chapters were organized in many parts of the country, and Congress received a steady flow of petitions urging favorable action. Despite growing popular support, the Marshall Plan was presented to a Republican-controlled Congress dedicated to reducing taxes and government spending. Vandenberg had to make the widest use of his highly developed parliamentary skill.

He listened to advice from all sides and proposed amendment after amendment to silence opponents and win doubtful votes. He suggested, with the agreement of the Administration, that instead of asking for seventeen billions and arousing the opposition of the economy bloc, five billions be appropriated the first year with the statement that it was the intent of Congress to appropriate further sums yearly. To counteract congressional criticism that China was being neglected, Vandenberg persuaded Truman to recommend some 463 million dollars for economic and military aid outside of the Marshall Plan.[7]

To forestall opposition to the State Department's administering the program, he suggested an independent agency with an administrator of cabinet rank. Then, late in February, 1948, the leaders of the Kremlin aided Vandenberg in his work with Congress when the Communists seized control of the government of Czechoslovakia.

By March 1, when Vandenberg spoke to a crowded Senate, he knew the bill would pass, but wanted the largest majority possible. The legislation, he told the Senate,

> . . . seeks peace and stability for free men in a free world. It seeks them by economic rather than by military means. . . . It aims to preserve the victory against aggression and dictatorship which we thought we won in World War II. It strives to help stop World War III before it starts. It fights economic chaos which would precipitate far-flung disintegration. . . . It recognizes the grim truth whether we like it or not — that American self-interest, national economy, and national security are inseparably linked with these objectives.

A Taft amendment to slash a billion dollars was defeated 56 to 31. On March 14, the Senate approved the legislation 69 to 17. Soon Truman, on Vandenberg's recommendation, appointed Republican Paul G. Hoffman, President of the Studebaker Corporation, director of the Marshall Plan. The cooperation between the Administration and Senator Vandenberg was based on a mutual respect of high order — a type of respect essential for a bipartisan foreign policy to succeed. The President and his former Senate colleague were leading the nation into uncharted paths. Vandenberg successfully persuaded more and more Republicans to meet the challenge of the new era. Late in 1949, however, Vandenberg underwent a serious operation. No longer was he able to carry the burden of leadership. His illness unhappily coincided with "disunity and internal disintegration" which threatened a stable foreign policy and led to the breakdown of bipartisanship.

Russian aggression, which remolded American attitudes during 1946-1948, also had a major impact on European leaders. Faced with the overwhelming might of the Red Army, Great Britain, France, Belgium, the Netherlands, and Luxembourg signed the Brussels Pact in March, 1948, pledging economic, social, and cultural cooperation and collective self-defense. Without participation by the United States, however, it was a frail alliance. In April, at a White House Conference attended by Vandenberg, agreement was reached on the need of a North Atlantic regional pact. Vandenberg and Under Secretary of State Robert A. Lovett collaborated closely in the drafting of the proposal for submission to the Senate.

In May, 1948, Vandenberg introduced his resolution urging the Administration to proceed to the "Progressive development of regional and other collective arrangements for individual and collective self-defense in accordance with the purposes, principles, and provisions of the Charter." [8] It passed the Senate 64 to 6 on July 11 after the rejection of an amendment by Claude Pepper to strike out all references to possible American military aid.

While this resolution was being discussed by the Senate Foreign Relations Committee, the Soviet Union intensified the cold war by halting all overland traffic from Western Germany to Berlin. For the Allies to withdraw from Berlin would have been an immense victory for the Russians with catastrophic implication of uncontrollable Soviet aggression. Truman rejected both the idea of withdrawal and the suggestion that the Army fight its way to Berlin. Instead, he resolved to supply goods to Western Berlin by air, thus leaving to the Russians the decision for peace or war. From June, 1948, to May, 1949, when the Soviet leaders admitted defeat and ended the blockade, the Royal Air Force and the U. S. Air Force performed a remarkable feat in supplying the city. The airlift in addition encouraged free nations to resist Soviet threats.

The Soviet blockade had the effect of enlarging the Senate majority supporting the North Atlantic Treaty. It was ratified on July 21, 1949, by a vote of 82 to 13. Eleven of the negative votes were cast by Republicans. "I get so damned sick of that little band of GOP isolationists," Vandenberg wrote that July.

The inclusion in the treaty of the statement that an attack against one nation was an attack against all the member nations indicated how far the United States had moved from the neutrality legislation of the previous decade. And, although it was affirmed that such a regional alliance was "in accordance with the purpose of the Charter of the United Nations," the economic aid program and the North Atlantic Treaty Organization had now become the primary instruments of American foreign policy and the UN a subordinate instrument. In October, 1949, the North Atlantic Treaty was implemented by the passage of the Mutual Defense Assistance Act with an initial appropriation of a billion and a half dollars for aiding the European nations to rebuild their military establishments.

Congress, in the preamble to the Act, endorsed the extension of containment through "the creation by the free countries and free peoples of the Far East of a joint organization, consistent with the Charter of the United Nations, to establish a program of self-help and mutual cooperation designed to develop their economic and social well-being, to safeguard basic rights and liberties and to protect their security and independence." But this proposal ran into determined opposition in Asia. Such new nations as India, Indonesia, Burma, and Ceylon refused to join the bipolar system. Instead, they preferred to be a third force in world politics uncommitted to either side in the power struggle.

They were willing, however, to accept economic aid provided it did not involve them in alliances with the West. In January, 1949, Truman proposed as a fourth point in American policy that the nation should "embark on a bold program for making the benefits of our scientific advances and industrial progress available for the improvement and growth of underdeveloped areas." "Democracy alone," he added, "can supply the vitalizing force to stir the peoples of the world into triumphant action, not only against their human oppressors, but also against their ancient enemies — hunger, misery, and despair." Labeled immediately the Point Four Program, it was approved by Congress in 1950. Although in financial terms it was never as comprehensive a program as circumstances warranted, Point Four technicians performed valuable services in a number of underdeveloped countries.

---

25. Climax in the Far East

By 1950, the Truman Doctrine, the Marshall Plan, the Berlin airlift, and the North Atlantic Treaty Organization indicated success in containing Soviet power in Europe. But in Asia, the Chinese Communists had succeeded in overrunning the mainland and the remnants of Chiang Kai-shek's forces had fled to Formosa.

All during World War II, the United States alone had considered China a major power. To achieve this, the Administration encouraged formation of a unified China. By early 1945, there was a wide division among American policymakers as to method. Patrick J. Hurley, Ambassador to China, and General A. C. Wedemeyer, commander of American forces in China and Chiang's Chief of Staff, favored working closely with Chiang. Many foreign service experts in China, however, believed that the Nationalist government was hopelessly corrupt and inefficient, without any popular base. These diplomats felt the Communists would prevail because they were more representative of the Chinese people. They appealed to Washington over Hurley's head to force Chiang to come to terms with the Communists, or, if he refused, to support the Communists. In March, 1945, however, Roosevelt endorsed Hurley's position.

By late 1945, American policymakers faced the possibilities of using American military force to support Chiang; of withdrawing entirely; or of trying to halt the war by mediation. The first alternative was precluded by the rapid demobilization of American armed forces and public opposition to participation in the civil war. The second ran counter to the concept of building China as a great power to fill the vacuum created by the defeat of Japan. This left only the hope of mediation, although there was always doubt that this could be successful.

General Marshall was sent to China in December, 1945, to press for a truce and to help establish a coalition government. He was directed to tell Chiang that American aid would be withheld if he did not seek agreement with the Communists. The Communists were to be warned that if they were not reasonable, America would aid Chiang. But, in addition, Marshall was told that the United States would continue to aid Chiang even though the Nationalists were not conciliatory. After months of fruitless negotiations, Marshall abandoned the mission in January, 1947.

That summer General Wedemeyer reported to the Administration that there was danger of Communist success and warned that this would imperil American interests in the Far East. He advised against working for a coalition government and recommended that effective American aid go to Chiang provided the Nationalists initiated basic political, economic, and military reforms. But this recommendation was rejected by State Department experts since Chiang continued to resist reforming his government. Instead they now favored a non-intervention policy in China.

A crisis in policy had been reached, but neither Congress nor the public was informed about it. At the very time that formation of European policy involved close congressional participation, Far Eastern experts in the Department of State deliberately avoided seeking congressional support — either Democratic or Republican — for their China policy; as did Truman. Gradually, Republican criticism of failure to aid the Nationalists became more outspoken, particularly from Congressman Walter Judd, once a medical missionary to China. William Bullitt's "A Report to the American People on China," *Life*, October 13, 1947, was a powerful indictment of the Administration's policy and a demand for increased aid to Chiang.

Congress, in 1948, adopted a program of economic and military aid for Chiang. This was the compromise developed by Vandenberg and others to widen Senate support for the European Recovery Program among those who were opposed to it unless China also received aid. But the Truman Administration delayed action on aid to China, thereby losing the opportunity to demonstrate the futility of such an aid program to a rootless, inefficient, and corrupt government. And Truman's failure gave Republicans the political ammunition to charge that they had tried to save China but had been sabotaged by the Democratic Administration.[1]

After Chiang fled to Formosa in 1949, the Department of State defended its policy in a White Paper. Secretary of State Dean Acheson observed in his summary letter to it:

> The unfortunate but inescapable fact is that the ominous result of the civil war in China was beyond the control of the government of the United States. Nothing that this country did or could have done within the reasonable limits of its capabilities could have changed that result; nothing that was left undone by this country contributed to it. It was the product of internal Chinese forces, forces which this country tried to influence but could not. A decision was arrived at within China, if only a decision by default.[2]

Now the Administration tried to fight loose from entanglements with Chiang. On December 19, 1949, the Department of State sent out a paper to its missions advising them to minimize the importance of Formosa since its fall "is widely anticipated." On January 3, 1950, this paper was "leaked" to the press by General MacArthur's command in Tokyo. The previous day, Herbert Hoover had advocated American naval defense of Formosa, a position endorsed by Senator Taft. But on January 5 the President announced that we would not provide military aid for Formosa.

The China issue now inflamed partisanship and reduced the Administration's flexibility in the Far East. By 1950, Chiang had become an integral part of American politics. And although the Truman Administration wanted to adopt a non-intervention policy toward Formosa, it was never in a political position to do so since Chiang's powerful supporters in Congress could block or delay economic aid elsewhere unless Formosa were included.

Under bitter personal attack for his role in China policy, Acheson defended the Administration before the National Press Club in January, 1950. In his speech, he described the American defense perimeter in the Pacific as running from the Aleutians to Japan, to Okinawa, and to the Philippines. If any of these points were attacked, the United States would defend them, but it could not defend Korea and Formosa. If an attack occurred there, Acheson added, ". . . the initial reliance must be on the people attacked to resist it and then upon the commitments of the entire civilized world under the Charter of the United Nations which so far has not proved a weak reed to lean on by any people who are determined to protect their independence against outside aggression."

When the North Korean Communists attacked the Republic of South Korea on June 25, the United Nations Security Council met in an emergency session. Since, at the time, the Soviet Union was boycotting the Security Council because of its refusal to seat Communist China, the Council by a unanimous vote denounced the invasion of South Korea as an act of aggression and demanded the withdrawal of North Korean troops. Later that afternoon Truman ordered General MacArthur in Japan to furnish the South Koreans with arms and limited air support.

On the morning of June 27, the President called congressional leaders of both parties to the White House to tell them that he was determined to resist the invasion and that he would attempt to rally the UN to a collective effort. That afternoon the Security Council adopted an American-sponsored resolution calling upon all members to render assistance to South Korea. Truman wrote later:

> If the Communists were permitted to force their way into the Republic of Korea without opposition from the free world, no small nation would have the courage to resist threats and aggression by stronger Communist neighbors. If this was allowed to go unchallenged it would mean a third world war, just as similar incidents had brought on the second world war. It was also clear to me that the foundations and the principles of the United Nations were at stake unless this unprovoked attack on Korea could be stopped.[3]

The first response to Truman's action was exultant. Although a few Senators grumbled that Truman should have requested congressional approval, Knowland stated: "I believe that in the very important steps the President of the United States has taken to uphold the hands of the United Nations and the free people of the world, he should have the overwhelming support of all Americans regardless of their party affiliation."

The Korean struggle led to an extensive rebuilding of American military power which had declined seriously under Truman's Secretary of Defense Louis Johnson. It also brought a shift in emphasis from economic aid to the building of the military strength of free nations, the rearming of Western Germany, and the extension of defensive alliances. The United States, acting unilaterally, began discussions with Spain concerning military bases. On August 30, 1951, we signed a Mutual Defense Treaty with the Philippines and two days later a Tripartite Security Treaty with Australia and New Zealand (ANZUS). On September 8, the Japanese Peace Treaty was signed at San Francisco and the same day a Security Treaty was signed granting us the right to maintain land, sea, and air bases in Japan. And in March, 1952, Greece and Turkey became members of NATO.

The Korean conflict also forced the Administration to abandon its hoped-for policy of non-intervention in Formosa. Strategic consideration required the coupling of the defense of Korea with the defense of Formosa. And the need of harmony between the Ad-

ministration and Congress to prosecute the Korean war forced concessions to American supporters of Chiang.

---

26.   The American Image Overseas

"America has saved the world," Winston Churchill remarked in
1953. The nation discovered in the process that a great power was
seldom loved by others. It learned, too, that in addition to economic
and military rivalry, it was engaged in a struggle with the Soviet
Union for the minds of men. Among its allies and the uncommitted
nations, it discovered strange misconceptions of the United States
and seeds of misunderstanding and tension.

Throughout Western Europe, Asia, and the Middle East, there
was widespread comprehension of the commanding role the United
States had assumed in world decisions. At the same time there was
doubt that America possessed the wisdom to lead the free world and
anxiety lest American power be misused. The degree to which
anti-Communist feeling developed in the United States made leaders
in Europe and Asia fear that Americans would become disposed to
accept war with the Soviet Union as inevitable. All through the postwar years, the European allies felt there was still opportunity for
negotiation and they exerted considerable pressure on American
policymakers to achieve it.

Government leaders and the intellectual elite of Europe and Asia
also feared that the American political system was unstable. The
separation of powers between the executive and Congress seemed
frightening to those nurtured on the parliamentary system. They
were never comfortable when a congressional member of the President's party advocated a policy that differed from that of the Administration. And foreign leaders were apprehensive that the dependence of American politicians on a highly diverse electorate might
lead to the formulation of foreign policy not on the basis of an objective appraisal of the world situation but on the basis of con-
ciliating a bloc of voters.

The extent to which Americans boasted of being a capitalist

country dedicated to free enterprise sometimes prompted European and Asian liberals and socialists to charge that the United States was dominated by "reactionary Wall Street warmongers." Left-wing Socialists in Britain asked in 1946: "Must Europe . . . become Wall Street's colony . . . Is Washington, by economics and diplomacy, trying to convert all of the continent except Russia into an area for capitalist exploitation?" [1] There was little understanding of the vast social changes that had transformed America since 1933 and brought a redistribution of power and wealth. And, as European nations underwent painful adjustment to a secondary position in world politics, their dissatisfaction over the wealth and power concentrated in America led them to voice sharp criticism of "American materialism."

Although the status of the American Negro was improving rapidly, racial discrimination was a useful lever for Soviet propaganda against American democracy. Among non-Communists everywhere, but particularly in Asia, the Middle East, and Africa, the position of the American Negro was an important factor in raising doubts about American intentions. And the dropping of the atomic bombs on Japan was interpreted as further evidence of America's low regard for people of color.

Beginning in 1950, "McCarthyism" became a new word in the language of the world as the hysteria over Communism permitted Senator McCarthy to disgrace the nation. Although in retrospect it is now clear that the danger of McCarthy's destroying the Bill of Rights was exaggerated, his activities had a nearly disastrous effect on American diplomacy. And excessive restrictions in the McCarran Internal Security Act of 1950, passed over Truman's veto, which barred many foreign visitors, were taken as evidence that America was afraid of foreign influences. "These things represent a real loss of strength," one Italian journalist noted. "Europeans must not get the idea that American civilization upon which they base so much of their hope for the future, is introverted, calculating, narrow and obtuse, with no antennae for capturing ideas other than its own." [2]

Economic as well as political trends were watched closely. A mild recession in 1949, affecting America only slightly, led to a drastic fall in European imports and a devaluation of currencies. Any American tendency toward restricting imports was frightening to these nations. They needed trade not only with the United States but with the Communist bloc as well, and American security restrictions on such trade created much friction.

Even more complex than our relations with our Allies was the establishment of mutual understanding between America and the new nations. In Asia they were bitterly resentful of any remnants of Western imperialism. They denounced American military support of Chiang Kai-shek as naked colonialism and contended that America's blocking Communist Chinese membership in the United Nations was an affront to the new Asia. Our European Allies, it might be added, were also uneasy over America's identification with Chiang, seeing it as an alarming reaction to domestic politics. Asian nations were highly critical of American support to France while it held Indo-China and North Africa in its colonial empire. And they resented Western decisions affecting Asia made without consulting the countries concerned. Many of the new nations preferred to remain uncommitted in the power struggle and devote their resources to improving their standards of living. They were puzzled that, of all people, Americans who had remained neutral in the nineteenth century while developing their resources should be unsympathetic.

The countries of Asia, although weak economically and militarily, were proud of their ancient cultures and, with reason, were irate at arrogant propaganda about making the world over in the American image. Although there was gratitude both in Europe and Asia for economic aid, there was also suspicion of the panacea of American "know-how," since the American experience of transforming a virgin wilderness was unique. These countries, unlike America, had to overcome historic feudal traditions, a lack of social mobility, and pressure of population on resources. Since the American development was not analogous, Chester Bowles, after his experience as Ambassador to India, advised that the results of American aid "cannot be immediate, and we will experience only frustrations and bitterness if we fall prey to premature expectations." [3]

"Americans naturally tend to rely on their old experiences," an Italian journalist remarked in 1953. "The temptation is always with them to rush into whatever there is to be done, do it, and get it over with. Who will tell them the flames will never be extinguished and they will never go to bed." Then he asked: "Can the Americans make the shift from the psychology of the emergency, which is what their historical experience has taught them, to the psychology of the long pull?" [4]

Although both the Truman and Eisenhower Administrations presented their annual foreign aid requests to Congress in the spirit of emergency programs, thus implying their early demise, by December, 1955, the Secretary of State admitted: "I think it's a fair inference that we consider that both the economic aid and the military aid will need to go on for a considerable period of time at about the present level." The appointment of committees by both the President and Congress in 1956 to develop long-range plans indicated an adjustment was under way to the "psychology of the long pull." And in 1957 Congress chartered the Development Loan Fund to lend money to the less developed countries for specific projects designed to stimulate economic activity.

As never before in American history, it became vital to the national security to understand the minds of people in other societies and to have American aspirations and problems understood by others. No longer could the President be concerned solely with domestic pressures and reactions to American foreign policy.

The government entered into new activities in world propaganda and programs of cultural and educational exchange. The United States Information Agency beamed shortwave broadcasts on the Voice of America to the nations behind the Iron Curtain and to some free nations. The United States Information Service established American libraries in many countries with newspapers, periodicals, and books about America and by Americans. They showed documentary films and made available records of American classical, jazz, and folk music. They offered classes in English and provided lectures on various phases of American life. Foreign tours by ballet companies, jazz orchestras, and theatrical companies were also underwritten by the government.

With the compelling need for greater international understanding, Senator J. W. Fulbright of Arkansas in 1946 persuaded Congress to adopt an educational exchange program. He said: "The necessity for increasing our understanding of others and their understanding of us has an urgency that it has never had in the past. The adoption of this program by the Congress is a vital counterpart of the steps we are taking to increase our participation in world affairs." While the mass media — radio, television, newspapers, magazines, and motion pictures — all had a role in communicating aspects of American life to other nations, the exchange program hoped to create through the direct effect of people on people a deeper and more accurate understanding.

Under the Fulbright Program, from 1948 to 1955, over twelve thousand foreign students, teachers, and professors from twenty-eight countries came to the United States and over nine thousand Americans went abroad. In addition, Congress in 1948 adopted the Smith-Mundt Program extending the exchange of persons to some forty-two countries not covered by the Fulbright Program.[5] Under these two programs nearly forty thousand grants were made to Americans and foreign nationals between 1950 and 1955. In addition to educators, the Smith-Mundt Program made grants to newspapermen, labor leaders, civil servants of foreign governments, and members of foreign legislatures. Meanwhile, the Marshall Plan and later the Mutual Security Program brought businessmen, labor leaders, and technicians to the United States. At the same time, American universities and colleges, private foundations, such organizations as Rotary International, the American Association of University Women, and foreign governments were carrying on their own programs of exchange. As a result of all types of exchanges, nearly forty thousand foreign students were studying in the United States in 1957.

The Fulbright Program pioneered the government's exchange activities and quickly achieved respect among educators at home and abroad. It represented a characteristic American merger of government and private activity. While the Department of State's International Educational Exchange Service administered the program and did valuable work in over-all planning, policy was set and grants awarded by the Board of Foreign Scholarships appointed by the President, eight of whose ten members were educators. The Board relied on private agencies to screen applicants. These agencies in turn had the assistance of thousands of American educators in the screening process.

As the fact became known overseas that American educators — rather than government personnel — were influential in selecting American grantees, the prestige of the program increased and attacks on it as a propaganda weapon were reduced. The Department of State wisely made provisions for bi-national commissions consisting of citizens of the country and Americans resident there, including Embassy personnel. Leading educators and high government officials generally became members of these commissions. The presence of such prominent citizens on the commissions also weakened considerably the charge that the program was "cultural imperialism." [6]

To create better understanding of the United States, the Fulbright Program stimulated the study of American history, literature, and government in foreign educational institutions by sending them American lecturers and bringing their foreign colleagues to America to specialize in these subjects. In addition, conferences on American studies, headed by American scholars, were conducted with foreign scholars and students in many countries. And the teaching of English and linguistic studies were supported in a number of Asian countries.

Under the Fulbright Act it was possible to award grants to foreign nationals to attend American schools abroad. Nearly three thousand foreign students attended these schools, primarily in Greece and the Middle East. The American Farm School at Salonika trained young men for leadership in the villages, and the other American schools, including Athens, Anatolia, and Pierce Colleges, trained Greeks for business and the professions.

Although educational and cultural programs were overshadowed by the Truman Doctrine, the Marshall Plan, NATO, and the action in Korea, they were a constructive contribution by Congress to formation of foreign policy. Designed to meet the challenge of world leadership on the educational and cultural level, they were a recognition by Congress and Truman and Eisenhower that such activities were vital in maintaining the Allied coalition and achieving a more healthy and frank relationship with the uncommitted nations.

BOOK SIX

Failures of Leadership: Truman

27.   The Surprising Victory

A prominent Democrat, who had been in official Washington since 1913, once said: "Harry Truman, of all the Presidents I have known, could do the big things in the biggest way and the little things in the littlest way."

Truman had to assume office without the advantage of having been kept abreast of major developments or having been privy to Roosevelt's thoughts. He brought to the White House a devotion to work, unquestioned integrity, a fierce courage, a broad sympathy for the underdog, and a capacity to grow. At the same time he was a willful, bumptious partisan, given to rash outbursts which weakened his effectiveness as chief of state and exposed him to a mounting attack, particularly after 1948. In public he referred to a Washington correspondent as an "S.O.B."; he called the Hiss case a "red herring"; and he wrote a critic of daughter Margaret's singing, "I never met you. But if I do you'll need a new nose and plenty of beefsteak."

Truman lacked artistry in public relations. When he spoke, his gestures were as awkward as a penguin's waddle and his flat Midwestern twang jarred radio loudspeakers. He lacked, Alistair Cooke has remarked, "musicianship, of knowing when to pause, when to paragraph, when to go slow and easy, and when to lift into the big sentences." Handicapped by constant comparison with Roosevelt, he could say firmly and accurately: "It is awfully easy to 'demagogue' in favor of economy and against what is scornfully referred to as 'foreign aid,'" but he could not furnish the inspired leadership which convinced the public he was leading a just cause. And in the critical days after the collapse of Chiang Kai-shek and intervention in Korea, he was unable to explain Administration policies convincingly enough to lift the public out of its confusion.

While he drew many able and distinguished men into the Cabinet, the federal agencies, and the diplomatic service, he trusted too much in some of his intimate friends, among them General Harry Vaughan. He did not move quickly when some aides accepted mink coats and deep freezers from those seeking favors. Nevertheless, he grew in the presidency. And, by 1947, in foreign policy, the most important issue facing the nation, he began to provide constructive leadership. As he did, Washington correspondents reported that Truman was "becoming President of the United States."

But during his first year or so, he felt inadequate and failed to meet the challenge of being chief of state, party leader, and chief legislator. When complaints reached him, he flippantly remarked that he had not asked to be Vice-President and he had not asked to be President. "Washington has begun to turn against him," John Chamberlain wrote in *Life*, November 26, 1945. ". . . Harry Truman betrayed himself. Instead of fighting back, he began to complain before various audiences that he had never asked to be President and that everyone ought to pitch in and help him. This was the worst thing that Truman could have done, for pressure groups, like wolves, respond to any sign of weakness or hesitancy by closing in for the kill."

In these months, everybody seemed to be talking of reconversion, of shifting the nation back to a peacetime footing. The armed services were rapidly demobilized. Labor leaders advocated continuation of price controls but the ending of wage controls; businessmen clamored for free enterprise, meaning no price controls but ceilings on wages; farm leaders insisted that the purchasing power of the farmer be kept high. Although prewar tensions between New Dealers and anti-New Dealers came to the fore again, it was more significant that most conservatives agreed with liberals that the federal government had the responsibility for economic stabilization and a high level of employment. The editors of *Fortune* remarked: "The 1947 portrait shows that the trend toward minimizing individual financial risk and toward the belief that the government should assume responsibility for its citizens in time of need is found among all classes of society. And oddly enough, the greatest percentage-wise change in these attitudes is shown by the prosperous." [1] The Employment Act, adopted by Congress in February, 1946, affirmed the government's responsibility for prosperity and created a Council of Economic Advisers to advise the President and Congress on means of promoting economic welfare.

Despite such constructive legislation and the civilian control of atomic energy established in the Atomic Energy Act of August, 1946, to most people 1946 was a disagreeable year. Attacking price controls as socialistic, the conservative majority in Congress passed an impotent bill extending the OPA for one year but ordering it to decontrol prices "as rapidly as possible." Truman vetoed the bill and price control ended on July 1. Immediately, the country was swept by severe inflation. Late that month Congress passed a new price control law, but it was too feeble to stop skyrocketing prices or black market activities. Most irritating was the shortage of meat. To break the price ceilings on meat, cattle producers refused to ship beef to the slaughterhouses. "This was bad for the Democrats," David L. Cohn has written. "For as everybody knows, a housewife who cannot get hamburger is more dangerous than Medea wronged." [2]

And then there were the strikes. The United Automobile Workers shut down General Motors for weeks. And on April 11, John L. Lewis pulled his soft coal miners out of the pits. Within a month the economy began to slow down and the steel industry banked its fires. After forty days the strike was settled, but now a national railroad strike threatened.[3] Truman seized the railroads on May 17 and offered a compromise settlement, but the unions refused it and walked off the job. In an angry mood, Truman went before Congress and requested that he be empowered to declare a state of national emergency under which workers continuing to strike would lose employment and seniority benefits and be drafted into the Army. Just as he concluded his speech, the strike was settled.

Strikes, shortages, rising prices, and the black market were, per-haps, enough in themselves to defeat the Democrats that November. But, in addition, conservatives were hostile to Truman's request for an extension of Social Security, increases in the minimum wage and public housing, and a national health insurance program. At the same time, ardent New Dealers were disgruntled at the way Roosevelt appointees were leaving the government. On February 12, 1946, Harold L. Ickes resigned as Secretary of the Interior with a belligerent public letter denouncing the President for recommending the appointment of Edwin Pauley, California oil producer, as Under Secretary of the Navy.

When Ickes suggested his resignation become effective March 31, the President made it effective February 15. Washington, wrote the reporters, "has seldom seen such a sharp exchange between a cabinet member and his President." After the Democratic defeat in November, Ickes denounced Truman for collecting "a nondescript band of political Lilliputians" around him — including Robert E. Hannegan, George E. Allen, John W. Snyder, Harry Vaughan, Matthew J. Connelly, and Pauley. And, added Ickes, progressives felt that the Republicans could do no worse and voted accordingly. Truman must announce, concluded Ickes, that he would not be a candidate in 1948.[4]

Truman's firing of Henry A. Wallace in September, 1946, only increased the indignation of the New Deal wing. His adherents charged that Truman was trying to scrap the New Deal. Actually, Truman was advocating its extension, but he was doing it without the assistance of the political architects of the past decade.

As Hoover had discovered, the President became the butt of the people's anger when things went wrong. By November, 1946, Harry S. Truman was a mighty unpopular man. "Had Enough?" — liberally sprinkled in Republican speeches — produced torrents of affirmative response. And, in addition, the Democrats were denounced for being soft toward both the Soviet Union and Communists at home, and for being dominated by organized labor. Congressman O'Konski, speaking to a meeting of Polish-American voters, charged: "In this campaign there is no Democratic party as such. It has been taken over by the stooges of Moscow whose only interest is in the destruction of America . . . We are witnessing the abominable tragedy of Moscow playing the music to which the New Dealers dance." [5]

The Republicans captured both houses of Congress for the first time in eighteen years. The most powerful Republicans in Congress were men who, never having accepted the New Deal revolution, interpreted their victory as a mandate to undo it. Senator Styles Bridges, an authentic American Tory, hailed the election results as a repudiation of the Roosevelt-Truman policies. A conference of Republican congressional leaders proposed a slash of ten billion dollars from the budget, lower taxes, "abandonment of the philosophy of Government interference with business and labor," and the return to state and local governments of the "primary authority for the administration of housing, health, and social welfare programs."

Taft, the leader of the party on domestic issues in the Eightieth Congress, while insisting on budget cuts and tax reduction, favored retaining more of the New Deal measures than Congressman John Taber, Chairman of the Appropriations Committee; Congressman Jesse Wolcott, Chairman of the Banking and Currency Committee; Senator Kenneth Wherry, majority whip; and Bridges, Chairman of the Appropriations Committee. Nevertheless, during these years, Taft became the symbol of extreme conservatism and isolationism. His following included those old-stock Americans who had not taken well to the new power of the unions and the minorities in the big cities. Although he was not as dogmatically conservative as most of his supporters pictured him, nor to the degree the Democrats and his Republican opponents, including Governor Dewey, encouraged the public to believe, his forthright exposition of his views made him appear so.

He made a virtue of being forthright rather than devious, candid rather than ingratiating. He viewed tact as a kind of dishonesty. While this was refreshing, he could be direct to the point of political ineptness. When asked what the public should do about soaring meat prices, he said: "Eat less."

World politics irritated Taft. He called himself a nationalist and became the hero of those who mourned the departure of pre-1914 America. Eric Sevareid has said of Taft:

> Many people who disagreed with Taft's most basic policies still voted for him, out of an instinctive feeling that even for them it was important to have such a man in the Senate. The feeling, I

think, was this: they saw government grow vast and involve their lives deeply; they saw their country plunging into new and strange enterprises in a desperate attempt to control a world in revolutionary turmoil. They did not really know how things could otherwise be done, but they were a little frightened, and to them Senator Taft seemed a kind of safety device, a brake; and intuitively they wanted him there as an anchor to windward.[6]

The leadership of the congressional Republican party misinterpreted the meaning of the 1946 election. A low vote was cast — thirty-four millions — reflecting general discontent with the lack of leadership from Truman and irritation over shortages, strikes, and inflation. It meant that Democrats did not bother to vote; not that they voted Republican.[7] Shortages disappeared in 1947, strikes declined, and the hesitant Truman was replaced by the forceful Truman, whose policy of containment checked uneasiness over Democratic "softness" to the Russians.

But, presuming their election indicated public dissatisfaction with the New Deal, Republican Congressmen attacked the reforms of the depression decade in full battle array. The Taft-Hartley Act was passed over Truman's veto. It allowed the union shop but outlawed the closed shop; employers could petition the National Labor Relations Board for elections to determine bargaining agents and to speak out during organizational campaigns; it provided for "cooling-off" periods and the presidential use of the injunction in strikes imperiling the national security; it prohibited contributions from union dues to political campaigns and it required non-Communist affidavits from union leaders before unions could avail themselves of NLRB procedures.

Although it was not the "slave labor act" pictured by labor leaders and Truman and unions continued to prosper after it was passed, it did mobilize the A. F. of L., CIO, and the railroad unions behind the Democrats in 1948. The leaders of the railroad brotherhoods had announced their determination to defeat Truman after his speech at the time of the 1946 railway strike, but by passing the Taft-Hartley Act the Eightieth Congress drove them to the Democrats.

Appropriations for soil conservation and crop storage were slashed; price supports at 90 per cent of parity were maintained to 1949, but after that they were to be flexible, ranging from 60 to 90 per cent of parity. And Congress refused to allocate funds for public housing, extend Social Security, pass an anti-lynching bill, eliminate the poll tax, establish a permanent Fair Employment Practices Commission, or furnish aid to education.[8] It refused the President the anti-inflation program he requested. The tax bill, passed over his veto, favored the high income groups. T. R. B. commented in the *New Republic*: "This Congress brought back an atmosphere you had forgotten or never thought possible . . . Victories fought and won years ago were suddenly in doubt. Everything was debatable again."

As the Republicans assembled to nominate a presidential candidate in 1948, they presumed they were in fact nominating the next President. They passed over Taft again to renominate Governor Dewey after General Eisenhower had refused to run. "I am not available for and could not accept the nomination," Eisenhower said. ". . . The necessary and wise subordination of the military to civil power will be best sustained when life-long professional soldiers abstain from seeking high political office."

The brief platform pledged a fight against inflation, monopoly, and government waste. It advocated federal aid to housing and farm prices, increased Social Security, the passage of laws establishing fair employment practices, and the outlawing of the poll tax.

Republican faith in victory was increased by the apparent disintegration of the Democrats. Extreme left-wingers had organized the Progressive party around Henry A. Wallace. And when Hubert Humphrey led a successful floor fight at the Convention to insert a strong plank on civil rights, thirty-five Southern delegates waved Confederate flags and walked out. Meanwhile, big city bosses, including Jacob A. Arvey of Chicago and Frank Hague of Jersey City, and some labor leaders, fearing certain defeat if Truman were nominated, tried to draft Eisenhower. Americans for Democratic Action urged the President to retire to Independence, Missouri. But Truman was adamant. The Convention, unable to do anything else and expecting certain defeat, reluctantly nominated the President and his chosen running-mate, Alben Barkley.

At two in the morning, Truman spoke to the dispirited delegates in a confident tone. "Senator Barkley and I will win this election," he cried. "The Republican party . . . favors the privileged few and not the common every-day man. Ever since its inception that party has been under the control of special privilege; and they have completely proved it in the 80th Congress. They proved it by the things they did *to* the people and not for them." Then the President ended his acceptance speech with a surprising statement: "On the twenty-sixth day of July, which out in Missouri they call Turnip Day, I'm going to call that Congress back." The plan, he explained, was to ask "that Congress" to pass the laws advocated in the Republican platform.

When he spoke to Congress, he insisted on "strong, positive" action against inflation, aid to education and housing, expansion of Social Security and increase in the minimum wage, civil rights legislation, a health insurance program, and a long-range farm program. But, after doing as little as possible, the Republican leaders adjourned Congress.

Immediately after the Democratic Convention, "Dixiecrats" met at Birmingham and nominated Governor Strom Thurmond of South Carolina and Governor Fielding Wright of Mississippi as the candidates of the States' Rights Democratic party. And on July 22 the Progressive party, controlled by Communists and fellow travelers, nominated Wallace and Senator Glen Taylor of Idaho on a platform calling for gradual nationalization of basic industries and a change in foreign policy from containment to friendship with the Soviet Union.

Amidst the confusion in Democratic ranks, the Dewey "Victory Special" journeyed calmly and efficiently across the nation with the candidate exuding confidence. He expressed not anger but sadness over Truman's limitations: "We know the kind of government we have now," Dewey said in sorrow. "It's tired. It's confused. It's coming apart at the seams . . . It cannot give this nation what it needs most — what is the real issue of this election — unity." The country, he explained, had been very patient with what he called "the Administration which happens to be in power at the moment." Near the close of the campaign, the Dewey staff expressed concern over the damage Truman might do between election day and January 20, which led a reporter to ask: "How long is Dewey going to tolerate Truman's interference in the government?"

While the smugness of Dewey's campaign cost him some votes, the outcome of the election was shaped by Harry S. Truman. The President campaigned with an intense appeal directed to normally Democratic groups, many of whom had not voted in 1946. He traversed the country using a shrill tone and the most bellicose language heard in a presidential campaign in the twentieth century.

Truman concentrated on one subject, the Eightieth Congress. "The record of the 80th Congress," Truman harangued in his Missouri twang, "is a sad tale of the sell-out of the people's interest to put more and more power in the hands of fewer and fewer men. . . . The Republican 80th Congress repeatedly flouted the will of the people. And yet the Republican candidate has the gall to say: 'The 80th Congress delivered as no other Congress ever did for the future of our country.' " Then he punched home his point:

> I'll say it delivered. It delivered for the private power lobby. It delivered for the big oil company lobby. It delivered for the railroad lobby. It delivered for the real estate lobby. That's what the Republican candidate calls delivering for the future. Is that the kind of future you want?

In urban areas Truman asked: "Do you want to carry the Taft-Hartley law to its full implication and enslave totally the working-man, white collar and union man alike, or do you want to go forward with an administration whose interest is the welfare of the common man?" In farm areas, Truman charged: ". . . they have already stuck a pitchfork in the backs of the farmers by cutting down on funds for crop storage . . . I warn you, that's their real attitude. First the little cuts, then all price supports would be thrown out." To first- and second-generation voters, he denounced the refusal of Congress to admit displaced persons and he flayed the "anti-Semitic, anti-Catholic" immigration bill it had passed. Emphasizing the pressing necessity of civil rights legislation, he was the first major party candidate to stump Harlem.

As election day approached, public opinion polls, newspapers, and magazines all inflated Dewey's confidence. *Life*, the week before election, carried his picture, the "next President," on its cover. On election night, the *Chicago Tribune* printed an eight-column headline: "DEWEY DEFEATS TRUMAN."

Truman, however, went to bed early, serene in his expectation of victory. The early returns were Democratic. Radio commentators, led by their excitable "Dean," H. V. Kaltenborn, explained that this was to be expected, but wait until the rural returns came in. As midnight passed, these returns revealed slim Dewey majorities or Truman victories in such states as Iowa. Although the President lost Alabama, South Carolina, Mississippi, and Louisiana to Thurmond, the rest of the South and a sizable bloc of Western and Midwestern states were his. By dawn, the electoral vote of New York, California, or Ohio would put him across. At breakfast time, Ohio went for Truman by a margin of seven thousand votes.[9]

"I just don't know what happened," George Gallup explained over the radio. Public opinion polls, in fact, had failed to catch a swing to Truman in the closing days of the campaign. He shrewdly took advantage of the political ineptness of Republican congressional leaders and, by his campaign, rallied some neutrals and Democrats, shaky in their allegiance, by convincing them that the Republicans could not be trusted to continue the social and economic reforms of the New Deal. Many German- and Irish-Americans, who had shifted to the Republicans in 1940 and 1944 because of foreign policy issues, now returned to the Democrats on the basis of the economic appeal of the New Deal. And Truman's speedy recognition of the new state of Israel in the spring of 1948 had increased Jewish loyalties to the Democrats.

The campaign of Barkley, too, was a factor in the victory. He concentrated on stimulating party workers to action. And in a number of states, candidates with a high voting appeal on the tickets strengthened Truman. In Illinois, Adlai E. Stevenson won the Governorship by a majority of 572,000; Paul H. Douglas won the Senatorship by just over 400,000, while Truman squeaked through to victory by a margin of 33,000 votes.

The rebellion of the two extreme wings of the Democratic coalition abetted, rather than jeopardized, Truman's victory. He and the National Democratic party were freed of the albatross of Southern reactionaries, and this enhanced the President's appeal to Negroes and other voters in the Northern cities. Chicago's Negroes cast approximately 71 per cent of their vote for Truman and the percentage was slightly higher in other Northern cities. And, at the same time, although votes for Wallace threw New York, Maryland, and Michigan into the Republican column, the existence of the Progressive party made the Democrats less vulnerable to the allegation of left-wing domination.

"I don't care how the thing is explained. It defies all common sense for the country to send that roughneck ward politician back to the White House," Taft announced after Truman's victory. Reluctantly, Republicans could accept defeat at the hands of Franklin D. Roosevelt, a gentleman even though he had "betrayed" his class, but defeat at the hands of "Give 'em hell, Harry" was too much.

---

28.   Politics of Revenge

After recovering from the initial shock of Dewey's defeat, many Republicans sought revenge. This desire for revenge, capitalizing on the anxieties of living in an atomic age and the aggravations of having to deal with world problems that could not be shelved, created a virulent public mood during the next three years.

Tensions over Truman's Fair Deal domestic program merged with tensions arising from the Cold War. Spurred by Republican campaign charges in 1946 that he was too lenient toward Communists, and by revelations of a Royal Commission in Canada that Soviet spy rings were in operation there, the President early in 1947 had ordered an investigation of all federal employees.[1] The probe, however, did not quiet the public alarm and two cases in 1949 increased the concern over Soviet espionage. Judith Coplon, a Department of Justice employee, was arrested for passing information about the FBI's counterespionage system to a Soviet agent. But of far greater impact was the Hiss case.

In August, 1948, *Time* editor Whittaker Chambers, a confessed former Communist spy, charged before the House Committee on Un-American Activities that Alger Hiss, a former official of the Department of State and now President of the Carnegie Endowment for International Peace, had been a member of the Communist party between 1934 and 1938. Hiss appeared before the Committee, confronted Chambers, and denied the charge. Then he instituted a libel suit against Chambers. At this point, Truman blundered, increasing the fear that he was not alert to the Communist menace, by telling his press conference that such investigations were a "red herring" to distract the public from the failures of the Eightieth Congress.

Late in 1948, Chambers re-examined his memory and expanded his charge. Hiss had been a member of a Soviet spy ring in the 1930s and had passed confidential documents to Chambers for transmittal to the Russians.[2] Chambers produced copies of secret documents, some of which he alleged were in Hiss's handwriting, while others, he said, were typed on a machine belonging to Hiss. Hiss was accused now, not only of belonging to the Communist party during the depression, a not uncommon affiliation of young intellectuals in that period, but of betraying his country.

Truman stubbornly stuck to his story: the investigation was still a "red herring" and the Committee was just seeking headlines. On December 15, 1948, a New York grand jury indicted Hiss on a charge of perjury for saying that he had not passed on "numerous secret, confidential and restricted documents" and for denying that he had seen Chambers after January 1, 1937. Although the statute of limitations prevented Hiss from being indicted for espionage, the public knew what the indictments meant. The first trial began in May, 1949, but the jury could not agree. The second trial began in November and Hiss was found guilty in January, 1950.

The Hiss case crowded out all other conversation, and Hiss the individual was transformed into Hiss the symbol. An increasing number of people, disturbed over the social changes of the New Deal and holding the Democrats responsible for the crisis with the Soviet Union, made Hiss the representative of the New Deal and Fair Deal eras. To many, Hiss illustrated that Democrats were susceptible to treason. On the other hand, those who felt that Democratic domestic and foreign policies were eminently wise also turned Hiss into "a representation of the Roosevelt-Truman years and pictured the achievements of that era as now under assault from dark reactionary forces. For both these groups, the Hiss symbolism provoked fierce, blinding emotions." [3]

Four days after Hiss's conviction, Secretary of State Acheson, a friend of Hiss and a member of the same law firm as Hiss's brother, was asked if he had any comment on the case. He refused to discuss the legal aspects of the trials but said: "I should like to make it clear to you that, whatever the outcome of any appeal which Mr. Hiss or his lawyers may take in this case, I do not intend to turn my back on Alger Hiss." His conduct would be determined, he explained, by the twenty-fifth chapter of Matthew, starting with verse thirty-four where Christ explained to his followers that the man who turned his back on anyone in trouble also turned his back on Him. The Secretary's position, while courageous and Christian, was politically unwise. It was deliberately misconstrued in the tense, feverish atmosphere of the time and seized upon as additional proof that the Truman Administration underestimated the Communist threat.

The Hiss trials coincided with the collapse of Chiang Kai-shek and the announcement in September, 1949, that the Soviet Union had exploded an atomic bomb. On January 31, 1950, ten days after the conviction of Hiss, the President revealed that the nation was working on the deadly hydrogen bomb. Albert Einstein appeared on television and warned that "radioactive poisoning of the atmosphere and, hence, annihilation of any life on earth has been brought within the range of technical possibilities. . . . General annihilation beckons."

Then, four days later, the British arrested Klaus Fuchs — an atomic scientist who had been sent to Los Alamos in 1944 to help make the atom bomb — for turning over to Soviet agents secret information from 1943 to 1947. "How much more are we going to have to take?" Senator Homer Capehart raged on the floor of the Senate. "Fuchs and Acheson and Hiss and hydrogen bombs threatening outside and New Dealism eating away the vitals of the nation. In the name of Heaven, is this the best America can do?"

On February 9, 1950, Senator Joseph McCarthy spoke to the Republican women of West Virginia. He explained all the difficulties in one sentence: "The reason we find ourselves in a position of impotency is not because our only powerful potential enemy has sent men to invade our shores, but rather because of the traitorous actions of those who have been treated so well by this nation. . . . In my opinion," he added, "the State Department . . . is thoroughly infested with Communists." Acheson, that "pompous diplomat in striped-pants, with a phony British accent," is the most dangerous person in the Department, McCarthy charged.

Reporters present insisted that McCarthy said he had a list of two hundred and five Communists in the State Department. The Senator spoke from notes and later could not find even these. On February 10, at Salt Lake City, he charged there were "57 card-carrying members of the Communist party" in the State Department.

Newspapers headlined the charges, Acheson denied them, and a Senate Committee headed by Millard Tydings investigated. On March 27, Senator Bridges asserted: "The spies of communism in our Government had laid their lines deep, and they are still effective. The wreckage of our diplomatic and military efforts in Europe and Asia is no accident. Stalin is not a superman. He had help from inside our ranks. . . . We must find the master spy, the servant of Russia who moved the puppets . . . in and out of office in this Capital of the United States, using them and using our State Department as he wills." Bridges closed by announcing that the first battle to win the Cold War "must be won in our own Department of State."

Unable to point out any Communists then in the State Department, in a lengthy speech on March 30, McCarthy shifted his attack. Professor Owen Lattimore was "the top Russian espionage" agent in the United States and a man who had long been "one of the top advisers on Far Eastern policy." "He is undoubtedly the most brilliant and scholarly of all the Communist propagandists," McCarthy accused, "and also the most subtle of the evangelists who have deceived the American people about the Chinese Communists." Amidst all the furor created by McCarthy's charge, the fact became obscured that the Department of State had consulted Lattimore only infrequently during the Truman Administration and generally had ignored his advice.

In addition, the speech contained a blistering attack on the Institute of Pacific Relations, diplomat John S. Service, and Professor Philip Jessup, serving as Ambassador-at-Large to the United Nations, who had helped prepare the State Department's White Paper on China. Although McCarthy's accusation in West Virginia had not mentioned China, the Senator explained on March 30 that the important thing to be determined was "to what extent our far eastern policy has paralleled the Communist party objectives." [4]

The atmosphere of the Senate, one reporter wrote:

> . . . is something to remember. No one who sees this show will ever underestimate young Mr. McCarthy again. He is the most formidable figure to hit the Senate, we think, since Huey Long. He has the galleries with him. The Republicans around him beam. Taft and Bridges exchange enthusiastic smiles as he side-steps hostile questions again and again . . . It would seem easy to pin down the preposterous utterances, but no; McCarthy is as hard to catch as a mist — a mist that carries lethal contagion.[5]

John Duncan Miller described the situation in *The Times* of London as a revolt of the primitives against the intelligent in the complexities of foreign affairs. And several Washington correspondents reported that Taft remarked: "McCarthy should keep talking and if one case doesn't work out he should proceed with another." Taft immediately protested that this statement misrepresented him. After the Korean intervention, Taft said that Truman had the bad judgment to "assume the innocence of all the persons mentioned in the State Department. Whether Senator McCarthy has legal evidence, whether he has overstated or understated his case, is of lesser importance. The question is whether Communist influence in the State Department still exists." [6]

On April 5, 1950, Knowland, although carefully avoiding McCarthy's accusation that Lattimore was a spy, charged: "Yet consistently and insistently Owen Lattimore has played an important part in the undermining of the Republic of China. He has done it in his writings, and in such positions as he has occupied as would permit him to help influence public opinion on United States policy."

After weeks of listening to the charges of conspiracy, Margaret Chase Smith delivered a Declaration of Conscience to the Senate on June 1. She criticized confusion arising from the lack of effective leadership from the White House, of its "complacency to the threat of communism here at home," and of "its petty bitterness against its critics." But she stated: "Certain elements of the Republican party have materially added to this confusion in the hopes of riding the Republican party to victory through the selfish political exploitation of fear, bigotry, ignorance, and intolerance." [7]

On July 17, the Democratic majority on the Tydings Committee submitted its report rebuking McCarthy for making unsubstantiated, distorted charges. McCarthy had no list of Communists in the State Department and "there is not one member of the Communist party or of a 'spy ring' employed in the State Department known to the Secretary of State or other responsible officials of that department." The allegations against Philip C. Jessup were "completely unfounded and unjustified," the report added.[8]

Owen Lattimore was not an employee of the State Department, he was not the "architect of our Far Eastern policy," nor was there evidence to support the charge that he was the "top Russian spy" or any sort of spy.[9] While John S. Service was indiscreet in supplying classified information to *Amerasia*, this was not sufficient "to brand an otherwise competent and loyal employee . . . as disloyal, pro-Communist, or a security risk." [10] And McCarthy's allegation that John Carter Vincent was a member of an espionage ring in the State Department was "absurd."

The charges, the Democrats concluded, were "A fraud and a hoax perpetrated on the Senate of the United States and the American people. They represent perhaps the most nefarious campaign of half-truths and untruth in the history of the Republic." [11]

The report enraged the exponents of the conspiracy thesis and only increased their vituperative attack. Jenner denounced Tydings for conducting the "most scandalous and brazen whitewash of treasonable conspiracy in our history" and insisted that the "crowd of master conspirators" in the State Department had not only "sold out China" but now they were undermining Korea. "The sad thing about it . . ." the Senator declared, "is that those who are being pushed now in Korea are the sons of the mothers of America." [12]

After 1949, however, much more than the conspiracy thesis was involved in the deeply felt emotions toward Communist China.

Americans were profoundly shocked as the Chinese Communists angrily denounced them as "fascist imperialists." The United States had made China its ward at the turn of the century and helped save it from imperialist depredation. In a spirit of altruism, the indemnity from the Boxer Rebellion had been devoted to educating Chinese in America and missionaries had brought education, medicine, and the Christian religion to the "heathen." And, during World War II, America had insisted that China was a great power. "The way in which the American record in China is today traduced naturally embitters American feelings," *The Times* of London has observed. "These feelings are of a people suddenly and unjustly cast out of China." [13]

Those who were insisting that Chiang's loss of China was caused, not by his internal problems, but by pro-Soviet Americans, offered a convenient explanation of China's rejection of our paternalism. Now Far Eastern experts in the Department of State, by their past refusal to seek political support from Congress and the public for their China policy, reaped a whirlwind. And the Department of State was in no position during Truman's second Administration to withstand the onslaught.

And, of course, the Department had never been popular. The widely held stereotype of the striped-pants-clad, tea-drinking, Ivy League Foreign Service officer hobnobbing with foreign aristocrats was anathema to log-cabin democracy.[14] And, since the Department was the vehicle through which troublesome foreign problems were brought to the nation's attention, it came under incessant attack when the world failed to conduct itself in the manner ordained by Americans.

Beginning in 1950, many Republicans conducted a guerrilla campaign of partisan politics against the State Department. Revenge for the defeat of Dewey required the destruction of the Roosevelt coalition. Finding their economic appeal ineffective, some Republicans utilized the Chinese situation, the Hiss case, the allegations of disloyalty in the Department of State to shake allegiance to the Democratic party.

The attack on the Department centered increasingly on Dean Acheson. He had played a major role in establishing the Truman Doctrine, the Marshall Plan, and NATO. He was hailed by many in

America and outside as the best Secretary of State in modern times. But he was the prime example of those who called for an adjustment of older ideas to the new situation. "We have got to understand," he said in 1946, "that all our lives the danger, the uncertainty, the need for alertness, for effort, for discipline will be upon us. It will be hard for us."

Senator Hugh Butler of Nebraska protested: "I watch his smart-aleck manner and his British clothes and that New Dealism, ever-lasting New Dealism in everything he says and does, and I want to shout Get Out, Get Out. You stand for everything that has been wrong with the United States for years." Acheson has observed: "The Republicans, quite naturally, were seeking political leverage with which to obtain power. Their interest turned inward to the domestic political scene, where the forces which could be exploited were the reaction from the burdens and discipline of war and the reluctance to assume heavy and novel commitments far beyond our shores and our experience." [15]

Skilled as a diplomat and policy formulator, Acheson did not tolerate fools easily, nor those who were purposely obstructionists; this was apparent in his replies at Congressional hearings. But neither he nor Truman was able after 1949 to explain foreign policy in a way that won mass support and freed it from the crippling restrictions imposed by public emotion. Instead, congressional Republicans, rather than the President, became the principal source of news and opinion. Among other things, as Douglass Cater has written, the shift in public attention from the White House to the pronouncements of certain Congressmen "created serious doubts at home and abroad whether the President did in fact stand at the helm of government during a critical time in world affairs." [16]

Three days after the aggression in Korea, Taft announced that had Truman requested congressional support he would have voted for it. But he denounced Truman for ordering American troops into action without congressional approval. He blamed the Administration for the fall of Chiang, Far Eastern troubles, and the "sympathetic acceptance of communism." He called for the resignation of the Secretary of State, asserting that Acheson's statement that Korea was not in the American defense perimeter had been a green light to the Communists.

Meanwhile in Korea, after weeks of retreating to a defense perimeter around Pusan, UN forces under MacArthur in September launched a brilliant amphibious operation at Inchon. Soon North Koreans were surrendering by the thousands or running to the 38th parallel. Although the evidence is still incomplete, the 1950 congressional election may well have been the determining factor that UN forces would cross the parallel. Taft and other Republicans made it clear that it would be wrong to stop at the parallel.

On October 7, the United Nations Assembly approved the crossing of the parallel. A week before the decision, China warned that it might intervene and this warning was repeated on October 11. Four days later, the President met with MacArthur on Wake Island. Just what was said it still the subject of bitter dispute.[17] Apparently, MacArthur thought the Chinese would not intervene, but, if they did, they would be slaughtered. On this advice from MacArthur, Truman approved the advance into North Korea up to a few miles from the Yalu River.

Although the Chinese were being engaged in increasing numbers, the congressional election was held before massive intervention occurred. The Democrats held control of both houses but lost twenty-seven House and five Senate seats. Majority Leader Scott Lucas lost in Illinois to a bitter foe of the Administration's foreign policy, Everett M. Dirksen, and Congressman Richard Nixon captured the California Senate seat in a campaign in which allegations of pro-Communist sympathies were made against his opponent, Congresswoman Helen Gahagan Douglas.

In Maryland, Tydings was defeated in a campaign of abuse and implied dishonesty. A fraudulent composite photograph showing him with Communist leader Earl Browder was widely circulated in a tabloid, *From The Record*. A Senate Committee investigated and stated that "such campaign methods and tactics are destroying our system of free elections." *From The Record*, they added, contained "misleading half-truths, misrepresentations, and false innuendos that maliciously and without foundation attack the loyalty and patriotism" of Tydings. The report also stated that McCarthy took an active part in the campaign, "making his staff available for work, for research, pictures, composition, printing of the tabloid, *From The Record*." The report recommended the adoption of rules making "acts of defamation, slander, and libel sufficient grounds for presentment to the Senate for the purposes of declaring a Senate seat vacant." [18]

On November 24, 1950, MacArthur announced a final offensive that would end the war by Christmas. Two days later, the Chinese struck back with large forces and the UN retreat was on. Early in 1951, UN lines held south of Seoul and there they started a slow, difficult advance toward the 38th parallel. All through these critical weeks a debate raged on foreign policy. When Truman announced he was sending additional troops to Europe, Taft called for a re-examination of foreign policy. On December 15, Senate and House Republicans demanded the dismissal of Acheson. Five days later, Hoover proposed that America should "hold the Atlantic and Pacific oceans with one frontier on Britain (if she wishes to cooperate); the other on Japan, Formosa and the Philippines."

On January 5, 1951, Taft stated: "In the first place, we should be willing to assist with sea and air forces any island nations which desire our help. Among these islands are Japan, Formosa, the Philippines, Indonesia, Australia and New Zealand; on the Atlantic side, Great Britain, of course." But, he insisted: "The commitment of a land army to Europe is a program never approved by Congress into which we should not drift."

On February 15, a majority of House Republicans signed a manifesto endorsing Hoover's proposals. As the debate continued, it exposed deep fissures in the Republican party. John Foster Dulles, Governor Dewey, Governor Earl Warren, Harold E. Stassen, and Senator Henry Cabot Lodge parted company with the Hoover-Taft position. And Dewey called for strengthening the armed forces "since the defense of America is in India, Africa, South America and Asia, and primarily in Europe and Japan."

In the midst of the debate, Eisenhower, recently appointed as Supreme Commander of NATO forces, reported to Congress on his tour of Europe. There was no acceptable alternative, he stated, "to the rearmament and defense of western Europe."

At the time of Truman's nomination of Eisenhower as Supreme Commander, James Reston had written that one of the misfortunes of the political wrangle over Acheson was that it diverted attention from the basic questions of foreign policy. The entrance of Eisenhower, Reston predicted, was likely to have considerable effect on this situation since Eisenhower had what Acheson lacked: "political support in the country. Moreover, he had Republican support, a commodity that has been in short supply at the State Department ever since Senator McCarthy, Republican of Wisconsin, invaded West Virginia last spring." [19]

On April 4, the Senate approved the sending of four additional divisions to Europe for Eisenhower's command, although it admonished the President against dispatching any more without "further Congressional approval." [20] This controversy, however, was mild compared with the furor in the country after April 11.

On that morning, the President — Captain Harry of Battery D — dismissed General of the Army Douglas MacArthur, announcing to the press that MacArthur "is unable to give his wholehearted support to the policies of the United States Government."

The audacious, irascible General opposed the policy of a limited war in Korea and publicly said so in *U.S. News & World Report*, on December 6, 1950. That day a policy directive went from Washington to "military commanders and diplomatic representatives" to clear all but routine statements with Washington and "to refrain from direct communication on military or foreign policy with newspapers, magazines, or other publicity media in the United States."

But MacArthur was implacable. On February 14, 1951, the *New York Times* quoted him in a further criticism of Administration policy: "The concept advanced by some that we should establish a line across Korea and enter into positional warfare is wholly unrealistic and illusory." In a public statement on March 24, the General denounced the orders that UN forces were not to bomb Chinese bases north of the Yalu River. Then, with full knowledge that the Administration was discussing with its Allies a settlement with the Chinese, MacArthur issued a statement that the enemy's army had "less stamina than our troops," lacked the industrial power essential to modern war, and offered to confer in the field with the Chinese commander to achieve the unification of Korea under Syngman Rhee.

The Chinese reacted so violently that negotiations were precluded and America's Allies protested at MacArthur's interference with policy. Then the General provoked the President further by allowing the release of a letter he had written Republican leader Joseph Martin. Again he rejected the concept of limited war. "As you pointed out," he told the Congressman, "we must win. There is no substitute for victory."

An initial outburst of rage greeted MacArthur's removal. Since congressional approval had not been sought for the Korean action, Republicans were not committed to support the Administration when the war stalemated. Two months before he died, Vandenberg wrote to Lodge: "The President's great mistake was in not bringing his Korea decision to the immediate attention of Congress (as Wilson did at Vera Cruz). At *that* time, the country and the Congress overwhelmingly agreed with him and would have said so. Much of the intervening controversy would itself have been avoided." [21]

MacArthur's position now furnished additional ammunition for the bitter partisan warfare designed to destroy the Democrats. Taft and other Republicans agreed that MacArthur should be invited to address Congress and there must be an investigation of Administration policy. "In addition," Martin explained to the newspapermen, "the question of impeachments was discussed." The way he emphasized the plural left no question that Dean Acheson was included with the President. [22]

When MacArthur's plane landed at San Francisco, he received a thunderous ovation. Cheering people turned out to meet him there and in Chicago, New York, and Washington. On April 19, the General addressed a wildly applauding Congress. Reminding his audience of the singularity of America, he said that "here are centered the hopes and aspirations and faith of the entire human race." Communism must not be appeased, he observed. It was imperative that Formosa not fall under Communist control. When China intervened in Korea, it "created a new war and an entirely new situation." But diplomatic decisions to permit "the realistic adjustment of military strategy" were not forthcoming, he charged. Then he expressed his impatience with any doubt of American omnipotence: "Once war is forced upon us, there is no alternative than to apply every available means to bring it to a swift end. War's very object is victory, not prolonged indecision."

From May 3 to June 25 a Senate Committee heard over two million words of testimony from MacArthur, Generals Marshall and Bradley, Acheson, and dozens of others. After MacArthur testified he went off on a speaking tour. He denounced "the insidious forces working from within" and criticized the Administration for underestimating the peril. Meanwhile, as the hearings developed, the Joint Chiefs of Staff took the offensive for the Administration. They emphasized that the General had publicly opposed official policy and thus violated the basic principle of the Constitution that the military must be subordinate to the civilian Commander-in-Chief.

Secretary of Defense Marshall warned that MacArthur "would have us, on our own initiative, carry the conflict beyond Korea against the mainland of Communist China, both from the sea and from the air. He would have us accept the risk of involvement not only in an extension of the war with Red China, but in an all-out war with the Soviet Union. He would have us do this even at the expense of losing our allies and wrecking the coalition of free peoples throughout the world." Bradley, in his mild manner, affirmed that MacArthur's proposals "would involve us in the wrong war, at the wrong place, at the wrong time, and with the wrong enemy."

At the end of the hearings, the eight Republican members of the Committee issued a statement denouncing the dismissal of MacArthur, our Far Eastern policy, and the idea of limited war. But, by this time, the country had recovered somewhat from its initial emotion. Truman was not popular, but the Constitution was; and MacArthur had disobeyed orders. Moreover, though many people were responsive to the General's development of the conspiracy theory, his attitudes on domestic policies sounded dangerously reactionary. Uproot spies and conspirators, yes, but the majority wanted no uprooting of the Roosevelt revolution.

Leading Republicans, including Taft and Dewey, enjoyed the General's onslaught against the President and eagerly added their voices to the chorus critical of the "disastrous failure of leadership in Washington," but they were careful not to identify Republican chances in 1952 too closely with the General. Public opinion polls showed a shift away from him and MacArthur-for-President talk subsided.

Although the General faded away to the Waldorf Astoria Towers, the impact of his dismissal did not. The Administration had failed to make the public understand that this limited war was an alternative to submission to Communist aggression or an atomic war of annihilation. America had always won wars. It was good old-fashioned Americanism to want a swift, total victory and MacArthur symbolized for many their impatience to get the job over with, to "solve" foreign problems and return to a simpler day. He "left behind him," Herbert Agar has observed, "the feeling that, even if he had been wrong this time, 'limited warfare' was also wrong."

The Administration became a prisoner of some of the General's policies. It tried to mollify its opponents by adopting a position closer and closer to theirs. Diplomatic negotiations with the Chinese Communists were now precluded since they signified appeasement. On May 18, 1951, Assistant Secretary of State Dean Rusk announced that the Communist regime "is not the government of China . . . It is not Chinese." Walter Lippmann in his column five days later observed that this speech "made the issue with Red China not the repulse of its aggressions in Korea but that of its survival. Regimes do not negotiate about their survival."

Aid to Formosa was speeded up. In a further demonstration of its new intransigence, Acheson pledged that the Administration would resist seating the Chinese Communists in the United Nations and several Foreign Service officers associated with past China policy, including John S. Service, were dismissed. The Foreign Service *Journal*, in July, 1951, denounced the Department for its failure to protect its employees. Remove the disloyal if they exist, it wrote: "But if the rest of us are loyal, let the department have the courage to defend our loyalty." [23] And the *Washington Post* remarked that Acheson "has seemed to be striving to appease the most vociferous of his critics, i.e., the most reactionary of MacArthur elements in the Republican party." [24]

The Administration's actions failed, however, to stem the torrent. On June 14, 1951, McCarthy assailed Marshall as being part of "a conspiracy so immense, an infamy so black, as to dwarf any previous such venture in the history of man." It was directed, he insisted, "to the end that we shall be contained, frustrated and finally fall victim to Soviet intrigue from within and Russian military might from without. . . . It was Moscow, for example, which decreed that the United States should execute its loyal friend, the Republic of China. The executioners," McCarthy asserted, "were that well-defined group headed by Acheson and George Catlett Marshall." On June 23 Taft said while he did not agree with McCarthy's accusation of treason, he felt that Marshall's policy in China "was the most stupid possible policy, and it showed the same complete lack of understanding of what communism is; the same failure he and Hopkins and Harriman displayed at Yalta. Subsequent events in Formosa and the war in Korea stemmed directly from that stupidity." Then, he charged: "This Korean War is a Truman war."

---

29. Repudiating the Democrats

By 1952, the situation was ripe for revolt against the Democrats. Not only were they on the defensive over China and the stalemate in Korea, but some of Truman's cronies were guilty of lax standards, if not of corruption. His military aide, Harry Vaughan, accepted a deep-freeze from a company that could use a kind word in the right place in Washington. An investigation of the Reconstruction Finance Corporation, headed by Senator Fulbright, exposed corrupt influence in the granting of loans and revealed a group of "five percenters" who sold their influence to get government favors for their clients.

In 1951-1952 corruption was exposed in the Bureau of Internal Revenue, and it was revealed that the Assistant Attorney General in charge of income tax evasion cases had accepted gifts, including two mink coats for his wife, from influence "fixers" and persons accused of income tax frauds. While Truman reorganized the RFC and the Bureau of Internal Revenue, he seemed to act slowly and reluctantly. And "deep freeze" and "mink coats" became powerful campaign charges as Republicans resolutely hammered at "the mess in Washington."

Outside of Washington, too, scandals seemed to be rampant. College basketball players were exposed for taking bribes from gamblers; ninety cadets at West Point were dismissed for cheating at examinations; and beginning in the spring of 1950 a Senate Committee, headed by Estes Kefauver, investigated organized crime and revealed to a nationwide television audience embarrassing connections between criminals and Democratic city machines in New York and Chicago.

Late in 1951, a group of Republican governors decided that Eisenhower — because of his decency, his unassailable integrity and his military fame — was the only person who could save the nation from further degradation under the Democrats.[1] A number of party leaders, newspaper owners, including the publisher of the *New York Herald Tribune*, and businessmen visited Eisenhower at NATO headquarters in France and pointed out that it was his duty to run.

Although the General's political affiliation was in doubt, on January 6, 1952, Senator Lodge, just back from a visit to him, told a crowded press conference that at Governor Sherman Adams's request he was entering Eisenhower's name in the New Hampshire primary. Lodge announced that the General "assured me he is a Republican . . . I am speaking for the General and I will not be repudiated."[2] Immediately, reporters besieged Eisenhower in France. He agreed he was a Republican, stated he would not campaign for the nomination because of his duties, but affirmed that Lodge and his associates had the right to organize "in pursuit of their common convictions in an attempt to place before me next July a duty that would transcend my present responsibility."

Although the *New York Times, Chicago Sun-Times*, and many other papers immediately announced their support of the General, those who had been espousing the conspiracy thesis rallied around a "real" Republican, Robert Alphonso Taft. Despite Eisenhower's absence in Europe and Taft's active campaign in New Hampshire, Eisenhower bested him in that state's primary by over ten thousand votes. A week later, although Stassen won the Minnesota primary, over a hundred thousand write-in votes were cast for the General.

But in Wisconsin on April 1, Taft won twenty-four delegates to six for Governor Warren, and the same day in Nebraska where the Senator and the General were both write-in candidates, Taft ran ahead. In May, Taft won the Ohio and West Virginia primaries and Eisenhower carried Oregon. And on May 27, the Taft forces controlled the Texas State Convention. But Eisenhower supporters, who had outnumbered and outvoted Taft supporters at a number of county conventions, and who had been denied seats at the State Convention, held their own Convention and nominated a rival slate of delegates. Most of Eisenhower's supporters in Texas — as well as other parts of the South — were in fact Democrats. Republicans in the South mainly were a small group of professional politicians who controlled the party machinery and received federal patronage when Republicans held the presidency. They, therefore, naturally opposed any broadening of party membership. And, historically, at presidential conventions, since they had no local patronage and power base of their own, they were easy for the Republican National Committee to manipulate.

Eisenhower's supporters asserted immediately that Taft had stolen the Texas vote. By now the Senator's strength was such that Eisenhower could no longer wait for a draft and his supporters persuaded him to return on June 1 to take an active role. In Dallas on June 21, he declared that the Texas backers of Taft were guilty of "a betrayal of the whole Republican party and its principles" when they "deliberately and ruthlessly disfranchised" the majorities who had voted for another candidate at the precinct and county conventions.

As delegates converged on Chicago, the Associated Press listed 458 uncontested votes for Taft to 406 for Eisenhower. But a Gallup poll released on June 19 showed voters favoring Eisenhower over Senator Kefauver or Governor Adlai Stevenson, with both Democrats leading over Taft. Eisenhower's supporters quickened their urgent insistence that he was the only candidate who could defeat the Democrats.[3] But the Taft forces, in control of the machinery of the Convention, ignored public opinion polls, the power of the mass media, and concentrated instead on winning undecided delegates by stressing the Senator's Republicanism.[4] They named MacArthur to

deliver the keynote address; McCarthy to speak; appointed Taft's
West Virginia manager as temporary Chairman, a position enabling
him to seat the contested delegates who might determine the outcome; and urged the nomination of a real Republican to conduct
an offensive against the "complete failure of the Truman, Acheson,
and Marshall" foreign policy and the socialism of the New Deal
and Fair Deal.

The eyes of the nation were on the fight for the disputed delegates. While the Eisenhower forces, master-minded by Dewey,
Herbert Brownell, James Hagerty, and Lodge, executed well-planned
moves, the Taft forces blundered, creating the impression they
were trying to steamroller the Convention by improper tactics.
When the National Committee met to hear the arguments of the
disputed delegations from Texas, Georgia, and Louisiana, the Taft
majority ruled there could be no television cameras or reporters
present.

Eisenhower's supporters now had the issue given them: "Fair
Play."

They drew the picture of Taft, operating in secrecy to rig the
Convention, guilty of the same type of political conniving as Truman, in contrast to Eisenhower's innate honesty and decency. Already on June 25, Lodge had prepared the way for this adroit move
by saying, "In the interest of fair play and decency, we will support at the opening session a resolution to amend the rules and to
bar these contested delegates from voting to seat themselves or
other contested delegations — regardless of whether they are for us
or for Senator Taft."

It was a carefully planned strategy. The Eisenhower leaders knew
they would lose the contests before the National Committee. Under long-standing convention rules, the roll of delegates approved by
the National Committee provided the basis for opening the Convention. Delegates on this roll, contested or uncontested, could vote
on any question except one. When the credential committee's report on permanent seating reached the Convention floor, contested
delegates on the temporary roll could not vote on their own contest.
They could still vote, however, on the other contests. Thus, in the
contest on Georgia, the Taft delegates in dispute from Louisiana
and Texas could vote to seat the Taft delegates from Georgia.

Georgia and Texas could then vote to seat the Taft delegates from Louisiana, and Georgia and Louisiana could vote to seat the Taft delegates from Texas.

The annual conference of Governors coincided with the National Committee's meeting to decide the delegate question. Dewey wired on July 1 urging that the hearings be opened to television: "Let the people see and hear the evidence." On July 2, twenty-five Republican Governors insisted that contested delegates be barred from voting in the Convention until after the contests had been settled. Two days later Hoover proposed that each side select an eminent citizen to "sit with me and see if we could find a basis of agreement."

Lodge, speaking as Eisenhower's manager, rebuked the former President: "I cannot imagine anything more undemocratic than for three men in a private meeting to arrogate unto themselves the power to disfranchise many thousands of Americans." A letter from Taft proposed the Texas contest be compromised by awarding twenty-two delegates to him and sixteen to Eisenhower. Lodge replied: "General Eisenhower is a no deal man."

Over television and radio and through the press the Eisenhower managers exploited the issue of "Fair Play" and "Taft Steals Votes." And the General, at every whistle stop en route from Denver to Chicago, denounced "chicanery," "star chamber methods," and "smoke-filled rooms." It had telling effect. Voters began wiring and phoning their delegates to support the fair play amendment. On July 7, the opening day of the Convention, delegates committed to neither Taft nor Eisenhower joined the General's supporters and the fair play amendment was adopted. Two days later, Taft's attempt to seat his Georgia delegation was rejected. Fearful that another defeat would ruin his chances, Taft gave in and accepted the Texas Eisenhower delegation.

Meanwhile, the Eisenhower managers, experienced in the use of television, paraded Governors before the delegates and the cameras and chose good-looking young men to give short speeches while the Taft people paraded the same tired old faces, Bricker and Dirksen. "We were trying to dramatize our point: the Ike people are young and vigorous, opposing the Old Guard," one Eisenhower manager said. When the balloting started, Ike's supporters knew they were just short of the 604 votes needed for victory. At the end of the roll call, before the results were made official, Eisenhower had 595, Taft 500, Warren 81, Stassen 20, MacArthur 10. Now the Minnesota delegation demanded recognition and changed its Stassen votes to Eisenhower. It was all over save for the rush of other states to switch and get on the record for the General.[5]

By attempting to rig the machinery of the Convention and failing to recognize a moral issue in the contest over the disputed delegates, the Taft supporters failed to realize how profoundly disturbed millions of citizens were by the revelations of corruption around them. Eisenhower, however, symbolized the demand for a renewal of faith in "spiritual values." [6] And, after his nomination, his resolute pledge to the delegates that he would conduct a great crusade to restore integrity to the government met with a tumultuous ovation.

As the Republicans moved out of Chicago, the Democrats moved in searching for a man to nominate. None of the candidates — Senator Richard Russell, Senator Estes Kefauver, and Averell Harriman — could secure votes beyond their factional following. And Vice President Barkley, a popular figure who could appeal to all elements, was considered too old. Meanwhile, a group of Chicago citizens opened unofficial campaign headquarters to draft their Governor Adlai E. Stevenson. As newspapers, radio, and television increasingly discussed the possibility of a draft, leaders from Pennsylvania, New Jersey, Indiana, and Kansas began working with the unofficial Draft Stevenson Committee.

When Stevenson appeared before the Convention on the opening day to welcome the delegates to Illinois, his speech, sparkling with insight, wit, and common sense, electrified the crowd. Praising the constructive achievements of the Democrats over the past twenty years, he reminded the delegates that the Republicans said it was all "a miserable failure. For almost a week pompous phrases marched over this landscape in search of an idea, and the only idea they found was that the two great decades of progress in peace, and of victory in war, and of bold leadership in this anxious hour, were the misbegotten spawn of bungling, of corruption, of socialism, of mismanagement, of waste and of worse."

Then, he added: "They captured, they tied and they dragged that ragged idea here into this hall and they furiously beat it to death.

for a solid week. After listening to this everlasting procession of epithets about our misdeeds, I was even surprised the next morning when the mail was delivered on time. I guess our Republican friends were out of patience, out of sorts, and need I add, out of office."

But he admonished his party that its past achievements were not enough: "We dare not just look back to great yesterdays. We must look forward to great tomorrows. What counts now is not just what we are against, but what we are for. And who leads us is less important than what leads us — what convictions, what courage, what faith — win or lose. A man does not save a century or a civilization, but a militant party wedded to a principle can."

Despite his frequent and adamant statements that he did not want the nomination because he was a candidate for re-election in Illinois, the Convention four days later ignored his wishes. He made no deals, no commitments, and gave no gestures of encouragement to those who led the draft. And he refused President Truman's support and that of other party leaders before and during the Convention. Local and state leaders, undaunted by Stevenson's attitude, drafted him as the most formidable man they had. He was not associated with the "mess in Washington"; he was a coalition leader who had been elected to the governorship by the largest majority in Illinois history; he had been a vigorous Governor; and he was a man of integrity and intelligence.

After his nomination, he stood before the Convention and said:

> The ordeal of the Twentieth Century — the bloodiest, most turbulent era of the Christian age — is far from over. Sacrifice, patience, understanding and implacable purpose may be our lot for years to come.
> Let's face it. Let's talk sense to the American people. Let's tell them the truth, that there are no gains without pains, that we are now on the eve of great decisions, not easy decisions, like resistance when you're attacked, but a long, patient, costly struggle which alone can assure triumph over the great enemies of man — war, poverty, and tyranny — and the assaults upon human dignity which are the most grievous consequences of each.

He viewed the campaign, he explained, not as a crusade to exterminate the opposition "but as a great opportunity to educate and elevate a people whose destiny is leadership, not alone of a rich, prosperous, contented country, but of a world in ferment." Then, during the campaign, with speeches of a literary quality unmatched in American politics since Woodrow Wilson's, Stevenson affirmed the need for discipline and a realization that there was no easy road to peace and security.

He praised the Truman Doctrine, the Marshall Plan, and NATO for contributing to a secure Europe. "I wish I could say the same for Asia, but there would be no greater disservice to the American people than to underestimate the gravity of the dangers that America faces in this area, perhaps for many years to come. . . . In Korea we took a long step toward building a security system in Asia," he remarked. "As an American I am proud that we had the courage to resist that ruthless, cynical aggression; and I am equally proud that we have had the fortitude to refuse to risk extension of that war despite extreme communist provocations and reckless Republican criticisms. Whatever unscrupulous politicians may say to exploit grief, tragedy and discontent for votes, history will never record that Korea was a 'useless' war, unless today's heroism is watered with tomorrow's cowardice. . . . It would seem to me, my friends, that the Republican critics could better demonstrate the good faith of their concern for Asia by doing something about India and Pakistan today rather than talking about China yesterday. I don't think that tearful and interminable post-mortems about China will save any souls for democracy in the rest of Asia, the Near East and in Africa."

He championed civil rights legislation including a compulsory Fair Employment Practices Commission. He told his audience in Richmond, Virginia: "I should justly earn your contempt if I talked one way in the South and another way elsewhere. . . . I shall not go anywhere with beguiling serpent words." He also advocated the repeal of the Taft-Hartley Law, but with the courage that characterized his campaign he told a Labor Day rally in Detroit: "I don't say that everything in the Taft-Hartley Act is wrong. It isn't, and I don't think it's a slave labor law, either. But I do say that it was biased and politically inspired and has not improved labor relations in a single plant."

The sparkling wit in his speeches was an irritant to the opposition, a delight to his admirers. Eisenhower's acceptance of much of the New and Fair Deal led him to remark: "I have been tempted to say that I was proud to stand on that record, if only the General would move over and make room for me." But he could be stern as well. He told the American Legion that patriotism "is based on tolerance and a large measure of humility." McCarthy's attack on "our great wartime Chief of Staff, General Marshall," was shocking. At Salt Lake City, Stevenson criticized Republican speechmakers for describing the nation as "half-defeated, half-bankrupt. . . . They thus betray the conquering, hopeful, practical yet deeply moral America which you and I know."

He won a devoted following of intellectuals — "eggheads," the opposition sneered. He spoke with a clarity and eloquence the Truman Administration lacked, appealed to the best in the national character, and made fewer concessions to self-interest and greed than most candidates. As he defined the basic issues and reformulated many ideas, the Illinois Governor was more concerned with the literary quality of his speeches than with the projection of himself over television. Rapidly developing TV since the 1948 election had become a powerful new medium, emphasizing the visual image of the candidate, particularly such superficial aspects as a smile and warmth or lack of it. But Stevenson, master of artful prose and the well-turned phrase, never made a wholly successful adaptation to these demands of television.

Nor did Truman help. They were deeply different human beings. Where one was reflective and loathed partisan warfare, the other gloried in rash and bitter forays. Abhorring the Stevenson type of campaign, Truman, unwanted but undaunted, took off on a whistle stop tour reminiscent of 1948. Vociferously he attacked Eisenhower for "betraying his principles" to win the support of the McCarthys and Jenners, and he explained that a military man was not equal to the task of being president. As Truman hammered away, Republican spokesmen, aware that he was a liability to Stevenson's campaign, were quick to besmirch Stevenson with "the mess in Washington." And Life, in one October issue, carried not one picture of Stevenson! Instead, the issue featured Eisenhower versus Truman.

At the outset, the Republican campaign was beset with difficulties. The platform, while reflecting much of Taft's attitude on foreign policy, met the Eisenhower position for support of Europe by pledging, "we shall encourage and aid the development of collective security forces there, as elsewhere." Both wings of the party agreed on assailing Truman for "appeasement" of Communism at home and abroad.

The demand by the Taft supporters for a sharp attack on Truman's foreign policy was reflected in the planks denouncing the Democrats for undermining Chiang, for inviting the attack in Korea, for the military stalemate and the "ignominious bartering with our enemies." The doctrine of containment was rejected as a "negative, futile and immoral policy" since it abandoned "countless human beings to a despotism and Godless terrorism." Instead, the Republicans promised a "dynamic initiative" and looked forward "to the genuine independence of those captive peoples." All elements of the party agreed on promising a balanced budget, a reduction of the national debt, and the ending of corruption in Washington "to restore honest government to the people."

The extreme Taft supporters left Chicago in a bitter mood over the rejection of their candidate. The Senator took a lengthy vacation, and petulant old Colonel McCormick protested that Eisenhower's "chief newspaper supporters are Democratic New Deal papers" who wanted "the continuation of the Marshall Plan." On August 23, he proposed in his *Chicago Tribune* that the public ignore both presidential candidates and vote for the "patriotic candidates" for Congress including McCarthy, Jenner, Knowland, and Bricker.

In the West, at his temporary campaign headquarters in Denver, Eisenhower announced his support of the social gains of the past but explained that Truman was too far to the left. America instead must take a straight road "down the middle." And the Truman Administration had made "really terrible blunders that led up to the Korean War. But I do not see how these conditions, having occurred and having been created, how you could stay out of the thing, I don't know."

On August 22, Eisenhower stated: "George Marshall is one of the patriots of this country . . . Maybe he has made mistakes. I do not know about that . . . I have no patience with anyone who can find in his record of service for this country anything to criticize." The reporters asked would he support McCarthy for re-election? "I will support him as a member of the Republican organization," Eisenhower explained, but "I am not going to campaign for or give blanket endorsement to any man who does anything that I believe to be un-American in its methods and procedures." He added that a Republican President needed a Republican Congress: "For that reason, I have to accept the decisions of the voters of a state, as much as I can."

The pro-Eisenhower Scripps-Howard chain of newspapers immediately ran a front-page editorial declaring: "Ike is running like a dry creek." The speeches were those of "just another me-too candidate." If Eisenhower did not know whether Marshall had made mistakes, "he had better find out. For that's one of the big issues of the campaign. Ask any mother, father, or wife of a soldier in Korea."

In a speech to the American Legion on August 26, while Eisenhower spoke out against disloyal elements, there was no criticism of Korean policy. The doctrine of containment, however, came under an oblique attack. After listing the nations subjugated by the Soviet Union, he said: "The American conscience can never know peace until these peoples are restored again to being masters of their own fate." And he spoke of haunting the Kremlin with nightmares of punishment that could be visited by "the retaliatory readiness" of powerful American forces.

On September 12, to enlist the positive support of Taft, Eisenhower conferred with the Senator for the first time since the Convention. Taft submitted a list of issues to ascertain the General's position. After the meeting, Taft announced he would heartily cooperate in the campaign. Eisenhower agreed, Taft told the press, that the main issue was "liberty against creeping socialization." The General pledged, Taft added, a drastic reduction in government expenditures. The Senator explained that while he did not agree with all of Eisenhower's views on foreign policy, "I think it is fair to say that our differences are differences of degree."

After the meeting, as Democrats asserted that the General had surrendered to Taft, Eisenhower increasingly concentrated on Korea, corruption, and Communists in government. He dropped his support of universal military training and implied that the Republicans would end the fear that American boys would have to serve overseas in the future. While the changing campaign tactics dis-

turbed some of the early Eisenhower enthusiasts, James Reston remarked: "There is nothing in any of this that is different from the
normal. The point is merely that the Eisenhower crusade is turning
into just another political campaign, featuring all the old back-
platform tricks, all the old debating points, all the old slogans and
all the old compromises."

In Wisconsin, McCarthy rode on the campaign train and persuaded Eisenhower to delete a paragraph praising Marshall from
his speech in Milwaukee. The differences between himself and Mc-
Carthy were well known, Eisenhower explained in a speech at
Green Bay. But, "I want to make one thing very clear. The purpose
that he and I have of ridding this Government of the incom-
petents, the dishonest and, above all, the subversive and the disloyal
are one and the same. . . . The differences apply to method." In
Indiana, with Jenner on the platform, Eisenhower avoided mention of the Senator by name, but urged the Republicans to "spare
no effort" to see that all Republican candidates were elected.

Korea now ran through almost all of Eisenhower's speeches. "The
seven years since the war have been a record of catastrophe, with its
climax in Korea," he said on September 22 and charged that Acheson by defining the defense perimeter as excluding Korea had
thereby invited aggression. Truman struck back by saying that the
General had shared in the making of policy since the war and
carried a share of the responsibility for the decisions he was now denouncing. Eisenhower answered that he had given purely military
advice and the decisions made were political.

On October 2, he stated that South Koreans, not Americans,
should man the front lines. Stevenson and Truman replied that
South Korean troops were being used to their full effectiveness and
Eisenhower knew this and was guilty, therefore, of a cheap political trick. Stevenson, on October 16, explained that withdrawal
from Korea would be a sign of weakness and to expand the conflict
would involve America in a futile war with China. The only course,
he insisted, was to build up both American and South Korean
strength, continue truce negotiations, and rotate American troops.

Ten days before election, at a rally in Detroit, Eisenhower accused
the Democrats of giving the "false answer . . . that nothing can be
done to speed a secure peace." If elected, he announced: "I shall

go to Korea." The cheers of the crowd indicated the enthusiasm for the proposal. The Democrats, on the defensive, denounced it as pointless. But in the next few days Eisenhower dwelt on the theme. He explained on October 27 that Truman's attitude "has been my rudest lesson in partisan politics. I had thought that all Americans shared one simple feeling of mine. That feeling is this: If a journey to Korea and a close study of our military and political problems there can save the life of a single American soldier and bring peace of mind to a single American family, I must make that journey."

Correspondents, during the campaign, described the "magic in that three-lettered word, Ike." When he stepped out on the platform and his features broke into their genial grin, the crowds responded with enthusiasm. Although reporters groaned over Ike's "little moral lectures" and "dynamic platitudes," the public, James Reston wrote, "like his angry little outbursts against corruption, and his essays on America."

CBS commentator Eric Sevareid observed that Eisenhower was projecting a father image, and Cabell Phillips remarked that while Stevenson relied on the content of his speeches, Eisenhower relied on the mood: "One tries to persuade his hearers, the other to move them." Without histrionics or rhetorical flourishes, Phillips wrote: "he conveys a sense of indignation, of sincere and honest anger over trusts that have been violated, over tragedy induced by stupidity or wickedness. The 'mess in Washington' must be cleaned out; disloyal public servants and thieving tax collectors must be ruthlessly punished; means must and will be found to end the slaughter 'of your sons and husbands on the blood-soaked fields of Korea, which the present Administration has the effrontery to call a police action.'" And, added Phillips: "The crowd is with him. Idolatry shows in their solemn, upturned faces." [7]

The public's confidence in Eisenhower's ability to set things right resulted in a landslide on election day. He received 33,824,351 popular votes and 442 electoral votes. Stevenson received 27,314,987 popular votes, carrying only nine states: South Carolina, Georgia, Alabama, Mississippi, Louisiana, Arkansas, North Carolina, Kentucky, and West Virginia. Despite widespread discontent with the

Truman Administration and Eisenhower's own personal appeal, the voters showed no great trust in the Republican party. In the congressional voting, Republicans won the House by a margin of eight and in the Senate they had a tie.

More significant than Eisenhower's smashing of the South was his support from Northern urban dwellers who had been voting Democratic for twenty years. He made significant inroads among skilled and semi-skilled workers, union members, and Catholics. He raised the Republican big city vote some six percentage points over 1948. Except for Philadelphia, Stevenson's majorities in the large cities were far below those Truman received in 1948. In Philadelphia, the Democratic party had vigorous, young, reform leadership. Mayor Joseph Clark, Jr., District Attorney Richardson Dilworth, and President of the City Council James A. Finnegan ended the long reign of the Republican machine in 1951. In view of the local Republican record of mismanagement, Republicans had so little appeal that Stevenson received far more votes than Truman and surpassed Roosevelt's 1944 vote.

In the suburbs, grown some nine million in population between the two elections, Eisenhower had nearly a complete sweep. As a result, for the first time since the decade of the '20s, the Republicans carried the urban states, the backbone of the Roosevelt coalition.[8]

Many of those who had been voting Democratic since 1932 had now become comfortable, home-owning citizens. Appeals to New Deal loyalties — "Don't Let Them Take It Away" — were no longer as powerful as in 1948. And urban ethnic groups with ties to nations swallowed up by the Russians were attracted by the Republican pledge to replace containment with a "dynamic initiative." The Democratic allegiance of these same, predominantly Catholic groups, was also shaken by allegations that Truman was blind to the Communist menace within.

The assertion that the Democrats were responsible for the fall of Chiang struck a responsive chord among many. And the Administration's decision to fight a limited war in Korea that it dared not lose but dared not win had become intolerable. The election, Samuel Lubell has remarked, was not a "vote for peace at any price. It was more a vote of impatience with the frustrating state of neither war nor peace." [9]

Although the Democrats insisted that the training of a military man precluded Eisenhower from mastering the presidency, his military experience as well as his honesty and decency gave assurance to a majority of the voters that he was the ideal leader to guide the nation through turbulent waters. His crusade would restore integrity to government; it would renew faith in the vigor of democratic institutions; it would end the stalemate in Korea; and replace blundering in foreign policy with a new dynamism.

BOOK SEVEN

The Changing Electorate:
Truman and Eisenhower

---

30.   Transforming the Middle Class Base

"What an age! What a land!" Walt Whitman wrote in *Democratic Vistas*. A restless people always on the move, Americans expanded from 75 million in 1900 to 173 million by 1958 and forsook their rural past for the city and the suburb. The value of the goods and services they produced expanded fivefold during this half-century, and in the years after the great depression the American bonanza was more equitably distributed.

After 1940, to use Adolph A. Berle's phrase, the nation was in the throes of "galloping capitalism." With less than 7 per cent of the world's population, the nation had become the master technologist producing nearly half the world's factory-made goods. Geography, resources, politics, thought, and fate all played their role in this achievement, as did the absence of an aristocratic disdain for trade and business. So did the driving, furious energy of a hybrid population spreading rapidly over a new continent creating a climate favorable to innovation, to risk-taking, and to investing capital.

Increasing productivity, a huge consumer demand for homes, automobiles, and other products of the new technology, business investment in capital equipment, increasing expenditures by local and state governments, and the steady expenditure by the federal government (10 to 15 per cent of the gross national product) all contributed to the boom conditions.

The enormous increase in the wealth of the country reflected it-self, among other things, in the growing nationalization of life. While there were still islands like Li'l Abner's Dogpatch where modern equipment and methods had not penetrated, these were isolated relics. Modern technology was supplying the same material goods everywhere. And, at the same time, the automobile, the airplane, motion pictures, radio, and television contributed to the diminution of regional differences.

The prosperity seemed unbelievable to many of the depression generation. Factory workers, with working wives, were driving expensive automobiles, investing in the stock market, and earning more money than some of their companies' junior executives.[1] By the 1950s the nation had achieved a standard of living beyond the comprehension of most of the rest of the world. Even that perpetual complainer, *The Nation*, wrote about "Perpetual Prosperity"; and in 1953 the value of the gross national product reached $367.2 billions — two decades earlier it had been $123.4 billions.[2]

At the same time, a dramatic shift had occurred in the dispersion of this wealth. As the national output expanded after 1939, the lower 95 per cent of the population gained a larger share of a steadily growing pie. At the core of the dispersion of wealth was the expansion of the middle income group. By 1953, after taxes, 43 per cent of all non-farm families had incomes of $4000 to $7500. Sixty per cent of these particular families were headed by blue-collar workers. And 58 per cent of all families enjoyed incomes between $3000 and $10,000 a year, where in 1929 only 31 per cent had such an income in dollars of the same purchasing power.

The expanding income of the middle group came largely from wages and salaries. To a startling degree this group consisted of people defined by the Marxists as proletarians. ". . . it is time to change the stereotype of the American middle-income consumer," the editors of *Fortune* said in May, 1954, "he is not, and has not been for some years, a small landlord or drugstore proprietor. If any stereotype at all is meaningful, it might be the machinist in Detroit."

By the 1950s, although some eighteen million industrial workers were unionized, they were not a militant, "class-conscious" force. Union members had no interest in ideologies. With rising wages and benefits, many blue-shirted workers joined the migration from the city to the suburbs and thus made it difficult for labor's political action workers to rally their votes. Organized labor had more success in local and congressional than in presidential elections. In key city districts, where unions had funds to spend and members to work as precinct captains, this frequently meant the difference between victory and defeat. And the recessions of 1953-1954 and 1957-1958 helped labor leadership to persuade their membership to vote for labor-endorsed candidates.

But when the issue was more abstract, the leaders did not have notable success in delivering votes. In Ohio in 1950, CIO leaders blundered in trying to defeat Taft. Although they charged that Taft-Hartley was a "slave labor" law, workers knew that this was nonsense. Taft won by impressive margins, winning votes from both union members and others alarmed at the arrogance of the CIO. Eight years later in the same state, however, when pressure from wealthy contributors forced Republican candidates to support right-to-work legislation which threatened to end the protection given by unions, labor leaders were able to rally the workers and defeat such a strong vote-getter as Senator John W. Bricker.

Although labor leaders frequently accused the Eisenhower Administration of being dominated by big business, it could not be said that Eisenhower was antagonistic to labor. While the Administration generally adopted a strict hands-off, settle-it-yourself attitude toward management-labor disputes, it did not do so when the strike in steel in July, 1956, threatened a protracted shut-down. Behind the scenes, Secretary of the Treasury George Humphrey and Secretary of Labor James Mitchell induced the steel companies to improve their wage offer and other benefits to the union. Most of the leading steel officials were Republicans and they were persuaded that a lengthy strike might force the President to take steps that would arouse union members in an election year.

Prosperity in 1956 limited the effectiveness of both the Democrats' economic appeal to workers and the trade union leadership's endorsement of Stevenson. Union leaders had to accept the fact that union membership was only one factor influencing political response and that affiliation with churches and social clubs and the influence of family and neighbors were competing pulls. Other issues, including Eisenhower's personal magnetism and the belief that peace was more assured in his hands, were powerful factors determining voting behavior. Eisenhower won two thirds of the non-union labor vote and 48 per cent of the votes of union members.

In spite of prosperity, the postwar years could hardly be termed utopian. There were not only the problems of the Soviet Union, China, atom and hydrogen bombs, and guided missiles, but at home there were too many automobile accidents, still too many marginal income families, too many urban slums crying for rebuilding, tense racial situations, too few schools and hospitals, too little medical care at a reasonable cost. And there was an increasing shortage of teachers, the only occupational group whose real earnings fell after 1940.[3]

John Kenneth Galbraith protested in *The Affluent Society* (1958) that the American preoccupation with high and mounting production and consumption of *private* goods was outdated and resulted in a serious social imbalance whereby the production of *public* service — including adequate education, schools, parks, and public safety — remained far too low.

And, of immense import for the future, the gap between the American living standard and that of much of the rest of the world was widening. The late Premier Liaqat Ali Khan of Pakistan said on a visit to the United States in 1950:

> As I let myself ponder over this, I suddenly see the United States of America as an island — a fabulously prosperous island. And round this island I see the unhealthy sea of misery, poverty and squalor in which millions of human beings are trying to keep their heads above water. At such moments I fear for this great nation as one fears for a dear friend.

Despite charges that foreign aid programs were bankrupting America, the actual percentage of the American national product that flowed into international economic cooperation and assistance was "so imperceptible that one blushes to mention it," Leon Keyserling has written.[4]

Increasing job mobility, a rapidly expanding national income, and a large new middle income group were only a few of the momentous changes in the postwar years. Another was the rapidly expanding birth rate. Approximately 23,500,000 babies were born between 1950 and 1956, almost as many as the total number of births in the 1930s. And people were living longer. By 1950, the average life expectancy was sixty-eight years. Between 1940 and 1950 the population increased from 131,669,275 to 151,132,000, and by 1958 it reached 173,260,000. Most notable was the population increase in California and the Pacific Northwest. With heavy migration from the East, California replaced Pennsylvania as the second most populous state.

In these years, unlike earlier periods of rapid American development, immigration accounted for only a fraction of the population growth.[5] The decline of immigration, beginning with the institution of the quota system in the 1920s, had long-range implications. Among other things, the choking off of the European labor supply provided Negroes with the opportunity to fill industrial jobs once held by the immigrants. And, without a continuous, large supply of newcomers, ethnic groups were losing their identity. While appeals to them, particularly in the formation of foreign policy, were still profitable, the dispersal of the second generation into the total population suggested the diminution of this in the future.

The decline in immigrant numbers did not signify an end to the pressure-cooker aspect of assimilation into American society. European migration as a source of labor for expanding industries was replaced by what the sociologists termed in-migration to cities. From the rural and small-town South came both Negroes and whites. At the same time, Puerto Ricans swelled the flow to urban centers, particularly to New York.

Between 1940 and 1950 the metropolitan areas of the country absorbed 81 per cent of the total national population growth, and 97 per cent between 1950 and 1955. But within the metropolitan areas there was a quickening of the decentralization of population. Between 1940 and 1950 suburbs grew two and a half times as fast as the central cities and seven times as fast from 1950 to 1955.

Beginning in 1947 over a million white- and blue-collared workers a year fled to the suburbs in a headlong torrent. In the process, the depression-born Democratic appeal to the "common man" had less and less to offer the new suburban dwellers, many of whom had been Democrats in the big cities. Those moving upward in the social scale found the political coloration of the suburbs more Republican than their former neighborhood and with alacrity adopted the prevailing sentiments. By 1958, with some forty-seven million Americans living in suburbs, the suburbanite approximated that person of fiction — "the average American."

The Democratic party in the North, with its strength historically resting in the big cities, found it difficult in the 1950s to adjust to the growth of the suburbs. Its traditional city type of party organization was not transferable. After the defeat of Stevenson in 1952, a number of liberals who had supported him launched Democratic clubs independent of the regular party organization. In California, particularly, but also in Illinois and New York, this club movement successfully incorporated some suburban voters as well as certain upper income city dwellers who remained aloof from traditional party activities.

Both parties were altered by the expansion of the middle income group. Neither had a clear-cut majority during the 1950s. Under Eisenhower the Republican party accepted most of the Democratic reforms and thus broadened its support from middle income voters. Many conservative Republican Congressmen from secure districts were quick to express their dismay over Modern Republicanism. But its acceptance was vital if the party were to control the presidency. To secure support from the more liberal industrialized areas, it had to ignore its extreme conservatives. At the same time, the Democratic congressional leadership ignored the more extreme Northern liberals in its ranks. With the Republicans holding the presidency, the Democratic record was set largely by conservative or moderate Congressmen. The refusal of Lyndon Johnson and Sam Rayburn to join the Advisory Council of the Democratic National Committee was an indication of the historic division between the national and congressional wings of the party.

There was a shifting equilibrium of political behavior in the 1950s. The Democrats were on the defensive over foreign policy and the danger of inflation, while the Republicans suffered as the economy went into two recessions. By this decade the growing nationalization of American politics — one of the signal consequences of the New Deal revolution and the expanding urbanization and industrialization of the country after 1940 — revealed itself in the voting patterns.[6] Eisenhower, for instance, carried middle income districts in the urban South with nearly the same majority with which he won comparable districts in the urban North. Despite Southern opposition to civil rights, which delayed the region's progress toward full nationalization politically, by the end of the decade, differences over foreign policy and over the role of the government in society were replacing traditional religious, ethnic, and regional factors in molding political behavior.

---

31. The Negro and Politics

The position of the Negro underwent rapid change in the postwar years. Gunnar Myrdal predicted in *An American Dilemma* (1944) that "not since Reconstruction has there been more reason to anticipate fundamental changes in American race relations, changes which will involve a development toward the American ideals."

Economic prosperity and a high level of mobility in the population, reducing the number of communities where there was a fixed sentiment against the Negro, contributed to the rapid change. Outward mobility from the areas where they suffered the most discrimination was an additional factor. Although in 1900 nine tenths of the Negroes had been in the South, a half-century later only slightly more than half remained. Other forces in the rapid change after 1945 were the growing political power of the Northern urban Negro, educational and propaganda efforts for more equality of civil rights, decisions of the Supreme Court and executive actions by the Presidents.

There was a growing awareness among Americans that the nation's position of world leadership was jeopardized by racism at home. The Catholic Church and some trade unions in the South assisted

Negro organizations in the fight against segregation. The United Packinghouse Workers, under the leadership of Ralph Helstein, banished segregation throughout Southern as well as Northern locals and, in 1955-1956, the national leadership of the Oil, Chemical and Atomic Workers forced the ending, over the protests of Southern white locals, of the ban against Negroes in skilled positions. In spite of these developments, Southern white workers proved to be the strongest foes of racial equality and this brought the AFL-CIO organizing campaign in the area to a near standstill.

Between 1940 and 1950 Northern industrial centers absorbed nearly a million new Negro workers. By mid-century 60 per cent of the Negroes were living in cities — Northern and Southern. By 1950, Negroes numbered 50,000 or more in 27 cities and in each they were 10 per cent or more of the population. Negroes were not only streaming out of rural areas, but they were also improving their economic status. The per capita income of Negroes, in dollars of the same purchasing power, by 1956 was nearly three times their prewar earnings. But while improving their position more rapidly than white workers, they were still far behind. Eighty-one per cent of all the Negro familes — as against 48 per cent of white families — had incomes of less than $4000 in 1956.[1] And the nearly three million Negroes still on Southern farms were an exception to the generalizations about Negro economic progress.

Eli Ginzberg has pointed out in his excellent study, *The Negro Potential* (1956), that the Northern city offered the Southern Negro more than a higher income. There was a broader range of job opportunities and superior schooling provided the chance for Negro children to develop skills leading to higher living standards. Although most Negroes were still employed in the lower paid, less skilled occupations, between 1940 and 1950 more came to be employed as craftsmen, foremen, and clerks. There was also a small trained elite of professional people. There were few Negro business leaders, however, in fields other than real estate and insurance. Half the Negro professionals were teachers and professors. Of the 23,000 engineers graduated in 1955, only one hundred and fifty were Negroes, while about two hundred Negroes became lawyers and another two hundred became doctors.[2]

Basic to many of the difficulties faced by the Negro in the

North was the problem of adequate housing. Of the sixty thousand new houses built in metropolitan Philadelphia between 1953 and 1955, only four hundred were made available to Negroes who comprised 18 per cent of the population. And when Negroes could buy homes, they found that the price was 10 to 20 per cent higher than for whites. For apartments, too, they had to pay higher rents for less space and service than the whites, reflecting the real estate owners' knowledge of their pressing needs. Chicago's Negro population, doubling in 1940-1950, swelled already crowded slums and then burst out at points into white sections. This resulted in a frightening sequence of near riots. And violence and continuing threats of violence menaced Chicago's most sensitive spot, Trumbull Park, where a few Negro families moved into a public housing project hitherto all-white.

For all the difficulties involved, the Negro was making progress toward achieving full citizenship. While a number of whites, including Southern governors and legislators and Northern real estate brokers, were impeding the forward march, the Negro, as never since Reconstruction, was branded on the national conscience.

The Negro remained more vulnerable than the whites to any faltering of the economy. Unemployment among Negroes was higher in the three postwar recessions than among whites. Skilled jobs were difficult to secure in face of systematic discrimination by such unions as the Railway Brotherhoods and most of the A. F. of L. metal and building trades. Nevertheless, in the industrial unions each year of continued prosperity meant another year of job security for the Negroes trained for skilled work.

Older patterns of discrimination were being breached. In 1953, President Eisenhower created the President's Committee on Government Contracts to help eliminate discrimination in businesses receiving any of the six million government contracts. Although handicapped by the lack of investigators, this Committee ended a number of flagrant abuses. And presidential action achieved integration in the armed forces. Under President Truman's leadership it was almost completed by 1952.

The federal courts were more often instrumental than the Presidents in broadening Negro rights. Until 1944 few Southern Negroes participated in politics. That year the white primary, which restricted the vote in Democratic primaries to white citizens, was held unconstitutional by the Supreme Court. South Carolina's legislature struck back immediately by repealing all laws pertaining to the primary and a Democratic state convention adopted rules organizing Democratic clubs to conduct primaries. Under this fiction, that the Democratic party was a private association, it was possible to continue excluding Negroes from the Democratic primary.

In 1947, federal District Judge J. Waites Waring, a Charlestonian of impeccable connections, outlawed this move: ". . . private clubs and business organizations do not vote and elect a President of the United States, and the Senators and members of the House of Representatives of our national Congress; and under the law of our land, all citizens are entitled to a voice in such selections." And he concluded: "It is time for South Carolina to rejoin the Union." [3]

With the striking down of the white primary, the states of the Deep South adopted several tests for voter registration. An Alabama law adopted in 1951, in addition to the customary qualifications of age, residence, and lack of criminal record, provided that the following persons should be qualified to register:

> . . . those who can read and write any Article of the Constitution of the United States in the English language which may be submitted to them by the Board of Registrars, provided, however, that no person shall be entitled to register as electors except those who are of good character and who embrace the duties and obligations of citizenship under the Constitution of the United States and under the Constitution of the State of Alabama, and, provided, further, that . . . each applicant shall be furnished . . . a written questionnaire. . . . Such questionnaire shall be answered in writing by the applicant, in the presence of the Board without assistance.

With variations, other Southern states adopted similar legislation which provided registrars with opportunities for continued discrimination. In rural areas, particularly, while white registrants were quickly approved, most, or all, Negroes were rejected.

Despite the various stratagems to prevent Negroes from gaining political power, 1,321,731 were registered to vote in eleven Southern states by 1958. This was approximately 25 per cent of the Negroes of voting age. About 80 to 85 per cent of these voters were concentrated in urban areas. In Atlanta, in the 1950s, the Negro president of Atlanta University, Dr. Rufus Clement, was twice elected to the city's school board and carried white as well as Negro wards. Negro voters were vital to the re-election of the mayor of the city. As a result, in 1958, two Negroes were appointed to the previously all-white county Democratic committee.

But in the rural and small-town South, the barriers to voting remained. In 1957 Congress established the Federal Civil Rights Commission to investigate the denial of voting and other rights. Ralph McGill, editor of *The Atlanta Constitution*, wrote, "through the turbulent years immediately ahead, the nation will badly need such a board." [4]

The National Association for the Advancement of Colored People, which had long struggled to widen Negro voting in the South, also led the attack on the inferior education provided for Negro children in segregated schools. It moved first against segregation in higher education and won a number of cases before the Supreme Court opening hitherto white institutions to Negroes. By 1954 over two thousand Negroes were enrolled in these Southern universities and colleges.

With this barrier breached, the NAACP now focused its attack on segregated public schools. In May, 1954, the Supreme Court delivered the historic decision that segregated schools were unconstitutional, since the Fourteenth Amendment guaranteed the equal protection of the law to all persons. "Separate educational facilities are inherently unequal," Chief Justice Earl Warren announced in the unanimous decision. A year later the Court stated that there was no specific time set for compliance by the seventeen states and the District of Columbia that had segregated schools, but the federal courts and local school districts were instructed after assessing their situations and recognizing the administrative complexities to ensure a "prompt and reasonable start" and carry out the decision with "all deliberate speed" as quickly as was "practicable."

The District of Columbia, on initiative from the President, ended segregation immediately; Delaware, Maryland, West Virginia, Kentucky, Missouri, Tennessee, Arkansas, Oklahoma, and Texas achieved by 1956 a policy of partial integration in three hundred and fifty school districts. Meanwhile, in some Southern states integration was opposed by "white councils" and the Ku Klux Klan. The Governors of Virginia and the states of the Deep South secured the passage of a variety of laws designed to circumvent the decision. These Governors muttered about "state sovereignty," and, in terms reminiscent of John C. Calhoun, threatened "nullification" and the "interposition" of state authority to prevent federal enforcement. Saner heads in the South were unwilling, however, to sacrifice the rapidly growing economic and cultural progress of the region to the nostalgic memory of the antebellum South.[5] Progress toward integration was, however, fraught with difficulties. Southern tempers were edgy.

When the schools opened in September, 1957, Governor Orval Faubus of Arkansas provoked a serious challenge to federal authority by calling out the Arkansas National Guard to prevent nine Negro children from attending Little Rock's Central High School, thus "interposing" state authority against an order of the federal District Court to proceed with integration. Although the Governor insisted that he had acted to prevent violence, the Mayor of Little Rock, the chief of police, and federal authorities testified before the federal judge that there had been no such threat.

Three weeks later Faubus withdrew the troops under a federal court order, but by now he had provoked resistance and an unruly mob prevented the Negro children from entering the school. When on the following day the mob ignored a presidential proclamation to disperse, Eisenhower placed the Arkansas National Guard under federal authority and also ordered federal troops to Little Rock to enforce the court order.

Moderate spokesmen in both the North and the South were critical of the President for moving so slowly and for having said at a press conference on July 17 that he could not visualize a situation requiring the use of federal troops in the South. "The President," the New York Times remarked, "did, belatedly and powerfully, what he might not have had to do at all if he had previously made his position unmistakably and publicly understood." And Virgil T. Blossom, Superintendent of Schools in Little Rock from 1953 to 1958, has written: "There must be leadership that will open the countless minds now closed." [6]

As the 1958 school year approached, the Little Rock School Board and the Superintendent of Schools petitioned the federal District Judge to postpone their plans for desegregation for two and a half years since extreme public hostility, which they stated had largely been engendered by official attitudes and actions of the Governor and the state legislature, made it impossible to maintain a sound educational program with Negro students in attendance. The District Judge granted the request but the Court of Appeals overruled it.

The case went immediately to the Supreme Court, which stated on September 29, 1958: "It necessarily involved a claim by the Governor and Legislature of a state that there is no duty on state officials to obey Federal court orders resting on this court's considered interpretation of the United States Constitution." The Court cautioned that the desegregation decision "can neither be nullified openly and directly by state legislators or state executive or judicial officers, nor nullified indirectly by them through evasive schemes for segregation whether attempted 'ingeniously' or 'ingenuously.' "

And the Court warned: "No state legislator or executive or judicial officer can war against the Constitution without violating his undertaking to support it." Moreover, striking at Southern plans to close all public schools and substitute "private" segregated schools with state support, the Court announced: "State support of segregated schools through any arrangement, management, funds or property cannot be squared with the [Fourteenth] amendment's command that no state shall deny to any person within its jurisdiction the equal protection of the laws."

Nevertheless, Governor Faubus continued to deny federal authority and he closed the Little Rock high school rather than accept integration. And the Governor of Virginia in the fall of 1958 closed several high schools where the federal courts ordered integration to proceed.

On January 19, 1959, the Virginia Supreme Court, while deploring "the lack of judicial restraint" by the United States Supreme Court, struck down the law enacted by the Virginia legislature that empowered the Governor to close schools where integration had been ordered. The Virginia Constitution, the court stated, "requiring the General Assembly to 'establish and maintain an efficient system of public free schools through the state' is still in the organic law and must be complied with."

Although the General Assembly held an emergency session, the Governor now cautioned against further extremist action. A few days later, the closed high schools reopened with token integration of a few Negro students.[7] In a state under the control of the most efficient political machine in the nation, there was no violence when the Negro children entered hitherto white schools.

Virginia — unlike its neighbor North Carolina which had proceeded with token integration earlier — had pioneered the way for the Deep South in "massive resistance." Now, in 1959, although its acceptance of token integration was belated and reluctant, the Old Dominion's action portended similar developments in other states.

All through these difficult years, important Southern newspapers including the *Louisville Courier-Journal, Atlanta Constitution, Nashville Tennessean, Arkansas Gazette,* and the *Raleigh News and Observer* urged compliance with the law. And an encouraging number of Southern clergymen and educators protested the massive resistance legislation. But in Virginia, Arkansas, and in the Deep South, political leadership failed to offer the guidance that was essential and, instead, rallied extremist opposition to the Court's decision.

The inflammatory activities of Southern politicians had an immediate impact on the way Negroes voted. In 1956, President Eisenhower halted the twenty-year Democratic trend of Northern Negro voting. He received 8 per cent more of the Negro vote than he had in 1952. And in Southern cities the increase was 28 per cent.[8] An extraordinary shift occurred in Atlanta and New Orleans. In the predominantly Negro precincts of Atlanta, Stevenson had received 74.3 per cent of the vote in 1952, but in 1956 Eisenhower captured 86.35 per cent. In New Orleans the shift was from 67 per cent Democratic in 1952 to 57 per cent Republican in 1956.

Although high levels of employment, the rapid development of a stable middle income group, and increased Republican campaigning all contributed to these gains, the civil rights issue was paramount. White Citizens Councils, the Ku Klux Klan, and rabid segregationists including Senators James O. Eastland of Mississippi and Herman Talmadge of Georgia, and Congressman James C. Davis of

Atlanta, drove Negroes out of the Democratic party in presidential elections.

The Republican failure in 1956 to win control of Congress indicated the necessity of breaching one of the two blocs of "safe" Democratic seats. It seemed more possible that they could accomplish this in the Northern urban districts, which had the heaviest Negro concentrations, than in the South.

By accentuating the strains between the Dixiecrats and the rest of the Democrats, the Republicans were in a position to strike at the heart of the Democratic party in the Northern cities. Ever since 1938, conservative Southern Democrats and conservative Northern Republicans had formed a tacit coalition in Congress to block economic legislation unattractive to the latter and civil rights laws offensive to the former. In 1957, however, the White House pushed for a civil rights bill and the coalition broke down.

Faced with a threatened filibuster from extreme Southerners and the likely disruption of the Democratic party, Lyndon Johnson persuaded Southerners to abandon the filibuster and many Western Democrats to accept a compromise bill largely confining Eisenhower's proposed bill to protecting Negro voting rights in the South. For the time being, Johnson had shaped a workable compromise between the incorrigible Southern extremists and the liberal Northern Democrats, but the potential of the civil rights issue for disrupting the Democratic party remained.[9]

By 1959, six Southern states, with a total of 57 electoral votes, had adopted legislation freeing electors from obligation to vote in the Electoral College for the Democratic presidential candidate. In a close election, such as Wilson's in 1916, this plan could keep the nominee from receiving a majority in the Electoral College, throwing the decision into the House of Representatives. Southern extremists calculated this would intimidate the convention and force it to nominate a conservative candidate whose views on civil rights, taxes, labor legislation, and public welfare issues would be acceptable to them.

But their scheme appeared less threatening to Northern Democrats than they believed. Many Northern Democrats, including Paul Butler, Chairman of the Democratic National Committee, recognized that the electoral vote of the industrialized North was more significant than that of the South. Further, Republican inroads on the vote of Northern Negroes and urban liberal forces would be more costly than the votes gained by the appeasement of Southern extremists. And Northern leaders were not unmindful of the fact that the Dixiecrat revolt of 1948 had enhanced Truman's appeal in metropolitan areas where presidential victories were determined.

Intermittent Leadership: Eisenhower

32.   Modern Republicanism

During its first term, the Eisenhower Administration, much like the Conservative party in Great Britain, adopted most of the policies of the opposition, tried to make the programs less expensive, placed conservative-minded men in charge of them, gave these programs a new slogan — Modern Republicanism — and claimed it was all wholly new. In spite of his right-of-the-middle views before taking office, by 1954 the President was led by the pressure of events and good politics to support the welfare state and a managed economy.

Old Guard Republicans did not like it. George Sokolsky, a journalistic spokesman, complained that under Eisenhower the Republican party "has gone so modern that it is indistinguishable from the New Deal." Representative Noah Mason of Illinois, a veritable antique Republican, lamented: "Essentially Ike's New Republicanism is a form of bribery, a program to buy votes with the voter's own money." To which Eisenhower replied on April 11, 1957: "I happen to believe that in this day and time we cannot use the governmental processes that were applicable in 1890. We have got to adapt the great principles of the Constitution to the inescapable industrial and economic conditions of our time, and make certain that our country is secure, and our people participate in the progress of our economy."

Although Eisenhower was not as conservative in the presidency as he had sounded in the 1952 campaign, there were warring pulls in his philosophy. As he expressed it, he wanted to be conservative on fiscal matters and liberal in human relations. When he was campaigning in 1952, he had said: "Isn't it time we had, in Washington, an administration which knows how to keep spending down?" Yet non-defense expenditures, beginning in 1956, were raised higher than under Truman. The President's apology for his $71.8 billion request for fiscal year 1958 was clearly the pull within him between the desire to reduce government spending and the belief that the government should promote the general welfare.

With the exception of the budget prepared for fiscal 1953 by the Truman Administration, which reflected the costs of the Korean war and preparation for unabated cold war, the Eisenhower budgets were larger than those of the Fair Deal. But military expenditure was not responsible for the increase. In fact, expenditures for defense were reduced in the Eisenhower Administration below what they had been in fiscal 1952-1953. To a degree, the Eisenhower Administration financed Modern Republicanism by reductions in the defense area. It was not actions by the Soviet Union that determined reductions in military spending but the Republican desire to hold down government spending.

In 1953, the Eisenhower Administration was more conservative than in later years. Secretary of the Treasury George Humphrey insisted that the economy must be freed of the price and wage controls instituted during the Korean war and that expenditures and taxes must be cut. Defense appropriations were slashed and the government tightened up on credit. These two steps contributed to a recession in late 1953 and through half of 1954.

But after the recession set in, the Administration took positive steps to prevent another 1929. Credit restrictions were eased, the Social Security program expanded, and business, local governments, and consumers encouraged by Humphrey and others to increase their spending. Although Democrats recommended more direct intervention through programs of public works, the Administration's actions were a turning point and not only stimulated a bounding prosperity by late 1954 but established the fact that the policies of Andrew Mellon were not in control of this Republican Administration.

Through the first term, the rhetoric used by the businessmen in the Cabinet made them sound far more to the right than they actually were. And the increasing influence of economist Gabriel Hauge, the chief theoretician of Modern Republicanism, and of Arthur F. Burns, Chairman of the Council of Economic Advisers, indicated by 1955-1956 that the Administration had moved toward the center.

Eisenhower believed that the federal government strengthened the economy when it widened opportunity for the less fortunate; stimulated, in cooperation with the states, expenditures for highways, hospitals, and schools; encouraged private initiative, avoiding encroachment on the private sector; and generated confidence by relying on fiscal policies rather than direct controls to prevent inflation or deflation. The government, he felt, should apply restraint, with active intervention justifiable only in the extremity of an impending crisis.

With businessmen dominating the Cabinet and various federal regulatory agencies, critics were quick to denounce the "businessman's government." While the government was kind to business in many ways, it had learned from the decade of the 1920s that the interests of other groups could not be ignored if the Republicans were to remain in power.

Although farm income dropped during Eisenhower's presidency, it was not because the Administration failed to treat farming as a special interest deserving special attention. At the outset Secretary of Agriculture Ezra Benson believed that the farm economy was weak because high price supports had resulted in excessive stocks of wheat, corn, cotton, tobacco, and other crops held by the government. Lower price supports would discourage production and solve the problem. Congress was induced to adopt a more flexible parity ratio — 82 to 90 per cent in 1955 and 75 to 90 per cent in 1956. But this did not discourage production, and in 1956 the Administration spent about two billion dollars to raise farm prices.

The drop in farm income stirred political protest. The farming Midwest, almost continually Republican since the Civil War, now began to be doubtful territory. The more politically minded members of the Administration intervened in farm policy and insisted over Secretary Benson's objections upon a program to pay farmers for removing acreage from production and putting them in a soil bank, hoping that this would allow the domestic and foreign market to absorb the surpluses on hand.

In 1955, the President had vetoed a soil bank program proposed by the Democrats as well as a Democratic bill fixing parity at 90 per cent. In 1956, however, the Administration introduced its own soil bank bill, less expensive than the Democratic version, and price supports on major crops were set at only a few percentage points below 90. The Republicans were now spending more for the farmers than was ever spent by the Democrats, and Stevenson was robbed of the farm issue in his campaign. Eisenhower carried every farm state outside of the South except Missouri, although many farmers reflected their dissatisfaction by voting for Democratic Congressmen and Governors.

The basic difficulty in farming was that the earnings of farm people for their labor and entrepreneurship were not comparable to the returns to workers in other sectors of the economy. And, although farm population had shrunk ten millions in the past two decades, there were still too many people in agriculture. In a technological revolution that required fewer and fewer people to produce more and more, both Democrats and Republicans preferred to debate the degree of price supports rather than take measures to speed the flow of people out of agriculture.

Aside from farming, resources and power policies were the most explosive issues of the first four years. "The best natural resources program for America," Eisenhower said in his first State of the Union Message, "will not result from exclusive dependence on Federal bureaucracy. It will involve a partnership of the states and local communities, private citizens and the Federal Government, all working together."

But the President's catchy term "partnership" soon was attacked by the equally catchy term of the Democrats, "giveaways." The offshore submerged oil lands were granted to the coastal states. The budget of the Bonneville Power Administration for long-range planning in the vast Columbia River basin was slashed. A number of dam projects, already approved by Congress, were abandoned or shelved. The Democratic plans for a high federal dam in Hell's Canyon were blocked and the area was turned over to the Idaho Power Company.

And the Administration, in accord with this philosophy, restricted the expansion of the TVA in favor of private power. But the Administration became devious, indirect, and soon stumbled into trouble.

Memphis needed more power, but the Administration refused to allow the TVA to build a steam plant. Then, instead of empowering the TVA to contract with a private group for the power, the Atomic Energy Commission was authorized to do it. On November 11, 1954, the AEC signed a contract with the Dixon-Yates combine. Before the contract was signed, Democrats were already attacking the arrangement. After a meeting of the Senate Democratic Policy Committee on November 9, Johnson, now the majority leader, said: "We had hoped that the A.E.C. could be kept out of the political field and that it could use its time in assuring America's maintenance of superiority in the atomic field." [1]

With the attacks increasing, the President instructed the Bureau of the Budget to make a "complete disclosure" of the history of the contract. But the Bureau omitted one important item in its report. In February, 1955, Senator Lister Hill of Alabama unearthed the crucial point missing from the "complete disclosure." Nowhere in the report was the name Adolphe H. Wenzell mentioned; it had been omitted, investigation revealed, at the request of the AEC. Wenzell had served as an unpaid special consultant to the Bureau of the Budget when it prepared the contract. At the same time, he was an official of the First Boston Corporation, the investment house that was to act as financial agent for the Dixon-Yates combine.

With this revelation, it was clear the Adminstration was in need of a graceful way to get out of the entire affair. The city of Memphis provided it by announcing it would build its own generating plant. On July 11, 1955, the President canceled the contract. When the AEC, which has always maintained the legality of the contract, now contended it was illegal because of a "conflict of interest" on the part of Mr. Wenzell, Dixon-Yates went to court to recover preliminary construction costs. On July 12, 1956, the Justice Department told the Court of Claims that the contract had been "contrary to the public interest" and illegal from the start!

The West, in particular, reacted strongly against the Administration's resources policy. While Eisenhower himself swept to victory in 1956, Democrats in the West won nearly 60 per cent of the state and local races. The President's hand-picked candidates for the Senate — Douglas McKay of Oregon, Dan Thornton of Colorado, and Arthur B. Langlie of Washington — went down to defeat.

In their power and resources policies, the Republicans ignored the pressing needs of the Pacific Northwest. With its population growing 10 per cent faster than that of the rest of the nation, it needed more cheap water power to provide for new industry and additional water for irrigation. "We are moving too fast," a Seattle banker said, "to be able to afford any kind of status quo." Shortly after the election the Associated Press reported that an anonymous White House official had said that the Administration was starting a complete review of its power and resources policies. And a Seattle Republican leader remarked: "There now are no Republicans left in Congress who are willing to fight for 'partnership.' "

The 1954 mid-term elections revealed that the nation had two evenly competing parties. The bare Republican majority achieved two years before provided no cushion to absorb the usual mid-term losses. The Democrats captured two Senate and seventeen House seats, which the Republican incumbents had won by narrow margins in 1952. Where the impact of the recession was most acute, the Republicans suffered losses, but elsewhere held their own or gained votes. Although unable to close the 1952 gap between itself and Eisenhower, the Republican party did not fare badly.

Candidates identified with McCarthyism, however, did poorly across the country. Sharpening the very issues that Eisenhower chose to blur, Vice-President Nixon led the attack on the Truman-Acheson foreign policy, Korea, Communism, and corruption. Particularly in the mountain states where Republican economic appeal was weak, Republican orators stepped up this assault on the Democrats.

He set the issue of Communism in a more usable text than McCarthy's "Twenty Years of Treason." "Communism should not be a political issue," Nixon said. "There is no difference between the loyalty of Democrats and Republicans. But —" and here, Cabell Phillips reported, he lowered the boom gently into place — "some misguided officials of the previous Administration were blind or indifferent to the danger. They ignored the repeated warnings that J. Edgar Hoover and others including myself brought to them. . . . But this Administration is *cooperating* with J. Edgar Hoover and the F.B.I. We have not only fired the Communists and fellow-travelers and security risks off the Federal Payroll by the thousands; we don't hire them in the first place. I can assure you that no one in this Administration regards Communism as a red herring." [2]

This type of campaign achieved spotty results. The voters elected in most cases the candidates who were most abused by the Republicans. When the President was asked at a press conference on October 27 whether he had approved the change in Republican strategy from praising the Eisenhower program to charging the Democrats with being soft on Communism, he looked puzzled.

He replied that he had heard two or three speeches in Washington and had not heard the word Communist mentioned. He added that he had not read the recent speeches, nobody had discussed with him the details of their talks, but his colleagues knew his views, and he assumed they were presenting the case as they saw it. James Reston commented that the President would never imply that the Democrats winked at treason, nor would he knowingly condone it, "but things are done in his name that he knows not of."

The 1954 election freed the President from the restraints of the extremists in his own party. And Modern Republicanism, while still amorphous, took more form in the next two years than it had been able to do with a Republican Congress. The Eisenhower Administration, not Congressmen from small-city or rural America, now set Republican policy.

By 1956, peace and prosperity replaced Korea, Communism, and corruption as themes of Republican oratory. Over television and radio, and with cross-country tours, Eisenhower put on an active campaign that belied attacks that his health was impaired. The majority of citizens "liked Ike"; in addition, his proposals for a soil bank, public housing, a vast federal highway construction program, and federal aid for school buildings revealed that the President had acquired the political acumen to negate the Democratic monopoly on social welfare legislation. During the campaign, the President whipped up wild enthusiasm.

Stevenson, renominated by the Democrats, tried to focus the campaign on the necessity of expanded slum clearance, federal aid to education, and federal activity in the field of health. He warned of the lack of initiative in foreign policy from the White House, of the weakening of the alliance with other free nations since 1953, of the unformulated policy in the smoldering Middle East, and of the absence of respect for the uncommitted nations.

The public, obviously, was in no mood to listen to talk about problems. With prosperity for almost all, and with peace, however shaky, the nation favored tranquillity with Eisenhower. Near the close of the campaign, the Hungarian uprising against Soviet domination, the Israeli attack on Egypt, and the British-French action in the Suez added to the conviction that Eisenhower was the man of stature necessary to deal with such upheavals.

While Stevenson launched a vigorous campaign late in August, Eisenhower waited until mid-September to start his. A month later, Eisenhower's was reaching its peak while the Democratic campaign, after its initial vigor, was sagging noticeably. Stevenson was rarely able to win a response like that of four years before. He was not as persuasive. At times he seemed ill at ease. And he was tired. He had been campaigning for a year, going through grueling primary fights with Senator Kefauver and a tense and wearing Convention struggle with Truman and Governor Harriman of New York. His 1956 speeches lacked the elation and resounding conviction of four years before. Moreover, he was hampered by the Democratic congressional support of Eisenhower's policies which furnished no distinctive record for the national wing of the party to build on.

Eisenhower's nine and a half million margin of victory demonstrated how seriously the old New Deal coalition had been shattered and indicated that American politics was moving into a new era.[3] Democrats emerged stronger than before in hitherto rural Republican strongholds, capturing the Governorships of Kansas and Iowa, but more significant were the heavy Republican gains in the hitherto powerful Democratic cities. In the twelve largest cities, Eisenhower drew 49 per cent of the vote, registering gains among Catholics, union members, young people, and those of lower income level; and he actually carried such former Democratic strongholds as Chicago and Jersey City.

While Eisenhower received a powerful vote of confidence, he was the first President in over a century to be without a congressional majority at the start of his term. The voters saw the Republican party as a whole as less deserving of support than the President. Although he carried 329 of the nation's 435 congressional districts, his party won only 201 seats in the House. In the forty-one states carried by Eisenhower, the Republicans won seventeen Senate races and lost eleven, and won fourteen and lost thirteen gubernatorial races.[4]

Eisenhower had not accomplished by 1956 what Roosevelt had achieved in 1934 when he transformed his personal following into a rebuilt Democratic party with a decisive national majority.

---

33. Security and McCarthy

The mood of well-being, repose, and moderation, which came to characterize the first Eisenhower Administration, was not achieved quickly or easily. The acrimony which had made the closing years of the Truman era inglorious and dangerous continued to infect American politics.

On November 6, 1953, Attorney General Herbert Brownell contrasted the Administration's new security program with Truman's, and charged: "Harry Dexter White was known to be a spy by the very people who appointed him to the most sensitive and important position he ever held in Government service." Since Truman had appointed White, there was a furious outcry. At a stormy press conference on November 11, when asked if he thought Truman knowingly appointed a Communist spy to high office, Eisenhower eased some of the rancor when he replied: "No, it is inconceivable."[1]

A month later, Governor Dewey, after denouncing Truman and the Democrats for "bungling our country" into the Korean war and for the loss of China, said: "Remember that the words Truman and Democrat mean diplomatic failure, military failure, death and tragedy." And, on a speaking tour arranged by the Republican National Committee to commemorate Lincoln's Birthday, Senator McCarthy assailed the Democrats for "twenty years of treason": "The hard fact is that those who wear the label — Democrat — wear it with the stain of an historic betrayal."

At his press conference on February 10, 1954, the President tried to steer the nation away from this virulent mood. He knew that Democratic leaders would not cooperate in government if Republicans turned party contest into a war of political extermination. To suggest that all Democrats were tinged with treason or were all security risks, Eisenhower said, was "not only completely untrue, but very unwise" since "the Administration needed Democratic votes to get its program through Congress." He then added that it was obvious that he was "not very much of a partisan. The times were too serious . . . to indulge in partisanship to the extreme."

Despite his soothing words, the Administration's security program inflamed partisanship. Having agreed with the extremists in 1952 that there were Communists and security risks in the government, the Eisenhower aides diligently tried to demonstrate that they were ousting such influences. Under Truman, there had been separate loyalty and security programs. The former covered all employees and dismissal occurred when there was a reasonable doubt of loyalty. The latter applied to eleven "sensitive" agencies, including the Departments of Defense and State, and provided for dismissal of employees if their habits — loose talk, drunkenness, and homosexuality, in addition to subversive activities — made them risks to the national security. The Eisenhower Administration eliminated the separation between the two programs, issuing Executive Order 10450 which covered personal habits, integrity, and subversion and applied it to all government positions.[2]

Then began what the Democrats and some non-Democrats called the "numbers game." On October 23, 1953, the White House stated that 1456 government employees had been dismissed or had resigned under Eisenhower's security program. During the next year, the Administration raised the figure to 2200, to 6926, to 8008, and finally stopped the statistics at 9600. While Republican orators clutched the figures with sheer delight, newspapermen clamored for information as to how many were actually dismissed as Communists, former Communists, or fellow travelers. The Alsops denounced it as "Security-Firing Fakery" and asserted: "The privately admitted purpose of these 'security firings' has been to 'grab the Commie issue away from Sen. McCarthy.'" [3] Under hammering from the press and Democratic Congressmen, Brownell said on February 7, 1954, that the 2200 discharged came under eight or nine categories and by no means were all of them Communists or spies.

The Department of State reeled under the full blast of the hysteria in 1953-1954. Apparently to undercut McCarthy's attacks on the Department, Dulles and his security chief, Scott McLeod, announced that 306 employees had been released for security reasons, and by February, 1954, the figure had reached 534. But, when called before a secret session of a House Appropriations Subcommittee, Department officials explained that only eleven had been dropped for loyalty reasons and no active Communist had been found.[4]

The entire security program was criticized hotly not only by Democratic leaders but by writers, educators, scientists, and lawyers for undermining constitutional rights, forcing conformity of opinion, impeding scientific research and depriving the government of the services of able citizens. And from former right-wing Republican Senator Harry Cain, appointed by Eisenhower to the Subversive Activities Control Board, came devastating criticism. By 1955, he was convinced that the internal security system was doing more harm than good. He charged that the program was brutal and ruthless and was "unnecessarily destroying individuals."

In the spring of 1955, the Administration announced some procedural changes in the security system, including the right of the accused to confront and cross-examine witnesses who supplied derogatory information except when the national security might be jeopardized. The Senate voted unanimously, and the House without debate, for a bipartisan study of the whole security system. With the need to secure cooperation from a Democratic-controlled Congress, no more statistics were issued by the Administration about uprooting security risks. In effect, the Administration now conceded that its security figures had been misleading or false.

The Civil Service Commission admitted that more than 90 per cent of those 9600 employees described as security risks had left the government by regular civil service procedures without hearings to test any security charges. Up to September 30, 1955, only 1016 employees actually had been charged under the security program. And, of these, only 342 were dismissed under security procedures. The interesting fact was that more than 50 per cent of the 9600 had been hired during the Eisenhower Administration.[5]

For the first two years of the new Administration, not only did McCarthy continue his ruthless onslaught on the loyalty of many citizens, but he also tried to usurp the powers of the presidency and wrest control of the Republican party from Eisenhower. From his chairmanship of the formidable Permanent Subcommittee on Investigations, McCarthy immediately launched an attack on the Administration. At first, Eisenhower tried either to ignore the Senator or cooperate with his investigations. It was the President's "passion," his aide C. D. Jackson said, "not to offend anyone in Congress."

When McCarthy announced that a good security officer was needed in the Department of State to clean out Communists, John Foster Dulles complied by appointing Scott McLeod. Such appeasement failed to stop the attacks. McCarthy denounced the appointment of James B. Conant, President of Harvard University, as High Commissioner to Germany. He fought the appointment of Charles E. Bohlen as Ambassador to the Soviet Union as a "security risk" and accused Dulles of "untrue statements" in defending Bohlen.

Throughout these early weeks, McCarthy — with a battery of television cameras recording the hearings — assailed the Information Program of the Department of State. In April he sent his aides, Roy M. Cohn and G. David Schine, on an eighteen-day whirlwind tour through Western Europe to ferret out "subversion" in the information program. McCarthy proclaimed "appalling infiltration" and a number of able people were released by the Department.

In an earlier move to appease McCarthy, the Information Agency on February 19 issued a directive that "No material by any Communists, fellow-travelers, et cetera, will be used under any circumstances." But there was no definition of a Communist or a fellow traveler, or what an "et cetera" was. This produced so much criticism at home and abroad that when Robert Johnson took charge in March as the new director of the Information Agency he asked Dulles for clearer instructions. Dulles's reply omitted the "et cetera" but ordered the removal of books by those "who obviously follow the Communist line or participate in Communist front organizations" and the withdrawal of any magazine containing "material detrimental to the U. S. objectives." The words "detrimental" and "objectives" again were not defined. While the lists of books and magazines were being drafted, frightened officials overseas removed items that were never to appear on the lists and some books were burned. None of this satisfied McCarthy who had his own list, and who charged on May 5 that "30,000 to 40,000 books by Communists and fellow-travelers" were in the overseas libraries.

While the book episode was raging, Eisenhower's appointee, Robert Johnson, tried to enlist help from the White House only to be told the President was solidly booked for two weeks ahead. Finally, with the aid of writers and publishers, Johnson worked out a policy on books which Dulles approved on July 8. It explained that the Information Agency would not exclude books as Communist or communistic which contained criticism of American policies or institutions: "We must begin with the content of a book. We must examine its special usefulness in terms of our overseas needs." Moreover, books by Communists or Communist sympathizers might be included "if such authors may have written something which affirmatively served the ends of democracy." By this statement, the policy was again essentially the one that had been followed prior to February.

McCarthy stepped up his assault over TV and radio on November 24, 1953, by saying that while Eisenhower was doing "infinitely" better than Truman in ousting security risks, there were a few cases where the batting average was "zero." As to Eisenhower's statement a week before that Communists in government would not be an issue in the 1954 campaign, McCarthy replied bluntly that the "raw, harsh, unpleasant fact" was that Communism would indeed be an issue. Next, he leveled his guns at the Administration's foreign policy and denounced the continuance of mutual assistance to Britain while the British traded with Communist China. Instead of cutting off aid to Britain, the scowling Senator rasped, we are sending "perfumed notes."

With the approval of the President, Dulles now fought back, pointing out that we were dealing with free nations as sovereign equals. The next day Eisenhower, urged by one adviser to mention McCarthy by name, refused, saying: "I will not get in the gutter with that guy." He told the press that to coerce our Allies would be the mark of an "imperialist rather than of the leader." As to Communists in government, the Administration would remove any discovered, but it would protect the basic rights of loyal citizens.

By now, McCarthy was launching an attack on the Army. He asserted that there were "earmarks of dangerous espionage" in the Signal Corps at Fort Monmouth. The Secretary of the Army, Robert Stevens, trying to work with McCarthy, suspended those accused, even though the Federation of American Scientists warned that the suspensions resulted in "a serious disruption of the scientific work at the laboratory." On February 18, 1954, McCarthy, at a hearing, shouted at a distinguished General, Ralph Zwicker: "You are a disgrace to the uniform. You're shielding Communist conspirators. . . . You're not fit to be an officer. You're ignorant."

No longer could the Administration ignore McCarthy's attempt to dominate the executive and be master of the Republican party. The Army, with the support of the White House, struck back. On March 3, the President, who considered it inconsistent with the dignity of his office to mention McCarthy by name, stated: "In opposing Communism, we are defeating ourselves if either by design or through carelessness we use methods that do not conform to the American sense of fair play."

On March 11, at the suggestion of Presidential Assistant Sherman Adams, the Army charged that McCarthy, Roy Cohn, and the Subcommittee staff director, Francis Carr, had tried by improper means to force the Army to grant preferential treatment to G. David Schine who had been drafted the previous fall. McCarthy, who now was accusing the Army of "coddling Communists," fired back with forty-six charges.

The Senate Subcommittee voted to investigate the Army-McCarthy charges, with Karl Mundt temporarily replacing McCarthy as the Chairman. The televised spectacle transfixed the nation for thirty-six days. The hearings became, as one newspaperman has written, the national business, the national pastime, and the national disgrace. Among the performers who gained respect was Senator John McClellan of Arkansas, who revealed with rasping logic how the Secretary of the Army had tried to appease the friends of a buck private.

But, above all, there was the image of McCarthy in millions of living rooms, bars, and public places. Scowling, interrupting with "Point of order, point of order, Mr. Chairman," seizing the floor, flinging smears while accusing others of smearing, he became more reckless in his charges. When McCarthy, in a flagrant encroachment on the executive, demanded records of privileged conversations in the White House, the President refused and asserted those rights which "cannot be usurped by any individual who may seek to set himself above the laws of the land."

By now no one, including Eisenhower, was immune to the charges of being soft on Communists. On May 30, McCarthy spoke of "the evidence of treason that has been growing up over the twenty . . ."— he paused, scowled, and with great deliberation added "Twenty-one years." Now even those Republicans who disagreed with him were treasonable.

As the hearings ground on, McCarthy's popular support was weakened both by his own ruthless tactics as well as by presidential opposition.[6] Still, McCarthy might have preserved some of his following had he not thrown a wild haymaker at Joseph Welch, Chief Army Counsel, and senior partner of a distinguished Boston law firm. Welch's deft questioning infuriated McCarthy. Near the close of the hearings, as Welch led Roy Cohn through a destructive cross-examination, McCarthy interrupted and attacked a member of Welch's law firm for once having belonged to the Lawyer's Guild, "which was named, oh, years and years ago, as the legal bulwark of the Communist party."

With his face white with anger, Welch replied: "Until this moment, Senator, I think I never really gauged your cruelty or your recklessness . . . Little did I dream that you could be so reckless and so cruel as to do an injury to that lad . . . I fear he shall always bear a scar needlessly inflicted by you. If it were in my power to forgive you for your reckless cruelty, I would do so, I like to think I am a gentleman, but your forgiveness will have to come from someone other than me."

As McCarthy tried to break in, Welch, with emotion, said: "Let us not assassinate this lad further, Senator. You have done enough. Have you no sense of decency?" When McCarthy tried to ask him about his partner, Welch cut him off with cold scorn and said: "Mr. McCarthy, I will not discuss this with you further . . . If there is a God in heaven, it will do neither you nor your cause any good."

There was a hush over the room broken suddenly by a storm of applause. McCarthy slouched in his chair, and with bewilderment in his voice turned to someone and said: "What did I do wrong?" "Joseph McCarthy would never know," Eric F. Goldman has written in *The Crucial Decade*. "And that June day, 1954, millions at their TV sets learned once and for all that Joseph McCarthy would never know." [7]

On August 2 the United States voted to form a select committee to weigh a motion of Senator Ralph Flanders to censure McCarthy. On September 27, Senator Arthur Watkins submitted a unanimous report recommending censure. After thirteen days of acrimonious debate, the Senate voted 67 to 22 to censure McCarthy. The arrogant Senator was not censured for attacking the Bill of Rights, for accusing without proof, for dividing the nation or for denying the oldest traditions of the English-speaking heritage, but for abusing the 1951 Senate Subcommittee on Elections and for attacking the special Watkins Committee in language that reflected on the dignity and integrity of the Senate. After the Senate vote, this self-styled man of destiny dwindled into a forlorn figure.

The merit of Eisenhower's approach to the problem of McCarthy will long be debated. While he had disdain for McCarthy, Eisenhower felt that he had to calm public opinion rather than excite it by engaging in a fight with the Senator. Instead, McCarthy was allowed to destroy himself by his own excesses. With his immense prestige, Eisenhower might have been able to isolate McCarthy in 1953 and prevent his outrages. But, while the Senator was playing himself out, countless citizens were subjected to unjust attacks, the machinery of government thrown into confusion, the standards of legislative investigations debased, and an ugly picture of America exported to the world.

---

34.   Paralyzing Pressures on Foreign Policy

For the first two years of the Eisenhower Administration, foreign policy formation was at the mercy of domestic politics. The savagely partisan and irresponsible Republican attacks on the limited war in Korea, on China policy, and on the loyalty of State Department officials continued to be nearly disastrous liabilities to sound foreign relations.

Eisenhower, with a public support that Truman had lacked, failed to mobilize it to free foreign policy from the paralysis imposed by the extremists, and instead succumbed to a degree, as he had during the later stages of the 1952 campaign. Inexperienced in politics, he assumed that the Democrats were his opposition in matters of foreign affairs, when his real opposition was the majority of Republicans in Congress. And valuing Republican unity more than bipartisanship, members of the Administration blessed the extremists' attempts to stigmatize Democrats as condoners of treason.[1] As part of appeasing the Knowlands and the Bridges in his own party, Eisenhower cooperated with the congressional investigations that undermined the personnel of the Department of State, supported Dulles in eliminating many able diplomats and appointing irreconcilables to key positions. And, to satisfy his Republican opposition, he proclaimed a "dynamic" foreign policy, often reiterated but never implemented.

Dulles used the public relations technique of issuing spectacular announcements designed to appease the Republican opposition. But the language — "liberation," "dynamic foreign policy," "instant massive retaliation," "unleashing Chiang Kai-shek," "agonizing reappraisal"— proved to be meaningless, since Eisenhower was too responsible to do what the irreconcilables desired. Dulles's statements, however, had the unfortunate effect of frightening the Allies that action might conform to official pronouncements. In fact, they frightened all those who did not grasp the intricacies of intraparty politics.

And, as Hans J. Morgenthau has written: "This 'foreign policy by hoax' has served to confuse the American people. It has raised doubts in the minds of many about the reliability of public pronouncements on anything and has thus led to the beginnings of a crisis of confidence which endangers democratic government itself." [2]

The conflict between international realities and internal Republican party politics appeared in Eisenhower's first State of the Union Message. As part of a "new, positive foreign policy," the United States, he said, would "never acquiesce in the enslavement of any people in order to purchase fancied gain for ourselves." The Korean army would be enlarged and the Seventh Fleet would "no longer be employed to shield Communist China" from attack from Formosa. [3]

The new "dynamism," he explained, was based on the lesson that "the free world cannot indefinitely remain in a posture of paralyzed tension." Later in the speech, however, Eisenhower promised less government spending and a balanced budget, which precluded a more aggressive policy. And he pledged the extension of the Reciprocal Trade Agreements Act and mutual security aid to other nations, for as he said, denying the neo-isolationist belief in unlimited American power: "the policy we pursue will recognize the truth that no single country, even one so powerful as ours, can alone defend the liberty of all nations threatened by Communist aggression from without or subversion within."

Although the Administration compromised with its irreconcilable wing with words, its actual achievements were in not going to war with China; in not fighting in Indo-China; in not replacing containment with a policy of liberation; in not following the advocates of preventive war; and in not ending the alliance with Western Europe. Fears of the Western Allies that Republican victory would mean a reinstatement of isolationism were supplanted by relief that Western Europe had an alliance not only with the Democratic party but with the United States.

Secretary of State John Foster Dulles, more than any single figure in the Administration, furnished the rhetoric which proclaimed the new dynamism in foreign policy. He pioneered the appeasement of the Republican opposition while essentially he steered old policies along old channels. Contemporary comment on Dulles ranged the spectrum. The President called him the greatest Secretary of State he "knew anything about." The Vice-President once remarked: "Isn't it wonderful to have a Secretary of State who stands up to the Russians?" Democratic Senator Henry M. Jackson, however, contended that he was "the original misguided missile, traveling fast, making lots of noise, and never hitting the target."

During 1953-1954, Dulles was determined to avoid such hostile attacks as had destroyed Acheson's effectiveness. He retired career diplomats John Carter Vincent and John Paton Davies, not because of lack of loyalty, but on the ground that they had become too burdensome for a Secretary to carry in his relations with right-wing Republicans. And the security program, under his appointee Scott McLeod, undertook to force conformity on the Department and the foreign service.

The frightening drop in morale that resulted prompted five distinguished retired career diplomats — Norman Armour, Robert Woods Bliss, Joseph C. Grew, William Phillips, and G. Howland Shaw — to warn in a public letter to the New York Times that the foreign service was being destroyed. They expressed their deep concern over the dismissal of many officers, who in the past had reported conscientiously, only to have their loyalty and integrity challenged now. Those who remained in the service, they warned, were writing ambiguous and cautious reports to escape persecution from Washington. "When any such tendency begins its insidious work," they observed, "it is not long before accuracy and initiative have been sacrificed to acceptability and conformity. The ultimate result is a threat to national security." [4]

In addition to removing experienced diplomats, Dulles appointed a number of men to high positions whose main attributes were their sympathies with the extremists. These included the Assistant Secretary of State for Far Eastern Affairs — Walter S. Robertson, a Virginia Democrat — who opposed any negotiations with Communist China. These men, in time, imprisoned Dulles in the straitjacket of old policies when opportunities for a fresh initiative occurred.

Dulles dominated both the making and the conduct of foreign policy far more than his recent predecessors. He was the strongest personality in the Administration and an effective advocate in the National Security Council and the Cabinet. He combined the traditional functions of the principal Cabinet officer with the functions of a traveling presidential agent. In foreign affairs, he was not only Eisenhower's chief adviser and his chief representative on Capitol Hill, but also the President's negotiator in the councils of the Western alliance. With Dulles, Eisenhower did not need a Harry Hopkins.

Dulles sought to dramatize American leadership by becoming a peripatetic secretary-at-large. He flew a total of 479,286 miles outside the United States. While he was admitted to be a redoubtable negotiator by his critics, they insisted that his activities overseas led him to neglect the Department and weakened the effectiveness of the foreign service officers in the various capitals of the world.

Dulles was a man of strong moral conviction and complete confidence in his own judgment. Unlike Acheson, he shut himself off from regular State Department channels of information and advice pertaining to many major decisions. With the exception of his recommendation to risk military action in Vietnam in 1954, Dulles's policy suggestions were followed explicitly by Eisenhower.

With the greatest possible regularity, the Secretary of State held Tuesday morning press conferences, and he met with reporters in off-the-record sessions far more often than other Cabinet members. His statements were the more significant because he spoke with an authority seldom granted a Secretary of State. At his Wednesday press conferences, Eisenhower often merely repeated what Dulles had said the day before or referred the questions to Dulles.

As Dulles presided over the transition of congressional Republicans from isolationism to collective security, he extended American commitments far beyond those made by the Democrats. In 1954, he extended military aid to Pakistan, a decision of far-reaching consequences. It alienated India, forced the Indian government to transfer scanty funds from economic development to defense, and added new difficulties to the settlement of the Kashmir dispute. And the formation that year of the Southeast Asia Treaty Organization, with no major Asian nations participating, stimulated the Afro-Asian Conference at Bandung (1955) with its heavy anti-Western implications. The Baghdad Pact (1955), fathered by Dulles, but which the United States did not fully enter, was a propaganda boon used by the Soviet Union in exploiting Arab nationalism. "In this," Walter Lippmann has written, "Dulles has shown himself to be not a prudent and calculating diplomat but a gambler who is more lavish than any other secretary of state has ever dreamed of being with promissory notes engaging the blood, the treasure, and the honor of this country." [5]

Admirers of Dulles pointed to his "brink of war" doctrine as evidence of his mastery of foreign policy. "You have to take chances for peace, just as you must take chances in war," Mr. Dulles remarked. "Some say that we were brought to the verge of war. Of course we were brought to the verge of war. The ability to get to the verge of war without getting into the war is the necessary art. If you cannot master it, you inevitably get into wars. If you try to run away from it, if you are scared to go to the brink, you are lost. We've had to look it square in the face — on the question of enlarging the Korean War, on the question of getting into the Indo-China war, on the question of Formosa. We walked to the brink and we looked it in the face." [6]

This statement provoked a violent response at home and abroad. Critics maintained that it was fundamentally a false account. Although Dulles described the events in terms of unilateral deterrents by the United States, both sides actually were held in check by mutual deterrents. While the Communists were halted by fear of our atomic retaliation, Syngman Rhee, Chiang Kai-shek, and those Americans who wanted to intervene in Vietnam were restrained by the fear of Soviet retaliation.

Paul Nitze, Chairman of the Policy Planning Staff under Acheson, has suggested that a distinction must be made between the "declaratory policy" and the "operational policy" of Dulles. When there was a revolt among the East Germans in the summer of 1953, the "operational" policy demonstrated that America had no intention of going to war to liberate the satellites. Chiang was encouraged to send his troops to the Tachen Islands and step up raids on the mainland, but at the same time Dulles privately explained that the real policy was one of disengagement from the mainland of Asia. Disengagement started with the Korean truce signed on July 29, 1953. It was not possible, however, to withdraw entirely.

The focus of attention shifted to Vietnam, where the French had been fighting a hopeless war since 1946 against Communist leader Ho Chi Minh who rallied support with a nationalistic appeal against French colonialism. After the Korean truce, the Chinese Communists increased their military aid to Ho's forces. America, in turn, poured in military aid to bolster the French and the Vietnamese government.

Dulles warned China that, if it sent troops to Vietnam, such an aggression "could not occur without grave consequences which might not be confined to Indo-China." Then in a speech before the Council on Foreign Relations on January 12, 1954, Dulles explained that the "new look" in military policy placed its emphasis on air-atomic power, on the "deterrent of massive retaliatory power" to supplement "local defensive power." The United States now would "depend primarily upon a great capacity to retaliate, instantly, by means and at places of our own choosing." [7] Dulles's declaratory policy was aimed again at satisfying extremists and further reflected the feeling that the 1952 election had repudiated the concept of limited war.

His warning did not hinder the Chinese Communists from continuing their aid to Ho. On April 16, 1954, Nixon suggested to the American Society of Newspaper Editors what the operational policy might be: "If, to avoid further Communist expansion in Asia and Indochina we must take the risk now by putting our boys in, I think the Executive has to take the politically unpopular decision and do it."

The reaction was violent. Admiral Arthur Radford, Chairman of the Joint Chiefs of Staff, faced with the danger that the French fortress at Dienbienphu would fall to Ho, recommended an air strike to relieve it. The British refused to join such a plan; key members of Congress, leading newspaper editors, and Generals Matthew B. Ridgway and Nathan F. Twining of the Joint Chiefs of Staff all opposed intervention; and the President thereupon vetoed such unilateral action. In July at a Conference at Geneva an armistice was signed, and Ho's forces gained the northern half of Vietnam. Dulles attended the Conference, but he did not enter into the agreement that led to the armistice.

To put at rest the minds of those Senators, led by Knowland, who feared American recognition of Communist China, Dulles reported that he had not even glanced at the Chinese delegation at the Conference. The inflexibility in American relations with Communist China, which had set in under Truman, became even more rigid under Eisenhower. While bold declarations against China were pleasing to Republican extremists and some Democratic Senators, they were not the massive American support needed by Chiang Kai-shek to attack the mainland. And despite the neo-isolationists, by late 1954 the Administration's policy was one of "leashing Chiang" to prevent him from raiding the mainland. When Chiang said he expected American logistical support to invade the mainland, Eisenhower told his March 2, 1955, press conference: "The United States is not going to be a party to an aggressive war."

During the previous December the United States had signed a mutual defense treaty with Chiang which stated that an attack on the territory of the "Republic of China" would be a threat to American security. While the defense of Formosa and the Pescadores Islands was included in this territory, the Administration retained the option on the question of defending the offshore islands, including Quemoy and Matsu.

The People's Republic of China denounced the treaty as aggression and threatened to "liberate" Formosa. As tensions mounted, the President secured a resolution from Congress in January, 1955, approving the use of armed force to protect Formosa and the Pescadores. He explained in his message to Congress that our clear intentions "will reduce the possibility that the Chinese Communists, misjudging our firm purpose and national unity, might be disposed to challenge the position of the United States, and precipitate a major crisis which even they would neither anticipate nor desire."

The resolution and the President's message left the Chinese Communists guessing as to American actions toward the offshore islands. "The authority that may be accorded by the Congress," Eisenhower said, "would be used only in situations which are recognizable as parts of, or definite preliminaries to, an attack against the main positions of Formosa and the Pescadores." [8]

The situation in the Formosa Straits remained a powder keg. At the Bandung Conference in April, 1955, America's Formosan policy came under strong attack. The People's Republic of China, too, was subjected to pressure for peace in the Formosa Straits. Premier Chou En-lai assured the conference that China did not want war and was willing to enter negotiations to relax tensions.

The Department of State at first insisted that any negotiations would have to include the Nationalists. Walter George, Chairman of the Senate Foreign Relations Committee, warned Dulles that he could not hope to please everyone in the United States and still maintain leadership of the non-Communist world. At this point, Democrats and Eisenhower Republicans, by insisting on excluding the Nationalists from the meetings, freed the Administration from the trap of the neo-isolationists.

The conference of ambassadors began in August, 1955, but the Administration refused to discuss any subject, including tensions in the Formosa Straits, before effecting the release of Americans in Chinese prisons. The general inflexibility toward China remained. Robert J. Donovan has explained in his semi-authoritative book, *Eisenhower: The Inside Story*, that the President was not convinced that the best interests of America were realized by non-recognition of Communist China. But he made no move to alter this policy in view of Knowland's threat to resign as Senate Republican leader to campaign publicly for American withdrawal if the United Nations were to admit the Peking government.

Reacting to the past hysteria, the Administration averted war, but failed to devise new policies that would place relations with China on a more practical basis. Instead, by treaty it allied America with Chiang's defeated faction and committed the nation to a lost cause. While most other countries recognized that the Chinese Communists had consolidated their rule and tried to make accommodations to their increasing power, the United States behaved as though Chinese Communism were a passing phenomenon.

Between 1948 and 1953, public fear and suspicion in the nation precluded negotiations with the Soviet Union. The explosion of hydrogen bombs by the two nations, with the resulting danger of mass annihilation, however, propelled the United States and the Soviet Union toward a meeting. In May, 1953, Winston Churchill proposed a meeting with the Soviets at the "highest level."

Eisenhower, however, moved warily. Many Republicans, obsessed with the evil image they had created of the Roosevelt-Truman meetings with Stalin, objected strenuously. But public opinion in the country, as well as among the Allies and the uncommitted nations, clamored for a relaxation of tensions. And, in January, 1954, the Foreign Ministers of the Big Four met for the first time since 1949. Eisenhower, with the Knowlands and the McCarthys insisting that negotiation at a conference was synonomous with appeasement, moved with caution. But after the mid-term congressional elections, the Democratic leadership exerted its power to free Eisenhower from the paralyzing restraint imposed by his own party.

At his press conference on December 2, 1954, the President said: "let us recognize that we owe it to ourselves and to the world to explore every possible peaceful means of settling differences before we even think of such a thing as war." The Administration, however, continued to delay as the irreconcilables demanded that the satellite nations had to be liberated before other matters could be negotiated.

McCarthy proposed a resolution to the Senate designed to prevent the President from taking up any subject with the Russians until they agreed to solve the satellite issue. Knowing that this would be defeated, Knowland, Jenner, Capehart, and Hickenlooper tried to bury it in committee. But Lyndon Johnson forced a vote, saying that the issue was clear: "It is whether the President of the United States shall be sent to the Big Four Conference in a straitjacket."

The Republican extremists now had to decide between Eisenhower and McCarthy. On the vote, McCarthy, who was advocating perpetuation of the tensions of the cold war, lost 77 to 4. Many dared not oppose Eisenhower, knowing that Republican success in 1956 depended on him.

At the Summit Conference at Geneva in the summer of 1955, the President assured the Russians that America would "never take part in an aggressive war. . . . No doubt there are among our nations philosophical convictions which are in many respects irreconcilable," he said. "Nothing that we can say or do here will change that fact. However, it is not always necessary that people should think alike and believe alike before they can work together."

When he returned from the conference, the President spoke of the "evidence of a new friendliness in the world" and newspapers described the "Geneva spirit" as heralding a less tense world situation. Soviet policy soon ended this illusion. Another dangerous illusion that emanated from Geneva was that the United States and the Soviet Union had agreed tacitly, but positively, not to resort to all-out atomic war as an instrument of national policy. Instead, the fact emerged that under the *present conditions* of atomic stalemate neither could win such a war and, therefore, neither would *deliberately* start such a war.

Shortly after Geneva, the Soviet leaders launched a new cold war (or cold peace) of maneuver. They initiated a vigorous diplomatic and economic offensive in Asia and the Middle East, denounced Western imperialism, and offered trade and economic aid. Within two months of the Summit Meeting, the Soviet Union aggravated tensions in the Middle East. After the Israeli-Arab fighting had ceased in 1949, an uneasy truce filled with border incidents and hatred had prevailed. Israel, to the Arabs, was the latest manifestation of Western imperialism. While they felt that Israel intended to expand further at their expense, the Israelis believed that the Arabs wanted to push them into the sea. The nearly one million Arab refugees who had fled from Israel during the 1948-1949 fighting and existed in miserable refugee camps were a festering sore. Between 1950 and 1955, we developed no adequate policy to bring a settlement between the two.

Then, in September, 1955, the Communists became a factor in

Middle Eastern affairs when Czechoslovakia sold Egypt jet airplanes, tanks, and other equipment. Now the delicate balance existing between Israel and the Arab states was menaced. Hoping to keep Egypt, under Colonel Gamal Nasser, from moving closer to the Soviet bloc, America and Britain offered economic aid to build the Aswan dam on the upper Nile. Nasser delayed in accepting the offer while he tried to destroy the British position in Jordan and in the rich oil sheikdoms on the Arabian coast. At the same time, he armed Arab nationalists fighting the French in Algeria and trained commandos and sent them across the Israeli border to kill and plunder.

In July, 1956, when Nasser asked for the proffered aid to build the dam, Dulles abruptly canceled the offer. Nasser struck back by seizing control of the operation of the Suez Canal. Fearing Nasser's control of this lifeline vital to their economies, the British and French favored retaking the canal by force. But, upon consultation, Dulles recommended negotiation.

The British and French, convinced that the Administration's noble intentions and pronouncements would not produce a solution, decided they must act to protect themselves. When Israel attacked Egypt on October 25, Britain and France, keeping their plans secret from us, issued an ultimatum to Israel and Egypt, demanding their withdrawal from the Suez area and the acceptance of temporary Anglo-French occupation of the canal zone. The next day Anglo-French bombers attacked Egyptian airfields as a prelude to invasion.

Eisenhower, then in the closing day of his campaign for re-election, took the issue to the United Nations, and the Soviet Union joined in the vote that called for a cease-fire, the termination of the Israeli, British and French expeditions, and the creation of a UN emergency force to supervise the cessation of hostilities and prevent raids across Egyptian-Israeli boundaries.

The failure of the British and French to consult with the United States, "though understandable, was a fatal error," Dean Acheson has written. "Their action and ours brought near the breaking point an alliance that had been under strain for a number of years." Although our Allies had to yield to our "moral onslaught," such users of force as the Soviets in Hungary and Egyptians raiding into Israel could not "within the President's limitations, be *effectively* opposed because the users are immune to our moral and political pressure." Referral of the political issue to the UN, he added, was no adequate substitute for an American policy in the Middle East.[9]

Just before the Middle East crisis, trouble erupted in the Soviet satellites. Not only were there severe stresses within the Soviet system, but Nikita Khrushchev, the First Secretary of the Communist Party, added to the strains early in 1956 by suddenly denouncing Stalin as a brutal tyrant.

The previous year the new Russian leaders had apologized to Tito for breaking relations in 1948 and seemingly agreed with Tito that independent, national Communism was possible. When, in mid-October, 1956, the Polish Communists replaced Russian-oriented leaders with national Communist leaders who had been purged earlier for "Titoism," Khrushchev flew to Warsaw and threatened to suppress them by force. The national Communists defied him, however, and insisted that Soviet troops be withdrawn from Warsaw to border positions. The Russians complied.

The next day, an uprising shook Hungary. Fighting broke out with students, workers, and many Hungarian soldiers challenging Soviet might. The Russians overwhelmed the Hungarians in bloody fighting, placed new puppets in power, and ignored the demand of the United Nations for a cessation of their action. In spite of the crushing of Hungary, the rumblings behind the Iron Curtain indicated the need for the Western nations to reassess the old view of the Communist world as a solid bloc.

And, again, as in the case of the East German uprising three years earlier, America's hands-off operational policy was a far cry from the declaratory policy of "liberation."

During the first term, the Democratic leadership of Congress generally conformed to the Administration's foreign policy except in its concessions to Republican extremists. Some of the younger Senators, however, occasionally protested the emphasis on military alliances and the failure to adapt old policies to swiftly changing situations. When Dulles told the Senate Foreign Relations Committee early in 1956 that the Soviets were losing the cold war and were not making progress in the Middle East, Senator Fulbright asked: "Does the skillful way the Soviet Union has posed as the champion of Asiatic peoples represent a triumph for Western diplomacy as Mr. Dulles suggests? It does not."

A democratic public, Fulbright warned, was not well served when the Secretary of State "misleads public opinion, confuses it, feeds it pap, tells it that if it will suppress the proof of its own senses, it will see that Soviet triumphs are really defeats, and Western defeats are really triumphs." He queried: "Will such a public opinion be prepared to make new sacrifices when the Secretary of State implies that the battle against the Soviet bid for world domination has been won?"

---

35. The New Look

The dynamic foreign policy proclaimed in 1953 was accompanied by a New Look in military policy. The Republican approach to the budget forced an abandonment of balanced forces and emphasis on nuclear air power — "a bigger bang for a buck." Since severe cuts on domestic programs were not only more difficult to achieve but also politically unwise, it was easier to reduce expenditures for national security.

In the spring of 1953, Secretary of Defense Charles Wilson and the Director of the Bureau of the Budget reduced the military budget prepared by the Truman Administration without consulting the Joint Chiefs of Staff. In August new men were appointed to the Joint Chiefs and asked to reconsider military requests. But they recommended almost the same expenditures as advocated by the previous Joint Chiefs.

The National Security Council, under the leadership of Secretary of the Treasure Humphrey and Budget Director Dodge, rejected the recommendations and ordered a less expensive defense budget. Civilian economic ideas, rather than military judgments, started the New Look. "The fact is," General Matthew Ridgway has written, "the 1955 budget was a 'directed verdict,' as were the Army budgets for 1956 and 1957. The force levels provided in all three were not primarily based on military needs." General Ridgway has added that in view of his opposition he was "nonplussed" by the President's phrase in the State of the Union Message in 1954 that "the defense program recommended in the 1955 budget . . . is based on a new military program unanimously recommended by the Joint Chiefs of Staff." [1]

Secretary Dulles elaborated the New Look in his "massive retaliation" speech in January, 1954. The present level of defense expenditures, he explained, could not be maintained indefinitely "without grave budgetary, economic and social consequences." [2] To reduce military expenditure, it was necessary to be "selective in building our military power." The aggressor had to be warned that "he cannot always prescribe battle conditions that suit him." There would be "more reliance on deterrent power, and less dependence on local defensive power." Hence, the National Security Council had decided to "depend primarily upon a great capacity to retaliate, instantly, by means and at places of our own choosing."

The New Look in military policy that shaped the Eisenhower budgets during the first term equated military force with nuclear power. When the Administration took office, there was approximate military equilibrium between America and its allies and the Soviet Union and its allies. By 1956, American capacity to fight a limited war had been sharply reduced, Soviet naval expansion had decreased the ability of Allied fleets to control the seas, and America was losing its air supremacy to the Soviets. While American military expenditures were reduced, Russian expenditures mounted. The personal and military prestige of the President was such that when he gave assurances that the reductions would not endanger the national security, they were approved by Congress in spite of objections from Senators Stuart Symington and Henry Jackson.

In June, 1955, General Matthew Ridgway, retiring Army Chief of Staff, assailed the "overemphasis" on air power and massive retaliation with nuclear weapons at the expense of greatly reduced ground forces at a time when the Soviet Union was building up all elements of its military power. After describing the commitments to the NATO nations, to the Americas, to the SEATO nations, Korea, Japan, Formosa, and others, he warned that present "United States military forces are inadequate in strength and improperly proportioned to meet the above commitments, specific or implied." And he added that "the commitments which the United States has pledged create a positive requirement for an immediately available mobile joint military force of hard hitting character in which the versatility of the whole is emphasized and the preponderance of any one part is de-emphasized." [3]

His successor as Chief of Staff, Maxwell D. Taylor, said on June 30, 1957, that because of the suicidal nature of general nuclear war it was "increasingly unlikely that any nation will deliberately embark on such a war with its prospect of reciprocal annihilation." But he warned that the danger of local or limited aggression appeared to be an "increasingly serious threat to world peace. This form of aggression, if not arrested, may lead to the erosion of the free world and to our loss, piecemeal, of that which we are pledged to defend. If resisted, it must be resisted promptly and successfully; otherwise it may spread to that general atomic war which it is our purpose to avoid."

Others also insisted that while the nation was equipping itself with devastating retaliatory striking power, it was losing its capacity to fight a limited war at a time when the Soviets were capable of either a total nuclear war or a non-atomic conflict. Henry Kissinger emphasized in *Nuclear Weapons and Foreign Policy* (1957) that the fallacy of the massive retaliation theory was that national survival became involved in every diplomatic conflict that verged on the use of force. And, since America recoiled from this, there was the resulting danger that it would surrender step by step to the pressures of the Communist world. The alternative to allowing the Communists to nibble away at the rest of the world piece by piece, Kissinger added, was not only the ability to meet an all-out attack with an all-out counteraction, but to meet limited aggression with limited warfare: "The purpose of limited war is to inflict losses or to pose risks for the enemy out of proportion to the objectives under dispute."

In October, 1957, Dulles indicated that a shift was taking place from sole reliance on "massive retaliation." Tactical nuclear weapons could be used "to defend countries" so "as to make military invasion with conventional forces a hazardous attempt." But critics warned that America might hesitate to use tactical nuclear weapons, fearing that they would lead to all-out war. A special committee appointed by the President in 1957 to study Soviet capabilities recommended, among other things, that to avoid a situation in which America would hesitate to use tactical nuclear retaliation against small attacks, conventional armaments be expanded and the nation be ready to fight old-fashioned infantry actions comparable to Korea whenever necessary.

Although the Administration justified its reductions in the Army on the basis that "primary emphasis" was to be placed upon the Air Force and the creation of "massive retaliatory power," appropriations requested were not sufficient to maintain American air superiority over the Soviet Union. When Secretary Wilson testified before the Senate Armed Services Subcommittee on July 2, 1956, that "we are ahead of the Russians and we expect to keep that way," General Nathan F. Twining, Air Force Chief of Staff, told the Committee:

> The Communists have thousands more combat airplanes than we do. If being ahead is related to aircraft production, we are again only second best. . . . Even more important, if being ahead is related to rate of progress, we have fallen behind. Of course we can outproduce the Communists, there is no question about that. Our production potential is not the reason we are falling behind. One of the reasons we are dropping behind is that the Communists are making scientific and technological advances at a faster rate than we are.[4]

Although the Truman Administration had cut new weapons research in the years before the Korean fighting, it had secured appropriations of $533 million for Air Force Research and Development in 1953. But the Eisenhower Administration in its budget for 1955 reduced this amount by more than one hundred million. American development of guided missiles, particularly of the intercontinental ballistics missile, lagged, while the Soviets gave it top priority. A committee of leading scientists, headed by James R. Killian, Jr., President of Massachusetts Institute of Technology, concluded in the summer of 1955 that the Soviet Union was overtaking the United States in missile development and in the years 1960-1965 would have a sizable lead based primarily upon "a decided superiority in intercontinental ballistic missiles."

The powerful Air Force Association, the pressure group of the Air Force, accused the President in October, 1957, of not providing direction on the problem of national survival. The Association asked: "How could the President let the shortage of scientific brain power be 'solved' by reducing the demand for it through research budget reductions . . . how could he allow the aviation industry . . . to be undermined by a rash of directives compromising efficient and economic performance?" [5]

The rhetoric of the New Look appealed to those who desired a reduction in the budget and to those who objected to limited wars like Korea. It also reinforced those who comforted themselves with the illusion of American omnipotence. Until the sputniks in 1957, the Administration by its public statements increased this illusion. Official policy assumed until 1958 that the United States could keep ahead in the arms race without merging the missile programs of the armed services, without interfering too much with the domestic economy, and without pooling the scientific knowledge of the Allied world. The Administration ignored warnings that its excessive security restrictions limited the effectiveness of scientists and deprived the government of the services of outstanding individuals including Robert Oppenheimer. And it ignored warnings that the shortage of teachers, low salaries, and limited research funds were handicapping education in general and scientific education in particular.

But, regardless of all this, obviously a "peasant" people like the Russians could never match American scientific and productive achievements. When Congress pressed Secretary of Defense Wilson in January, 1956, to explain or deny reports that the Russian air force was ahead of us in its capacity for nuclear war — reports which had been accepted as accurate by General Twining and General Curtis LeMay, Chief of the Strategic Air Command — Wilson patronizingly replied that the Communist world was "making some progress undoubtedly" in the industrial revolution.

And the President, by abstaining from action except in a crisis, just as in domestic policy, lulled the country into a false sense of security by an equally false sense of superiority. Ignoring much intelligence information, the Administration contributed to the public belief that Russia was a shambling nation incapable of huge scientific and industrial strides.[6]

Although in his State of the Union Message in January, 1959, Eisenhower set forth his belief that "America can be sure of the strength and efficiency of her armed forces," the House Select Committee on Astronautics and Space Exploration said in its final report on January 10:

> This Committee is pleased with what has been done so far. But it is also concerned whether this is enough. It has worked to see that the Congress fully appreciates the stakes that are involved. The Committee is also concerned whether the Executive branch is driving home to the public the realities we face in a way which will create the broadbased support needed for carrying on a national effort of the magnitude we require.

36.   Politics of Postponement

During the second term, problems began to press in on Eisenhower as never before, and he compounded the difficulties by ineffective leadership. His increased budget request in January, 1957, provoked a violent response. He had made no effort to prepare the public, Congress, or newspaper editors before the budget was submitted. His own Secretary of the Treasury, George Humphrey, publicly criticized its size. At his press conference, Eisenhower astonishingly invited Congress to suggest "sensible reductions," undermining confidence in the integrity of the Executive Budget. This left his wing of the party in Congress without support from the White House for the President's own budget.[1] Months passed before he defended it, but by this time he was unable to persuade the public or Congress of the necessity of his original requests.

Nor did he fight for federal aid to education, a "major goal" of his Administration. And again, by his delaying until the closing weeks of the session his attempt to awaken the country and Congress to the compelling need of his request for foreign aid, the amount appropriated was less than he felt necessary for national security. After submitting a broad civil rights bill to Congress, he lost control of the issue by telling reporters that he did not agree with all aspects of the legislation. ". . . the fiasco of his program is in some part due to his own indecision and seeming unsureness in support of it," *Life* lamented on August 26, 1957.

A few days after Congress adjourned, the Governor of Arkansas confronted Eisenhower with the crisis over the Little Rock schools. Later that autumn, the Russian success in placing Sputniks I and II in orbit around the earth jolted public confidence in the soldier-President's judgment in the field he was supposed to know best, the nation's security. The impact of the Soviet scientific achievement came as a shock to a people complacent over the superiority of "American know-how." What Denis Brogan has called "the illusion of American omnipotence" had been cultivated during the five years of the Eisenhower Administration by an elaborate tranquillizing campaign with assurances that American military strength was outstripping the Soviet Union.

The Russian sputniks dealt a mighty blow to the illusion, and for almost the first time the President began to be criticized in person. With the United States in grave danger from the outside, public relation techniques no longer could protect the President. Eisenhower's attempt to calm public reaction by a series of television broadcasts was cut short by a mild stroke. Then, in January, 1958, he delivered his State of the Union Message, a disappointment to those who hoped for a bold program of national revival in education and scientific research. Instead, he concentrated on a recommendation for a reorganized Defense Department and increased expenditures for missile development. Senator Fulbright warned that "the real challenge we face involves the very roots of our society. It involves our educational system, the source of our knowledge and cultural values. And here, the Administration's program for a renaissance of learning is disturbingly small-minded."

Shortly after the President recovered from his stroke, the economy, which had been faltering for months, descended into the most serious recession since the war and unemployment reached five million. The Administration took such remedial measures as substituting low interest rates for credit restraint and reducing down-payments on government-insured housing mortgages; but critics observed that the Administration failed to take as speedy action as in the milder recession of 1953-1954. Congress, as it had in 1957, took more aggressive action than the executive. It reshaped and redirected the President's legislative proposals on the recession and voted larger appropriations for defense than Eisenhower had requested.

Eisenhower did, however, exert leadership to secure passage of his Department of Defense reorganization bill and a substantial foreign aid program. He called Congressman John Taber, long the chief congressional foe of foreign aid, to the White House and persuaded him to lead the fight against any cuts in the appropriation. Congress, led by Speaker Rayburn, supported the President's request to extend the Reciprocal Trade Agreements Act for five years.[2] But the Administration's over-all foreign policy faced mounting criticism from the Democratic-controlled Congress. Congress early in 1957 voted its approval of the Eisenhower Doctrine. It authorized expansion of economic aid to Middle Eastern nations and use of American forces to assist any nation against aggression from a country controlled by international Communism. But the foreign policy debate revealed the latent distrust over the wisdom of such military pacts.

Critics called for a thorough review of Middle Eastern policy, expressing the belief that the Eisenhower Doctrine ignored the realities of Arab nationalism and the poverty of the area. They warned that this resolution and the Baghdad Pact, while aimed at preventing Soviet encroachments in the Middle East, disregarded the pervading neutralism of the Arabs and the danger that Arab nationalism would react by sweeping away all Western ties. Shortly after the proclamation of the Doctrine, Colonel Nasser upset the existing situation by merging Egypt and Syria into the United Arab Republic and stimulating Arab nationalism against Western interference.

In July, 1958, when a military *coup d'état* removed the pro-Western leaders of Iraq, the Administration countered by landing troops in Lebanon at the request of the incumbent but outgoing president, who had been the only Middle Eastern leader to accept the Eisenhower Doctrine. But four months later, by the time American troops were withdrawn, the Lebanese had selected a neutralist president and prime minister.

In September, while troops were still in Lebanon, the Eisenhower policy of maintaining the status quo brought America to the verge of war when the Chinese Communists stepped up their bombardment of Quemoy and other offshore islands. Between the Formosan resolution of 1955 and this renewed assault from the mainland, the Administration had been content to allow China policy to drift and had failed to withdraw from supporting Chiang's forces in the offshore islands. By insisting upon Chiang as the proper representative of China in the United Nations, the Administration declined to acknowledge that Communist China's participation in international deliberations was necessary for the solution of some of the world's most pressing problems.

During 1957-1958, Dulles's refusal to alter outdated policies, his moralizing, and his alternating complacency and "brinkmanship" alienated a number of Senators. Fulbright, Hubert H. Humphrey, Mike Mansfield, John Kennedy, John Sparkman, and Wayne Morse, who had reluctantly supported Administration policies, now voiced their open opposition.[3]

In August, 1958, Fulbright — who was to become a few months later Chairman of the Committee on Foreign Relations — charged that our foreign policy was "inadequate, outmoded, and misdirected. . . . it reflects a dangerous apathy and a quite incomprehensible unwillingness to look facts in the face," he added. "Time and again we have put things off. Time and again we have drifted until circumstances reached an intolerable state, and then we have rushed to the brink." And he concluded: "unless there is a drastic, sweeping revision of our foreign policy and in the execution of that policy, we are heading for far graver troubles than these in which we now find ourselves."

The missiles race with the Russians, the growing recession, and continuing crises in foreign policy ended one of the longest honeymoons in the history of the presidency. A ten-day vacation trip to Georgia met widespread criticism. *Time*, one of Eisenhower's most enthusiastic adherents in two elections, concluded in its February 24, 1958, issue: "Conspicuously absent was a badly needed feeling of presence — specifically, the presence of the President of the U. S. at his desk, giving attention to the daily details that make long-range plans and policies work." And *Newsweek's* March 10 issue reported "a swelling tide of discontent with the way the White House is being run." Few of those interviewed blamed "the man they all call Ike. But they wonder if he is up to the job; and also if the men around him are giving him the best information and advice."

The growing criticism of the lack of leadership from the White House was an inevitable reaction from the universal adulation Eisenhower had enjoyed in his first term. By the second term, his approach of "not making decisions until after the event reaches you" [4] aggravated already disturbing domestic and international questions.

While Eisenhower continued to evoke personal affection and praise, there was uneasiness in the nation, beset by problems beyond its control. Not only partisan Democrats but many Eisenhower supporters, Samuel Lubell discovered, were voicing what troubled much of the nation: "Things are in an uproar, but what is Eisenhower doing? All you read about is that he's playing golf. Who is running the country?" [5]

On November 4, the voters, by an overwhelming margin, elected a Democratic Congress, the first time in American history that a President had had three Congresses controlled by the opposing party. During the last two weeks of the campaign, Eisenhower essayed the hitherto neglected role of party leader and tried to rally sagging Republican efforts by denouncing what he called the "radical" wing of the Democrats. In Los Angeles he said: "Either we choose left-wing government or sensible government, spendthrift government or responsible government."

But the public responded by electing fifteen new Democratic Senators and some forty-six additional Democrats to the House.[6] Only in New Deal days had the Democrats exceeded such margins. Republican stalwarts, including John Bricker of Ohio, George W. Malone of Nevada, Frank A. Barrett of Wyoming, and Chapman Revercomb of West Virginia went down to defeat while modern Republican Senatorial candidates won in New York and Pennsylvania. And the Democrats unseated Republican governors in California, Maryland, Nevada, New Mexico, Ohio, South Dakota, Wisconsin, and Wyoming to give them control of thirty-three states.

The most notable Republican victory was the defeat of Governor Harriman by Nelson A. Rockefeller. Throughout his vigorous campaign, the liberal-minded Rockefeller carefully dissociated himself both from national issues and the Eisenhower Administration and was elected by an impressive margin of over half a million votes.

While a diversity of local issues affected the outcome, discontent over agricultural policies continued to weaken Republicans in their former rural strongholds. The recession, the high cost of living, and support of right-to-work laws cut deeply into Republican strength in industrial areas. In the largest cities outside the South, excluding New York, the vote for Republican candidates for the House dropped 17 per cent from 1954. In the suburbs of twelve major cities, the Republican vote declined 4.6 per cent. The Gallup poll found in its sampling that the Democrats received more votes than in 1954 from business and professional men and white-collar workers.[7]

Discontent at Eisenhower's presidentship as well as Dulles's drifting from brink to brink manifested itself in the 1958 elections. "The 'lack of leadership' issue has considerable more validity than blaming the recession on the Republicans," John S. Knight, strong Eisenhower supporter in 1952 and 1956, insisted in his chain of newspapers.[8]

---

37. Projecting the Image of the President

Dwight D. Eisenhower's great strength as President was as a unifier of the nation, an accommodator rather than a provoker of controversy, a man of decency and dignity, a man who blurred issues, a tranquillizer rather than a stimulant. He was a man who, when he saw a cloud on the horizon, looked for the silver lining, a man who, after a generation of depression, war, contention and divisions in the nation, was an optimistic and attractive mediator.

Without Eisenhower as the head of the Republican party, the venom that disgraced democratic politics in the closing years of Truman's presidency would have been rife in the nation. He purged national life of rancor. And by presenting himself continuously as standing at the moderate and reasonable center of American life, he was able to tune in on the deepest instincts of the people, who, at this stage in their history, desired pause, comfort and repose;

a mood which reflected the spectacular expansion of the middle class base of American life.

To the economic euphoria of mid-century America, Eisenhower contributed political euphoria. Where Roosevelt excited, aroused, and involved people in politics in a different era, Eisenhower soothed a public that relished complacency. With the good fortune of a bounding prosperity for the majority, the mass of voters were eager to leave complicated issues to the President. T. R. B. wrote in the *New Republic* on February 18, 1957: "The public loves Ike. The less he does the more they love him. That, probably, is the secret. Here is a man who doesn't rock the boat."

By the time Eisenhower became President, television was added to press conferences, radio, and newsreels, offering an unprecedented opportunity for expansion of direct presidential influence. By this time, as well, advertising and public relations experts — "the Madison Avenue Boys" — were being employed to apply their techniques to both political campaigning and the projection of the image of the President.

Television did not become a substitute, however, for personal contact. To be an effective campaigner, a President still must meet the public at rallies, speak to them at whistlestops, and confer with local party leaders to stimulate them to action. And he still had to consult with Congressmen to secure backing for his policies. But with television, the mass of the people now had before them a living, moving picture of the man they chose for their President, the symbol of their national unity, and the arbiter of their major problems.

Television and radio overcame the problem of reaching a population spread across a vast continent. And to politicians relatively unknown to the nation, including Truman, suddenly thrust into the presidency in 1945, or Stevenson, drafted by the Democrats in 1952, the mass media furnished the opportunity of becoming well known overnight.

Technology, by the time of the Eisenhower Administration, supplanted the inanimate printed word — and all the ancient conventions of vocabulary, syntax, and rhetoric — with the living voice and the living face. Most Americans now had more firsthand evidence on which to judge the personality of their President than any but a minute portion of the population had possessed a century before.

Eisenhower was made for television. Although critics insisted there was little intellectual content in his speeches, they had to agree that his infectious grin radiated over the TV screen and peeled off right into the room. But his prose was convoluted. It has been suggested that the Gettysburg Address as transformed into Eisenhower's style would have begun:

> I haven't checked these figures, but 87 years ago, I think it was, a number of individuals organized a governmental set-up here in this country, I believe it covered certain Eastern areas, with this idea they were following up based on a sort of national independence arrangement and the program that every individual is just as good as every other individual.[1]

Although his sentences at press conferences wandered across the landscape without consideration for syntax, what did come through was the fact that the President was a warm, kindly, decent human being who said simple, friendly things. He could communicate a belief in homely virtues; and to the public, at least during his first term, this seemed more important than penetrating analyses of issues or the development of far-seeing policies.

While he was not usually effective in delivering a prepared speech on complicated domestic issues, when he spoke about peace, prosperity, unity, his sincerity was obvious and convincing. Gradually, he developed a preference for the "informal talk"; using notes or speaking from memory rather than reading a speech from a prepared text. Aided on television by the advice of actor-producer Robert Montgomery, and at the press conferences by his press secretary, James C. Hagerty, after 1952 his effectiveness as a speaker increased. In time he became poised and relaxed on TV. He projected a warm, reassuring image. His voice became well modulated, his diction clear, his timing excellent; and millions drew inspiration and comfort from it all.

During the first year, he was ill at ease and on the defensive at his press conferences. After that he gained confidence and with it a certain mastery. When asked in 1956 about their value, the President replied: "I think this is a wonderful institution . . . I rather like to get the questions because frequently I think they represent the kind of thinking that is going on."

During his first term he held one hundred press conferences and beginning in 1955, for the first time, television cameras were admitted to provide the public with an intimate view of the President under questioning. Although his prolix answers did not always make for clarity and his personality was lost in the maze of the printed transcript, his words sounded better than they read. While the President gave a blurred rather than a sharp delineation of the Administration's position, the TV viewer could see the President at the press conference as large as life in his own living room. "To a political Confucius like Hagerty," one correspondent remarked, "this is worth all the 4,000 printed words of the conference." [2]

The press corps generally felt the President was more at ease in answering questions about foreign and military affairs than questions about domestic matters. On many touchy questions, he gradually developed an excellent sense of timing. When one reporter mentioned in 1957 that the President's older brother Edgar had criticized the size of the budget and the liberal influence of brother Milton and Presidential Assistant Sherman Adams, the President, with the flicker of a reminiscent smile, replied: "Edgar has been criticizing me since I was five years old." Every TV news program played the vignette of "Little Ike and Big Edgar." As one correspondent said, the President showed his "genius in public relations, in getting himself liked."

Where Truman had been caustic in many of his replies to reporters and Roosevelt scornful of a stupid question, Eisenhower tried to answer all questions ranging from delicate to insipid. He seldom used "No comment," which in some situations might have been more advisable than the answer given. Moreover, the addition of television cameras added to the risk of the President's making an unguarded reply which might upset sensitive diplomatic negotiations or throw America's allies into a turmoil.

As everyone was extremely polite to him, it was not until the second term that he faced the trenchant questioning that had characterized the Roosevelt-Truman press conferences. Difficulties with the Russians and Chinese, troubles in the alliance structure, resistance to school integration, and the recession of 1957-1958 produced blunter questions, and the President's replies indicated rising annoyance with the criticism of his Administration.

Occasionally he became angry and fairly sputtered with rage. When a reporter asked him in 1958 about charges in Congress that his plan to reorganize the Defense Department might make it possible for some other President to set up a kind of personal army, he replied sharply: "I've got one question to ask you. Have you read the law?" When the correspondent replied that she had, the President cut her off: "No you haven't I don't think." When the next questioner asked if he would comment on the charge by Senator Mike Mansfield that while the Administration asserted it had produced peace in the Far East no more than a tenuous truce existed in Korea, Formosa, and Vietnam, the President flushed, hesitated and replied: "No." [3]

Only at the press conferences were the reporters in a position to penetrate the formidable palace guard around Eisenhower. And they performed the unusual function of bringing a number of controversial issues to Eisenhower's attention for the first time. When this happened, he was so painfully honest that he replied: "Now you are telling me something about my own Administration I never heard of." Frequent responses of this nature indicated that official government sources failed to inform Eisenhower on important public issues. At the same time, he lacked the antennae to derive information from a variety of private sources. Unlike Roosevelt, who had innumerable informants from a range of backgrounds and carefully balanced their views with official information, Eisenhower with minor exceptions relied for his unofficial information upon a few friends who were successful corporation leaders. "Variety is something the President plainly lacks in his intake of information . . ." one Washington correspondent has written. "Curiosity may be fatal to cats, but it is indispensable in a President." [4]

Eisenhower's critics, unlike those of F. D. R. or Truman, charged him with doing too little, never too much. But what he lacked in legislative and party leadership, he contributed in personality. In fact, his personality became a substitute for presidentship, dominating the scene for the majority of people. Faults of omission or commission were readily overlooked or attributed to his assistants, not to the President himself.

The favorable public image of Eisenhower was to an important degree shaped by the activity of the most powerful White House press secretary in our history. The news about the President was carefully managed by Hagerty. Twice a day he held informal press conferences producing a steady flow of news. Between presidential press conferences and speeches, day in and day out Hagerty "is the authentic voice of the White House and, to an extent rarely recognized, of the whole Administration," *Time* remarked on January 27, 1958.

Bending every effort to show the President at his best, Hagerty transferred the blame for mistakes to other government agencies and appropriated credit for achievements to the White House. An example was the handling of the news about rocket development. Launching failures were announced by the armed services, but the news of the first satellite to orbit came from the White House. And Hagerty also released the news that the *Nautilus* had traveled under the polar icecap. "From the way they told it," one correspondent remarked, "you'd have thought the President designed the sub and placed Hagerty at the helm." [5]

Hagerty was adept at timing the release of big and favorable stories to blanket unfavorable news. On Eisenhower's prolonged vacations at Augusta or Gettysburg, Hargerty took along executive orders, appointments, reports, and cost-of-living surveys and issued these carefully on a day-by-day basis to make news. "He did anything and everything, in short, to keep the subject of golf and fishing far down in the daily stories about the President," *Time* has written.

Douglass Cater, in his thoughtful study of Washington journalism, reported that one major newspaper felt obliged to reduce the number of front-page stories coming out of the White House because the editors judged they were creating a false impression of immense presidential activity. Hagerty, concluded Cater, "has made of public relations an end in itself rather than a means to an end. . . . For prolonged periods, he has attracted public attention away from compelling problems of leadership with a succession of make-shift and inconsequential diversions." [6]

---

38. Presidentship

There was no disagreement that Eisenhower used the press conferences, radio, and television to wrap the nation in an aura of good feeling. He vastly enlarged the scope of the President's communication with the American people and with people overseas. Although he mastered the art of communicating through the mass media, his conception of the presidency did not include vigorous party leadership nor continuous pressure on Congress for his legislative program.

His attitude toward the office varied decidedly from that of his two immediate predecessors. Truman understood thoroughly the President's function as chief legislator and head of party, but his failure to appreciate the role of chief of state contributed much to the bitterness of his era. Roosevelt, like his relative Theodore and like Abraham Lincoln, understood both roles and was able to veer back and forth between them deftly and with considerable success. Eisenhower clearly preferred the role of chief of state and exercised the other functions only intermittently. Although more forceful in foreign policy, he adopted an air of passive benevolence in the conduct of domestic affairs. "What will we refrain from doing now?" in general, typified his outlook.

Quarrels were unseemly to a man of Eisenhower's temperament. Feeling that the wranglings between the White House and Congress under Truman had weakened respect for the presidency, he attempted in his first year a honeymoon with Congress. While the President spoke of the equality of the two branches of the government, the Republican leadership quickly moved to assert the supremacy of Congress over the executive. It was not only that the Republican Congressmen represented a party which, with the exception of Lincoln and Theodore Roosevelt, had never had strong presidential leadership, but, in addition, they were eager for Congress to recover the power and prestige that it had lost during the Roosevelt era.

For the short time that he lived to be majority leader, Senator Taft, instead of being the President's spokesman in the Senate, led in forming Administration policy on a number of issues. He was followed by Senator Knowland, who attempted to do the same but with less effect. Eisenhower for the first year clearly reigned but did not rule. Many of his suggestions were ignored, and, to his chagrin, such important measures as foreign aid were rescued for him by Democratic votes. By the close of 1953, the President was indignant at most Republicans in Congress and debated whether he should form a new party. Slowly, however, after 1953, and until his heart attack in September, 1955, the President inclined somewhat toward being the chief legislator, if not the party leader as well.

Regular meetings with Republican leaders were instituted, with Eisenhower becoming a bit more assertive in persuading recalcitrants to support his program. But this required endless effort, and his illnesses and frequent golfing expeditions away from the White House — forty per cent of his first three years were spent away from Washington — made it difficult to sustain.

Actually, Eisenhower did not enjoy political maneuvering. When he sent proposed legislation to Congress, he felt that it should be accepted on its merits without the necessity of constant pressure on the Congress. "I don't feel like I should nag them," he told his press conference on January 29, 1959. Although the President went to the public in behalf of his program, he failed to telephone wavering Congressmen often enough to secure their vote or call them to the White House to persuade or cajole. He thus neglected to provide Congressmen, under pressure from constituents to oppose legislation, with the convenient reply that the President had explained to them in person that a favorable vote was necessary for the national welfare.

Many of the original Ike supporters of 1952 expected that he would remodel the Republican party, making it an effective instrument for government. To an extent he did. By adopting the essences of the New Deal and Fair Deal and largely accepting the containment policy of the Truman Administration, Eisenhower rescued the party from the regressive record set by the majority of Republican Congressmen during the previous two decades. But his detached view of the presidency made him unwilling to assume the task of party discipline. He refused steadfastly to criticize opponents, including even McCarthy. Nor did he intervene in party primaries to encourage Modern Republicans to run against more conservative incumbents, although he did suggest that supporters of his program run where there were Democratic incumbents.

At his first press conference after his re-election in 1956, Eisenhower reaffirmed his opposition to being the party leader. He said that he interpreted the voters' decision to keep Congress under Democratic control as indicating that the public "has not yet been convinced that modern Republicanism is with us and is going to be the guiding philosophy of the Republican party." Old Guard Republicans, he hoped, would read the returns in the same light. But he rejected a suggestion from a reporter that he should exert greater control and insist that Republican Congressmen support his program. "I am not one of the desk-pounding type that likes to stick out his jaw and look like he is bossing the show," he stated. Congressmen, as one Eisenhower associate put it, "were scared of Roosevelt, and even Truman. They're not scared of Ike." The knowledge that the President disliked using his power to punish and reward explains in part why many Republican Congressmen were "not scared of Ike."

In fact, Eisenhower created an aura of moral sanctity over his refusal to commit himself to party leadership. When asked at a press conference on May 16, 1957, if he intended in the 1958 elections to oppose those Republicans who fought his program and support those who supported him, he replied: "I don't think it is the function of a President of the United States to punish anybody for voting what he believes."

After a meeting with the President in October, 1958, leaders of the Republican National Committee issued the statement: "Nationalization and socialization of industry is the clear alternative to a Republican Congress." When asked at his press conference whether he subscribed to it, the President replied: ". . . it was not my statement, it was theirs, and I think politicians do love to make things very positive."

The burden of campaigning for the Republican ticket was left to Vice-President Nixon. When Administration foreign policy came under attack, Nixon explained to the press on October 15, 1958, that since it was the duty of the President to mobilize the entire country behind him, it was "proper" that he not hit back. But, Nixon added: "For us who have the responsibility of carrying the weight of this campaign to stand by and allow our policies to be attacked with impunity by our opponents without reply would lead to inevitable defeat."

In the closing two weeks of the campaign, however, Eisenhower delivered what his press secretary termed "fighting" speeches. Although he labeled Northern Democrats "radicals" and "spenders," his hard words, often accompanied by apologetic smiles, were not convincingly delivered. "It was like a Truman concoction flavored with vanilla instead of vinegar," Edwin A. Lahey reported.[1]

A few weeks after the Democratic victory in 1958, the President told a meeting of the Republican National Committee that he deeply regretted "that some people look upon our party as a kind of hibernating elephant who wakes up with a mighty trumpet blast at election time and then rests calmly until the next election." Political activity, he added, must be a matter for "unremitting effort" 365 days a year. After the President's message had been read, Representative Richard M. Simpson, Chairman of the Republican Congressional Campaign Committee, told the group to loud and sustained applause:

> I call upon the White House to give us some of that "unremitting effort" on behalf of the Republican party.

But in 1959, with the loss of two strong-willed advisers, Eisenhower at last took a firmer grasp of both foreign and domestic policy. On January 27, Dulles held his last press conference. Thereafter Eisenhower assumed the direction of policy in the crisis over Berlin precipitated by the Soviet demand that Allied troops be withdrawn from the city. Eisenhower's pronouncement that we would stand firm on our occupation rights caused a sharp rise in his prestige and in public confidence that the President knew how to defend the country and prevent war.[2]

Until 1959, Eisenhower had entrusted to the "Assistant to the

President," Sherman Adams, many of the duties which Roosevelt and Truman had discharged themselves. Using him as a chief of staff to cut down the length and number of papers to be studied, reduce the decisions to be made and the number of people to be seen, Eisenhower partially abdicated. No earlier President ever depended on a subordinate to this degree. After Adams came under attack in late 1958 for accepting gifts from a man who had cases pending before federal agencies, the President, while agreeing that this had been "imprudent," told the press: "I need him." After Adams's resignation, the change in Eisenhower was noted by a reporter: ". . . the business of the presidency is getting his personal attention." [3] Congressmen and Republican party leaders, who had been unable to get past Adams, now found access to the President easier.

Instead of the "pattern of spongy Presidential leadership" of the past six years, Eisenhower unexpectedly brought a new vitality to 1600 Pennsylvania Avenue. "He has got 'tough' with Congress where he used to be wishy-washy," Cabell Phillips noted in the *New York Times* on August 16, 1959. "He has come to grips with the *substance* of many of the big issues before him, whereas it had often seemed he was familiar with the form only. He has acquired a new sense of the institutional quality of the Presidential office and a new respect for its prerogatives."

Not only did he challenge Congress by his determined use of the veto and his strong public appeal for substantial labor legislation, but he took foreign policy into his own hands by inviting Premier Khrushchev to the United States. The President's leadership in trying to abate the tensions of the cold war and avoid an ultimate clash of nuclear arms, as well as the new vigor on domestic issues, dampened the criticisms of his ineffectiveness during 1957-1958. And as reporters and editorial writers turned to analyzing the "new" Eisenhower, a Gallup poll in the summer of 1959 showed that 62 per cent of those interviewed approved the way he was handling the presidency.

By 1959, the economy had made a brisk recovery from the recession. On January 7, just before Eisenhower delivered his annual message to Congress, Senator Johnson gave his own State of the Union message to his Democratic colleagues. He remarked that "our nation is at the edge of what can clearly be its greatest age of expansion, growth and abundance." "American industry and business are pouring forth billions in research to discover new capabilities," Johnson added. But government "is moving hardly at all . . . Great minds of the nation are not being mobilized to the challenges of self-government by free men." "There is no expense of government more costly or more intolerable than the burden of laggard government," he declared.

But Eisenhower rejected Democratic plans for enlarged government expenditures, demanding that spending be held within the confines of the nearly 80-billion-dollar budget that he submitted to Congress. From the outset of the Eighty-sixth Congress, he and other Republicans warned against "the wild spenders," the "radical wing" of the Democratic party.

Reinforcing his words, Eisenhower vetoed several bills carrying higher appropriations than he approved, and threatened further vetoes. Johnson thereupon forsook his position in favor of expansion of the economy through government action and concentrated instead on securing legislation that could not be condemned as "reckless spending." This was a defeat for those Northern Democratic Senators who believed economic growth depended upon additional government spending. They and others outside of Congress charged that Johnson's strategy of cutting appropriations to make them vetoproof threatened to blur the party's identity and might cost it the presidency in 1960. And they contended that Johnson had sacrificed a heaven-sent political issue — expansionism — to join Eisenhower's "reckless frugality spree."

But the majority leader countered that he would continue to work with Eisenhower to achieve "constructive and responsible legislation rather than indulge in a lot of political by-play. We were not sent to Congress," he added, "to paralyze government. We were not sent here to make a political record or to re-elect Senators or elect a President." [4]

Beginning with Roosevelt in 1933, and continuing under Truman, American politics had been marked by the greatest innovations since the Civil War. The American people were adapting themselves to these changes until the collapse of China and the Korean stalemate. The emotions aroused by these events had begun to endanger much-needed agreement on domestic and foreign policy at the time that Eisenhower took office. In spite of the Republican extremists, Eisenhower presided over a successful adjustment to the realities of world politics and consolidation of America's social gains. But presidential firmness to foster national awareness of new issues was absent until 1959.

Over the years, thoughtful observers at home and abroad have expressed their deep concern over the weaknesses created by the division of responsibility for foreign policy between the executive and the Congress, the undisciplined nature of the two political parties, and the crushing weight of the mass public. While these have frequently been liabilities, vigorous presidentship, at times, has converted them into a great strength.

The failure of the Presidents between 1920 and 1933 to lead Congress and public opinion created a situation in which even a powerful President such as F. D. R. found his freedom of action in foreign relations dangerously restricted. But under his purposeful guidance, the majority by 1939 came to recognize the need of revising America's attitudes toward the rest of the world.

The President had emerged after 1932 as the prime formulator of legislative programs and the principal budget-maker. And after 1939 the international burdens the nation had to assume brought about a gigantic increase of the President's power, reducing the role of Congress. He had the advantage over Congress of a large staff of experts and superior information from intelligence sources not available to them. And Congress, based on local and sectional interests, was unable to transcend these to cope with the larger domestic and international issues.

"I do not think there is the remotest chance for Congressional control of foreign policy," Senator Fulbright has said. While Congress could support, modify or obstruct proposals formulated by the executive, it could not assume his role and govern in his stead.

Under Eisenhower, the personnel of the Executive Office of the President was expanded by nearly 1500 over 1952. Secretariats were created for both the Cabinet and the National Security Council, and orderly staff work was emphasized. While these developments had positive aspects, they also tended to rigidify the presidential office. Woodrow Wilson's remark that the presidency is what the wisdom and ability of the occupant make it was unchanged by the proliferation of the White House bureaucracy. Under the American system the fact remained that only the President himself could coordinate the Cabinet, the National Security Council, and the federal bureaucracy.

One of the few political truths about the American system of government is that the President alone can give the nation an effective lead. While only a minority of outstanding men have been elected to the White House, it is on the greatness of a wise and skilled President, who can master the roles of chief of state, legislative leader, and head of party, that the progress and the survival of American democracy rest.

Notes

BOOK ONE

1. CRISIS IN AMERICAN DEMOCRACY

[1] Paul Y. Anderson, "Tear-Gas, Bayonets, and Votes," *The Nation*, August 17, 1932.
[2] General Glassford, in a series of articles later, states flatly that he had opposed the calling out of troops. President Hoover has stated just as flatly that Glassford "implored" the Commissioners to call for troops.
[3] *Sherwood Anderson's Memoirs* (New York: Harcourt, Brace and Co., 1942), p. 415.

2. COLLAPSE OF THE NEW ERA

[1] Automobile production increased 255 per cent; iron and steel products, 70 per cent; chemical products, 94 per cent; and rubber products, 86 per cent.
[2] About six hundred thousand families — 2.3 per cent — had incomes of $10,000 and higher. Two million families — 8 per cent — had incomes of $5000 and over. Twelve million families — over 42 per cent — received less than $1500. And six million families — slightly more than 21 per cent — had incomes of under $1000. Put another way, the six million families at the lowest income level received $3.5 billion in income while thirty-six thousand families at the top, all with incomes in excess of $75,000, received $9.8 billion.
[3] Helen Hall, "When Detroit's Out of Gear," *The Survey*, April 1, 1930.
[4] In 1926 he had warned in a public statement: "Psychology plays a large part in business movements, and overoptimism can only land us on the shores of overdepression."
[5] In 1931 Edward Angly gathered together the most optimistic assurances of Wall Street and Washington into a book with the derisive title *Oh Yeah!* A new magazine, *Ballyhoo*, appeared in 1932 to debunk the high-powered advertising of the '20s. In six months it achieved a circulation of two million.

3. THE DEEPENING DEPRESSION

[1] "Bacon and Beans and Limousines," *The Survey*, November 15, 1931.
[2] The statistics used in these particular pages are compiled from the

Federal Reserve Board *Bulletin* of February, March, and September, 1933; and Simon Kuznets, *Shares of Upper Income Groups in Income and Savings* (New York: National Bureau of Economic Research, 1950).

[3] Since the government then had no regular or complete unemployment registration, totals are only estimates. No one making estimates claimed infallibility since unemployment was increasing faster than it could be calculated. See Paul H. Douglas and Aaron Director, *The Problem of Unemployment* (New York: The Macmillan Co., 1934); U. S. Department of Labor, *Monthly Labor Review*, April, 1931 and, November, 1933.

[4] "Arkansas' Fight for Life," *Literary Digest*, January 24, February 28, 1931.

[5] "The Farmer Takes a Holiday," November 26, 1932.

[6] Many of Mrs. McCormick's writings on the domestic scene have been compiled by Marion T. Sheehan in *The World at Home* (New York: Alfred A. Knopf, 1956).

[7] *The Years of the Locust: America, 1929-1932* (Boston: Little, Brown and Co., 1933).

[8] Gilbert Burck and Charles Silberman, "What Caused the Great Depression," *Fortune*, February, 1955, pp. 94-95.

4. INEPTNESS IN THE WHITE HOUSE

[1] *Incredible Tale: The Odyssey of the Average American in the Last Half Century* (New York: Harper & Bros., 1950), p. 208.

[2] He summarizes his view of the presidency in *The Memoirs of Herbert Hoover: The Cabinet and the Presidency 1920-1933* (New York: The Macmillan Co., 1952), particularly pp. 169, 217, 279, 301, 315, 316.

[3] June 4, 1930.

[4] Michelson has written that President Hoover himself furnished the devastating ammunition for the picture drawn, since he was not the great politician needed in the presidency. Charles Michelson, *The Ghost Talks* (New York: G. P. Putnam's Sons, 1944), p. 32.

[5] Gilbert Burck and Charles Silberman have written, "If Mr. Mellon's formula had included business, it would have come close to being a description of what eventually happened." "What Caused the Great Depression," *Fortune*, February, 1955.

[6] Thomas C. Cochran, "Business and the Democratic Tradition," *Harvard Business Review*, March-April, 1956, is an able analysis of this point.

[7] National Conference of Social Work, *Proceedings*, 1931, pp. 38-39.

5. REPUDIATING THE REPUBLICANS

[1] *Time*, October 24, 1932, commented: "The 'deserving' was a new qualification. Last winter, again last September, he said, 'No one will starve,' but some did."

[2] "The Candidacy of Franklin D. Roosevelt," *New York Herald Tribune*, January 8, 1932; Frank R. Kent, "No Hero In Sight," *Scribner's Magazine*, June, 1932.

[3] Rexford G. Tugwell, "The Preparation of a President," *Western Political Quarterly*, June, 1948, and Raymond Moley, *After Seven Years* (New York: Harper & Bros., 1939), furnish much insight on the work and tribulations of the Brain Trust.

[4] While Roosevelt believed in the balanced budget, he was not as dogmatic about it as Hoover. After he took office, he realized that the difficulties of the continuing depression made it impossible. Yet his failure troubled him. When he retrenched government spending in 1936-1937 to carry out the dogma, he precipitated a recession.

BOOK TWO
6. "THE TREMENDOUS ENTRANCE"

[1] *Roosevelt and Hopkins: An Intimate History* (New York: Harper & Bros., 1948), p. 40.

7. REMAKING THE FACE OF THE NATION

[1] E. M. Douty, "FERA and the Rural Negro," *The Survey*, July, 1934.

[2] "In the Ditch," *New Outlook*, February, 1934.

[3] David Lilienthal, an original member of the TVA board, has in *TVA, Democracy on the March* (New York: Harper & Bros., 1944) an important discussion of this point.

[4] Rexford G. Tugwell explains this in "The Price Also Rises," *Fortune*, January, 1934.

[5] C. M. Pickett, "King Cotton's New Adventure," *New York Times Magazine*, August 27, 1933.

[6] Josephine Strode, "Kansas Grit," *The Survey*, August, 1936.

8. WASHINGTON — CENTER OF THE COUNTRY

[1] "Three Years of Dr. Roosevelt," *American Mercury*, March, 1936.

9. THE ROOSEVELT COALITION

[1] The membership of such farm organizations as the American Farm Bureau Federation increased from 163,246 members in 1933 to 409,766

by 1937, and trade union membership jumped from 2,857,000 in 1933 to 7,218,000 by 1937 and to 8,944,000 by 1940.

10. CHAMPION CAMPAIGNER

[1] The Revenue Act signed on August 30, among other things, increased the surtax only on net incomes over $50,000 on a graduated scale from 31 per cent at $50,000 to 75 per cent on incomes over $5,000,000. It also levied a graduated tax from 12½ to 15 per cent on corporations depending on the size of the net income.

[2] The violence of the attacks on government spending and the government deficits now sound a quaint note for anyone accustomed to government spending since 1940. This table, in billions of dollars, reveals why:

	Budget		Budget
1930	3.4	1945	98.7
1935	6.5	1951	44.0
1940	9.1	1956	66.5

The gross national debt was $23,350,000,000 in 1932. It reached $52,848,000,000 in 1940.

[3] Samuel J. Eldersveld, "The Influence of Metropolitan Party Pluralities in Presidential Elections Since 1920," *American Political Science Review*, December, 1949, is an important study. I have relied on his statistics and projections.

BOOK THREE

11. POLITICAL MISCALCULATIONS

[1] C. Herman Pritchett, *The Roosevelt Court: A Study in Judicial Politics and Values, 1937-1947* (New York: The Macmillan Co., 1948), p. 14.

12. THE ECONOMY IN A TAILSPIN

[1] Henry Ford proved to be a tougher proposition. He was a formidable foe of unions and his company police and spies smashed organizing efforts. In the autumn of 1940, the UAW organized the Ford workers. The next spring, Ford capitulated after a strike, and granted the union a closed shop and the checkoff of union dues.

[2] The value of the total gross national product in billions of dollars (based on 1953 dollars) was:

1929	175.9	1936	170.2
1932	125.3	1937	179.6

1933	123.4	1938	171.8
1934	136.3	1939	187.9
1935	150.3	1940	205.7

[3] *Income and Consumption* (New York: Henry Holt & Co., 1938), p. 127.

[4] Between 1933 and 1941 federal spending for relief and public works reached about fifteen billion dollars. In 1956, the Congress at the urging of President Eisenhower appropriated nearly thirty-three billions for a highway construction program to be extended over thirteen years.

[5] *Life*, June 5, 1939.

[6] *New Republic*, July 25, 1940.

13. PUBLIC OPINION AND FOREIGN POLICY

[1] Chile broke relations in January, 1943, and Argentina in January, 1944.

[2] Ralph Smuckler, "The Region of Isolationism," *American Political Science Review*, June, 1953, states that based on congressional voting from 1933 to 1950 North Dakota, Idaho, Nebraska, Kansas, Wisconsin, Ohio, Minnesota, and Nevada were the most isolationist. With exceptions he found people of German background were isolationists; rural areas were more isolationist than urban; and the majority of Republicans were isolationist.

[3] In 1944, Sidney Hillman, chief political spokesman for the CIO, in an alliance with the Communists, took control of the ALP from right-wing forces. Headed by George S. Counts and David Dubinsky, the right wing formed the American Liberal party. After Hillman's death, Marcantonio became state chairman of the ALP.

14. THE HIGH TIDE OF ISOLATION

[1] On a religious basis this same poll found 58 per cent of the Catholics sympathized with Franco and 42 per cent favored the Loyalists while 83 per cent of the Protestants sympathized with the Loyalists. For these polls see the highly useful compilation by Hadley Cantril and Mildred Strunk, *Public Opinion, 1935-1946* (Princeton: Princeton University Press, 1951).

[2] *The Inside Struggle, 1936-1939* (New York: Simon and Schuster, 1954), pp. 389-390.

[3] See Richard Hofstadter, *The American Political Tradition and the Men Who Made It* (New York: Alfred A. Knopf, 1948); Charles A. Beard, *American Foreign Policy in the Making, 1932-1940* (New Haven: Yale University Press, 1946).

15. PRESIDENTIAL LEADERSHIP AND FOREIGN POLICY

[1] When the public was asked by the Gallup poll how it would vote on the question of entering the war, the reply was:

	Stay Out	Go In
July, 1940	85	15
October, 1940	83	17
December, 1940	88	12
February, 1941	85	12

[2] *The Memoirs of Cordell Hull* (New York: The Macmillan Co., 1948), II, p. 684.

[3] The new law did not allow American merchant ships to go into combat zones. To those, including the Maritime Commission, who argued that the nation should support freedom of the seas, Hull replied that "the important thing is that Congress doesn't and the public doesn't." These restrictions on American merchant ships were not revised until just before Pearl Harbor. But by that time the need for more aid to Britain had led to evasions of the restrictions.

[4] *The Time for Decision* (New York: Harper & Bros., 1944), p. 119.

[5] In April, 1941, the Fight for Freedom Committee was organized from the nucleus of the Century group. It favored military intervention in the war. By this date, the new Committee felt that the Aid the Allies Committee was equivocating and no longer leading public opinion. The Right Reverend Henry W. Hobson served as Chairman; Francis P. Miller and Mrs. Calvin Coolidge were Vice-Chairmen; Ulric Bell was Chairman of the Executive Committee; Wayne Johnson was Treasurer; F. H. Peter Cusick was Executive Secretary; and Senator Carter Glass was Honorary Chairman.

[6] In addition to what I have touched upon, Cole describes attempts of Bundists and others to infiltrate America First. He writes: "The following of the America First Committee consisted of highly heterogeneous elements and among the worst of them were the pro-fascists . . . the Committee leaders earnestly sought to prevent these elements from working through their organization. And their efforts were more successful than most of its critics would concede."

[7] When Willkie testified before Congress for the Lend-Lease bill a few months later, isolationist Senator Bennett Champ Clark repeated some of these charges to Willkie. Willkie dismissed them with disarming candor by saying: "In moments of oratory in campaigns we all expand a little bit."

[8] *Working With Roosevelt* (New York: Harper & Bros., 1952), p. 242.
[9] His 26,890,401 popular votes was approximately 600,000 fewer than he had received in 1936 and his percentage of the vote dropped from the 60 of 1936 to 54. Willkie with his 22,381,018 popular votes received more votes than any other Republican until General Eisenhower in 1952.

16. AVOIDING THE IRREVOCABLE ACT

[1] The Gallup poll released on October 18 stated that 72 per cent of those interviewed favored arming mercant ships. On the question of permitting American ships to carry supplies to Britian, only 46 per cent were favorable, 40 per cent were opposed, and the remainder were undecided.
[2] *Roosevelt and Hopkins: An Intimate History* (New York: Harper & Bros., 1948), pp. 382-383.
[3] Grew, since that time, has justifiably criticized Hull and Hornbeck for their inflexibility over this point. Even if nothing had resulted from the meeting, it should have been attempted. Grew discusses this question in *Turbulent Era: A Diplomatic Record of Forty Years, 1904-1945* (Boston: Houghton Mifflin Co., 1952), Vol. II.
[4] Grew always believed that Japanese militarists "doctored" this note to persuade the Emperor and reluctant civilian leaders that the United States was determined to start a conflict. Prime Minister Yoshida was quoted on August 3, 1955, as stating "some of the Japanese leaders at the time of Pearl Harbor tampered with the text of the final U.S. note. This persuaded reluctant officers to agree to war. This was a fraud by the military and amounted to conspiracy."
[5] Hull and Hornbeck consistently underestimated the danger of a Japanese assault in spite of insistent and frequent warnings from Grew that the Japanese might launch a sneak attack.
[6] "War Came at Pearl Harbor: Suspicions Considered," *The Yale Review*, Spring, 1956.

BOOK FOUR

17. PRODUCTION AND MORE PRODUCTION

[1] During Roosevelt's second term, the older progressive doctrine of the regulation of business by re-establishing competition replaced the over-all centralized planning views of the early Brain Trust. Thurman Arnold, professor at the Yale Law School and author of *The Folklore of Capitalism* (1937), was appointed head of the Antitrust Division and given additional funds to launch major investigations.
[2] November, 1941.

[3] July 8, 1940.

[4] Private memorandum of conversations between Emmerich and Sidney Hyman, May, 1949.

[5] *New York Times Magazine*, August 24, 1941.

[6] *The Struggle for Survival: A Chronicle of Economic Mobilization in World War II* (New Haven: Yale University Press, 1951), p. 13.

[7] Nelson was removed as head of the WPB in August, 1944. Herman Miles, *Presidential Agency* (Cambridge: Harvard University Press, 1950), analyzes the work of the Office of War Mobilization and casts doubts on Nelson's contention that it was impossible for the civilian to control the military.

18. TRANSFORMING THE SOCIAL FABRIC

[1] *State of the Nation* (Boston: Houghton Mifflin Co., 1944), p. 5.

[2] It rose from $126.4 billion in 1941 to $213.7 billion in 1944 (in constant 1953 dollars the rise was from $239.2 billion in 1941 to $329.3 billion in 1944).

[3] In 1953 dollars, the per capita figure for 1944 was $1537. Not until 1953 was the 1944 per capita disposable income figure exceeded.

[4] "Who's Getting the Money?" *Harper's Magazine*, June, 1944.

[5] It provided for unemployment compensation, government guarantees of 50 per cent of any loans up to $4000 made for the purchase of a home, farm, or business, and government funds for the continuance of education.

[6] An example of the vindictiveness toward individual New Dealers occurred in 1943 when an amendment to a deficiency appropriation forbade the payment of salaries to three specifically named individuals. This was later declared unconstitutional by the Supreme Court.

19. THE INEXORABLE CALENDAR OF ELECTIONS

[1] November 15, 1943.

[2] October 5, 1943.

[3] Old Guard leaders demonstrated their antipathy to Willkie by not even inviting him to address the 1944 Convention. After the two Conventions, Willkie wrote "Cowardice At Chicago," *Collier's*, September 16, 1944, denouncing both parties for evasive statements on foreign policy: ". . . the fact is that our foreign policy is now and will be for generations the paramount, the absorbing question before us. *And upon its wise solution will depend the domestic welfare of the American people.*"

[4] *You're the Boss* (New York: Viking, 1947), p. 181.

[5] The Gallup Poll, *Chicago Daily News*, March 5, 1945.

20. THE VICTORIOUS COALITION

[1] *The Grand Alliance* (Boston: Houghton Mifflin Co., 1950), p. 663.

[2] *Roosevelt and Hopkins: An Intimate History* (New York: Harper & Bros., 1948), p. 363.

[3] Hanson Baldwin, *Great Mistakes of the War* (New York: Harper & Bros., 1950), insists that the fear of a separate peace was one of the false premises of American wartime policy.

[4] *Seven Decisions That Shaped History* (New York: Harper & Bros., 1950), p. 216.

[5] Not until the end of 1944 was SWNCC (a State, War, and Navy Departments Coordinating Committee) established in an attempt to overcome the separation between diplomatic and military policymaking in the American government.

[6] Eisenhower discusses the episode in *Crusade in Europe* (New York: Doubleday & Co., 1948), pp. 398-403.

[7] *A Soldier's Story* (New York: Henry Holt and Co., 1951), p. 336.

[8] In addition to American leadership in drafting the charter of the UN, to carry out the economic and social purposes of the Atlantic Charter, the United States was also instrumental in laying the groundwork for postwar economic cooperation at the Bretton Woods Conference, July, 1944, where agreements for the International Monetary Fund and the International Bank for Reconstruction and Development were drafted.

[9] "Hopes and Failures: American Policy Toward East Central Europe, 1941-1947," *Review of Politics*, October, 1955.

21. YALTA: MYTH AND REALITY

[1] The Churchill telegram appears in *Foreign Relations of the United States, Diplomatic Papers, The Conference at Malta and Yalta*, 1945 (Washington: Government Printing Office, 1955). The Stettinius statement is from Edward R. Stettinius, Jr., *Roosevelt and the Russians: The Yalta Conference* (New York: Doubleday & Co., 1949), which I edited. Unless otherwise noted, the material I use on Yalta is drawn from these two sources.

[2] *Triumph and Tragedy* (Boston: Houghton Mifflin Co., 1953), p. 402.

[3] Philip E. Mosely, "The Berlin Deadlock," *American Perspective*, December, 1948; "The Occupation of Germany: New Light on How the Zones Were Drawn," *Foreign Affairs*, July, 1950.

[4] *Decision in Germany* (New York: Doubleday & Co., 1950), p. 26.

[5] Secretary of State Stettinius was informed of these discussions but except for Ambassador Harriman, Foreign Service Officer Charles E. Bohlen,

who served as Roosevelt's interpreter, and Stettinius, the remainder of the State Department delegation did not participate in them nor were they informed of the Far Eastern Agreement signed on February 11.

6 Admiral Ellis M. Zacharias, formerly Deputy Chief of Naval Intelligence, charged in "The Inside Story of Yalta," *United Nations World*, January, 1949, that the Joint Chiefs made their decision on inaccurate and misleading intelligence reports. Arthur Krock wrote in the *New York Times*, August 12, 1949, that General Arnold sent a report to Yalta documenting Japanese weaknesses and "its purport was that the Russians were not required for a victory which would come much sooner than the high Army-Navy command believed." This report reached Harry Hopkins, but it is not clear whether it was shown to Roosevelt.

7 Wesley Frank Craven and James Lea Cate, editors, *The Army Air Forces in World War II: The Pacific: Matterhorn to Nagasaki, June, 1944 to August, 1945* (Chicago: University of Chicago Press, 1953), p. 711, state: "Because the invasion was to prove unnecessary and the Russian aid perhaps superfluous at the time and certainly embarrassing to U. S. policies later on, the advocates of that strategy have since come in for much criticism . . . In all fairness it must be realized that the decision on this strategy, like all adopted by the JCS, was a unanimous one and that it was supported by the experiences of the German war, by intelligence reports (remarkably correct) concerning the intact status of the Japanese Army, by the fresh memory of the fanatical resistance of enemy troops on Iwo Jima and Okinawa, and indirectly by American military tradition."

8 *Congressional Record*, May 14, 1951 (p. 5399), January 21, 1952 (p. 335), July 17, 1951 (p. 8450), contains examples of the attacks on secret diplomacy and power politics.

9 For examples of appeals to Polish-Americans, see the *Congressional Record*, February 11, 1952 (pp. A795, A803, A822), July 6, 1951 (p. 7935), February 14, 1952 (p. A856), April 30, 1952 (p. A2740), February 7, 1950 (p. A932).

10 For examples of the myth-making about the role of Hiss, see the *Congressional Record*, June 26, 1951 (p. A4071), May 3, 1951 (pp. 4957-4958), April 12, 1951 (p. 3825), February 17, 1950 (pp. A1227-A1228), February 7, 1950 (p. A935), February 6, 1950 (p. 856), January 26, 1950 (pp. A567-A568), January 25, 1950 (pp. 932-934).

11 The following note appeared at the bottom of the table of contents: "Neither the Members of the Republican Policy Committee nor other Republican Senators are responsible for the statements herein contained, except such as they are willing to endorse and make their own."

12 A statement which conveniently overlooked the many times that

Roosevelt and Churchill fought for governments representative of the people in liberated Europe and achieved Stalin's agreement to this. But the justness of their position availed little in the face of Soviet power.

22. THE ART OF PRESIDENTIAL LEADERSHIP

[1] "The President's Press Conference," *Survey Graphic*, July, 1939.
[2] "Selling the President to the People," *Commentary*, November, 1955.
[3] Anne O'Hare McCormick, *The World At Home* (New York: Alfred A. Knopf, 1956), p. 132.
[4] Within a week of the President's death, Pocket Books, Inc., published *Roosevelt: In Memoriam*, which contains this poem and much other useful material.

BOOK FIVE

23. USHERING IN THE NEW AGE

[1] These treaties were signed on February 10, 1947. They confirmed Western supremacy in Italy and North Africa and Soviet dominance in Hungary and the Balkans.
[2] "Hopes and Failures: American Policy Toward East Central Europe, 1941-1947," *The Review of Politics*, October, 1955.
[3] *Turbulent Era: A Diplomatic Record of Forty Years, 1904-1945* (Boston: Houghton Mifflin Co., 1952), Vol. II, pp. 1425-1426.

24. MAN OF GREAT DECISIONS

[1] *American Diplomacy: 1900-1950* (Chicago: University of Chicago Press, 1951), p. 73.
[2] "The Mainsprings of American Foreign Policy: The National Interest vs. Moral Abstractions," *American Political Science Review*, December, 1950.
[3] A Gallup poll revealed that the policy of firmness had solid support. *Chicago Daily News*, November 11, 1956.
[4] On March 6, 1946, for instance, Senators Claude Pepper, Glen Taylor, and Harvey Kilgore issued a statement calling the proposal "shocking." See, too, a speech by Pepper in the Senate on March 20. A year later Churchill wrote: "I was surprised that such mild, mellifluous, carefully shaped and guarded sentiments should have caused so much commotion, not only in America and in my own country but elsewhere." "If I Were an American," *Life*, April 14, 1947.
[5] A few days after the speech, Wallace released a letter he had written the President on July 23, 1946, urging a shift in our policy. He criticized

the atomic tests at Bikini and the size of military appropriations and said there was a "school of military thinking" that advocates a "preventive war": "These facts rather make it appear either (1) that we are preparing ourselves to win the war which we regard as inevitable or (2) that we are trying to build up a predominance of force to intimidate the rest of mankind."

⁶ Vandenberg's proposals on the UN reflected a popular feeling. The Gallup poll found that a majority of those interviewed were anxious "to see that the United Nations organization was not entirely bypassed." *Chicago Daily News*, April 14, 1947.

⁷ The Policy Planning Staff had concluded that China under the corrupt rule of Chiang Kai-shek lacked the type of economy that could be aided effectively by American aid.

⁸ Vandenberg, who had a high regard for the usefulness of the UN, wanted to keep the action within the Charter. Article 51 set forth the "inherent right of individual and collective self-defense" and Articles 52-54 permitted the existence of regional agreements. In 1947 at Rio de Janeiro the American nations had formed such a regional defense alliance embodying the concept that an attack on one nation would be viewed as an attack on all.

25. CLIMAX IN THE FAR EAST

¹ H. Bradford Westerfield, *Foreign Policy and Party Politics: Pearl Harbor to Korea* (New Haven: Yale University Press, 1955), is a valuable discussion of this point.

² *United States Relations With China, With Special Reference to the Period, 1944-1949* (Washington: Government Printing Office, 1949). It was released on August 5.

³ *Years of Trial and Hope: 1946-1952* (New York: Doubleday & Co., 1956), p. 333; copyright, Time, Inc.

26. THE AMERICAN IMAGE OVERSEAS

¹ Quoted in C. L. Sulzberger, "Europe Distrusts Us, But Wants Our Help," *New York Times Magazine*, June 23, 1946.

² Guido Piovene, in *What Europe Thinks of America*, ed. James Burnham (New York: John Day Co., 1953), p. 133.

³ "The Urgent Need for a New Approach to Foreign Aid," private memorandum, August 3, 1956.

⁴ Luigi Barzini, Jr., *Americans Are Alone in the World* (New York: Random House, 1953), p. 208.

⁵ In the early years, the Fulbright Act functioned only where foreign

governments owed the United States money for buying with their own currencies American surplus equipment at the close of the war. These currencies, not convertible into dollars, were used in part to finance the cost of Americans studying or teaching in these countries. The Smith-Mundt Program, in addition to extending exchanges to non-Fulbright countries, defrayed the dollar expenses in the United States of some of the foreign nationals from Fulbright countries.

[6] The Smith-Mundt Program varied decidedly in organization. Although it had an Advisory Commission on Educational Exchange, the Department of State was authorized by the law to set the policy and select the grantees. Overseas it had no bi-national commissions and the Embassy's cultural officer selected the foreign grantees. Lacking the bi-national features of the Fulbright Program, it was more exposed to the charge of "American propaganda."

BOOK SIX

27. THE SURPRISING VICTORY

[1] *Fortune*, January, 1947.

[2] *The Fabulous Democrats* (New York: G. P. Putnam's Sons, 1956), p. 170.

[3] The government seized the mines and signed a contract with Lewis later in May, 1946. In October, Lewis threatened a second strike. The government obtained an injunction to restrain Lewis, but he defied it. Lewis was fined. In June, 1947, the mines were returned to their owners and Lewis won a contract conceding his demands.

[4] *Chicago Times*, November 22, 1946.

[5] *Chicago Daily News*, November 1, 1946.

[6] *Small Sounds in the Night* (New York: Alfred A. Knopf, 1956), pp. 110-111.

[7] Louis H. Bean, "The Republican 'Mandate' and '48," *New York Times Magazine*, January 19, 1947.

[8] Taft sponsored the Taft-Ellender-Wagner bill, a program of public housing for lower income groups, but his followers rejected it.

[9] His total popular vote was 24,179,623, to 21,991,290 for Dewey, with 1,157,326 for Wallace and 1,176,154 for Thurmond. The Electoral College vote was 303 to 189 with Thurmond capturing 39.

28. POLITICS OF REVENGE

[1] When the investigation was completed in 1951, some two thousand employees had resigned and two hundred and twelve had been dismissed on the bases that there was reasonable doubt of their loyalty.

[2] The Soviet Union established a conspiratorial underground in Washington in the 1930s. Headed in turn by Harold Ware, Nathan Witt, and John Abt, cells were organized in some government agencies and documents were photographed or copied and passed on to the head of the Soviet underground, Colonel Boris Bykov.

[3] Eric F. Goldman, *The Crucial Decade: America 1945-1955* (New York: Alfred A. Knopf, 1956), p. 105.

[4] By now, McCarthy was receiving support from a group known as "The China Lobby," including Alfred Kohlberg, New York importer of Chinese fabrics. Edward A. Harris, "The Men Behind McCarthy," *New Republic*, April 24, 1950. The Administration's answers to McCarthy's charge are in the Department of State *Bulletin*, March 27, April 3, 10, 17, 24, June 12, 1950.

[5] T. R. B., *New Republic*, April 10, 1950.

[6] "This sort of thing was not the Taft one had known," his sympathetic biographer William S. White has written in *The Taft Story* (New York: Harper & Bros., 1954).

[7] Republican Senators Charles W. Tobey, George D. Aiken, Wayne C. Morse, Irving M. Ives, Edward J. Thye, and Robert C. Hendrickson joined her in the Declaration.

[8] In October, 1951, by a three to two vote, a Senate subcommittee refused to approve the appointment of Jessup as a delegate to the UN. Brewster voted against it without qualification. Democrat Guy Gillette and Republican H. Alexander Smith agreed that the attacks on Jessup's loyalty were unfair, but they voted against him to express their disapproval of "our over-all Far Eastern policy." Since the Senate did not have time to vote before it adjourned, Truman gave Jessup a recess appointment. On January 10, 1952, thirty-eight Republican Senators headed by Bridges recommended that he be recalled.

[9] The Senate Internal Security Committee reopened the Lattimore case in 1951-1952 and charged that Lattimore promoted Communist interests. An indictment charging Lattimore with perjury and seeking to further Soviet interests was obtained in 1953. The courts threw out the charges in 1955. Owen Lattimore presented his position in *Ordeal By Slander* (Boston: Little, Brown & Co., 1950).

[10] In 1945, it had been discovered that secret documents had been turned over to Philip Jaffe, editor of *Amerasia*, a Communist-sponsored monthly, established to influence Far Eastern policy. Jaffe was fined for receiving government property illegally.

[11] The Republican minority, Henry Cabot Lodge and Bourke Hickenlooper, filed a statement criticizing the investigation as "superficial and

inconclusive." They recommended a bipartisan committee to take "the whole matter out of politics" and get "a clean ending to the whole business, let the chips fall where they may." They praised John E. Peurifoy's running of the State Department's security program. On the basis of the investigation conducted, the allegations against Lattimore were not proved, they wrote. Service was indiscreet but "There is no proof of disloyalty and no rumor against his character."

[12] *Congressional Record*, July 20-21, 1950.

[13] August 25, 1958.

[14] See the contemporary articles by Hugh Morrow, "He's De-Snobbing the State Department," and Demaree Bess, "Why Americans Hate the State Department," *Saturday Evening Post*, August 27, 1949, and August 19, 1950.

[15] "The Parties and Foreign Policy," *Harper's Magazine*, November, 1955. See also Elmer Davis, "The Crusade Against Acheson," *ibid.*, March, 1951.

[16] *The Fourth Branch of Government* (Boston: Houghton Mifflin Co., 1959), p. 9.

[17] The President's account is in *Years of Trial and Hope* and the General's aide, General Courtney Whitney, has presented the MacArthur side in *MacArthur: His Rendezvous With History* (New York: Alfred A. Knopf, 1956).

[18] Nothing happened to this recommendation. "In fact it was not the impudence of McCarthy that was impressive; it was the silence of the Senate," Herbert Agar has written in *The Price of Power: America Since 1945* (Chicago: University of Chicago Press, 1957), p. 115.

[19] *New York Times*, December 20, 1950.

[20] The vote was 69 to 21; 27 Republicans, including Taft, voted in the affirmative, 19 against.

[21] *The Private Papers of Senator Vandenberg* (Boston: Houghton Mifflin, 1952), pp. 572-573.

[22] The *Chicago Tribune*, April 12, 1951, ran a front-page editorial demanding the impeachment of Truman. It concluded: "The American nation has never been in greater danger. It is led by a fool who is surrounded by knaves. Impeachment is the only remedy."

[23] The Supreme Court on June 17, 1957, held that Acheson violated the regulations of the Department of State in firing Service.

[24] April 28, 1951.

29. REPUDIATING THE DEMOCRATS

[1] This group included Dewey, Sherman Adams of New Hampshire, Dan Thornton of Colorado, Arthur B. Langlie of Washington, Walter Kohler of Wisconsin, Val Peterson of Nebraska, and Edward Arn of Kansas.

[2] Arthur Krock had written in the *New York Times*, November 8, 1951, that Truman had offered to support Eisenhower for the Democratic nomination.

[3] The *New York Times*, July 1-3, for instance, published three editorials outlining why "Mr. Taft Can't Win."

[4] In the *New York Times*, May 26, for example, the Taft forces ran an advertisement "You Know Where Taft Stands."

[5] The Convention immediately proceeded to the nomination of Senator Richard M. Nixon as the vice-presidential candidate. His youth underscored the new leadership of the party and his work as a member of the House Un-American Activities Committee in exposing Alger Hiss appealed to those apprehensive over allegations of Communists in government.

[6] Raymond McConnel, Jr., *Chicago Daily News*, July 10, 1952.

[7] See Reston's columns in the *New York Times*, September 17, 24, and Phillips's article "Eisenhower as Campaigner," *ibid.*, October 19, 1952.

[8] Angus Campbell, Gerald Gurin, and Warren E. Miller, "Political Issues and the Vote: November, 1952," *American Political Science Review*, June, 1953, observe that Eisenhower would have won by a narrow margin with the votes of new voters and non-voters of 1948, but the sweep was explained by former Democrats — some 25 per cent of the Eisenhower vote — who shifted.

[9] "Who Elected Eisenhower?" *Saturday Evening Post*, January 10, 1953.

BOOK SEVEN

30. TRANSFORMING THE MIDDLE CLASS BASE

[1] By 1956, twenty-two million women held one third of all the jobs. Half of these women were married. They held jobs ranging from executive, teaching, selling, office work to detailed factory work.

[2] These figures are in terms of 1953 dollars.

[3] In 1957, there were nearly three and a half million multiple-person families with incomes below $2000 and almost twelve million below $4000 — more than a quarter of all multiple-person families.

[4] "Eggheads and Politics," *New Republic*, October 27, 1958.

[5] Between 1901 and 1920 there were 14,531,197 immigrants; in 1921-1940, 4,635,640; and in 1941-1953, 1,676,710.

[6] Seymour Martin Lipset, *Political Man: Essays on the Sociology of Democracy* (New York: Doubleday Inc., 1960), Chapter 9.

31. THE NEGRO AND POLITICS

[1] In percentage terms, Negro income climbed from a previous 30 per cent of U. S. white income to a 53 per cent by 1956. *Employment and Economic Status of Negroes in the United States* (83rd Congress, 1st Session, Document 14, 1953).

[2] Otis Duncan and Beverly Duncan, *The Negro Population of Chicago* (Chicago: The University of Chicago Press, 1957), point out that the percentage of Negro women in domestic work dropped from 37.7 to 15.5 in 1940-1950; in clerical and kindred work, the percentage rose from 4.5 to 11.6; but in professional, technical, and kindred work it fell from 3.4 to 2.8. In cities like Chicago, the refusal of hospitals to admit qualified Negro doctors to their staff — only seven of the over seventy private "white" hospitals had Negro doctors on their staff in 1957 — was an example of continued discrimination against Negro professionals discouraging young Negroes from entering medicine.

[3] V. O. Key, Jr., *Southern Politics in State and Nation* (New York: Alfred A. Knopf, 1949), pp. 619-643, discusses the Southern reaction to the white primary decision.

[4] "If the Southern Negro Got the Vote," *New York Times Magazine*, June 21, 1959.

[5] As an example of a saner head, I have in mind Harry S. Ashmore, executive editor of the *Arkansas Gazette*. See his book, *An Epitaph for Dixie* (New York: W. W. Norton & Co., 1958).

[6] "The Untold Story of Little Rock," *Saturday Evening Post*, June 27, 1959.

[7] The federal District Court at Norfolk, one of the Virginia cities where schools had been closed, said on the same date as the state court's decision: ". . . we arrive at the inescapable conclusion that the Commonwealth of Virginia, having accepted and assumed the responsibility of maintaining and operating public schools, cannot act through one of its officers to close one or more public schools in the state solely by reason of the assignment to, or enrollment or presence in, that public school of children of different races or colors, and, at the same time, keep other public schools throughout the state open on a segregated basis. The 'equal protection' afforded to all persons and taxpayers is lacking in such a situation."

[8] Samuel Lubell, "The Future of the Negro Voter in the United States," *Journal of Negro Education*, Summer, 1957. This entire issue contains valuable articles on the Negro vote. Henry Lee Moon's estimates of the

Negro shift is higher than Lubell's. With sixty-three cities as his base, Moon finds a 36.8 per cent increase for Eisenhower in twenty-three Southern cities and a 9.9 per cent increase in forty non-Southern cities.

[9] C. Vann Woodward, "The Great Civil Rights Debate," *Commentary*, September, 1957, is a penetrating essay.

BOOK EIGHT

32. MODERN REPUBLICANISM

[1] David E. Lilienthal, former Chairman of the AEC, in a letter to the *New York Times*, November 10, 1954, deplored the way during the past year in the press and public discussions the AEC was being "thought of, for the first time in its history, in terms of the political affiliations or obligations of the members. . . . It certainly did not occur to anyone at the time the AEC came into being, in 1946, that a public body with such vast powers over the security, the science and the industry of the whole nation, operating largely in secret, should take into account the fact that its members had been appointed by a Democratic President nor that it should function as a bipartisan group of Democrats and Republicans."

[2] "One-Man Task Force of the G.O.P.," *New York Times Magazine*, October 24, 1954.

[3] Eisenhower polled 35,575,420 votes to Stevenson's 26,033,066. In 1952 Eisenhower polled 55.4 per cent of the major party vote, and in 1956, 57.7 per cent. Eisenhower gained nearly 1.7 million votes over 1952 while Stevenson lost 1.3 million. Stevenson carried only 7 states with 73 electoral votes in 1956; in 1952 he carried 9 states with 89 electoral votes. While he gained Missouri in 1956, he lost three states he carried in 1952 — Kentucky, Louisiana, and West Virginia. In the twelve largest cities, Stevenson's vote dropped 642,000. West of the Mississippi River, Eisenhower's vote declined.

[4] In the Senate, the division was 49 Democrats, 47 Republicans; in the House, 234 Democrats, 201 Republicans.

33. SECURITY AND MC CARTHY

[1] Brownell later denied on November 17 that he had implied that Truman was disloyal.

[2] The Supreme Court ruled on June 11, 1956, that Eisenhower exceeded his authority when he extended the security program to government workers in non-sensitive positions.

[3] *Chicago Sun-Times*, January 22, 1954; James Reston, "Security Risk Problem," *New York Times*, January 28, 1954.

[4] Yet, in that same month, McLeod told a Lincoln Day rally: "In the twenty years from 1933 to 1953, traitors had free run in high places and low."

[5] *Report of the Committee on Post Office and Civil Service* (U. S. Senate, 84th Congress, 2nd Session, Senate Report 2750).

[6] This support was probably overrated all along. For example, see "The Myth of McCarthy's Strength," *Look*, June 1, 1954; Louis H. Bean, *Influences in the 1954 Midterm Election* (Washington: Public Affairs Institute, 1954).

[7] Mr. Welch has set forth his impressions of the real lessons of the hearings with some amusing recollections in "The Lawyer's After Thoughts," *Life*, July 26, 1954.

34. PARALYZING PRESSURES ON FOREIGN POLICY

[1] Their desire to seek revenge on past policies was explained by Senator Taft in "What the G.O.P. Must Do to Win in 1954," *Look*, April 21, 1953.

[2] *Dilemmas of Politics* (Chicago: University of Chicago Press, 1958), p. 332.

[3] The President obviously overstated the situation here since under President Truman raids from Formosa against the mainland had occurred.

[4] January 17, 1954.

[5] *New York Herald Tribune*, August 12, 1958.

[6] James Shepley, "How Dulles Averted War," *Life*, January 16, 1956.

[7] In the speech there was a balancing passage which did not attract attention: "If we can deter such aggression as would mean general war, and that is our confident resolve, then we can let time and fundamentals work for us." See also Dulles's article in *Foreign Affairs*, April, 1954.

[8] Although the President constitutionally did not need this resolution, he obtained it to avoid the abuse heaped on Truman for not asking for a congressional resolution when the Korean fighting broke out.

[9] "Foreign Policy and Presidential Moralism," *The Reporter*, May 2, 1957.

35. THE NEW LOOK

[1] Charles J. V. Murphy, "Eisenhower's Most Critical Defense Budget," *Fortune*, December, 1956, pointed out that there was nothing unusual in the complaint of the armed forces that their effectiveness was being crippled by economies: "But what was especially disquieting about the situation, after four years of Eisenhower, was that so large a gap should still separate the judgments of the military chiefs and a President, who, for most of his life, was one of them."

[2] Gerhard Colm, *Can We Afford Additional Programs for National Security?* (National Planning Association, October, 1953), insisted, however, that the country could spend twenty to thirty billions additional on defense without dislocating the economy.

[3] *New York Times,* July 15, 1955.

[4] Reporters who publicized official reports on the progress of Soviet science, which were at variance with public statements by the Administration, were condemned by Administration officials and subjected to investigations. Joseph and Stewart Alsop, "That Washington Security Curtain," *Saturday Evening Post,* February 19, 1955.

[5] *London Observer,* October 20, 1957.

[6] Albert Perry, "Why Should We Have Been Surprised?" *The Reporter,* October 31, 1957, analyzes the information ignored by the Administration.

36. POLITICS OF POSTPONEMENT

[1] A Hoover Commission task force report on the budget stated in 1955: "An essential part of his [the President's] function is to exercise national leadership and to counterbalance the sectional and special interests which might otherwise exert undue influence on Congressional decisions."

[2] The vote on this bill was 184 Democrats and 133 Republicans for; 39 Democrats and 59 Republicans against.

[3] I have in mind, for instance, Kennedy's speech, "United States Military and Diplomatic Policies — Preparing for the Gap," *Congressional Record,* August 14, 1958; Fulbright's "On The Brink of Disaster," *ibid.,* August 6; Humphrey's "A Chronology of Failure," *The Reporter,* August 7; and Mansfield's on the German situation, *Congressional Record,* February 12, 1959.

[4] See the President's reply to Chalmers Roberts at the September 3, 1958, press conference.

[5] *Chicago Daily News,* September 30, 1958.

[6] The outgoing Eighty-fifth Congress had 49 Democratic, 47 Republican Senators; the House 235 Democrats, 200 Republican members. The admission of Alaska as a state resulted in two additional Democratic Senators and one Congressman.

[7] A research report issued by the Republican National Committee concluded that the election setback came largely from "an urban revolt." *New York Times,* April 7, 1959.

[8] *Chicago Daily News,* November 1, 1958.

37. PROJECTING THE IMAGE OF THE PRESIDENT

[1] Doris Fleeson printed in its entirety: "The Gettysburg Address As It Would Have Been Written by President Eisenhower," *Chicago Daily News*, June 14, 1957.

[2] John Herling, *New York Times Magazine*, June 9, 1957.

[3] Press conference of April 23, 1958; see also the conference of March 27, 1957.

[4] Frederic W. Collins, "Our Om-nescient President: Some Forces of His Not-Knowing," *New Republic*, June 1, 1959.

[5] Joseph Kraft, "The Dangerous Precedent of James Hagerty," *Esquire*, June, 1959.

[6] *The Fourth Branch of Government* (Boston: Houghton Mifflin Co., 1959), pp. 163-164.

38. PRESIDENTSHIP

[1] *Chicago Daily News*, October 21, 1958.

[2] Samuel Lubell, *Chicago Daily News*, May 8, 1959.

[3] Felix Belair, Jr., "White House Changes With Persons on Job," *New York Times*, February 1, 1959.

[4] *New York Times*, June 24, 1959.

Selected Bibliography

I am grateful to the many participants who have written useful memoirs and to the journalists and scholars who have published helpful articles and books. In my footnotes or in the text I have indicated my indebtedness to many of them. I do not usually repeat these references in this bibliographical essay. I have found the *Congressional Record*, many congressional hearings, *The Congressional Quarterly*, and a number of government publications immensely useful. The *New York Times* was an invaluable aid to me as were some other newspapers and a number of magazines.

BOOK ONE

Essential sources for study of American life and society during the late 1920s and the early 1930s are *Recent Social Trends* (1933); *Social Changes*, annual volumes 1928-1933, ed. W. F. Ogburn (1929-1934); and *Social Changes During Depression and Recovery* (1935), also edited by Ogburn.

Statistical studies of a basic nature are Paul H. Douglas and Aaron Director, *The Problem of Unemployment* (1931); Isadore Lubin, *The Absorption of the Unemployed by American Industry* (1929), a valuable study of the jobless in the last days of "prosperity"; M. Leven, H. G. Moulton, and C. Warburton, *America's Capacity to Consume* (1934), a pioneer attempt to determine income distribution. Simon Kuznets's *Shares of Upper Income Groups in Income and Savings* (1950) is indispensible.

Robert Lynd's *Middletown* (1929) is an excellent study of a community and his and Helen Lynd's *Middletown in Transition* (1937) contains candid shots of the depression. F. L. Allen, *Only Yesterday* (1931) and *Since Yesterday* (1940), contain lively material. The best single article on the human aspects of the depression is "No One Has Starved," *Fortune*, September, 1932. Virtually every issue of *The Survey* has valuable material as do *Social Forces* and *The Family*. Other important articles on unemployment include Louis Stark, "All I Want Is Work," *New Republic*, February 4, 1931; "New York in the Third Winter," *Fortune*, January, 1932; M. A. Hallgren, "Mass Misery in Philadelphia," *The Nation*, March 9, 1932, and "Panic in the Steel Towns," March 30,

1932; J. L. Heffernan, "The Hungry City," *Atlantic Monthly*, May, 1932. Samuel Stouffer and Paul Lazarsfeld, *The Family in the Depression* (1937), O. M. Hall, "Attitudes and Unemployment," *Archives of Psychology*, March, 1934, and Paul L. Benjamin, "The Family Society and the Depression," *Annals of the American Academy of Political and Social Sciences*, March, 1932, are all useful studies.

Murray R. Benedict, *Farm Policies of the United States, 1790-1950* (1953), is a major contribution. Theodore Saloutos and John D. Hicks, *Agricultural Discontent in the Mid West, 1900-1939* (1951), examines the sources of farm troubles, and the following describe the situation in the early depression: U. S. Department of Agriculture, *The Agricultural Situation*, various issues 1930-1933; "When the Farmers' Fury Explodes," *Literary Digest*, February 4, 1933; Josephine Herbst, "Feet in the Grass Roots," *Scribner's Magazine*, January, 1933; and Mary H. Vorse, "Rebellion in the Corn Belt," *Harper's Magazine*, December, 1932.

The Autobiography of Lincoln Steffens (1931) and John Chamberlain, *Farewell to Reform* (1932), reflect disillusionment with the American experiment and enchantment with collectivism. Jonathan Norton Leonard, *Three Years Down* (1939), is a bitter account.

Arthur M. Schlesinger, Jr., *The Crisis of the Old Order: 1919-1933* (1957), has excellent material on the 1920s. Eric F. Goldman, *Rendezvous With Destiny: A History of Modern American Reform* (1952), is a lively history of liberalism. Richard Hofstadter, *The Age of Reform: From Bryan to F. D. R.* (1955), has penetrating insights. William Leuchtenburg, *The Perils of Prosperity 1914-1932* (1958), is a valuable brief study. John Kenneth Galbraith, *The Great Crash: 1929* (1955) is a detailed analysis. James W. Prothro, *The Dollar Decade: Business Ideas in the 1920's* (1954), and George Soule, *Prosperity Decade* (1947), are studies of the economic thinking of the 1920s. Broadus Mitchell, *Depression Decade* (1947), analyzes the Hoover policies. Harris Gaylord Warren, *Herbert Hoover and the Great Depression* (1959), is a balanced account. *The Memoirs of Herbert Hoover: The Cabinet and the Presidency 1920-1933* and *The Great Depression 1929-1941* (1952) are invaluable for Hoover's view of the presidency. William Starr Myers and Walter H. Newton, *The Hoover Administration: A Documented Narrative* (1936), and Ray L. Wilbur and A. M. Hyde, *The Hoover Policies* (1937), are strong Hoover defenders. W. E. Binkley, *The President and Congress* (1947), has useful material on Hoover's relations with Congress. Sydney Hyman, *The American President* (1954), is a discerning study; Clinton Rossiter, *The American Presidency* (1956), and Pendleton Herring, *Presidential Leadership* (1940), are important analyses. E. E. Robinson, *The Roosevelt Leadership* (1955), is critical of Roosevelt and favorable to Hoover.

For Hoover's handling of newspapermen and his views on public relations the following are valuable: James E. Pollard, *The Presidents and the Press* (1947), Irwin H. Hoover, *Forty-Two Years in the White House* (1934), and Walter Lippmann, "The Peculiar Weakness of Mr. Hoover," *Harper's Magazine,* June, 1930.

BOOK TWO

Frank Freidel's volumes, *Franklin D. Roosevelt: The Apprenticeship* (1952), *Franklin D. Roosevelt: The Ordeal* (1954), *Franklin D. Roosevelt: The Triumph* (1956), are invaluable. James A. Farley, *Behind the Ballots* (1938), is an engaging account. His later book, *Jim Farley's Story* (1948), is marred by bitterness. Edward J. Flynn, *You're the Boss* (1947), is a delightful book. Samuel I. Rosenman, *Working With Roosevelt* (1952), is excellent for all the campaigns and for insights on Roosevelt's leadership. Lela Stiles, *The Man Behind Roosevelt: The Story of Louis M. Howe* (1954), unravels the role of this adviser. Albert Romasco, "The Image of Roosevelt: 1932 Pre-Convention Campaign" (unpublished M.A. thesis, University of Chicago, 1957), is a fine summary of contemporary attitudes. Roy V. Peel and Thomas C. Donnelly, *The 1932 Campaign, An Analysis* (1935), is useful.

Robert E. Sherwood, *Roosevelt and Hopkins: An Intimate History* (1948) is one of the best studies by a Roosevelt adviser. Samuel I. Rosenman, ed., *Public Papers and Addresses of Franklin Delano Roosevelt* (1938-1950), 13 volumes, is the standard compilation. Rexford G. Tugwell, *The Democratic Roosevelt: A Biography of Franklin D. Roosevelt* (1957), is superior to most of the books written by Roosevelt advisers. Frances Perkins, *The Roosevelt I Knew* (1946), is chatty. Harold L. Ickes, *The Secret Diary of Harold L. Ickes: The First 1000 Days* (1953) is the irresponsible Ickes, but it must be used with care. Jonathan Daniels, *The End of Innocence* (1954), is an able account.

Contemporary newspapers and magazines are the best source of the spirit of the nation on March 4th and during the Hundred Days. In addition, the following are useful: Benjamin Duffy, *The World's Greatest 99 Days* (1933), Ernest K. Lindley, *The Roosevelt Revolution: First Phase* (1933), and Earle Looker, *The American Way: Franklin Roosevelt in Action* (1933). Walter Johnson, *William Allen White's America* (1947) and *Selected Letters of William Allen White* (1957), contain the reactions of a liberal Republican. Arthur M. Schlesinger, Jr., *The Coming of the New Deal* (1959), is written in a lively style.

Among the valuable writings on Roosevelt's skill in public relations are Leo Rosten, *The Washington Correspondents* (1937), James E. Pollard, *The President and the Press* (1947), and Frank Luther Mott, *News in America* (1952). Mrs. Roosevelt's *This I Remember* (1949) is revealing. Grace Tully, *F. D. R. My Boss* (1949), and Ira T. Smith, "*Dear Mr. President . . .": The Story of Fifty Years in the White House Mail Room* (1949), are useful.

Edward S. Corwin, *The President: Office and Powers* (1958), is a basic study. James MacGregor Burns, *Roosevelt: The Lion and the Fox* (1956), is a provocative work. Roosevelt's ideas on public policy can be seen, in part, in his papers and speeches. The books by his associates cast light on his philosophy as do the scholarly studies by Freidel, Burns, and Schlesinger, Jr. The last two differ sharply in point of view. Daniel R. Fusfeld, *The Economic Thought of Franklin D. Roosevelt and the Origins of the New Deal* (1956), is a careful study.

Dixon Wecter, *The Age of the Great Depression* (1948), is an able account of the social impact of the New Deal. Denis W. Brogan, *The Era of Franklin D. Roosevelt* (1950), is the best short volume. Grace Abbott, *From Relief to Social Security* (1941), Paul H. Douglas, *Social Security in the United States* (1936), and Seymour E. Harris, *The Economics of Social Security* (1941), are valuable. Donald S. Howard, *The WPA and Federal Relief Policy* (1943), discusses the revolution in relief policies. Harry Hopkins described the work relief program in *Spending to Save* (1936). Nathan Straus, *Seven Myths of Housing* (1944), surveys the federal housing program.

Among the useful contemporary articles on the relief program are Corrington Gill, "Unemployment Relief," *American Economic Review*, March, 1935; "The Crisis in Civil Works," *Literary Digest*, February 3, 1934; Gertrude Springer, "For Welfare and Security," *The Survey*, March, 1934; "On the Dole: 17,000,000," *Fortune*, October, 1934; Raymond Clapper, "Harry Hopkins and His Four Million Jobs," *Review of Reviews*, January, 1934; *Social Work Year Book*, 1937 (1937); Beulah Amidon, "WPA — Wages and Workers," *Survey Graphic*, October, 1935; "Balance Sheet of the New Deal," *New Republic*, June 10, 1936.

The best articles on public works are to be found in *The American City*, an engineering and public utilities journal. C. Herman Pritchett, *The Tennessee Valley Authority: A Study in Public Administration* (1943), and Gordon Clapp, *The TVA: An Approach to the Development of a Region* (1955), are valuable. There is useful contemporary material on the farm program in Edwin G. Nourse, Joseph S. Davis, and John D. Black, *Three Years of the Agricultural Adjustment Act* (1937); U. S. Department of Agriculture, *Agricultural Adjustment* (1934), and subsequent annual reports. Henry A. Wallace, *New Frontiers* (1934), and Russell Lord, *The Wallaces of Iowa* (1947), explain his viewpoint. Arthur F. Raper and I. deA. Reid, *Sharecroppers All* (1941), Carey McWilliams, *Factories in the Field* (1939), and "Bryan! Bryan!! Bryan!!! Bryan!!!!," *Fortune*, January, 1934, explain the plight of submarginal farmers. Among more recent studies are Theodore W. Schultz, *Agriculture in an Unstable Economy* (1945) and *Production and Welfare of Agriculture* (1952).

The literature about the NRA, like so many of the New Deal agencies, is voluminous. Most useful are Leverett S. Lyon *et al.*, *The National Recovery Administration* (1935); "Codes At Work," *Business Week*, June 9, 1934; James Rorty, "Throttle Bottom and the Infusoria," *The Nation*, March 21, 1934; "NRA Examined," *American Economic Review, Supplement*, March, 1935.

The changing labor scene is discussed in Leon C. Marshall, *Hours and Wages Provisions in NRA Codes* (1935), Robert R. R. Brooks, *Unions of Their Own Choosing: An Account of the National Labor Relations Board and Its Work* (1939) and *When Labor Organizes* (1937), Leo Wolman, *Ebb and Flow in Trade Unionism* (1936), and Herbert Harris, *Labor's Civil War* (1940). *Handbook of Labor Statistics*, Bulletin 916 (1947), contains valuable statistical information. C. Wright Mills, *The New Men of Power* (1948), and Eli Ginzberg, *The Labor Leader* (1948), are studies of the new labor leadership. Charles O. Gregory, *Labor and the Law* (1946), is a major contribution. Harry A. Millis and E. C. Brown, *From the Wagner Act to Taft-Hartley* (1950), is useful, as is Milton Derber and Edwin Young, eds., *Labor and the New Deal* (1957).

Ferdinand Pecora, *Wall Street Under Oath* (1939), and J. T. Flynn, *Security Speculation* (1934), outline the need for reform of the stock market. William O. Douglas, *Democracy and Finance* (1940), describes the Holding Company Act and the regulation of the security exchanges. Marriner S. Eccles, *Beckoning Frontiers: Public and Personal Recollections*, ed. Sydney Hyman (1951), is an important memoir. Monetary policies and pump-priming are described in H. H. Villard, *Deficit Spending and the National Income* (1941), John K. Galbraith and G. G. Johnson, Jr., *The Economic Effects of the Federal Public Works Expenditures, 1933-1938* (1940), Arthur E. Burns and D. S. Watson, *Government Spending and Economic Expansion* (1940), James D. Paris, *Monetary Policies of the United States 1932-1938* (1938), Kenneth D. Roose, *The*

Economics of Recession and Revival (1954), Alvin H. Hansen, *Fiscal Policy and Business Cycles* (1941), and Seymour E. Harris, ed., *Saving American Capitalism* (1948). The ideas of Keynes are evaluated in L. R. Klein, *The Keynesian Revolution* (1947), Alvin H. Hansen, *A Guide to Keynes* (1953), and Seymour E. Harris, *John Maynard Keynes* (1955). Joseph Dorfman, *The Economic Mind in American Civilization, 1918-1933* (1959), Thomas C. Cochran, *The American Business System: A Historical Perspective, 1900-1955* (1957), and Lewis H. Kimmel, *Federal Budget and Fiscal Policy, 1789-1958* (1959), are basic studies. David Lynch, *The Concentration of Economic Power* (1946), Thurman W. Arnold, *The Bottlenecks of Business* (1940), and Walton H. Hamilton, *Antitrust in Action* (1940), discuss the government's antitrust program.

Samuel Lubell, *The Future of American Politics* (1952), is a major contribution. E. E. Robinson, *They Voted for Roosevelt: The Presidential Vote, 1932-1944* (1947), is a useful compilation, as is Cortez A. M. Ewing, *Congressional Elections* (1947). Louis Bean, *Ballot Behavior: A Study of Presidential Elections* (1940), is a careful analysis. Insights into the forces behind the Roosevelt coalition can be found in Arthur N. Holcombe, *The Middle Classes in American Politics* (1940), James K. Pollock and S. J. Eldersveld, *Michigan Politics in Transition* (1942), H. F. Gosnell, *Grass Roots Politics* (1942), Dayton D. McKean, *The Boss: The Hague Machine in Action* (1940), and Harold F. Gosnell, *Machine Politics* (1937). James Michael Curley, *I'd Do It Again* (1957), should not be ignored. V. O. Key, Jr., *Southern Politics in State and Nation* (1949), is a superb study. Max M. Kampelman, *The Communist Party vs. the C. I. O.: A Study in Power Politics* (1957), and Matthew Josephson, *Sidney Hillman: Statesman of American Labor* (1952), reflect the impact of the New Deal on labor.

Factors behind the shift in the Negro vote are discussed in Henry Lee Moon, *Balance of Power: The Negro Vote* (1948), Gunnar Myrdal, *An American Dilemma* (1944), John Hope Franklin, *From Slavery To Freedom* (1950), and Walter White, *How Far The Promised Land?* (1955). Chicago Negro politics are treated in detail in St. Clair Drake and Horace Cayton, *Black Metropolis* (1945), Harold F. Gosnell, *Negro Politicians: The Rise of Negro Politics in Chicago* (1935), Harry W. Morris, "The Chicago Negro and the Major Political Parties, 1940-1948" (unpublished M.A. thesis, University of Chicago, 1950), and Elmer W. Henderson, "A Study of the Basic Factors Involved in the Change in the Party Alignment of Negroes in Chicago, 1932-1938" (unpublished M.A. thesis, University of Chicago, 1939). Wilson Record, *The Negro and the Communist Party* (1951), is a balanced study.

Donald R. McCoy, *Angry Voices: Left-of-Center Politics in the New Deal Era* (1958), analyzes demagogues. Among the useful contemporary writings on them are Raymond G. Swing, *Forerunners of American Fascism* (1935); John Spivak, *Shrine of the Silver Dollar* (1940); *Every Man a King, The Autobiography of Huey P. Long* (1933); and Hartnett T. Kane, *Louisiana Hayride* (1941). Donald D. Egbert and Stow Persons, eds., *Socialism and American Life* (1952), contains material on the rise and fall of Communism in the 1930s. Eugene Lyons, *The Red Decade, The Stalinist Penetration of America* (1941), is exaggerated. Nathaniel Weyl, *Treason, The Story of Disloyalty and Betrayal in American History* (1950) and *The Battle Against Disloyalty* (1951), are useful, as is John R. Carlson, *Undercover* (1943).

Thomas Paul Jenkin, *Reactions of Major Groups to Positive Government in the United States, 1930-1940* (1945), is useful for the response to the New Deal. Some of the conservative criticism can be seen in Herbert Hoover, *The Challenge To Liberty* (1934) and *American Ideals vs. the New Deal* (1936), James P. Warburg, *Hell Bent for Election* (1935), David Lawrence, *Stumbling Into Socialism* (1935), and Marquis W. Childs, *They Hate Roosevelt* (1936). Frederick Rudolph, "The American Liberty League," *American Historical Review*, October, 1950, is a scholarly appraisal.

Harold F. Gosnell, *Champion Campaigner: Franklin D. Roosevelt* (1952), is a good political biography. For insights on some of the factors in the 1936 campaign see, in addition, Stanley High, *Roosevelt — And Then* (1937), and Ernest K. Lindley, *Half Way With Roosevelt* (1936).

BOOK THREE

The contemporary literature on the Supreme Court controversy includes William R. Barnes and A. W. Littlefield, eds., *The Supreme Court Issue and the Constitution* (1937), Joseph Alsop and Turner Catledge, *The 168 Days* (1938), Drew Pearson and Robert S. Allen, *Nine Old Men at the Crossroads* (1936), Merlo J. Pusey, *The Supreme Court Crisis* (1937), Walter Lippmann, *The Supreme Court, Independent or Controlled?* (1937), and Edward S. Corwin, *Court Over Constitution* (1938). Among the important biographies are Merlo J. Pusey, *Charles Evans Hughes* (1951), A. T. Mason, *Brandeis* (1946) and his *Harlan Fiske Stone* (1956). Robert K. Carr, *The Supreme Court and Judicial Review* (1942), and Edward S. Corwin, *Constitutional Revolution, Ltd.* (1941), are useful scholarly studies.

The 1938 attempt to purge conservative Democrats is discussed in a number of books already mentioned. Jasper B. Shannon, "Presidential Politics in the South: 1938," *Journal of Politics*, I, 1939, is most useful. V. O. Key, Jr., *American State Politics: An Introduction* (1956), is valuable for the local and state basis of political power.

In addition to the books already mentioned that treat labor in the 1930s, Robert R. R. Brooks, *As Steel Goes* (1940), and Edward Levinson, *Labor on the March* (1938), explain the new power of unions. George Blackwood, *The UAW* (unpublished University of Chicago doctoral dissertation, 1951), catches the dynamics of the auto workers. His "The Sit-Down Strike in the Thirties," *South Atlantic Quarterly*, October, 1956, is a good appraisal. Among the useful contemporary articles are Louis Stark, "Sit-Down Strikes," *Survey Graphic*, June, 1937; Phil S. Hanna, "Six Months After the Strike," *ibid.*, June, 1937; and "It Happened in Steel," *Fortune*, May, 1937.

Gabriel A. Almond, *The American People and Foreign Policy* (1950), is a revealing study. Selig Adler, *The Isolationist Impulse: Its Twentieth Century Reaction* (1957), is a useful book. Robert A. Dahl, *Congress and Foreign Policy* (1950), has valuable material. Robert H. Ferrell, *American Diplomacy in the Great Depression: Hoover-Stimson Foreign Policy, 1929-1933* (1957), is excellent. D. F. Fleming, *The United States and the World Court* (1945), is a valuable study. Sumner Welles, *The Time for Decision* (1944), is excellent on the Good Neighbor policy. Dexter Perkins, *Hands Off: A History of the Monroe Doctrine* (1941), and E. O. Guerrant, *Roosevelt's Good Neighbor Policy* (1950), are useful studies.

Hadley Cantril and Mildred Strunk, *Public Opinion, 1935-1946* (1951), is a compilation of public opinion polls. The various issues of *Public Opinion Quarterly* are valuable. Elmo Roper, *You and Your Leaders: Their Actions and Your Reactions, 1936-1956* (1957), is a study of shifting attitudes.

The Memoirs of Cordell Hull (1948) and Summer Welles, *Seven Decisions That Shaped History* (1951), have valuable material and reflect their disagreements over policy. The following publications by the Department of State are helpful: *Peace and War: United States Foreign Policy, 1931-1941* (1943); *Papers Relating to the Foreign Relations of the United States: Japan, 1931-1941* (1943); *The United States and Italy, 1936-1946* (1946); *Diplomatic Papers: The Soviet Union, 1933-1939* (1952); *Documents on German Foreign Policy, 1918-1945* (1949); and the annual *Foreign Relations*.

Among the important books on Far Eastern policy are Herbert Feis,

The Road to Pearl Harbor (1950), and Ambassador Joseph C. Grew, *Turbulent Era: A Diplomatic Record of Forty Years, 1904-1945*, ed. Walter Johnson (1952). Henry L. Stimson, *The Far Eastern Crisis: Recollections and Observations* (1936), and his collaborative work with McGeorge Bundy, *On Active Service in Peace and War* (1948), are first-hand accounts. Highly critical of Stimson is Richard N. Current, *Secretary Stimson: A Study in Statescraft* (1954). Sara R. Smith, *Manchurian Crisis, 1931-32* (1948), and Reginald Bassett, *Democracy and Foreign Policy, the Sino-Japanese Dispute, 1931-33* (1952), are significant studies.

Donald Whitehead, "U. S. Foreign Policy, 1933-1937" (University of Chicago doctoral dissertation, 1951) is based heavily on unpublished State Department material. Charles A. Beard, *American Foreign Policy in the Making, 1932-1940: A Study in Responsibilities* (1946), differs sharply from my account. Donald F. Drummond, *The Passing of American Neutrality, 1937-1941* (1955), Basil Rauch, *Roosevelt: From Munich to Pearl Harbor* (1950), and Edwin W. Wade, "Presidential Leadership and the Neutrality Legislation, 1935-1941" (M.A. thesis, University of Chicago, 1956), contain detailed accounts of the neutrality legislation.

The isolationist-collective security question produced many contemporary books. Samples include Allen W. Dulles and Hamilton Fish Armstrong, *Can America Stay Neutral?* (1939), C. G. Fenwick, *American Neutrality: Trial and Failure* (1940), Charles A. Beard, *Giddy Minds and Foreign Quarrels* (1939), and Jerome Frank, *Save America First: How To Make Democracy Work* (1938). F. Jay Taylor, *The United States and the Spanish Civil War, 1936-1939* (1956), is good.

The files of *The Communist* and the *Daily Worker* are invaluable for the evolution of the popular front doctrine, as are Earl Browder's *Build the United People's Front* (1936) and *The People's Front* (1938). Jay Lovestone, *The People's Front Illusion* (1937), is an attack on it. Among the exposés of Communist infiltration are Louis Budenz, *This Is My Story* (1947) and *Men Without Faces* (1948), and Martin Dies, *The Trojan Horse in America* (1940). More helpful are Murray Kempton, *Part of Our Time: Some Monuments and Ruins of the Thirties* (1955), Granville Hicks, *Where We Came Out* (1954), and Arthur M. Schlesinger, Jr., *The Vital Center* (1949).

Joseph Barnes, *Willkie: The Events He Was Part Of: The Ideas He Fought For* (1952), and Marry E. Dillon, *Wendell Willkie* (1952), are interesting studies. Also useful is the profile by Janet Flanner in the *New*

Yorker, October 12, 1940. Various aspects of the campaign are analyzed in Paul F. Lazarsfeld, Bernard Berelson, and Helen Gaudet, *The People's Choice* (1944).

By far the ablest scholarly studies of this period are William L. Langer and S. Everett Gleason, *The Challenge to Isolation, 1937-1940* (1952) and *The Undeclared War, 1940-1941* (1953). H. L. Trefousse, *Germany and American Neutrality, 1939-1941* (1951), is a useful volume, as is *The Moffat Papers: Selections from the Diplomatic Journals of Jay Pierrepont Moffat, 1919-1943*, ed. Nancy Harvison Hooker (1956). There is important information in *Pearl Harbor Attack, Hearings Before the Joint Committee on the Investigation of the Pearl Harbor Attack, 79th Congress, 2nd Session* and *Senate Document 244, 79th Congress, 2nd Session, Investigation of the Pearl Harbor Attack, Report of the Joint Committee* (1946).

The leading revisionist accounts are Charles A. Beard, *President Roosevelt and the Coming of the War: A Study in Appearances and Realities* (1948), and Charles C. Tansill, *Back Door to War — Roosevelt Foreign Policy, 1933-1941* (1952). Beard's account is slanted to justify his isolationist position, and Tansill's extreme position is not substantiated by the evidence he presents. Wayne S. Cole, "American Entry Into World War II: A Historiographical Appraisal," *Mississippi Valley Historical Review*, March, 1956, is an excellent analysis of the controversial literature. Among the articles challenging the revisionist interpretation are Arthur M. Schlesinger, Jr., "Roosevelt and His Detractors," *Harper's Magazine*, June, 1950, T. A. Bailey, "The Dilemma of Democracy," *American Perspective*, October, 1948, Dexter Perkins, "Was Roosevelt Wrong?" *Virginia Quarterly Review*, Summer, 1954, Sherman Miles, "Pearl Harbor in Retrospect," *The Atlantic*, July, 1948, and Samuel Eliot Morison, "Did Roosevelt Start the War?" *The Atlantic*, August, 1948.

Wayne S. Cole, *America First: The Battle Against Intervention, 1940-1941* (1953), is a careful study. My book, *The Battle Against Isolation* (1944), describes the Aid the Allies Committee.

BOOK FOUR

The story of American military action has been impossible to include in this book. It has been described in the memoirs of such participants as Eisenhower, King, and Bradley; correspondents' books including those of Ernie Pyle; the multi-volume work by Samuel Eliot Morison, *History of United States Naval Operations in World War II*; the hundred odd volumes, *The U. S. Army in World War II*; and the eight-volume *The Army*

Air Forces in World War II, eds. Wesley Frank Craven and James Lea Cate.

Selden Menefee, *Assignment: U.S.A.* (1943), and Jack Goodman, ed., *While You Were Gone* (1946), have insights into the mood of America at war. W. F. Ogburn, ed., *American Society in Wartime* (1943), and Reuben Hill, *Families Under Stress* (1949), are valuable studies.

The impact of the war on civil liberties is discussed in C. Herman Pritchett, *The Roosevelt Court*, in the annual reports of the American Civil Liberties Union, in E. S. Corwin, *Total War and the Constitution* (1947), and in Francis Biddle, *Democratic Thinking and the War* (1944). Dorothy S. Thomas and R. S. Nishimoto, *The Spoilage* (1946), Dorothy S. Thomas *et al, The Salvage* (1952), and Morton Grodzins, *Americans Betrayed: Politics and the Japanese Evacuation* (1949), are studies of the Japanese-Americans. Thomas Murphy, *Ambassadors in Arms* (1954), discusses the situation in Hawaii and the military contribution of the AJA's.

Wartime production figures and income can be found in *Historical Statistics of the United States: 1789-1945* (1949), in the annual *Statistical Abstract of the United States*, published by the Government Printing Office, in *The Economic Almanac 1951-52* (1953), and in Frederick Dewhurst, *America's Needs and Resources* (1947) and *Industrial Mobilization for War* (1947), Vol. 1. The monthly issues of *Fortune* in 1940-1941 and many articles in the *New Republic* reflect the struggles between New Dealers and businessmen as the defense program got under way. Donald Nelson, *Arsenal of Democracy: The Story of American War Production* (1946), and Bruce Catton, *The War Lords of Washington* (1948), are by two participants. U. S. Civilian Production Administration, *Industrial Mobilization for War* (1947), Vol. 1, is a factual analysis, and Joel Seidman, *American Labor from Defense to Reconversion* (1953), is a basic book on the war years.

John Lord O'Brian and Manly Fleischmann, "The War Production Board: Administrative Policies and Procedures," *George Washington Law Review*, December, 1944, is important for the legal aspects. Francis Walton, *Miracle of World War II: How American Industry Made Victory Possible* (1956), is a detailed account of war production. Harry A. Toulmin, Jr., *Diary of Democracy: The Senate War Investigating Committee* (1947), describes the Truman Committee. James P. Baxter, *Scientists Against Time* (1946), is excellent for scientific development.

Roland Young, *Congressional Politics in the Second World War* (1956), is a careful analysis. Michael Darrock, "What Happened to Price Control?" *Harper's Magazine*, July, 1943, recaptures much of the contemporary feeling about OPA. See also Chester Bowles, "Rationing & Price Control," *Life*, December 13, 1943, Paul M. O'Leary, "Wartime Rationing and Governmental Organization," *American Political Science Review*, December, 1945, and H. C. Mansfield *et al*, *A Short History of OPA* (1948). I have relied heavily on Simon Kuznets, *Shares of Upper Income Groups in Income and Savings* (1950), and U. S. Department of Commerce, *Income Distribution in the United States By Size 1944-1950* (1953), for the material on changing income patterns. Wartime changes in agriculture are discussed in W. W. Wilcox, *The Farmer in the Second World War* (1947), and T. W. Schultz, ed., *Food for the World* (1945).

Jonathan Daniels, *Frontier On The Potomac* (1946), contains insights into wartime Washington. Many of the studies of Roosevelt already mentioned in previous chapters are valuable for the 1944 campaign. In addition, Hadley Cantril, "The Issue Behind the Issues," *New York Times Magazine*, October 22, 1944, L. H. Bean, F. Mosteller, and F. W. Williams, "Nationalities and 1944," *Public Opinion Quarterly*, Fall, 1944, and H. E. Bateman, "Observations on President Roosevelt's Health During World War II," *Mississippi Valley Historical Review*, June, 1956, have useful material.

BOOK FIVE

Harley Notter, *Postwar Foreign Policy Preparation, 1939-1945* (1949), is the official account. Ruth B. Russell, *A History of the United Nations Charter* (1958), is a careful study. Senate Document 123, 81st Congress, 1st Session, *A Decade of American Foreign Policy, Basic Documents, 1941-49* (1951), supplements the various State Department publications. Redvers Opie *et al.*, *The Search for Peace Settlements* (1951), is an analytical account. Important scholarly studies on wartime diplomacy include Herbert Feis, *Churchill, Roosevelt, Stalin* (1957), H. Bradford Westerfield, *Foreign Policy and Party Politics: Pearl Harbor to Korea* (1955), William H. McNeill, *America, Britain and Russia: Their Co-operation and Conflict, 1941-1946* (1953), and John L. Snell, *Wartime Origins of the East-West Dilemma Over Germany* (1959).

Winston S. Churchill's *The Second World War*, 6 vols. (1948-1953), has valuable source material. Other useful books by participants include Harry S. Truman, *Year of Decisions* (1955), William D. Leahy, *I Was There* (1950), Lucius D. Clay, *Decision in Germany* (1950), and Walter Millis, ed., *The Forrestal Diaries* (1951). John Foster Dulles, *War or Peace* (1950), discusses the emergence of a bipartisan foreign policy, as do Arthur H. Vandenberg, Jr., ed., *The Private Papers of Senator Vandenberg* (1952), and James Reston, "Events Spotlight Vandenberg's Dual Role," *New York Times Magazine*, March 28, 1948.

John R. Deane, *The Strange Alliance: The Story of Our Efforts at Wartime Co-operation With Russia* (1947), and Chester Wilmot, *The Struggle for Europe* (1952), are highly critical of American policy. The best single scholarly book on Yalta is John L. Snell, Forest C. Pogue, Charles F. Delzell, and George A. Lensen, *The Meaning of Yalta: Big Three Diplomacy and the New Balance of Power* (1956). Among the useful articles are Louis Morton, "The Military Background of the Yalta Agreements," *The Reporter*, April 7, 1955, Oscar J. Hammen, "The 'Ashes' of Yalta," *South Atlantic Quarterly*, October, 1954, Raymond J. Sontag, "Reflections on the Yalta Papers," *Foreign Affairs*, July, 1955, and Rudolph A. Winnacker, "Yalta — Another Munich?" *Virginia Quarterly Review*, Autumn, 1948. Examples of the intemperate, polemic approach to Yalta can be seen in Felix Wittmer, *The Yalta Betrayal: Data on the Decline and Fall of Franklin D. Roosevelt* (1953), John T. Flynn, *The Roosevelt Myth* (1948), and William Henry Chamberlain, *America's Second Crusade* (1950).

Valuable scholarly studies on Far Eastern developments include Herbert Feis, *The China Tangle: The American Effort in China from Pearl Harbor to the Marshall Mission* (1953), Werner Levi, *Modern China's Foreign Policy* (1953), and Ernest R. May, "The United States, the Soviet Union, and the Far Eastern War, 1941-45," *Pacific Historical Review*, May, 1955.

Daniel J. Boorstin, *Genius of American Politics* (1953), is a provocative analysis of the theme of uniqueness in American society. Robert A. Taft, *A Foreign Policy for Americans* (1951), is an expression of this theme. Norman Cousins, *Modern Man Is Obsolete* (1945), is an eloquent plea for world government. Walter Lippmann, *The Cold War: A Study in U. S. Foreign Policy* (1947), Hans J. Morgenthau, *In Defense of the National Interest* (1951), C. B. Marshall, *The Limits of Foreign Policy* (1954), and George F. Kennan, *Realities of American Foreign Policy* (1954), are vigorous attempts at re-evaluating American foreign policy.

A discussion of the difficulties of working with the newly independent nations can be found in Barbara Ward, *The Interplay of East and West: Points of Conflict and Cooperation* (1957), F. S. C. Northrop, *The Taming of the Nations: A Study of the Cultural Bases of International Policy* (1952), Adlai E. Stevenson, *A Call to Greatness* (1954), and Chester Bowles, *Ambassador's Report* (1954). There is a growing literature on the foreign aid programs. William Adams Brown, Jr., and Redvers Opie, *American Foreign Assistance* (1953), is a detailed study. Dan Lacy, "Foreign Aid: Is It Still Necessary," *Harper's Magazine*, February, 1957, raises the basic issues. *Congressional Quarterly Weekly Reports*, February 10, 1956, has a convenient survey of aid since 1945. The *Hearings* of the U. S. Senate Special Committee to Study the Foreign Aid Program and the *Hearings* of the House Foreign Affairs Committee, *Mutual Security Act*, 1957, both published by the Government Printing Office in 1957, have valuable information. Jonathan Bingham, *Shirt-Sleeve Diplomacy* (1954), is an account of the Point Four program.

For the development of the policy of firmness toward the Soviet Union see James F. Byrnes, *Speaking Frankly* (1957), Arthur H. Vandenberg, Jr., ed., *The Private Papers of Senator Vandenberg* (1952), Harry S. Truman, *Year of Decisions* (1955), John Foster Dulles, "Thoughts on Soviet Foreign Policy and What To Do About It," *Life*, June 3, 10, 1946, and James B. Reston, "Negotiating With the Russians," *Harper's Magazine*, August, 1947. William Reitzel, Morton A. Kaplan, and Constance G. Coblenz, *United States Foreign Policy 1945-1955* (1956), is a careful, analytical study that is frequently critical. Philip E. Mosely, *Face To Face With Russia* (1948), and "Soviet-American Relations Since the War, Background of Rivalry," *Annals of the American Academy of Political and Social Science*, May, 1949, are highly informative. Henry A. Wallace, *Toward World Peace* (1948), opposed the firmness policy. Albert R. Sellen, "Congressional Opinion of Soviet-American Relations, 1945-1950" (1954, University of Chicago doctoral dissertation), is a useful study. The development of a bipartisan foreign policy is discussed in Dean Acheson, *A Citizen Looks at Congress* (1957). Joseph M. Jones, *The Fifteen Weeks (February 21 — June 5, 1947)* (1955), describes the events leading to the Truman Doctrine. Harry Bayard Price, *The Marshall Plan and Its Meaning* (1955), is a careful analysis. For an emotional attack on aid programs see Eugene W. Castle, *The Great Giveaway* (1957).

Herbert Feis, *The China Tangle* (1953), is an important study. Kenneth S. Latourette, *The American Record in the Far East: 1945-1950* (1952), contends that the United States could not have prevented the Communist victory, while Robert C. North, *Moscow and the Chinese Communists* (1953), is critical of American policy.

Educational Exchanges: Aspects of the American Experience (1956) contains useful material. Other sources include *Swords Into Ploughshares* (1956); "Special Fulbright Issue," Department of State, *The Record*, March-April, 1951; Cora Du Bois, *Foreign Students and Higher Educa-*

tion in the United States (1956); Guy S. Metraux, *Exchange of Persons: The Evolution of Cross-Cultural Education* (1952); John and Ruth Useem, *The Western-Educated Man in India* (1955); and Herbert Kubly, *An American in Italy* (1955), a delightful, informative account by an American Fulbrighter.

BOOK SIX

Mr. Truman's two volumes of memoirs are valuable for his view of the presidency and as background for the decisions he took. Herbert Agar, *The Price of Power: America Since 1945* (1957), is a stimulating account. Jonathan Daniels, *The Man of Independence* (1950), is a warm portrait. John Hersey's five-part "Profile" of Truman in the *New Yorker*, April 7 to May 5, 1951, is informative. See also Louis W. Koenig, ed., *The Truman Administration* (1956). Hostile to Truman and quite inaccurate is E. L. Dayton, *Give 'Em Hell Harry* (1956). Jules Abels, *The Truman Scandals* (1956), overstates his case.

Edwin G. Nourse, *The 1950's Come First* (1951), and Stephen K. Bailey, *Congress Makes a Law* (1950), deal with the Employment Law. The following are useful studies of the 1948 election: Bernard Berelson, Paul Lazarsfeld, and William McPhee, *Voting: A Study of Opinion Formation in a Presidential Campaign* (1954), Angus Campbell and Robert L. Kahn, *The People Elect a President* (1952), Louis H. Bean, *How to Predict Elections* (1948), and Jack Redding, *Inside the Democratic Party* (1958). Lindsay Rogers, *The Pollsters* (1949), examines why the public opinion polls were wrong.

Bert Andrews, *Washington Witch Hunt* (1948), is critical of the government's loyalty program and of the House Committee on Un-American Activities. See also G. Bromley Oxnam, *I Protest: My Experience with the House Committee on Un-American Activities* (1954). Robert K. Carr, *The House Committee on Un-American Activities, 1945-1950* (1952), and Eleanor Bontecou, *The Federal Loyalty-Security Program* (1953), are studies by scholars. The Hiss case has already provoked considerable literature, including Whittaker Chambers, *Witness* (1952), Alistair Cooke, *A Generation On Trial* (1950), Alger Hiss, *In the Court of Public Opinion* (1957), and Fred J. Cook, *The Unfinished Case of Alger Hiss* (1958).

Richard Rovere, *Senator Joe McCarthy* (1959), is critical, as are Jack Anderson and Ronald W. May, *McCarthy: The Man, The Senator, The "Ism"* (1952), James Rorty and Moshe Decter, *McCarthy and the Communists* (1954), and "McCarthy: A Documented Record," *The Pro-*

gressive, April, 1954. William F. Buckley, Jr., and L. B. Bozell, *McCarthy and His Enemies: The Record and Its Meaning* (1954), hails the Senator. Walter Gellhorn, *Security, Loyalty, and Science* (1950) and *The States and Subversion* (1952), criticizes the excessive fear of internal Communism. C. Herman Pritchett, *Civil Liberties and the Vinson Court* (1954), is excellent.

The testimony of the "MacArthur hearings" is published in U. S. Senate, *Military Situation in the Far East* (1951). Richard H. Rovere and Arthur M. Schlesinger, Jr., *The General and the President and the Future of American Foreign Policy* (1951), is favorable to the President. General Charles A. Willoughby and John Chamberlain, *MacArthur, 1941-1951* (1954), is adulatory.

Paul T. David, Malcolm Moos, and Ralph M. Goldman, *Presidential Nominating Politics in 1952* (1954), 5 vols., is a pioneer study of both conventions. I have described the Stevenson draft in *How We Drafted Adlai Stevenson* (1955). The following are valuable for the 1952 election: V. O. Key, Jr., "Solid South: Cracked or Broken," *New Republic*, December 1, 1952; "The Crucial States: What Happened," *ibid.*, November 17, 1952; Angus Campbell, "The Case of the Missing Democrats," *ibid.*, July 2, 1956; and Samuel Lubell, *The Revolt of the Moderates* (1956). Angus Campbell, *The Voter Decides* (1954), and Louis Harris, *Is There a Republican Majority?* (1954), agree that Democratic defections supplied the margin of victory. Alfred de Grazia, *The Western Public, 1952 and Beyond* (1954), analyzes differences between Westerners and other Americans. See also O. D. Weeks, *Texas Presidential Politics in 1952* (1953). Herbert Nicholas, "A British View of the Election," *Yale Review*, Spring, 1953, has shrewd insights. J. C. Davies, "Charisma in the 1952 Campaign," *American Political Science Review*, December, 1954, analyzes the personal appeal of Eisenhower as does R. E. Lane, "Political Personality and Electoral Choice," *ibid.*, March, 1955. Morris Janowitz and Dwaine Marvick, *Competitive Pressure and Democratic Consent: An Interpretation of the 1952 Presidential Election* (1956), is useful. For a discussion of the handling of the campaign by the press see Arthur Edward Rowse, *Slanted News* (1957), Nathan B. Blumberg, *One Party Press: Coverage of the 1952 Presidential Campaign in 35 Daily Newspapers* (1954), and Jean Begeman, "The One-Party Press Pays Off," *New Republic*, November 17, 1952.

BOOK SEVEN

Frederic Dewhurst *et al.*, *America's Needs and Resources* (1955), is a monumental study. *The Changing American Market*, by the editors of *Fortune* (1954), has important material. David Riesman, Nathan Glazer, and Reuel Denney, *The Lonely Crowd* (1950), Russell Lynes, *A Surfeit of Honey* (1957), A. C. Spectorsky, *The Exurbanites* (1955), and Robert C. Wood, *Surburbia: Its People and Their Politics* (1959), all have important things to say. Max Lerner, *America as a Civilization* (1957), reflects the introspection among Americans about their society. Conrad and Irene B. Taeuber, *The Changing Population of the United States* (1958), is a detailed summary of population trends.

C. Wright Mills, *White Collar: The American Middle Class* (1951), is an angry analysis. W. Y. Elliot, ed., *Television's Impact on American Culture* (1956), raises important questions. Edward L. Bernays, ed., *The Engineering of Consent* (1955) and his *Public Relations* (1952) have many insights on the strengths and limitations of public relations.

Daniel Bell, "The Language of Labor," *Fortune*, September, 1951; "Taft-Hartley, Five Years After," *ibid.*, June, 1952; "The New American Labor Movement," *ibid.*, April, 1953; and "The Capitalism of the Proletariat? American Trade Unionism Today," *Encounter*, February, 1958, are important articles. Warner Bloomberg, Jr., Joel Seidman, and Victor Hoffman, "The State of the Unions," a *New Republic* series beginning June 22, 1959, discusses the key issues facing labor. L. H. Fuchs, *The Political Behavior of American Jews* (1956), is a useful study of a group which votes heavily Democratic regardless of income status.

In addition to the literature already mentioned that deals with the Negro, there is a growing literature on the question of desegregation. The March, 1956, issue of the *Annals of the American Academy of Political and Social Science* is devoted to this. Harry Ashmore, *The Negro and the Schools* (1954), is a study that preceded the Supreme Court decision. Don Shoemaker, ed., *With All Deliberate Speed: Segregation-Desegregation* (1957), has articles by Southerners. Wilma Dykeman and James Stokely, *Neither Black Nor White* (1957), is a report of conversations and interviews with individuals in thirteen states. C. Vann Woodward, "The South and the Law of the Land," *Commentary*, November, 1958, is a significant study. Herbert H. Hyman and Paul B. Skeatsley, "Attitudes Toward Desegregation," *Scientific American*, December, 1956, analyzes public opinion findings by the National Opinion Research Center. Frederick B. Routh and Paul Anthony, "Southern Resistance

Forces," *Phylon Quarterly*, First Quarter, 1957, discusses the White Councils and similar movements. James McBride Dabbs, *The Southern Heritage* (1958), is an important book. Helen Fuller's "Southerners and Schools," a *New Republic* series concluded in the March 16, 1959, issue has valuable information as does the book by the Superintendent of Little Rock's schools, Virgil T. Blossom, *It Has Happened Here* (1959).

BOOK EIGHT

Robert J. Donovan, *Eisenhower: The Inside Story* (1956), is useful since he was allowed access to records of Cabinet meetings. Samuel Lubell, *The Revolt of the Moderates* (1956), is a valuable analysis. Marquis Childs, *Eisenhower: Captive Hero* (1958), is critical. Richard H. Rovere, *The Eisenhower Years: Affairs of State* (1956), has interesting insights. Eric Sevareid, *Small Sounds in the Night* (1956), contains excellent essays. Richard Fenno, Jr., *The President's Cabinet* (1959), is an analytical study of the Cabinet from Wilson's time through Eisenhower's.

The articles in the *New York Times*, July 21–August 2, 1956, on the Eisenhower Administration are extremely helpful, as are those by James Reston, *ibid.*, June 17–21, 1956, and December 2–4, 1957, on "The Presidency." Other useful contemporary material on the Eisenhower presidency includes John H. Steele, "Mr. President," *Dartmouth Alumni Magazine*, January, 1957, Douglass Cater, "The Folklore of an Electronic Presidency," *The Reporter*, July 12, 1956, Richard Strout, "The Administration's 'Abominable No-Man,'" *New York Times Magazine*, June 3, 1956, Marian D. Irish, "The Cipher in the White House," *New Statesman*, December 7, 1957, Richard L. Wilson, "Ike's Second Term Tragedy," *Look*, January 7, 1958, D. W. Brogan, "The Crisis in America," *Manchester Guardian Weekly*, January 9, 16, 23, 1958, Robert Bendiner, "Pennsylvania Avenue Gets Longer and Longer," *The Reporter*, February 20, 1958, and Sydney Hyman, "The Eisenhower Glow Is Fading Away," *ibid.*, September 19, 1957. The following articles by Lester Seligman contain valuable information: "Developments in the Presidency and the Conception of Political Leadership," *American Sociological Review*, December, 1955, "Presidential Leadership: The Inner Circle and Institutionalization," *Journal of Politics*, August, 1956, "The President Is Many Men," *Antioch Review*, Fall, 1956, and "Presidential Office and the President as Party Leader," *Law and Contemporary Problems*, Fall, 1956.

Eisenhower's press conferences and his use of the mass media are discussed in Henry F. and Katherine Pringle, "Mr. President!" *Saturday Evening Post*, June 15, 1957, Cabell Phillips, "President Then and Now — '53 and '57 Compared," *New York Times*, January 20, 1957, Merriman Smith, "Evolution of Eisenhower As Speaker," *ibid.*, August 7, 1955, Herling, "World's No. 1 Quiz Program," *ibid.*, June 9, 1957, James Reston, "A General Stands at Ease," "101st News Conference," *ibid.*, August 12, 1957, January 31, 1957. Charles A. H. Thomson, *Television and Presidential Politics* (1956), Stanley Kelley, *Professional Public Relations and Political Power* (1956) and his "After Thoughts on Madison Avenue Politics," *Antioch Review*, Summer, 1957, are valuable on the political questions raised by the growth of the mass media. See also Martin Mayer, *Madison Avenue, U.S.A.* (1958).

Arthur Larson, *A Republican Looks at His Party* (1956), is by a Republican "egghead." Stewart Alsop, "Just What Is Modern Republicanism?" *Saturday Evening Post*, July 27, 1957, is a succinct analysis. Lauren Soth analyzes the farm question intelligently in *Farm Problem* (1957). See also T. W. Schultz, "Homesteads in Reverse," *Des Moines Register and Tribune*, December 30, 1955, and D. Gale Johnson, "Government and Agriculture: Is Agriculture a Special Case?" *Journal of Law and Economics*, October, 1958. For a reasoned article on the Administration's resources policy, see Warren Unna, "Republican 'Giveaways': The Charges and the Facts," *Harper's Magazine*, May, 1956. From 1953 until his death in 1955, Bernard De Voto's passionate articles on conservation appear in "The Easy Chair," *Harper's Magazine*. E. W. Kenworthy, "Dixon-Yates: The Riddle of a Self-Inflicted Wound," *The Reporter*, January 26, 1956, summarizes the case and points up the key questions involved. See also Arthur Krock, "Dixon-Yates 'Blunders' Give Democrats Issue" and "The Mystery Story of the Dixon-Yates Contract," *New York Times*, July 17 and November 29, 1955.

Examples of growing criticism of the Government's security program include John B. Oakes, "This Is the Real, the Lasting Danger," *New York Times Magazine*, March 7, 1954, Lester Markel, "Report From 'Foggy Bottom,' " *ibid.*, March 28, 1954, Vannevar Bush, "To Make Our Security System Secure," *ibid.*, March 20, 1955, Leo Rosten, "Is Fear Destroying Our Freedom," *Look*, September 7, 1954, and "Secrecy, Security and Loyalty," *Bulletin of Atomic Scientists*, April, 1955. Among the important books dealing with aspects of the problem are John Lord O'Brian, *National Security and Individual Freedom* (1955); Robert E. Cushman, *Civil Liberties in the United States* (1956); E. N. Griswold, *The Fifth Amendment Today* (1955); *The Federal Loyalty-Security Program*, Report of the Special Committee of the Association of the Bar of New York City (1956); Edward Shils, *The Torment of Secrecy* (1956); Samuel A. Stouffer, *Communism, Conformity and Civil Liberties: A Cross Section of the Nation Speaks Its Mind* (1955); and John W. Caughey, *The Clear and Present Danger* (1958). Robert A. Horn, "The Protection of Internal Security," *Public Administration Review*, Winter, 1956, is a valuable article analyzing the literature on the subject. On the Atomic Energy Commission's barring of J. Robert Oppenheimer from government atomic secrets see Charles P. Curtis, *The Oppenheimer Case: The Trial of a Security System* (1955); *The Bulletin of the Atomic Scientists*, September, 1954; and Joseph and Stewart Alsop, "We Accuse!" *Harper's Magazine*, October, 1954. Michael Straight, *Trial By Television* (1954), discusses the Army-McCarthy hearings, and Richard Hofstadter, "The Pseudo-Conservative Revolt," *American Scholar*, Winter, 1954-1955, and Daniel Bell, ed., *The New American Right* (1956), analyze McCarthy's support.

V. O. Key, Jr., "The 'Moral Victory' of the Republicans," *New Republic*, December 6, 1954, Richard Rovere, "Letter From Washington," *The New Yorker*, November 13, 1954, and William Carleton, "The Triumph of the Moderates," *Harper's Magazine*, April, 1955, have insights on the 1954 election. Robert L. Riggs, "No Troubles in Our House," *New Republic*, October 25, 1954, William Lee Miller, "The Debating Career of Richard M. Nixon," *The Reporter*, April 19, 1956, Richard H. Rovere, "Nixon: Most Likely To Succeed," *Harper's Magazine*, September, 1955, Robert Coughlan, "A Debate, Pro and Con. Subject: Richard M. Nixon," *Life*, July 16, 1956, and David C. Williams, "Is There a New Nixon?" *The Progressive*, October, 1957, discuss Nixon's controversial career. Earl Mazo, *Richard Nixon: A Political and Personal Portrait* (1959), is more friendly.

William S. White, "Consensus American — A Portrait," *New York Times Magazine*, November 25, 1956; Max Lerner, "The Triumph of Conformity," *New York Post*, November 7, 1956; "Why They Like Ike," *Parade*, January 20, 1957; and Joe Miller, "How the Republicans Lost in the West," *The Reporter*, December 13, 1956, are valuable articles. Many of Adlai E. Stevenson's speeches are published in *The New America* (1957). "The 1956 Elections," prepared by the Research Staff, Republican National Committee, May, 1957, has interesting statistics. Samuel Lubell, "Can the GOP Win Without Ike?" *Saturday Evening Post*, January 26, 1957, and Joseph and Stewart Alsop, "The GOP Must Reform," *ibid.*, February 2, 1957, raise basic questions. *The Reporter*, November 27, 1958, has informative articles on the 1958 election. Eugene Burdick and Arthur J. Brodbeck, eds., *American Voting Behavior* (1959), analyzes voting habits. Duane Lockard, *New England State Politics* (1959), has important insights. Stephen A. Mitchell, *Elm St. Politics* (1959), is a discussion of the neighborhood political club movement by the former Chairman of the Democratic National Committee.

Norman Graebner, *The New Isolationism* (1956), traces the influence of the neo-isolationists. John Robinson Beal, *John Foster Dulles: A Biography* (1957), and James Shepley, "How Dulles Averted War," *Life*, January 16, 1956, are favorable to Dulles. More critical are Joseph C. Harsch, "John Foster Dulles: A Very Complicated Man," *Harper's Magazine*, September, 1956, Frederick Kuh, "Dulles — Great Secretary or Bungler?" *Chicago Sun-Times*, March 4, 1956, William Lee Miller, "The 'Moral Force' Behind Dulles's Diplomacy," *The Reporter*, August 9, 1956, and Chalmers M. Roberts, "The Pious Truculence of John Foster Dulles," *ibid.*, January 23, 1958. See also William L. Neumann, "Chiang's Seduction of America," *The Progressive*, November, 1958. Paul H. Nitze, " 'Impossible' Job of Secretary of State," *New York Times Magazine*, February 24, 1957, is an intelligent summary. Marvin Merson, *The Private Diary of a Public Servant* (1955), discusses the McCarthy attack on the Information Program.

Important studies dealing with warfare in the hydrogen age include Robert Endicott Osgood, *Limited War: The Challenge to American Strategy* (1957), William W. Kaufmann, ed., *Military Policy and National Security* (1956), Hanson W. Baldwin, *The Great Arms Race* (1958), and James M. Gavin, *War and Peace in the Space Age* (1958). Samuel P. Huntington, *The Soldier and the State: The Theory and Politics of Civil-Military Relations* (1957), is valuable. Ben T. Moore, *NATO and the Future of Europe* (1958), is a useful study.

World conditions requiring an adjustment in foreign policy are analyzed in Dean G. Acheson, *Power and Diplomacy: The World Today* (1958), Chester Bowles, *Ideas, People and Peace* (1958), C. L. Sulzberger, *What's Wrong With U. S. Foreign Policy* (1959), Walter Lippmann, "End of the Postwar World," *New Republic*, April 15, 1957, and Eugene Rabinowitch, "Ten Years That Changed the World," *Bulletin of Atomic Scientists*, January, 1956. George Kennan's views on the reassessment required are in *Russia, the Atom, and the West* (1958).

Acknowledgments

I am grateful to the book publishers and to the magazine and newspaper publishers who have granted me permission to quote material copyrighted by them. I am greatly indebted to my colleague Daniel J. Boorstin, to Frank Thistlethwaite, Fellow of St. John's College, Cambridge, and Thomas C. Cochran of the University of Pennsylvania for reading the manuscript and making many helpful suggestions. In addition, my colleague Stephen N. Hay and Wayne S. Cole of Iowa State College offered wise suggestions on portions of the manuscript. Leo Rosten, Herbert Emmerich, Leopold Haimson, Hans J. Morgenthau, David L. Cohn, Milton Friedman, Rexford S. Tugwell, Louis Gottschalk, Herbert Nicholas, and Herbert Agar are among those with whom I consulted while writing the book.

Paul Holbo, Albert Romasco, and Seymour Dresner were most helpful in aiding me in the research for certain sections. The Social Science Research Committee of the University of Chicago kindly furnished funds to assist on the research and typing expenses. I am grateful to Mrs. Edwin A. Stack and Miss Mary Nelson for their transcribing of the manuscript. My wife Bette spent many long hours reading the various drafts and performing valuable editorial tasks.

Index

DATE DUE

APR 1 '65			
DEC 14 '66			
MAR 2 '67			
OCT 29 '68			
DEC 8 '70			
MAY 8 '74			
GAYLORD			PRINTED IN U.S.A.